This book is a publication of

Indiana University Press
601 North Morton Street
Bloomington, Indiana 47404-3797 USA

www.indiana.edu/~iupress

Telephone orders   800-842-6796
Fax orders   812-855-7931
Orders by e-mail   iuporder@indiana.edu

© 1998 by Indiana University Press

The paper used in this publication meets the minimum
requirements of American National Standard for
Information Sciences—Permanence of Paper for Printed
Library Materials, ANSI Z39.48–1984.

Manufactured in the United States of America.

Library of Congress Cataloging-in-Publication Data

Philanthropy in the world's traditions / edited by Warren F. Ilchman,
Stanley N. Katz, and Edward L. Queen, II.
p.   cm.
Includes bibliographical references and index.
ISBN 0-253-33392-X (cl : alk. paper)
1. Charities—Cross-cultural studies.   2. Charities—History—
Cross-cultural studies.   3. Social service—Cross-cultural studies.
4. Social service—History—Cross-cultural studies.   5. Social
service—Religious aspects.   I. Ilchman, Warren Frederick.
II. Katz, Stanley Nider.   III. Queen, Edward L.
HV16.P46   1998
361.7′632′09—dc21   97-51241

1 2 3 4 5   03 02 01 00 99 98

PHILANTHROPY IN THE WORLD'S TRADITIONS

Edited by

Warren F. Ilchman,

Stanley N. Katz,

and

Edward L. Queen II

INDIANA UNIVERSITY PRESS   BLOOMINGTON AND INDIANAPOLIS

CONTENTS

PART FOUR: PHILANTHROPY AND SOCIAL CHANGE

PART FIVE: NEW SHOOTS, OLD ROOTS

INTRODUCTION

WARREN F. ILCHMAN, STANLEY N. KATZ, AND
EDWARD L. QUEEN II

This book represents a significant addition to the comparative study of philanthropy and culture. In no other volume have a variety of area specialists been asked to turn their attention to the role of philanthropy—of giving and sharing beyond the family—in the life of a particular culture at a particular time.[1] That so little attention has been paid to this subject is surprising. One need only consider the role that philanthropy has played in defining and sustaining numerous religious traditions, e.g., Buddhism, in the establishment of a wide range of educational and cultural institutions, and, perhaps most visibly, the construction of innumerable public buildings and facilities—roads, khans, fountains, etc. The sheer magnitude of this construction undertaken throughout history should have made that activity a prime candidate for study. However, such has not been the case.

The presumption at the outset of this work was that something called "philanthropy"—rooted in the ethical notions of giving and serving to those beyond one's family—probably existed in most cultures and in most historical periods, and that it often was driven by religious traditions. In making this presumption, however, the editors recognized the difficulty in choosing an appropriate generic term for the activities we hoped the authors would examine. In dealing with many cultures in a variety of historical periods, the editors realized that we would run up against the problem of overidentifying what was culturally possible. Just as it would be inappropriate to condemn those in the fourteenth century for failing to make the necessary hygienic responses to the outbreak of the Black Death, so it would be inappropriate to look for nineteenth/twentieth-century North Atlantic understandings of philanthropy in other times and places. For that reason, we have dispensed with the charity/philanthropy distinction. The distinction is of recent invention, linked with a belief in instrumental rationality, progress, and professionalization. Absent these realities, as well as the existence of the modern state, either the distinction makes no sense, or there can be no philanthropy. All that would be left for the subject matter of these essays would be charity, good deeds, and beneficence. This may be a valid way of approaching the issue, but it leaves open the question of what generic term identifies these seemingly related activities. The editors decided, therefore, to retain "philanthropy" as the most useful term to connect this set of behaviors and activities sharing marked family resemblances. Certainly in many ways it is a vague abstraction, but so are "the state," "the law," and "religion" and we find ways to talk about them. Although there remain ragged edges where clarity eludes us, we usually find these concepts understandable and useful both in ordinary language and in academic discourse. There is no reason why philanthropy should be any less useful.

In this volume "philanthropy," understood primarily as activities of voluntary giving and serving to others beyond one's family, is the collective term. In using it we owe a debt to Robert Payton's definition of philanthropy as "voluntary action for the public good."[2] Encompassing as it does the activities of voluntary giving, voluntary service, and voluntary association, this definition helps us analyze the role philanthropy plays in different cultures and in people's attempts to realize their understandings of the good through actions or donations. One of the significant results is that philanthropic acts become the preeminent means by which people attempt to realize their understanding of cultural values, to practice what their culture preaches.

People's attempts to realize these values through giving and serving often can be fraught with controversy and peril, especially when others view them as "factional" or when rulers interpret the activities as assaults upon the legitimacy or adequacy of their rule or as attempts to elevate oneself at the ruler's expense. These issues, raised in several of the essays, serve as a clear reminder that philanthropy as a public phenomenon is not always viewed as good by everyone.[3]

The task assigned to the various authors as specialists was to discern the distinctive form that philanthropy took in different historical periods and in different cultures, to describe the ways in which it worked, to articulate why it was formed this way or these ways, and, if possible, to address the relative importance of philanthropy within the culture and its predominant religious tradition. As these latter sentences suggest, the editors assumed that philanthropy was not a free-floating activity separated from the complex elements of the societies in which it resided, but was influenced, indeed structured, by the specificity of particular cultures.

In making this assumption the editors acted upon a particular set of understandings about culture, namely that culture is not primarily "complexes of behavior patterns," but "a set of control mechanisms—plans, recipes, rules, instructions—for the governing of behavior."[4] Members of particular cultures internalize these rules and then live their lives through them so that, to a great extent, culture becomes learned behavior or, perhaps more precisely, the learning of rules for determining behavior. This assumption made it imperative that the beginning of a study of the ways in which philanthropy operated in different cultures required a strong grounding in their specificity.

By focusing on philanthropy as socially and historically conditioned, we believed that the collection of essays could help us get a better handle on how to talk about philanthropy cross-culturally. Additionally, it would give us a deeper and more nuanced understanding of philanthropy as a phenomenon and make us more capable of seeing it in both its universal and particular aspects. Emphasizing the social and cultural roots of philanthropy enables us to see how philanthropic activities are related to people's conceptions of a good society, or a good life, making it possible to ask questions about what activities people undertake, absent state coercion or familial obligation, to effect some goal or purpose they believe is necessary for the achievement of a good society or a good life. The answers to those questions illuminate how the specific conditions of given societies call forth different philanthropic responses or, at least, color how philanthropic activities are perceived. Knowing this enables us to deal seriously with the fact that significant philanthropic activities in some societies might look fairly peculiar to people from other societies. A possible example of this is the voluntary association for the saving of animals. These organizations emerge from a particular vision of how society ought to be, in this instance a place where animals are not killed and are treated well. These activities rooted in the doctrine of *ahimsa*, would be major philanthropic activities in cultures deeply influenced by Hinduism and Buddhism.

Centering on the values of a society or culture also can help us to understand why, for example, the establishment of *madrasas*—teaching academies—was a preeminent purpose of the various *waqf*s, or foundations in Islamic societies. *Madrasas* helped to realize a basic good central to social identity, the strengthening of Islam. One can easily see how the understandings of what philanthropy can be is rooted in a particular cosmological vision, a point suggested in many of the essays and one which John A. Grim's essay argues directly. This point also explains the centrality of religion in so many of these essays. As a preeminent source of rules and principles for the living of lives, the religious constructions of philanthropy appear to have a particularly powerful resonance that manifests itself across cultures.

Although some have written about the role of philanthropy, of giving and serving, in the lives of various cultures—of their attention to the needs of the weak, the poor, and the stranger—little sustained attention has been devoted to the issue. Certainly some scholars have addressed the issues of giving, serving, and patronage, but few have struggled to understand a particular culture's understanding of philanthropy itself and its role in the culture. In this volume the various authors have undertaken that struggle—trying to understand the role of philanthropy in particular cultures at particular times and attempting to understand it as an integral part of the culture while describing the ways in which its forms reflected that culture's values.

What is reflected, however, varies immensely depending upon the mirror's direction. In Said Arjomand's essay it reflects the multiple goals of certain local elites who worked to maintain their status by donating funds to a culturally valued purpose—the support of Islam—and to do so in a manner that furthered their preferred method, legal interpretation, or instruction. This was done through a culturally and legally sanctioned form, the *waqf*, that received its status because of its prescription by the founder of Islam as the preferred method of supporting charitable activities.

Another issue that figures in several of the essays is the problem, both factually for the donors and conceptually for scholars, that emerges in states where the donative activities of elites are nearly inseparable from their governance functions as allocators of resources. For the donors this means that little could be done to protect their gifts from the predations of those regimes or individuals who succeeded them, especially through violence or conquest. The continuation of those institutions would have attested to the validity and even success of their predecessors, a situation that many successors found unacceptable.

For scholars of philanthropy it forces them to be clear, conceptually, on the fact that such contemporary distinctions as private, as opposed to government or dynastic, monies are fairly recent. As many of the authors struggled with a working definition of philanthropy, one element that presented itself was the inordinate emphasis placed upon the distinction between public and private or, more correctly, state and non-state in most contemporary discussions of philanthropy. Since many of these authors focused on dynastic or patrimonial states, where the issue of what belonged to the ruler as an individual and what as a sovereign is murky, the relativity of this distinction became quite evident. While the inadequacy of the public/private distinction for the premodern period should have been clear to anyone who worked in the history of medieval or early modern Europe, the fact was highlighted by bringing in the comparative dimension.

The mirror also tends to reflect powerful underlying cultural assumptions, many of which are not and often cannot be directly articulated. This comes out quite vividly in Adele Lindenmeyr's essay when she discusses the Russian term for objects of charity. The word, *neschastnye*, generically meaning unfortunates and applied specifically to beggars, criminals, convicts, and the poor as a whole, suggests a particular cultural understanding about misfortune—namely that it is random, undeserved, and likely to afflict anyone. Additionally, the existence of prisoners as appropriate objects of philanthropy, both under the tsars and the Communists, while undoubtedly owing much to the particular Orthodox understandings of duty and to a historical context in which the ransoming of prisoners taken in war or by pirates still had some vitality, seems also to argue for a general cultural view that imprisonment was not (necessarily) deserved but a random event that, like impoverishment, could strike anyone at any time. Charity/philanthropy toward prisoners, therefore, often could be seen as a challenge to the fundamental legitimacy of the state in imprisoning these people. Certainly the prison narratives of many political prisoners saw it that way as did the state, especially during the Soviet terror when any act of compassion toward an "enemy of the people" was punished severely.

These essays also show that philanthropy does not simply reflect a culture but the struggles and contexts in which a culture finds itself and of struggles between cultures. Like many other arenas it becomes a location where cultural values and norms are contested. The way philanthropy is done, the way it is structured, and its preferred objects often become battlegrounds for other issues. This becomes clear in several of the essays. In Derek J. Penslar's essay the theme is the way philanthropy becomes a process by which donors to and administrators of philanthropic enterprises attempt to transform, in a substantive way, the existing cultural reality. In the essay by Mark Juergensmeyer and Darrin M. McMahon we read how individuals attempting to act on certain personal values and goals find themselves caught up in conflicts in which they have no interest and identified as aiding people and purposes with whom they have no shared interests or concerns. This is extended in Gregory C. Kozlowski's and Amanda Porterfield's essays as they show how philanthropy can further certain purposes outside of particular cultures often taking on a transnational reach, by attempting to transform other peoples and other cultures or to bring certain cultural practices more in line with the desires of the donors.

A further element that permeates many of these essays and which deserves significantly more attention is the conception of the autonomy of the individual that lies behind the idea that individuals can choose those activities and organizations to which they give their money and their attention. Additionally, the presumption of inviolability of gifts that exists in several of these cultures, despite this often being factually violated, presents some idea about limitations on state power and the significance of the wishes of the individual. These facts imply something important about the role of philanthropy as the means by which individuals realize their values. The conflict between the attempts of individuals to do this and the ruling powers, between individuals and the state, suggests that philanthropic activities might play a significant role in the formation of civil society. Civil society here must be understood as that place where and those activities which individuals undertake to realize values and goals of importance to them. These activities also suggest some fundamental limitations or gaps in the state's abilities or its right to interfere with these activities, although this limitation historically has been recognized mostly in the breach. If these interpretations are valid, there remains significant work to be done on the relationship between a religious tradition's understandings of philanthropy and the ease with which the culture where it is predominant can develop a full-blown civil society. Linked with these ideas is the idea of *accepting* unknown others as legitimate. If civil society is the place where people struggle to realize their understandings of the good there must be the acceptance of others and their ability to pursue their values if the society is not to be constantly rent by violence. This giving of trust and acceptance, whether through necessity or conviction, constitutes a major basis of civil society as the realm or sphere where individuals undertake voluntary actions in concert with others to realize their vision of the public good.

Certainly this constitutes a subtext in many of these essays. As one reads through them it becomes obvious that the ways in which people try to realize certain values occasionally constitutes a contestation about the way in which the world should be constructed. People often must undertake these activities in the face of opposition by the ruling powers. The ways in which state apparatuses have acted to hinder and limit these activities or to control and channel them well demonstrates the truth of this claim. This suggests a need for more extended and detailed pursuit of these questions within specific traditions. Can one ask whether it has been the very pluriformity of Hinduism that has helped make India a relatively well-functioning democracy despite its innumerable difficulties and problems? Has not the history of multiple answers to religious questions constructed an ethos that enables Indians to live with the plurality and ambiguity that liberal democracy demands in a way that the Confucian tradition in China has perhaps helped to mitigate against? Certainly questions like this often make scholars apoplectic, especially when they seem to suggest failings in cultures and traditions for which long hours of study and reflection have generated much affection. If comparative studies are to have any value, however, they must indeed begin to address the significant question of what difference does difference make? Do certain traditions have a more expansive view of philanthropy than others? Is philanthropy more central, more defining, to certain traditions? Do particular cultural understandings lead more directly to institutionalization of philanthropy? How distinctive are the rationales and rhetoric within different traditions? This book, we believe, can begin to make it possible to ask such probing questions and to suggest directions for future research.

This book, therefore, must in the end be seen not as the final word, but as the first word. The essays by grounding the study of philanthropy and culture in specific times and places serve to illuminate and expand our understandings of philanthropy and the activity of studying it. In doing this, however, they raise for all of us new and exciting questions which we hope these and other scholars will pursue more fully in the future.

NOTES

1. For an attempt to do this solely within the Western cultural traditions, see J. B. Shneewind, ed., *Giving: Western Ideas of Philanthropy* (Bloomington: Indiana University Press, 1996).

2. Robert L. Payton, *Philanthropy: Voluntary Action for the Public Good* (New York: American Council on Education/Macmillan, 1988). As Payton writes he uses the term "philanthropy" in two ways: "first as comprehensive term that includes voluntary giving, voluntary service, and voluntary association, primarily for the benefit of others; and second as the prudent sister of charity, philanthropy and charity being intertwined thread throughout most of the 3,500 years of the philanthropic tradition in western civilization" (p. 32).

3. Publius (James Madison), "The Federalist, No. 10."

4. Clifford Geertz, "The Impact of the Concept of Culture on the Concept of Man," in *The Interpretation of Cultures* (New York: Basic Books, 1973), 45.

PART ONE
NON-LITERATE/ABORIGINAL TRADITIONS

.1.

Reciprocity and Assistance in Precolonial Africa

STEVEN FEIERMAN

Over the past 150 years, the creators of the human sciences have characterized the movement toward modernity in shifting, yet rich and interrelated sets of terms—as a movement from status to contract, from *Gemeinschaft* to *Gesellschaft*, from use value to exchange value, from gift to contract, and on through many other ways of defining a movement from authenticity to alienation, from a simpler division of labor to a more complex one, or from power exercised by a sovereign to power operating through technical knowledge. Underlying many of these distinctions has been the assumption that in the past the web of society itself, the fabric of reciprocal ties, constituted the safety net for those in need; only with the movement away from reciprocity has it been necessary to create specialized institutions for the care of those too ill or too poor, too young or too old to care for themselves. According to the *International Encyclopedia of the Social Sciences,* "In preliterate societies, the family, kin, caste, tribe, or clan looked after its own people as a natural duty."[1] The movement toward the creation of philanthropic organizations is, in this view, part of the movement toward modernity. Robert Wuthnow, in a more nuanced statement, wrote: "So interwoven were material interests and caring for others that it actually made sense to speak of a 'moral economy,' as students of traditional societies have come to recognize, rather than regarding the very notion as an oxymoron."[2]

The history of reciprocity past is not so much a reasoned analysis of the early history of philanthropy as it is an etiological myth—an origin tale of a kind more easily recognized among ethnologists—saying what we consider fundamental about ourselves, who we are at this moment, by telling an imagined story of how we came to be.

A moment's thought will tell us that the world never existed where reciprocity was a constant and reliable safety net. Indeed, it could not have existed. This is not to argue for the absence of a moral economy, nor is it to deny that local descent groups, kinship groups, or village communities looked after their own. It is to argue, however, that those looked after by their kinship groups were not the ones in need of a safety net. In a society constituted as congeries of kinship groups some of these groups are bound to be under stress at any given time—some die out when disease or maternal mortality strikes; others scatter in time of war; still others find themselves under attack by regional political leaders. When a kinship group is withering away, or when people are torn by circumstances from their supporting relatives, this is the time when a safety net is needed most, and it is the time when bonds of reciprocity are the least effective. In many cases the assumed logic of assistance is reversed. It is not so much that the unfortunate are family and therefore they are helped, but rather that they are helped, and therefore they are defined as family.

Sub-Saharan Africa, in the centuries before colonial conquest, was a region where voluntary giving was, in a majority of cases, grounded in reciprocity, and yet where inequalities existed, where kindly help was as double-edged as it is in the philanthropic West—a peculiar combination of caring and dominance, of generosity and property, of tangled rights in things and in people, all in a time and place where the strong would not let the weak go under, except sometimes.

In many places, the model for generous giving was that of a parent caring for children, so that even strangers might be taken in and defined as children. This way of giving care to the poor grew out of a perceived need for numerous and fruitful descendants—a need partially grounded in the religion of the ancestors as practiced in many (but not all) societies of precolonial Africa. Where the ancestors were honored an individual could not become an ancestor without descendants. These were an admission ticket for taking a place in collective memory. The greater the number of descendants, the more important the ancestor.

The evidence of expressed need for descendants is overwhelming—in ceremonial songs and ritual dramas, in oral narratives, and in reports by ethnographers all across the continent. Only a few localized illustrations are possible in this space. Kriel, summarizing central themes in Shona folktales from Zimbabwe, wrote that "the European may attain a status even if he is a bachelor—a muShona would not even leave a *mudzimu* [ancestral ghost] when he dies."[3] According to Devisch, writing about the Yaka of Zaire, "Inheritance and transmission of life are equally constitutive of personhood. It is this exchange which forms the basis of social individuation, of social identity and personhood. . . . The person is a stitch in the fabric of kin." Later in the book, he writes, "Seniority grows with multiplication of the self in descendants and initiates." When Yaka elders open their council, "a pair of senior men solemnly proclaim, dancing all the while. . . . *Thuna ha muyidika maambu*, 'We are here to generate things.'"[4] Among the Shambaa-speaking people of northern Tanzania, in the years before the general spread of Christianity and Islam, the officiant sang in the sacred rite of sacrifice, *Mpeho tuu, na wana*, "The cool of peace, and children." The assembled community would respond by singing of the ancestors, concluding, *Mpemba ing'we jamema kizumuo*, "One ear of (seed) corn fills a granary."[5] Such examples could be multiplied endlessly throughout sub-Saharan Africa.

The "descendants" valued in this way, however, were not only children, but also dependents who attached themselves to wealthy or powerful leaders. These included homeless people who attached themselves to a wealthy man, young men without prospects who came to work for the elder of a matrilineal village and to marry his daughters, or war captives taken into a wealthy household and treated as though they were sons, or daughters, or wives, or sons-in-law. In some instances, the disabilities of low-status refugees would be marked off in some way, so that they (and their descendants) would be recognized as different from, and inferior to, other descendants within the same kinship groups.

The value placed on "descendants," and therefore on caring for the poor, can be understood within the broader patterns of African demography and economy. Many historians argue that the emphasis on attracting people in Africa south of the Sahara—on building a kinship group—was appropriate to a continent rich in land and poor in population. This was a result of relying on labor-heavy hoe agriculture in the absence (in most places) of the animal-drawn plough. There is some justice to this picture, although the relative balance between land and people was, in fact, highly variable. Land which was irrigated, or carefully cleared, or located on favorable soils, or in a favorable spot with regard to rain, was often treated as a scarce resource, even though poorer land went unoccupied nearby. Nevertheless, in many societies the rich or powerful were defined as those with numerous followers; often the poor had access to land but lacked the labor to develop or farm it. In their relative abundance of land and relative scarcity of labor, most African societies were unlike early modern or modern European ones. They differed also in the significance of women's labor for daily farming activities.[6]

The language of caring did not, of course, refer to the shortage of labor for exploiting the land any more frequently than the need for an abundant and docile labor force figured into the language of philanthropy in early capitalist Europe. Reciprocity was grounded in old patterns of the relationship between giving and political allegiance, between exchange and marriage, between people and things. Kinship groups—the descendants of a future ancestor, or the followers of a wealthy big man—balanced their relationships to one another through the exchange of people and things. Injury inflicted by one such group on another usually was compensated through payment in livestock, cowries, metal currency, or woven raphia squares.

The larger set of exchanges of wealth and of labor included marriage. Unlike European dowry payments, which were made by the wife's family, African bridewealth was a form of compensation paid by the husband or his kinsfolk. In some cases the husband worked for his wife's family for a number of years; in others, the husband's family marked the establishment of a relationship with the wife's through the continuing payment of wealth in the form of livestock or one of the currencies. Payments were of different kinds and had different social meanings, but they all were part of an ongoing process by which groups, and networks of relationships, were defined by payments made and payments received. In Shambaa society different payments marked off the brother-in-law relationship and the husband's relation to his wife's mother, as well as the livestock payment given to the bride's patrilineage to be eaten commensally as a mark of their unity. There was also the "cow of affinity" (*ukwe*) which reproduced and had calves, in parallel to the birth of children in the marriage, so that the ongoing exchange of the calves paralleled the ongoing marriages of the daughters conceived in the marriage. Marcel Mauss, in the great classic on reciprocity, wrote, "The pattern of symmetrical and reciprocal rights is not difficult to understand if we realize that it is first and foremost a pattern of spiritual bonds between things which are to some extent parts of persons, and persons and groups that behave in some measure as if they were things."[7]

The method of tying people together through exchanges of wealth, and of building up followings through reciprocity, is clearly a very old one on the African continent. In the language scholars have reconstructed as proto-Bantu—ancestral to the large set of languages spoken all across eastern, central, and southern Africa—there is a word (-*gab*), thousands of years old, which has a cluster of meanings (with some variation in different places), including to divide, to give away, and to distribute, and referring also to patron-client relations. Another proto-Bantu word, -kúmú, refers to a rich man, someone who is honored, a leader; in some places the word refers to clientage. These words, and others, point to the existence of an ancient pattern in which people built leadership through the gift. The evidence for particular parts of this complex is, in some cases, absent until a later date: 1,000 c.e. for the institution of bridewealth in the equatorial forest, for example.[8]

Seen from afar, through the perspective of writings on Europe, voluntary giving grounded in reciprocal exchanges seems at first to bear little resemblance to philanthropy. J. B. Schneewind, in an essay on the intellectual history of property and charity in early modern Europe, explains why reciprocity differs from charity:

> In these societies there is accumulation of material objects by one person or family or clan, and transfer of these objects to other persons, without contractual repayment in kind or in money. The recipients will typically give the objects away to yet others, and eventually the initial donor will be a recipient; but none of this is charity as we think of it. The donors are not securely and predictably better off than the recipients, and the point of the giving is not to provide material assistance to the recipients. The whole cycle of giving and receiving is viewed as a way of securing honor, prestige, or recognized social standing; and the practice serves to reinforce solidarity and the sense of interdependence of the members of the community.[9]

This is a careful description of reciprocity as seen in Mauss's classic work, which is a profound analysis of the principles underlying certain forms of exchange. But these principles are located in Mauss's own essay in the world of an ahistorical other; Mauss finds them in "culture gardens" which are either outside history, or in the imagined time of an evolutionary past. If, instead, we study reciprocity as practiced by people who lived at particular historical moments, and who engaged in their own historically situated struggles, then reciprocity changes its aspect. The same principles can be seen as having been implicated in movements toward domination, as undergirding inequality, and as being invoked by those who gave material assistance to the poor and the powerless. In other words they are implicated in the very contradictions between helping the weak and preserving privilege which characterize "charity."

The contradictions are clearest in many African societies in the period just before colonial conquest. One reason for this has to do with the sources: encroaching Europeans left records of what they heard and saw; oral traditions, also, are relatively rich for this period. The patterns which emerge are strikingly clear, in the combination of generality and variability. Generality, because all across the continent big men (in some cases big women), lineage heads, chiefs, wealthy slaves, and traders worked to assemble large followings of people who depended on them and who, in return for dependency, received protection and help. This was so on the western side of the continent—in Lagos and the Yoruba kingdoms, for example, where men and women struggled to "build themselves up" by attracting people, and it was so among the voluntary Lemba associations of the Equatorial forest; the pattern held from southern Cameroon all the way across to central Kenya.[10] Proverbs in southwestern Uganda informed people that "Brotherhood means stomach," and "When you are rich you find so many relatives."[11] The large anthropological and historical literature on the central African matrilineal belt describes the tension between men as mothers' brothers, who tried to build their matrilineages by attracting their sisters' sons, and men as fathers, who tried to keep their children with them, so as to build up their followings in that way. The struggle to attract people meant that the weak, the poor, and the hungry could hope for some support. In a patrilineal region of central Kenya, men used their wealth to adopt dependents who had been left without support, and the person who bemoaned her fate (or his) was the one without a protector. The words of a women's work song in Kitui said, "I poor person. . . . I have not relatives to call."[12]

Along with the generality was diversity—not just between kingdoms and stateless societies, or matrilineal and patrilineal ones. In some societies, the process of assembling a following was cast in egalitarian terms, with an emphasis on open and shifting forms of leadership. In others, like the kingdom of Rwanda, the process of building a political following was connected to the emerging prestige of a dominant occupational group and with the rigid hierarchies of the state. There was diversity also in the particular cultural definition of wealth, or of people. In the Igbo language, in what later became southeastern Nigeria, the word *ùbá* meant "fruitfulness" or "plenitude," in crops, livestock, and persons, whereas *àkhu* meant "property acquisitions."[13] Within each language the terms for kinds of wealth, and the ways in which they were used to win people's allegiances, changed with time. Long ago Bohannan made the case, in writing about the Tiv of Nigeria, that media of exchange were divided among several categories and that only very special kinds of exchange objects could be given for rights in people. This in contrast to general purpose money in contemporary American society, which flows freely across a wide range of social domains. Other more recent authors have shown how categories of exchange objects which are ostensibly limited in circulation take on the more protean and boundary-breaking characteristics of money.[14]

There is no question that the patterns of exchange involved in bridewealth, in building a following, and in becoming a leader, were also at the heart of voluntary assistance to those in need. In the Xhosa-speaking regions of mid-nineteenth-century South Africa, people driven from their homes by disorders of many kinds sought refuge with local leaders, and gave their labor in return for protection and food. In the Zigua speaking parts of eastern Tanzania, as in the Xhosa-speaking parts of South Africa, the poor depended on their wealthier neighbors for food and for the loan of cattle.[15] In the northern part of Zambia people traveled many miles in famine seasons to take up residence with "relatives," so that they could "flee from hunger"—*ukubutuka nsala*.[16] It is not a mere fiction to say that those who received help were relatives. Knowledge of kinship linkages, however distant, was potentially life-saving. In a world where the gift was both moral and material, giving was a form of incorporation. Strangers *became* family, and so giving took place within the family.

Within the kinship group a framework of reciprocity held, even between rich and poor. These forms of reciprocity did not necessarily involve the equal exchange of goods—five baskets of grain given and five baskets received in turn. Reciprocity could mean food given and service returned; it could mean political protection given and praise-singing returned. Reciprocity in this sense involved gift and counterobligation; it involved people tied to one another through the exchange of objects which established a relationship deeply embedded in social values. The poor were given help, but through this help they were incorporated, or they assumed an obligation. This has the potential to be a higher form of philanthropy, because in it the poor are rarely in a situation where they receive without the opportunity to give in turn.

These issues have been discussed in a very interesting exchange about whether almsgiving existed during the years before colonial conquest among the Yoruba-speaking peoples of southwestern Nigeria. John Iliffe, in a general history of the poor in Africa, argued that Yorubaland

> had an indigenous tradition of begging which may have been unique outside Christian or Islamic regions. Begging in Yorubaland . . . was an exploitation by the poor of prevailing religious practices. The Yoruba beggar . . . was customarily described by missionaries as a "devil-monger." This was because the beggar normally carried or sat next to a figurine of Eshu, who was the intermediary between men and Olorun (Owner of the Heavens) but was misinterpreted by missionaries as the devil.[17]

John Peel, whose specialty is Yoruba religious culture, wrote in response to Iliffe that some of the "beggars" were in fact men of substance, that the "begging" was in actuality a form of mediation with a deity, and that "alms" were a form of sacrifice. The debate did not rest there. It continued in an article by Karin Barber, who argues convincingly that in a world where the transfer of money was a symbolic act of recognition, the payment was "a public acknowledgment of the claims of the god, on which the god's continuing reputation depended." She quotes Samuel

Johnson, a Yoruba intellectual who completed the first major history of his people in 1897. Barber quotes Johnson, writing about an instance where children received payments for the god Kori: " 'Thus the little children perpetuate the memory and worship of this deity, hence the ditty: . . . "But for the little children, Kori had perished." ' . . . It seems to have been explicitly acknowledged," Barber continues, "that only this recognition, solicited by the children, kept the god alive."[18] In this case even sacrifice, as a payment to the god, was embedded within an idiom of reciprocity—it was a payment which established a relationship of dependency, but in this case it was the god who was dependent for continued existence on both the "beggar" and person who gave that beggar "alms."

It is this pervasive and deeply rooted reciprocity which leads Barber to the perception that "charity" to beggars did not hold a significant place in the Yoruba moral imagination:

> It is striking that abject poverty is rarely signified in Yorùbá texts by the figure of the beggar, who is uninteresting because he is a terminal point in the circulation of wealth, with nothing to offer in exchange for money. The poor person is much more often represented by the *aségità*, someone who goes into the bush to collect sticks to sell as firewood. This is marginal, backbreaking, wretchedly paid, and shamingly low-status labor: but it is nonetheless an element in the cycle of production and exchange. To be a part of Yorùbá humanity, it is necessary to take part in this cycle.[19]

John Lonsdale, writing about a very different part of the continent, in central Kenya, comes to a similar conclusion. He writes, in his analysis of a body of Kikuyu proverbs, that "no more than three sayings in a thousand actually commended generosity to the poor. Tenfold more praised the quite different instinct of reciprocity."[20] Yet reciprocity was, as we have seen, a form of exchange within which the rich were led to care for the poor, and this was as true in Kikuyuland as elsewhere. But the care was given within a moral framework very different from a European one which emphasized asceticism, and self-abnegation, and the winning of religious merit through charity to the poor.

One small but interesting body of evidence on the range of reciprocity's uses is found in an article on Ozuitem, an Igbo-speaking village of southeastern Nigeria, in a somewhat later period. In 1938–39, an American anthropologist recorded the household budgets of sixteen village men and women.[21] Many of the items of income and expenditure had social ends, rather than narrowly economic ones. In one case a widow received money for food and for school fees from her dead husband's brother, even though he had no legal obligation to assist her. In some cases, the maintenance of a relatively balanced reciprocity seemed more important than assistance: a woman in need would receive payments from certain relatives, and then make roughly equal payments to them at another time and for another purpose. In other cases assistance was tied to control of labor: a wealthy man made loans to people in need, but then required the recipients to provide him with labor for his business. In this single, and very limited, set of cases we can see help for the needy, along with balanced reciprocity and business activity, all supported by the same idioms—by a single language of assistance and prestige, domination and reciprocity.

The safety net, organized according to principles of kinship reciprocity, is of course never perfect, although its weaknesses—the ways in which it fails—vary in each historical period, depending on the challenges faced. In the 1880s and 1890s (the period just before conquest), the northeastern part of modern Zambia experienced the most brutal excesses of the slave trade. The safety net at that time, as revealed in life stories collected by the first generation of missionaries, left many women unprotected. People cut off from their extended families were at risk, but some among these were more likely to receive support—young women still able to farm and bear children, for example. They were safer because men of substance, in secure groups, would take them in. Older women with grown sons could hope that their sons would have the resources to protect them. Older women without family were the least likely to win support. A young woman could gauge her status (at least in part) by the payment of bridewealth in her marriage; if she had a secure family, then her husband would pay bridewealth and she would have the added insurance of being backed by two local groups—her natal group and the group into which she married. The importance of having at least one supportive male-centered household (or better still, a larger kinship group) is clear from the autobiographical narrative told by a woman named Narwimba, whose husband had died, and who then spoke to his sister's son, a man named Mirambo, who undoubtedly had wives and children of his own at this point. Narwimba, in her own account, says she begged Mirambo "to take me to wife so that we might be protected."[22] This brutal calculus of kinship support and abandonment was not characteristic of African societies in general—not even characteristic of that particular region. It came during a particularly awful period of slave raiding and disorder; it was central Africa's scoundrel time.

In a much later period and farther to the south, the pressures of the southern African mining economy have presented different challenges and different patterns of entitlement to kinship assistance. In Lesotho, a major place of origin for men who worked as laborers in the gold mines, the children most at risk in the 1970s lived in women-headed households. In these, infant mortality sometimes reached 50 percent.

The survival of a woman's children, according to an anthropologist who carefully analyzed support networks during this period, depended not only on remittances from her husband, but also on reciprocal arrangements with neighboring women for sharing labor. The exchanges and feasts of ancestor rituals were also crucial for women as they worked to forge the links necessary for the survival of their children.[23]

The cases of northeastern Zambia in the early 1890s, and of Lesotho in the 1970s, demonstrate in a painful way something true (to a greater or lesser extent) in every time and place: if the poor relied only on those willing to bring them into the circle of reciprocity—only on those who would make them kinsfolk—then some would be left entirely without support. In fact, people cut off in this way could in many cases turn to broader institutions, extending beyond the circle of kin, and so receive life-giving help. In some states people in desperate straits could flee to the king's settlement to ask for sanctuary, and the capacity to give it was one of the marks of royal sovereignty. This was the case in the Shambaa kingdom, where the practice of giving sanctuary was important enough to affect high politics. In one case in the 1860s, the wife of an abusive but powerful chief fled to the capital but the king did not take her in. The capital's people and the king's rivals within the royal dynasty took this as a sign of his weakness. Opposing forces attacked him, leading ultimately to his death and to the fragmentation of the kingdom. A different pattern applied in the Lozi kingdom, in what is now Zambia, where the principle of sanctuary was seen as limiting the possibilities of royal abuse of power, and where none of the many sanctuaries were under the king's direct control. Refugees always had the possibility of fleeing to safety, even if they were being pursued by the king's men.[24]

During the slave trade period, many regions had shrines to which slaves, or people in danger of becoming slaves, could flee for protection. A European, traveling on the coast of West Africa in 1783–84, passed through the town of Malfi, where one of his own slaves sought refuge. The town, he reported, was "very famous because of the Fetish Temple there, wherein any slave, who can reach there, wins his freedom. This indeed happened to me, to my great sorrow."[25] Farther north, at Krachi on the borders of the Asante empire, the Dente shrine served as a sanctuary. In 1894 a missionary noted that the shrine priest's village "had just received an increase of some 40 slaves who had fled from their master Kwabena Panyin in Ateobu and sought sanctuary with the Fetish Odente."[26] The Dente shrine served also as a center for divination and for healing rituals.

The people who came to be healed brought gifts or tribute; those who sought refuge offered their labor. The Dente shrine was located in a labor-intensive yam-farming region, and refugees who came there spent some of their time growing yams for the benefit of the Dente Bosomfo—

the shrine priest. Once again, as in the cases of kinship assistance, the safety net did not depend on giving for its own sake, or for the sake of religious merit alone; the refugee servants of the Dente Bosomfo brought him recognition by their presence and by their labor. If the Dente Bosomfo had not had an entourage of refugees he would have lost his prestige, and his shrine would have lost its considerable efficacy.

Shrines, which could be found in many places across the continent, conformed to no single standard set of defining characteristics. Some, like the Dente shrine, provided healing services and sanctuary. Others, like the Mbona shrine of the Lower Shire Valley of what is now Malawi, are remembered for neither of these functions.[27] In this case the shrine's representatives were important critics of chiefly power holders. The medium at the shrine, or the spirit wife, fulfilled functions that, in another time and place, might have been thought appropriate to the public sphere. The medium was able to speak aloud at difficult times, saying things only whispered by ordinary folks—that chiefly actions were endangering prosperity, reproduction, or survival.

Spirit mediums and other shrine officials held their authority, in many cases, in a sphere separate and quite different from the authority of lineage elders or chiefs. The presence of an authority which derived from the ability to hear the words, or see the image, of an influential spirit, left open an important social space. It was not always possible for those with kinship authority or formal political authority to control either the spirit's message or to whom it spoke. For this reason, there were more women spirit mediums than women chiefs. In this alternative social space, shrine priests and spirit mediums might undertake to aid the weak, criticize the holders of power, preserve the fertility of the land and its people, heal the sick, and give sanctuary to slaves.

In each place, during each period, the possibilities would be exploited in different ways. In southwestern Uganda, the most prominent mediums of the Nyabingi spirit were able, at the turn of the twentieth century, to provide homes for childless women who otherwise had no secure place. Many people came to be healed, and some sought sanctuary at a leading medium's village or at a shrine. Oral traditions about the Nyabingi mediums tell of how hungry women with starving children sought the help of mediums and were blessed with food. The mediums helped men also. A court record of 1936 reports the story of a man who had lost his cattle in a rinderpest epidemic. This should not be seen merely as a loss of wealth but rather, when understood from within the system of reciprocal exchanges, as a loss of the capacity to reproduce. In this case a Nyabingi medium gave the man a heifer. In the normal course of things, those who received help from a Nyabingi medium gave labor, tribute, and/or service in return. Once again, as in the other cases mentioned here, help to the needy was not given as part of a unidirectional flow of goods; it was grounded in continuing patterns of reciprocity. Nyabingi mediumship was also a locus of social criticism and popular resistance. In the nineteenth century, mediums resisted the area's conquest by the armies of Rwanda's expanding kingdom. Then, in the decades after 1900—a time when colonial conquest led to the spread of smallpox, rinderpest, famine, and a dozen other plagues—the mediums articulated their critique of the colonizers and led the forces of resistance to European rule in battles which continued over decades.[28]

The implications of the assistance given at shrines and by spirit mediums are significant for our understanding of social patterns in Africa as well as for the general history of voluntary giving. In social contexts radically different from that of the bourgeois industrial nations of the nineteenth and twentieth centuries, and with understandings of rationality which were radically different from Western ones, there nevertheless existed a sphere within which it was possible to speak with some degree of autonomy about the actions of those who held power—there was a kind of public sphere—and it was often associated with assistance to the weak, to those who were not otherwise entitled to receive help.

There is yet another possibility, when we try to imagine sources of support for those who had moved beyond the web of kinship reciprocity. Healing associations, sometimes described by anthropologists as "cults of affliction," are known from twentieth-century ethnographies as being open to people in need. These associations vary widely in their forms of organization and membership, but an outstanding feature is that suffering qualifies an individual for membership. In some cases the suffering is infertility, in others it is illness, in still others it is bad luck at the hunt or in business. Some of the best ethnographies of these healing associations were written by Victor Turner, who called them "drums of affliction."[29] They were "drums" because of the centrality of the dance, and because the drum is often a symbol of healing authority, as well as political authority.

The afflicted join a healing association because they are in need of help, because they are suffering, but also sometimes because they wish to assume a position of leadership within the association. They learn the association's rituals, which define a place for their suffering within a framework of embodied meaning, or of religious experience, and which in most cases are meant to cure, to bring health and fertility. The ritual experts, the healers, the leaders of these associations, are themselves often people who entered as sufferers. Through their suffering they learned the rituals in which they later instructed others.

Any generalizations made about healing associations create a sense of homogeneity in what is really an enormously diverse cultural and social domain—with myriad forms of local practices, each with its own gender hierarchies, spheres of equality, and evocative symbolic language defining a context for misfortune. Nevertheless, the pattern often holds that people are initiated because they have been suffering, and that some move on from the role of suffering initiate to that of masterful healer. In some of the cults Turner described, on the basis of his work among the Ndembu of what was then Northern Rhodesia in the early 1950s, the most common reasons leading women to attend the rituals were "miscarriages, abortions, . . . an excessive menstrual discharge," and infertility, but also diseases such as leprosy.[30] Among those who had participated for some time many moved on to become what Turner calls "doctors"—leaders of the healing association. Relatives of the afflicted often took part in cult activities, but healing occurred only if a person received help beyond the limits of the web of kinship. In the particular Ndembu case the people joined together in a healing association shared, not a single ancestor, but a single mode of affliction, however diverse their ancestors.[31]

Those who suffered received help from those who previously had experienced similar suffering. In many societies ritual healing associations were an organizational form in which women assisted other women. Anita Spring makes this clear in her descriptions of Luvale healing associations, in an area adjacent to (and culturally similar to) the region described by Turner. Lihamba, among the Luvale, was an association led by women for women, and was especially designed to help in promoting natality—the capacity to bear living children and to see them survive. This in a region where infertility, fetal wastage, and infant mortality were major problems. Members would come voluntarily to the space outside the house of an afflicted woman and would perform the healing ritual for her. Women who seemed to be in the greatest immediate danger of losing a fetus or an infant would be placed in a kind of quarantine and required to remain inside a fenced area over months, or even a year. Within this area they followed a special diet, undertook special rituals, were prohibited from having intercourse, and were cut off from exposure to dangerous illnesses. According to Spring, who collected statistics on fetal wastage and infant and child mortality, the "big fence" ritual (as it was called) seemed to have had a positive effect on children's chances for survival. Women and children who had been through the "big fence" took special ritual names and entered a sisterhood of the chosen. In a related Ndembu ritual called *Chihamba* the adepts and the candidates they have guided form a special relationship, akin to blood-sisterhood or blood-brotherhood.[32]

Through these healing associations (more commonly called "cults of affliction"), people built relationships of quasi-kinship with one another: they provided one another with help and organized themselves into hierarchies. They extended the possibilities for reciprocity beyond the formal circle of kin. Many of these relationships were characterized by balanced reciprocity, as in Lihamba rituals described by Spring: "Women feel it is their obligation to help other women during these rituals so they may expect future assistance."[33] But other relationships combined assistance with inequality—with reciprocity as a way of building hierarchy.

Women living in a world of male-centered households faced extreme vulnerability if they chose to move outside the household structure, or if they were forced to do so. They were condemned to a life without kin-group insurance unless they could find a refuge. This need was met, in some places, by healing associations which controlled their own space and which took in women who had moved beyond the world of kinship reciprocity. In northern Nigeria, women on their own often moved to the compound of the Bori cult, usually headed by a senior woman whose title was Magajiya. Some younger women at the Magajiya's compound earned money by selling sexual services. Other women continued to live with their husbands, but visited to be healed through Bori dancing, and were not sexually available. Still others, beyond child-bearing years, found refuge there. The compound was thus the locus of a cluster of activities which would not have been combined in the same way in a European town. It was a place where sexual services were sold, but also a place to which afflicted women came to be healed. It was a place for honoring non-Islamic spirits, but most participants were Muslims; people sacrificed animals to the spirits, but then gave the meat as *sadaqa*, or alms, to "Qur'anic scholars and students, the homeless and the destitute, and devotees and musicians."[34] If we see Bori as grounded in reciprocity, then it combines the kindness of refuge with the hierarchical exchange of money for sex. Yet at the same time sacrifice, which was a gift from people to a god as a way of entering into a relationship of reciprocity with it, coexisted with the very different concept of alms, in which people honored God by giving gifts to one another in his name.[35]

There are two problems with taking the evidence on healing associations as demonstrating that there is a characteristically African form for the organization of assistance. The first, which has been mentioned already, is the enormous diversity of languages, and of cultural and social practices on the African continent. The second is that healing associations are usually located within a domain of non-literate communication, and so they are difficult to know about in past times. I am saying that this was a domain of non-literate communication, and not a set of non-literate societies, because the societies in question were often places in which people did read and write. Literacy is practiced in Hausaland today, and had been practiced (in Arabic) by some Hausa speakers for centuries before colonial conquest. But Bori, as a ritual association somewhat separate from Islam and from formal colonial structures, is not the subject of full and detailed documentation. Even in the realm of oral tradition, healing associations are not as well documented, in historical research, as the history of political organization and of formally political events. Given the weakness of the historical record, as it has been constructed until this point, it is fair to ask whether healing associations did indeed serve as a refuge for the weak in the centuries before colonial conquest, in the same way they do in the twentieth century. The question applies to the Bori associations, to Ndembu drums of affliction, to Nyabingi rituals, and to any one of a hundred other healing associations. Did these function as centers of refuge and of voluntary assistance, or are we reading twentieth-century understandings back onto the precolonial record? In some cases, the historical record shows that even when healing associations have grown out of precolonial roots, the more recent associations have differed in form from the earlier ones. The predynastic cult of the *iskoki* spirits in Hausaland, which preceded Bori, is thought to have supported descent-group organization, and not to have been the woman-centered association which it later became.[36] In western Uganda, the Chwezi healing associations, even in the twentieth century, have sometimes been seen as the support of local descent groups, with each group becoming a "patient."

In the Bantu-speaking regions the evidence for the antiquity of drums of affliction, in one form or another, is rich and impressive. The word *ngoma*—"the drum"—has been in existence since the proto-Bantu period, several thousand years ago. The historical depth of drums of affliction in this region is suggested also by the broad distribution, across many related languages and many societies, of therapeutic associations revolving around the dance, and in which those who come to be healed move on to become healers. Local people in many places claim that the "drums" are very old. In addition to the suggestive general evidence, there exist local studies of particular drums of affliction showing that they grow out of deep historical roots. Healing associated with the Chwezi spirits, in western Uganda and northwestern Tanzania, goes back at least five hundred years, and probably much longer. Lemba, as a healing association of equatorial Africa, is described in documentary evidence from the seventeenth century to the nineteenth. Kimpasi, a Kongo therapeutic association, also is noted in documentary evidence from the seventeenth century onward.[37]

The question is not whether healing associations existed, but whether the services they provided in earlier centuries were the same as those of the twentieth. What is in doubt, in particular, is whether loosely organized healing associations had the capacity to take in weak and vulnerable individuals and to protect them. To provide refuge in the precolonial period was radically different in its political implications from the seemingly identical act in more recent times. It was different because its political context was so different. The precolonial world was one (in many places) where political order emerged out of balanced competition, whether it was competition between local big men, or between local descent groups. In this world only the powerful were able to provide refuge. We must ask, therefore, whether healing associations exercised that sort of power in the past, for in the twentieth century most do not. Most contemporary healing associations are small in scale and loose in organization. Most do not have a corporate form of political organization, and most lack strong political leaders. If the healing associations were in fact able to provide refuge, then they must have been very different in their political form. Some might have achieved power as shrine centers, and others as nodes in networks of powerful people. Indeed we have already seen hints that these things happened. We have seen, for example, that Bori spirits in an earlier period probably had been assimilated to the authority of lineage elders. We also have seen that territorial shrines, in many places, served as healing centers, and that shrine priestesses, or priests, or their associates, accumulated the wealth and power needed if they were to offer sanctuary to the vulnerable. In other cases, senior healers acquired the wealth necessary to become big men, and provided refuge in this way. In the case of Lemba, the members of the healing association took great care to recruit the richest and most powerful men of the region, who then rose to the senior ranks of the association. Janzen explains that "Lemba's stance towards those wealthy who didn't wish to join was aggressively inclusive. They were invited, cajoled, harassed, even mystically threatened and forced to join."[38] Because of this, "Lemba membership consisted of the region's prominent merchants, priests, chiefs, judges and their wives."[39] Lemba then generated the political authority, in this setting, so that slaves and other people cut off from group support could be given ritual "fathers" within Lemba. There is only the hint of a possibility, in the records of Chwezi mediumship, that women could provide one another with assistance in a domain beyond the limits of shrines or lineages. Groups of itinerant and mendicant Chwezi priestesses were described in the mid-nineteenth century, in an account by a British explorer.[40] Perhaps these traveling groups were able to serve as a refuge for lone women without support, although this is by no means certain.

Yet another way people in sub-Saharan African societies provided help for those who could not count on family-based support, in the centuries before conquest, was through alms-giving. This was important in the parts of savanna West Africa where people had adopted Islam, and in Ethiopia, which had a long Christian history. In these regions we see both continuity with reciprocity-based traditions of assistance, and divergence from them. The giver of alms, who saw his or her act as meritorious before God, supported the expansion, continuity, and reproduction of a religious community which extended beyond any one kin group, whereas the giver who practiced kinship reciprocity extended the bonds of familyhood to the person in need, and so supported the continuity of the family.

It is of course dangerous to assume that "Islam" (or, alternatively, "Christianity") conforms to a single narrow meaning or narrow set of practices everywhere in the world. It is equally dangerous to assume that either religion was completely incompatible with local forms of reciprocity. That the "world" religions differed from place to place can be seen from the fact that the permanent charitable endowments called *waqf* appear to have been largely unknown in the Islamic parts of West Africa; they are mentioned only in a limited area around Timbuktu, Jenne, and Masina. Most Islamic African societies placed a much greater reliance on acts of charity which were impermanent. Iliffe, to whom we are indebted for the evidence on this issue, writes that the reason for the rejection of *waqf* might well lie "more in the strength of West Africa's traditions of personalised largess."[41] In some areas the imam constituted himself as a center of redistribution. He would collect charitable contributions from all Muslims and then redistribute the wealth, thus building his own prestige.

Religious charity was practiced also in Christian Ethiopia, where there is evidence about times when churches provided refuge for poor people, the disabled, lepers, the blind, and people with no families. Those who needed refuge sometimes lived in churchyards, in the huts built over tombs. The old, the poor, and the sick also sought help at monasteries, and could resort to the healing powers of Christian holy men.[42] It is impossible, of course, to distinguish sharply between Christian charity on the one side and the politics of reciprocity on the other. After all, monasteries in many parts of the Christian world, as in Ethiopia, used their wealth not only to care for the poor, but also to establish themselves as political presences. In the context of the current argument, it is significant that the alms offered by the church, or the monastery, served to define a moral community on a basis different from the family. In the wider history of Christianity, this seems to have been a crucial achievement of the church. Peter Brown tells how alms were used in postclassical Rome to define a religious community larger than any one city, or any one network of patrons and clients.[43] The Ethiopian monasteries defined community in terms which were not narrowly limited to family ties. But then so also did shrines all across Equatorial Africa, in regions which were neither Christian nor Muslim. In each case—that of central African shrines and Ethiopian monasteries—the place of refuge could survive and fulfill its purpose only if it were a secure node within its field of power. In Christian Ethiopia, where power often depended on the award of *gult*—of rights to the service of peasants living on a piece of land—monasteries of the early Solomonic period received *gult* in much the same way that army generals did, and *gult* land was used, by monks and by generals, as an instrument for building a following.[44]

The tension between the use of wealth as alms, given to honor God, and the use of wealth in a strategy to build power by accumulating dependents, played itself out not only in indigenous forms of Christianity, but also (in many parts of Africa) in the Christian practice of European missionaries. This tension was especially evident among missionaries who worked beyond the boundaries of empire—for example in eastern Africa during the decades before the completion of conquest. The mission records are filled with cases in which missionaries helping needy people saw themselves as bestowing charity, whereas the recipients saw themselves as becoming dependents. In other cases, the missionaries thought they were freeing slaves, but those seeking refuge understood themselves to be taking on new masters. Missionaries and their dependents then worked out a common language, a kind of social creole, for reconciling their divergent expectations.

Many of the greatest missionary successes of the nineteenth century came in regions recently unsettled by the slave trade, or among unsettled populations, among people who sought refuge at mission stations, and after doing so became converts. In these cases the missionary needed to provide the protection which in other contexts would have been given by a big man. A Catholic missionary in eastern Tanzania, in the late nineteenth century, reported that women seeking refuge would come to him with the plea, "*Blanc, achète-moi.*" Glassman explains that "Such perceptions were so common that the *mateka* and *watoro* [captives and runaways] who settled at the mission stations were often called the 'slaves of the Christians.' "[45] Giblin describes how a man approached the Spiritan missionaries in the southern Nguu Mountains of East Africa in 1883 and "pledged to become 'something like a vassal' if the missionaries would intervene to save his wife and children," who had become captives.[46] The missionaries did intervene and through their intervention became big men within the local system. Missionary practice depended just as much on the political context in precolonial Africa as had the practices of healing associations. In the same way that healing associations found it difficult to give refuge in the preconquest world unless they carved out zones of security for themselves—nodes of power—mission stations could give refuge only if the missionaries defended their political spaces.

The point is not that missionaries gave morally pure charity, which the refugees assimilated to a more suspect language of dominance, nor is it that missionaries corrupted themselves by being drawn into the language of slavery. It is that philanthropy inevitably has a two-sided character in which kindness and privilege experience an uncomfortable marriage to one another. One can certainly imagine the poor of industrializing Europe experiencing the charity of the church as one more way they were reminded of the privilege of the dominant classes. What was different in central or eastern Africa was not the double-sided nature of philanthropy, but the particular social context where privilege took the form of the ability to award personal protection, where those who were helped became dependents, and where (at some particularly difficult moments in time) dependency shaded into slavery.

The political context of philanthropy changed radically during the years after colonial conquest, and so the forms of philanthropy necessarily changed also. Colonizing Europeans attacked all forms of autonomous African power. To the extent that they succeeded they brought an end to the independent authority of big men and lineage heads, chiefs and kings, powerful healers and shrine mediums. After colonial conquest, every one of the philanthropic institutions described in this essay was transformed. The centralization of power under European governmental control led to the redefinition of the fields of political force within which ordinary people lived their lives. Neither the big man's settlement nor the medium's shrine survived in its old form. And the decline of the independent big man implied also the end of a form of Christian practice in which the mission station was a center of independent political authority.

The story of the changing social fabric of philanthropy during the colonial period is beyond the scope of this essay but what is clear, as part of the general history of philanthropy, is that philanthropy's forms are inextricably wedded to the particular forms of dominance and privilege in each historical time and each historical place. Certainly the history of philanthropy in each of the many regions of precolonial Africa reveals the contradictory nature of privilege which could constitute itself only by giving help, and the contradictions also in care to the weak, which could be instituted only by giving life to the forms of privilege.

NOTES

1. Aileen D. Ross, "Philanthropy," *International Encyclopedia of the Social Sciences*, vol. 12 (New York: Macmillan, 1968), p. 73.

2. Robert Wuthnow, "Rediscovering Community: The Cultural Potential of Caring Behavior and Voluntary Service," Essays on Philanthropy, No. 7 (Indianapolis: Indiana University Center on Philanthropy, 1992), p. 2.

3. Abraham Kriel, *An African Horizon*, Communication No. 35 of the School of African Studies, University of Cape Town (Rondebosch, Cape Town: Permanent Publishing House, 1971), p. 84.

4. Rene Devisch, *Weaving the Threads of Life: The Khita Gyn-Eco-Logical Healing Cult among the Yaka* (Chicago: University of Chicago Press, 1993). The quotation on inheritance and transmission of life is from page 133; the

quotation on seniority is from page 142; and the description of the elders' council is from page 4.

5. Feierman, field notes, rite of sacrifice, Mshihwi, Lushoto District, October 1966. The literal translation of *kizumuo* is a "large heap." See also Yohana Hoza, "Dini ya Kishambala, au Miviko ya Kishambala," manuscript, ca. 1960. Bethel Mission Archives, Bethel bei Bielefeld, F. Riese, "Die Opfer der Schambala," n.d. (ca. 1910). For additional examples of the centrality of descendants, see T. Beidelman, *Moral Imagination in Kaguru Modes of Thought* (Bloomington: Indiana University Press, 1986), p. 113. Fr. Marius Cisternino, *The Proverbs of Kigezi and Ankole (Uganda)* (Kampala and Rome: Comboni Missionaries, 1987), proverb no. 2062, "When a baby is born your clan is safe"; no. 2065, "The rich have to shout, but the father of many sits in peace"; no. 2059, "Children are more than wealth," and many others. For a very rich document on Zulu ancestors from the late 1850s and early 1860s, see Henry Callaway, *The Religious System of the Amazulu*, part 2, *Amatongo; or, Ancestor Worship, as Existing among the Amazulu, in their Own Words, with a Translation into English, and Notes* (Natal: John A. Blair, 1869).

6. John Iliffe, *Africans: The History of a Continent* (Cambridge: Cambridge University Press, 1995), p. 5. For an influential description of the contrast between hoe agriculture in sub-Saharan Africa and plough agriculture in Europe, and of the different forms of marriage and stratification which grew up around these, see Jack Goody, *Production and Reproduction* (Cambridge: Cambridge University Press, 1976).

7. Marcel Mauss, *The Gift: Forms and Functions of Exchange in Archaic Societies*, trans. Ian Cunnison (London: Cohen and West, 1954), p. 11.

8. Jan Vansina, *Paths in the Rainforests* (Madison: University of Wisconsin Press, 1990), pp. 103–104, 295, 274.

9. J. B. Schneewind, "Philosophical Ideas of Charity: Some Historical Reflections," seminar paper for "The Faces of Charity," Baltimore, Maryland, November 19, 1993.

10. The classic work on clientage is Sandra T. Barnes, *Patrons and Power* (Manchester: Manchester University Press for the International African Institute, 1986). See also Karin Barber, "How Man Makes God in West Africa: Yoruba Attitudes towards the *Orisa*," *Africa* 51 (1981), pp. 724–45; Vansina, *Paths*; John M. Janzen, *Lemba, 1650–1930: A Drum of Affliction in Africa and the New World* (New York: Garland, 1982); Charles Ambler, *Kenyan Communities in the Age of Imperialism* (New Haven: Yale University Press, 1988).

11. Cisternino, *Proverbs*, proverbs 1509 and 2069.

12. Ambler, *Kenyan Communities*, p. 26.

13. Jane Guyer, "Wealth in People, Wealth in Things—Introduction," *Journal of African History*, vol. 36 (1995), p. 88. On hierarchies in Rwanda, see Catharine Newbury, *The Cohesion of Oppression: Clientship and Ethnicity in Rwanda, 1860–1960* (New York: Columbia University Press, 1988).

14. Paul Bohannan, "Some Principles of Exchange and Investment among the Tiv," *American Anthropologist* 57 (1955), pp. 60–70. Arjun Appadurai, ed., *The Social Life of Things: Commodities in Cultural Perspective* (Cambridge: Cambridge University Press, 1986). Jane Guyer, ed., *Money Matters: Instability, Values and Social Payments in the Modern History of West African Com-*

munities (Portsmouth N.H. and London: Heinemann and James Currey, 1995). Sharon E. Hutchinson, *Nuer Dilemmas: Coping with Money, War, and the State* (Berkeley: University of California Press, 1996).

15. James Giblin, *The Politics of Environmental Control in Northeastern Tanzania, 1840–1940* (Philadelphia: University of Pennsylvania Press, 1992), pp. 37–39.

16. Audrey Richards, *Land, Labour and Diet in Northern Rhodesia: An Economic Study of the Bemba Tribe* (London: Oxford University Press for the International African Institute, 1939), p. 109.

17. John Iliffe, *The African Poor: A History* (Cambridge: Cambridge University Press, 1987), p. 86.

18. Karin Barber, "Money, Self-Realization, and the Person in Yoruba Texts," in Jane Guyer, *Money Matters*, 216. John Peel, "Poverty and Sacrifice in Nineteenth-Century Yorubaland: A Critique of Iliffe's Thesis," *Journal of African History* 31(1990), pp. 465–84.

19. Barber, "Money," p. 208.

20. John Lonsdale, "The Moral Economy of Mau Mau: Wealth, Poverty & Civic Virtue in Kikuyu Political Thought," in *The Unhappy Valley* (London, Nairobi, and Athens, Ohio: James Currey, Heinemann Kenya, Ohio University Press, 1992), p. 340; Lonsdale goes on to define reciprocity narrowly, as a system in which the rich give to each other. His essay is based on deep learning. It opens up a new and important subject area in the study of Kikuyu society, but on this point it underestimates the possibilities of reciprocity.

21. J. S. Harris, "Some Aspects of the Economics of Sixteen Ibo Individuals," *Africa* 14 (1944), pp. 302–35.

22. Marcia Wright, *Women in Peril* (Lusaka: National Educational Company of Zambia Limited, 1984), p. 2.

23. John M. Janzen, *Ngoma: Discourses of Healing in Central and Southern Africa* (Berkeley: University of California Press, 1992), pp. 158–59.

24. Steven Feierman, *The Shambaa Kingdom: A History* (Madison: University of Wisconsin Press, 1974), 155–56; Max Gluckman, *The Ideas in Barotse Jurisprudence* (Manchester: Manchester University Press, 1972), pp. 39–41.

25. D. J. E. Maier, *Priests and Power: The Case of the Dente Shrine in Nineteenth-Century Ghana* (Bloomington: Indiana University Press, 1983), p. 34.

26. Ibid.

27. J. Matthew Schoffeleers, *River of Blood: The Genesis of a Martyr Cult in Southern Malawi, c. A.D. 1600* (Madison: University of Wisconsin Press, 1992).

28. Jim Freedman, *Nyabingi: The Social History of an African Divinity*, Annales, Serie in 80, Sciences Humaines, No. 115 (Tervuren: Musée Royal de l'Afrique Centrale, 1984), pp. 51–52. Elizabeth Hopkins "The Nyabingi Cult in Southwestern Uganda," in R. Rotberg and A. Mazrui, eds., *Protest and Power in Black Africa* (New York: Oxford University Press, 1970), p. 261. S. Feierman, "Healing as Social Criticism in the Time of Colonial Conquest," *African Studies* 54 (1995).

29. Victor W. Turner, *The Drums of Affliction: A Study of Religious Processes among the Ndembu of Zambia* (Oxford: The Clarendon Press and IAI, 1968).

30. Victor W. Turner, *The Forest of Symbols* (Ithaca: Cornell University

Press, 1967), p. 12; V. Turner, *Schism and Continuity in an African Society: A Study of Ndembu Village Life* (Manchester: Manchester University Press, on behalf of the Rhodes-Livingstone Institute, 1957), p. 308.

31. V. Turner, *Schism*, chapter 10; see especially pages 293–95.

32. Turner, *Schism*, p. 307; Anita Spring, "Epidemiology of Spirit Possession among the Luvale of Zambia," in *Women in Ritual and Symbolic Roles*, Judith Hoch-Smith and Anita Spring, eds. (New York: Plenum Publishing, 1978), pp. 173–74.

33. Spring, "Epidemiology," pp. 171–72.

34. Fremont E. Besmer, *Horses, Musicians, & Gods: The Hausa Cult of Possession-Trance* (South Hadley, Mass.: Bergin & Garvey, 1983), p. 27. On Bori, see also Michael Onwuejeogwu, "The Cult of the 'Bori' Spirits among the Hausa," in Mary Douglas and Phyllis Kaberry, eds., *Man in Africa* (Garden City, N.Y.: Anchor Books, 1971), pp. 279–305; Guy Nicolas, *Dynamique Sociale et Appréhension du Monde au Sein d'une Société Hausa*, Muséum National d'Histoire Naturelle, Travaux et Mémoires de l'Institut d'Ethnologie, 78 (Paris: Institut d'Ethnologie, 1975); I. M. Lewis, Ahmed al-Safi, and Sayyid Hurreiz, eds., *Women's Medicine: The Zar-Bori Cult in Africa and Beyond* (Edinburgh: Edinburgh University Press for the International African Institute, 1991); Mary F. Smith, *Baba of Karo: A Woman of the Muslim Hausa* (New Haven: Yale University Press, 1981), pp. 63–65, 115–16, 155, 208–10, 226–30.

35. Mauss sees alms as closely related to sacrifice; *The Gift*, pp. 15–16.

36. Nicolas, *Dynamique*, pp. 107–13, 205–11.

37. Renee Tantala, "The Early History of Kitara in Western Uganda: Process Models of Religious and Political Change," Ph.D. dissertation, Dept. of History, University of Wisconsin-Madison, 1989. Janzen, *Lemba*. Peter Schmidt, *Historical Archaeology: A Structural Approach to an African Culture* (Westport, Conn.: Greenwood Press, 1978). Anne Hilton, *The Kingdom of Kongo* (Oxford: Clarendon Press, 1985), pp. 26–28.

38. John Janzen, "Ideologies and Institutions in the Pre-Colonial History of Equatorial Africa," *Social Science & Medicine* 13B (1979), p. 323.

39. Ibid., p. 322.

40. Iris Berger, "Rebels or Status-Seekers? Women as Spirit Mediums in East Africa," in Nancy Hafkin and Edna Bay, eds., *Women in Africa* (Stanford: Stanford University Press, 1976), p. 162.

41. Iliffe, *The African Poor*, p. 43.

42. Iliffe, *African Poor*, chapter 2; Steven Kaplan, *The Monastic Holy Man and the Christianization of Early Solomonic Ethiopia*, Frobenius Institut, Studien zur Kulturkunde, no. 73 (Wiesbaden: Franz Steiner Verlag, 1984).

43. Peter Brown, *The Cult of the Saints: Its Rise and Function in Latin Christianity* (Chicago: University of Chicago Press, 1981), pp. 44–47.

44. Steven Kaplan, *Monastic Holy Man*, pp. 54–59.

45. Jonathon Glassman, *Feasts and Riot: Revelry, Rebellion, and Popular Consciousness on the Swahili Coast, 1856–1888* (Portsmouth, N.H., London, Nairobi, Dar es Salaam: Heinemann, James Currey, E.A.E.P., Mkuki na Nyota, 1995), p. 108. On the general problems facing missions in this period, see Roland Oliver, *The Missionary Factor in East Africa* (London: Longmans, 1952).

46. Giblin, *Politics*, p. 80.

.2.

A Comparative Study in Native American Philanthropy

JOHN A. GRIM

> There's no other purpose for which a person lives. Again, I refer to what my heritage is. It's a central philosophy; you don't speak, you don't live except on behalf of your people. You can't live, you are not alone; only because of the people are you in existence. It doesn't just mean people as physical people, but people in terms of people and place, people and their religion, people as the source of who you are. Without that you are not really anything. So your voice is their voice, in terms of a collective communal spirit. Obviously, there is a contradiction, as there is in most everything. A person as a spokesperson, a person as an artist who has an ability, a gift given to him by his creator, by the All-Spirit, given to him to utilize, is going to do a lot of his work individually, but with the understanding that he doesn't exist without this context; without this wholeness and source he is nothing. That is essential.
>
> —SIMON ORTIZ,[1] ACOMA PUEBLO

While no one Native American thinker can articulate the diverse expressions of Native American philanthropy, the Acoma poet Simon Ortiz points toward the essential features for appreciating the depth of experience and thought which Native Americans have given to this issue.[2] Beginning with the intimate connections of an individual to his or her people, Ortiz locates that relationship in the context of a "collective communal spirit," "people and place," "people and their religion," "the source," "wholeness," and "the All-Spirit." This is not simply a string of unrelated terms but, I sense, an effort by an Acoma Pueblo poet to constellate ideas about human beings and human actions so that a non-native audience might understand their coherence as his people see it.

Embedded within this relationship between individuals, the people, and their spiritual source are centuries-old cosmological beliefs involving ancestors, sacred sites, liturgical acts, and mythic narratives. Even before the imposing mission church was built by the Spanish Christian missionaries in the mile-high pueblo plaza of Acoma, ancient belief systems inculcated philanthropic activity for the communal good. So it is that spiritual visions have been cultivated and transmitted by the indigenous inhabitants of the North American continent through cosmologies whose recitations are believed to bring rain for crops, vitality to newborn children, and to renew life ritually throughout the landscape.

PHILANTHROPY AND COSMOLOGY

The harmony and integrity of the whole, which is the context for philanthropic activity among North American Indian peoples, is an integral cosmology.[3] Philanthropy, in traditional Native American societies, flows from such an integral cosmology which acknowledges and celebrates the creative totality pervading existence. This differs markedly from western Euro-American settings where the term "philanthropy" while retaining cosmological resonances, emerged as a largely human-centered act of beneficence by individuals or by individuated associations and institutions. Moreover, native perspectives do not hesitate to identify truth with ethnocentric views, standing, thereby, in sharp contrast to secular postmodern philosophical positions which condemn totalizing perspectives as hegemonic. It is clear, however, that even within particular Native American traditions there often are many versions of a single cosmological narrative and many origin stories. Furthermore, the trickster narratives, found among most Native American peoples, often question orthodox views and subvert the cosmologies themselves, suggesting that hegemonic concerns are not exclusively postmodern. What unites the diverse cosmologies within any particular ethnographic tradition is their sense of the whole, within which actions for the public good are performed and understood.

Native American individuals and institutions appear not to separate philanthropic altruism as a humanitarian act from philanthropy as motivated by cosmological concerns reaching into all realms of life. The munificence of the hunter who ritually thanks the slain animal and often shares the meat with those in need, the concern of a Native American tribal government to provide scholarships for promising students, along with the family which seeks to honor an individual by a giveaway are philanthropic acts flowing from a traditional awareness of deeper values about giving within the cosmos itself. This is not to say that Native American philanthropy is fixed or unchanging. Like any exchange, thought, or act by an individual or segment of an indigenous society, Native American philanthropy constantly is ideologically reinvented, ritually performed, and contested by the practitioners. The dynamics within which Native American philanthropy occurs have unique cultural, environmental, and historical contexts. The term "lifeway" suggests this close interaction between human ideational, spiritual, and material realities in traditional societies.[4]

There typically is no separate abstract term indicating action for the public good in the ethnographies of native societies but contemporary narratives continue older story traditions about generosity, the heroism of sacrifice, and the condemnation of selfish behavior. Native American peoples have not separated voluntary service and sharing from their communal life or lifeway. An indigenous lifeway, in which cosmological values pervade political and economic life, tends to make individual and institutional acts of generosity communal and somewhat hidden. The task in this paper is to highlight these hidden histories and to explore Native American philanthropies within the worldviews of these diverse peoples rather than in terms of Euro-American conceptions of philanthropy. These opening remarks suggest that individual and institutional giving among the native peoples of North America derives from an integral cosmology which has a spiritual-material basis, implications for indigenous political economies, and ritual modes of celebration.

There is an enduring emphasis both by Ortiz above and by Native Americans generally on "the people" as the context in which cosmological benevolence is transmitted, understood, and carried out. The term "anthropocosmic"[5] may be used to stress this sense of human values as embedded within, and reciprocal to, the dynamics of the universe. This can be seen in the circle metaphor widely used to symbolize cosmological wholes by native peoples, such as the Lakota. So also the carved box metaphor of the Pacific Northwest Coast civilization images the human body as a carved box with inner and outer dimensions set within the village-community box itself set within a sequence of increasingly larger concentric boxes of spirit-animal-plant-and-mineral communities.[6] A philanthropic act, such as curing by a healing practitioner, is experienced and understood by these northwest coast Native American peoples with a depth of concern for larger realities whose outer manifestations and inner realities meet at the transactional axes of the lids of boxes, the places which open to cosmological power. Cosmology and community are inseparable threads in the web of the creative benevolence and violence of life in which Native American philanthropy occurs.

A COMPARATIVE STUDY

Seeking to give expression to diverse Native American voices, this article is a comparative study in philanthropy. By "comparative" I refer to two points. First, there are no indigenous peoples in North America who are "Native Americans," rather there are numerous diverse peoples native to this continent. There are no "American Indian" people but rather specific nations such as the Anishnabeg (Ojibway, Pottawatomi, Ottawa), Hodenosaunee (Iroquois), Tsistsistas (Cheyenne), Apsaalooke (Crow), and others of the over five hundred distinct indigenous peoples in the United States alone. Discussions of Native American thought often struggle awkwardly to frame general conceptions in light of the particular ethnography and thought of the diverse indigenous nations of North America. Any attempt to speak of a Native American idea or practice immediately involves one in a comparative project in which the different ideational and material practices of these native peoples are considered.

Terms such as "pan-Indian" suggest historical convergences and increased communication between native peoples from the early nineteenth century to the present—such as Tecumseh's alliance building, the so-called "prophetic movements" (e.g., Tenskwatawa, Smohala), the Ghost Dances of Wodziwob and Wovoka, the Native American Church, or Peyote Way, and American Indian voluntary associations for acculturation into mainstream America. In vastly different ways these developments knit together diverse native peoples in their ritual, political, and economic life. However, two comments are appropriate: first, native peoples of the Americas were in prolonged interaction long before the nineteenth century; and, second, this comparative project suggests that one can identify shared characteristics of diverse indigenous peoples of North America without erasing their significant religious, political, and cultural differences. Thus, Native American philanthropy is not presented here as a "pan-Indian" idea or Western-influenced development but as an integral cosmological dimension of the First Peoples of the North American continent. "Comparative," then, indicates a concern to consider the question of giving for the public good as an inherent idea and practice within the indigenous thought of American Indian peoples.

A second point, namely, the fact that this article has been written by a non-native person, clearly makes it comparative in its method of understanding and interpretation. No amount of fieldwork or goodwill can bring a non-native intellectual to a Native American reading of this issue. This author holds the position that comparative work can bridge ideological gaps between native and non-native views leading to awareness of present differences, and meaningful reflection on past historical interactions.

THE GREAT LAKES ANISHNABEG-OJIBWAY

Taking seriously the mound-building cultures of the Mississippi River drainage system radically transforms the narrative of American history.[7] These riverine civilizations, apparently entirely indigenous in their early manifestations, begin from the current era to show influence from the Meso-American city-states. Throughout the eastern woodlands, from the south to the north, currents of cultural influence and material trade undoubtedly linked the village-band groups who have been viewed as separate "tribes" in the historical period. Corn, tobacco, and the cults associated with these plants and other materially based symbol systems, radiated throughout the riverine regions along with mortuary symbolisms, segmentary kinship, and leadership hierarchies. Cosmological perspectives framed the diffusion of these diffused items as evidenced by stories of the "dying and rising" corn plant, the gifts of the three sisters—corn, beans, and squash—and other agricultural and technological "gifts" of the Creative Mystery.

These centuries of interaction make it difficult to locate the roots of the Algonquian-speaking Anishnabeg, let alone one of the "Three Fires" of this people, such as the Ojibway-Chippewa who seem to have coalesced as a distinct nation in their migration from the Great Lakes region westward between the seventeenth and nineteenth centuries. While transmitting ancient material and cultural ideas from a circumpolar culture, such as ecstatic shamanism, snow shoes, and bear ceremonialism, the Ojibway also carried mound-building influences among which may have been a solar cosmogony. The Ojibway scholar Basil Johnston writes:

> In lifegiving, the sun is the father of all. Just as the Anishnabeg rendered prayers of thanks in the morning, so did they give thanks in the evening for the gifts received during the day.
>
> But the analogy of sun and man-father goes beyond the obvious and the physical to symbolize the relationship of the begotten to God or Kitche Manitou. The sun served only to symbolize this relationship and this theological understanding.
>
> Prayers of thanksgiving were part of daily life and living, not separate from man's labor or recreation, nor cribbed in ritual. As the giver gave freely and generously, so the receiver must acknowledge his gratitude in the same spirit. To the Anishnabeg there was no gift or giving without a recipient. At the same time the recipient must know how and in what terms to acknowledge benefits. The gift of life may be given once, but it is renewed daily in each dawning.

> There is yet another aspect to the gifts bestowed by Kitche Manitou. Everyone shares in the gifts of light, life, and warmth. Thus no one person may presume that the gift is intended for him alone or deny the enjoyment of such gifts to another. All have received, all must acknowledge the great bounty.[8]

Returning to the concept of philanthropy, before developing some specific cultural implications of Johnston's remarks about his Ojibway people, let me draw out the cosmological features of giving suggested in his remarks.

As mentioned earlier, philanthropy, acts of mercy to relieve suffering and voluntary assistance to improve the quality of life, is not separated out from daily life in indigenous thought systems. Here Johnston articulates this lifeway context as gift, thanksgiving, and relationship. The Great Creative Mystery, or Kitche Manitou, gives merciful sustenance through the sun, and that giving becomes the paradigm for the Ojibway lifeway. The cosmological gift of life functions in all aspects of the lifeway, not simply in ritual moments or public displays of giving. Private thanksgiving addressed to the sun symbolizes awareness of the gift of life but, interestingly, Johnston speaks of the sun and "man-father" images as analogies which seek to express deeper relationships and understandings. He does not want his people's insights to be interpreted simply as univocal icons or worship of the physical sun as object as they continue to be understood by some Christian missionaries and Western philosophers.

Seeing lifeway as another analogy for that creative relationship of which this Ojibway scholar speaks, we can also draw out his final remarks on the philanthropic character of the gifts of life which require reciprocity. Giving, according to this Ojibway thinker, required from the recipient acknowledgment of the gift and an awareness of the interdependent quality of the gifts of life. These observations by Johnston resonate with the penetrating questions asked by Marcel Mauss, namely, "What rule of legality and self-interest . . . compels the gift that has been received to be obligatorily reciprocated? What power resides in the object given that causes its recipient to pay it back?"[9] In thinking about a "total social phenomenon" such as gift exchange, Mauss conceived of the need to think synthetically about the force behind any exchange in an indigenous context. Using the Polynesian term, *hau*, Mauss groped to articulate that unperceived totality which both binds those involved in exchange and surmounts the dichotomizing into camps of a "self" and an "other" between whom exchanges occur.

From Johnston's remarks it appears that the Ojibway cultivated altruism as a cosmological insight in which giving established a relationship among humans analogous to that of the giving of Kitche Manitou through the sun to all of life. The inherent contradiction of perceiving gifts as one's own, or one's "self" separate from an "other," and the act of giving as merely a dialogic act between the self as possessor and the other as recipient, is surmounted by the Ojibway understanding that the sequence of gift-thanksgiving-relationship express the inherent mystery, or *manitou*, that courses through all of life. Indeed, in this thought system giving promotes life.

Some critics might charge that the Ojibway do not actually practice philanthropy, as the West has understood it, because they do not personally or consciously choose to extend help to those in need but are simply compelled by cosmological forces. However, the powers that the Ojibway call *manitou* are not simply ideological drives but those forces in the natural world and the larger cosmos that bring us what, as Johnston says below, we are entitled to. Integral to human participation in this cosmological endowment is the freedom to decide for oneself or, as the Ojibway say, *inaendaugwut*, "it is permitted." Most important to the Ojibway was the preservation of personal freedom, the capacity to decide. Transmitting teachings about the world of the *manitou*, as the Ojibway ancestors had perceived that mystery, was crucial for preserving the capacity for freedom and for philanthropic reciprocity. As Basil Johnston has observed:

> Regarding the universal question of "what is man as a man entitled to," the Anishnabeg would probably have replied, food, clothing, shelter, personal inner growth, and freedom. To all other matters respecting man's relationship to other men and women and to society in general they would have said, "inaendaugwut," it is permitted: or "inaendaugozi," he is permitted of himself. Such term [sic] was predicated of many aspects of life, living, and relationships: it was a mode of understanding and interpretation.
>
> Events were permitted by forces outside of man himself; the exercise of personal talents and prerogatives permitted by men. . . .
>
> The Anishnabeg's society was based upon what he considered to be his basic rights; his relationships upon the preservation of his personal freedom to grow in soul-spirit and in accordance with the world.[10]

Awareness of what was permitted might come to an Ojibway in a variety of ways, visions during a fast, dreams, teachings by family elders, storytellers, or political leaders, and personal reflections. *Manitou* experiences might themselves become a source of philanthropic activity such as transferring medicine knowledge. Medicine, in this sense, might refer to prayer, vision songs, or the manipulation of material objects believed to bring spiritual forces to bear on a person's needs. Such medicine knowledge might involve special knowledge of plant properties or animal behavior revealed privately to an individual by the *manitou*-spirit of the plant or animal. This knowledge could be taught to another person by the recipient of the spiritual revelation if she or he also had received permission to transmit that knowledge to others. The revelation, given by cosmological powers, was completely gratuitous and the transmission to another person was considered *inaendaugozi*, that is permitted of one-self, a personal choice, a voluntary philanthropic act for the welfare of another. While the Anishnabeg peoples have a wealth of examples of such benevolence, perhaps no clearer expression of institutional philan-thropy can be found among them than the Grand Medicine Society, Midewiwin.

Healing and caring for the sick are abiding examples of the altruistic behavior which serves to help define the very meaning of philanthropy. While large moneyed gifts often constitute the current popular image of philanthropy in the United States, the innumerable merciful acts by individuals and voluntary associations to alleviate human suffering and misery probably have benefited human communities more than finan-cial outlays. Among indigenous communities, in whose economies money was not exchanged for goods and for whom commodities as life-less objects did not exist, the exchange of goods as well as the exchange of healing knowledge in rituals became a conduit for cosmological forces. While indigenous communities may today be dependent on the global consumer market for goods, and while a materialist commodifi-cation-of-everything may seem to pervade reservation and urban Indian lives, the maintenance of an integral cosmological vision in traditionally minded native peoples is most evident in the enduring healing teach-ings and practices of the Ojibway Midewiwin.

The term Midewiwin, a compound of *mide*, "the sound of the drum," and *wiwin*, "doings," refers to the institution, or Mide Society, com-posed of recognized healing practitioners and those who have gained entrance to the society by passing through at least one of the eight "earth" and "sky" degrees of the graded ceremony.[11] *Midewiwin* also refers to the ceremony itself, which took eight days to perform and was conducted in the spring or late summer or whenever there arose a need for curing. Finally, Midewiwin refers to the oral narratives transmitted by individual healers and practitioners of the Mide Society. This mythic tradition conveyed some of the oldest cosmogonies of the Ojibway peo-ple. The oral narratives of Midewiwin also told how this ceremonial was transferred to the people through the cure of the trickster, Nanabush (Nanabozho, Man-abo-sho, Wedjakid).[12]

Traditional Ojibway Midewiwin, sacred by virtue of its origins among the *manitou* and secret due to the prohibition on profane mention of ceremonial matters, was performed publicly so that all Ojibway could view and hear the proceedings. The long Mide Lodge, *midewigan*, sym-bolized the cosmic powers in the four directions, open to the celestial regions at the top and to the powers of the earth as participants sat on the ground. With each degree the candidates passed through the numinous regions of the *manitou*, some of whom were helpful while others were considered harmful and dangerous. Paper-birchbark scrolls recorded the mnemonic symbols whereby officiants instructed initiates about the *manitou* and the moral teachings of the Mide Society.[13]

The ritual lore of *midewiwin* told of the cosmic struggles to assemble the ceremony and to transmit it to humans. Simultaneously, Midewiwin narrated the history of the Ojibway migration in which specific locations in the western movement were cardinal points on which hinged validation of the migration itself. These locations, known as "stopping places," marked settlements of the migrating Ojibway as well as sacred sites of the *manitou*-powers involved in the cosmogonic drama by which they established the ceremony. In effect, Midewiwin became the means for legitimating the Ojibway movement westward

The highpoint of the eight-day *midewiwin* ceremony came when the patient-participant was symbolically "shot" with the *manitou* powers of the assembled Mide Society members. Mystically "dead" the patient revived as one now able to participate in the ceremony and to learn the accumulated lore of Midewiwin. As with many philanthropic acts that have a public character, status and privilege accrued to participants in Midewiwin through their gifts to the officiants who manifested the *manitou* through ritual drama, and by sponsoring the public thaumaturgy through which the Ojibway celebrated themselves as a people with purpose.

Three points clarify the philanthropic character of Midewiwin: first, the ritual complex of activities whose liminal states generated a depth experience of community; second, the redistribution of goods in the giveaways associated with Midewiwin which augmented the political economy based on shared prosperity; and, third, the articulation within Midewiwin of profound lifeway values in an ethical passage through life symbolized in the Mide path of "eight stops." Two criticisms will be considered below, namely, that Midewiwin was exchanged for goods given by the patient-participant, which seemingly compromises the philanthropic character of the act, and that there was ideological abuse of Midewiwin during its history by self-aggrandizing individuals.

Victor Turner's analysis of ritual focuses on liminal, ecstatic states generated by ritual, and on *communitas*, a heightened sense of community resulting from crossing normative boundaries in ritual liminality. Midewiwin brought such experiences to the Ojibway people as a public good.[14] Not only were familiar rituals such as sweat lodges, giveaways, chanting, medicine bundle openings, and ritual dancing folded into *midewiwin*, but the ceremonial complex also staged a visual reenactment of the cosmogonic events through which creation was differentiated into cosmic levels and Midewiwin first performed. Through the collective effort of knowledgeable individuals, who apart from Midewiwin often were recognized healing practitioners in their own right, this public ceremony affirmed the Ojibway ethos, promoted communal identity, and brought healing energies to bear upon individual and community illnesses.

From the perspective of political economy, which seeks the roots and explanations of cultural institutions such as the Ojibway Midewiwin in production, trade, and consequent political conflict, an alternative picture emerges with significant implications for understanding Midewiwin's philanthropic nature. The Midewiwin vision would have us believe that the Ojibway received a revelation that validated their movement as middlemen in the emerging western trade networks of the seventeenth through the nineteenth centuries. From what we know of this period from the standpoint of other Great Lakes peoples and the French missionary, trade, and diplomatic documents, many tribal lifeways fragmented in the contested "middle ground" of the Old Northwest.[15] In earlier periods it had not been unusual for seemingly contradictory forms of intertribal exchange, such as warfare and gift-giving, to exist simultaneously, but the period of the Ojibway migration saw an unprecedented emphasis on warfare. The resulting tribal fragmentation affected both internal social systems and the symbiosis necessary for regional trade. Migration, warfare, and the eventual relocations of some peoples disrupted the voluntary trade and mutual assistance between groups such as the Menominee and Pottawatomi or between the more southern Sauk and Fox.

Previously, Midewiwin had been transmitted to several of these neighboring tribal groups as a component of their trade relations. In this sense Midewiwin continued older trade and diplomatic liaisons between village groups established by the Algonquian Feast of the Dead, where the bones of dead ancestors were disinterred, ritually carried to villages designated for trade and political alliance, and reburied with the ancestral bones of that village. While Midewiwin had a ceremonial for the passage at death its major concerns were life-restoring. Midewiwin allowed the Ojibway to transcend the difficulties which beset their neighbors because the public-spirited ritual complex enabled internal redistribution of goods during the ceremony thus alleviating the dependence on adjacent peoples. Moreover, the society-ceremony vision enabled the Ojibway to bridge the gaps of this uncertain time by compensating for erratic trade patterns through elaborate ritual mechanisms that connected Ojibway villages, or "stopping places" in Midewiwin terminology. Finally, Midewiwin gave expression to a political economy in which the Ojibway first saw themselves as a coherent interband tribe whose worldview challenged them to accommodate changing ecological niches and prospective trading opportunities as they moved westward into the territories of such tribes as the Santee Nakota and Cree. From this perspective the political economy of Midewiwin provided the Ojibway with a symbol system based on intertribal altruism. Midewiwin compensated for the exigencies of the times to promote movement as a reaction to reduced trade and production opportunities.

Before the final remarks on the lifeway symbolism of Midewiwin, let me consider two critiques of Midewiwin's philanthropic character, namely, that payment was made for advancement in Midewiwin and that the organization was used for self-aggrandizement. Philanthropic voluntarism, as an ideal in the West, has a philosophical emphasis on individualism and autonomy. That is, acts to relieve suffering and enhance the quality of life typically are understood as moral acts by individuals who in their autonomy of decision-making choose to undertake this public good.

Goods distributed during Midewiwin are not motivated simply by autonomous individual freedom, *inaendaugwut* a permitted act, reciprocating other humans. Rather, the logic of the cosmology within Midewiwin says that the *manitou*, in the persons of the Midewiwin Society officiants, are being gifted. Thus, the philanthropic act of the participant is not in his or her giveaways to humans in need but as the patient-conduit for healing forces which spread out to benefit the whole community. Just as Nanabush, the first patient, experienced a reversal of his foolish trickster guise through bringing the "grand medicine" to the people, so also the feeble initiate sought to reverse the maladies of his family and his tribe. The patient's most significant ritual role occurred when reenacting the cosmological sacrifice of being "shot" by numinous powers which internalized the vision of Midewiwin. This dramatic event empowered the patient and the community and was reciprocated by gifts to the assembled *manitou*.

The charge that Midewiwin eventually became self-serving and abusive of the people usually is based on reservation documents from the mid-twentieth century. Describing it as "witchcraft," U.S. government agents of the civilization program discouraged Midewiwin. Members of the Mide Society were persecuted actively by Christian missionary personnel or solicited by museum collectors seeking Mide paraphernalia and lore. While the accusation of decay against Midewiwin cannot be dismissed summarily, since it comes from Ojibway people themselves, the desperate economic conditions on the reservations, coupled with the openly hostile agency policies regarding Native American religious and cultural practices help place the charge in historical perspective.

Ojibway healers had traditional reputations as numinous power figures whose *manitou* capacities might heal or harm. Midewiwin was structured around this shamanic ethos whose altruistic healing orientation did not exclude the possibilities for self-aggrandizing tendencies by individuals. Extremely stressful conditions such as those existing throughout Ojibway country from the mid-1800s on, increased the temptation to abuse those powers. Needless to say, Ojibway reflection on the human condition evident in the cosmological narratives and in the trickster stories recognized these possibilities. In the face of these deviations Midewiwin members who held to the tradition did not condemn these errant wanderings from a Western Christian ethical position. Rather, they evoked the message and symbolism of the Mide path of life.

The cycle of life without end, as the Ojibway say, has "four hills" for the human, namely, birth, youth, mature adulthood, and the aged. Midewiwin developed this basic Ojibway teaching into the Mide path of life. Symbolized by a linear drawing, often ornamented with beadwork flowers at the "stopping points," the line drawing has seven to nine digressions off the main path until the final circle of fire. Each stopping place marks an errant turn in life which, upon reflection, becomes a place to call friends together and "lecture" them about digressions from the true path.

That this vision has been transmitted intact into the contemporary period is evident in the philanthropic work of the White Earth Land Recovery Project. An Ojibway voluntary association dedicated to collecting funds to purchase land lost on the White Earth Reservation in Minnesota to non-native occupants, it has maintained the altruistic cosmology in changed times and new situations of need. Winona LaDuke, an Anishnabeg who directed the White Earth Land Recovery Project and cochaired the Indigenous Women's Network, has written:

> The ethical code of my own Anishinabeg community of the White Earth Reservation in northern Minnesota keeps communities and individuals in line with natural law. *"Minobimaatisiiwin"*—it means both the "good life" and "continuous rebirth"—is central to our value system. In *minobimaatisiiwin,* we honor women as the givers of lives, we honor our *Chi Anishinabeg,* our old people and ancestors who hold the knowledge. We honor our children as the continuity from generations and we honor ourselves as a part of creation. Implicit in *minobimaatisiiwin* is a continuous habitation of place, an intimate understanding of the relationship between humans and the ecosystem and of the need to maintain this balance.[16]

Winona LaDuke's resistance to her people's loss of land and their way of life hearkens back to the ancient philanthropic lifeway of her people. Her awareness that Ojibway altruism does not simply spring from humanitarian values but from a complex of cosmological values connecting people with their ancestors, the land, and the whole of creation. Her remarks about the balance maintained with the ecosystem bring us to our next case study in Native American philanthropy, namely, the *Ashkisshe* ceremonial of the Crow, often translated as the "Sun Dance."

JOHN A. GRIM

THE NORTHERN PLAINS APSAALOOKE-CROW

The high unemployment, alcoholism, and poor health endemic on contemporary Native American reservations throughout the upper Missouri River drift plains provide numerous occasions for philanthropy. For the Apsaalooke of south central Montana, known to the English-speaking world as the Crow, philanthropy may take many forms.[17] Not only are there late-twentieth-century forms of philanthropy such as the American Indian Tribal College Fund, which assists Little Big Horn College, the Apsaalooke tribal college located at Crow Agency, there are various voluntary religious associations. Tied to mainstream Christian denominations these local voluntary groups cross between reservation boundaries and, at times, overcome the prejudice against native peoples in the nearby urban centers of Billings, Montana, and Sheridan, Wyoming, to bring public assistance to needy reservation families. Apsaalooke people are involved on both sides of these mainstream American philanthropic activities. They both give time, money, and effort to these charities and accept, when needed, the beneficence of these donors. In this chapter I want to note other forms of philanthropic relief that arise from the Apsaalooke people's sense of themselves as a spiritual nation brought to a fertile, productive land. These are complex issues whose formulations tax an Apsaalooke intellectual, let alone an outsider like myself who has been allowed to visit Crow families and talk a little bit about these matters.

The Crow people have many forms of cosmological stories. These crucial containers of tribal wisdom and thought were constantly contested and reinvented as they were transmitted orally across the centuries.[18] Extended families among the Crow still transmit versions from their elders that differ slightly throughout the current six divisions of the reservation which replaced the older band organization of these people. Family cosmologies are carried into urban Indian country across the United States. Teasing clans in the Crow way, that is, relatives on one's father's clan side, have some relationship to the cosmological stories in which Old Man Coyote made this world as it is today. Unlike modern engineering concerns for rational efficiency and scientific method, Coyote's techniques ambiguated creation with contestation and spontaneity at every turn. Teasing is related to this trickster-transformer paradigm among the Crow. Teasing became a way for the people to have a good time and, for the one being teased, to stand firm and show his or her stamina.[19]

It may seem a strange interpretation to cite teasing as an example of philanthropy but the Apsaalooke understand that quality of life is forged in trying circumstances. A related Apsaalooke practice similar to Western ways of giving, and a significant Crow philanthropic activity, is the unlimited giving associated with one's matrilineal kin. Relatives on one's mother's clan side are expected to provide material sustenance just as the father's clan side provides spiritual support, instruction, and teasing challenge. These ideal kinship forms of philanthropy are woven into the Apsaalooke clan system in the form of giveaways, which continue to this day. All of these forms of assistance make demands upon individuals and families. In fact, one Apsaalooke elder once remarked to me, "Everything about the Crow way is hard! You burn up in the sweat lodge, you die of the fast in the Sun Dance, you hurt your back sitting all night in the Peyote meeting. Nothing about our ways are easy!"

Of course the underlying moral of his remarks is that life is not easy and spiritual relations with the powers in the landscape and in the larger cosmos are not acquired without effort. This effort is exemplified in another Crow cosmological story, the Earth-Diver narrative, well known among indigenous peoples influenced by the old circumpolar culture. In that story a group of animals are gathered with Coyote, or Trickster, in a boat floating upon the flood waters which the Trickster released through his foolish behavior. Wishing to restore dry land the animals volunteer to dive down and bring up some earth. While the names of the animals vary, both those who try and the one who succeeds, the point is that one animal manages to bring up a bit of earth often gripped in the last moments of life underwater and held fast as the animal floated up dead. Restoring life to the animal-quester and extending that small handful of soil into the land in the four directions, Trickster-Coyote transformed and remade the earth. So also the individual seeker in Apsaalooke religious ceremonies such as the solitary vision quest and the communal Sun Dance, undertakes the heroic journey to acquire something to renew the people. Yet, to endure hardship in a ritual manner is not simply an individual feat, according to the Apsaalooke, but a philanthropic transaction which benefits all the people.

Foremost among the Apsaalooke rituals which manifest this traditional philanthropy is the *Ashkisshe* or Sun Dance of the Crow.[20] This four-day ceremonial, returned to the Apsaalooke in 1941 from the Shoshoni of Wyoming after the Crow lost their traditional Sun Dance in 1875, usually occurs during the full moons of the spring.[21] During the four days, male and female dancers who have entered the specially constructed "Big Lodge" of the ceremonial go without food or water for three nights and into the fourth day according to the dream-intuition of the sponsor of the *Ashkisshe* in consultation with a Sun Dance Chief.

The historical, experiential, and ritual dynamics of the *Ashkisshe* ceremonial are aspects that the dancers might discuss among themselves during the breaks in the dancing. These features coalesce in a central concern to do something for the people which constitutes a cosmological act which at its heart is philanthropic. As the Sun Dance Chief, Thomas Yellowtail, said:

> In the Sun Dance way, the individual benefits from his prayers, but this is not all. The entire tribe benefits from the Sun Dance, because one part of our prayers is especially for the tribe and for all creation. Without these prayers from all the different Indian tribes, the world might not be able to continue. You can see how important the Sun Dance is. In our morning Sunrise Ceremony, when we sing the four sacred songs after we have greeted the rising sun, we bring forward all of the Medicine Fathers, and all of the sacred beings in the universe hear our prayers. When I say the morning prayer after we finish the songs, I ask that the tribe and the entire creation be blessed for another year until the next Sun Dance. All of the other dancers share in this prayer. This is a very important time, and anyone who is present can sense that we are all at the heart of creation during these prayers.[22]

To understand the way in which the Apsaalooke interpret participation in this ceremonial as an act for the public good, it is helpful to disentangle the cosmological, transactional, and ritual processes without attempting to separate them analytically as separate constituents. Rather, a synthetic critical method attempts to demonstrate that the whole is interacting in and through all the parts. Understanding ceremonial segments requires considering them in relation to the whole purpose of the ritual complex. For example, the whole from an Apsaalooke perspective can be articulated as *Acabadadea,* "Maker of All Things Above."

The senior anthropologist, and student of Crow lifeway for over fifty-five years, Fred Voget discusses the concept of *Akbatatdea* [*Acabadadea*] in this manner:

> An original creator set the stars in their heavenly places and created the earth and all within it. He was known as First Maker, Starter or Maker of All Things, The One Above, The Old White Man Above, The Above Person with Yellow Eyes, He That Hears Always, and He That Sees All Things. First Maker had so made the universe that stars, stones, insects, animals, birds, and even men and women could take on the form and behavior of spirits. Spirits were endowed with a special sacred energy or power, *makpay* [*maxpe*], characteristic of their original animal natures and capabilities. They could appear interchangeably in their human or in their material earthly forms. Spirit persons with such "medicine" were known as Those That Have No Bodies, and their earthly counterparts were the Without Fires People, who appeared as buffalo, otters, hawks, eagles, rattlesnakes, and the myriad forms of animal life as well as rocks, trees, and plants.[23]

In this discussion Voget suggests that there are a sequence of spiritual entities, according to Apsaalooke understanding, between whom spiritual transactions occur. These spiritual relationships bring benefit not simply for humans but for all beings through the ecosystem. The Creator, *Acabadadea*, has placed spirits throughout creation who may establish special relations with humans thereby transferring the power, *maxpe*, which enables the individual to do something for his or her people.

During the *Ashkisshe* individual dancers are aware, and encouraged by family outside the lodge and by announcers at the eastern open door of the "Big Lodge," to quest with "determination and sincerity" so that "something can happen." This encouragement is similar to that given a faster who undertakes the isolated quest for a vision experience. Both the isolated vision faster and the dancer at an *Ashkisshe* seek a personal, experiential contact with spirit power, *maxpe*. However, the public character of the *Ashkisshe* heightens the philanthropic aspect by bringing the quester in full public display during the difficult personal journey across the three nights and into the fourth day without food or water. The Apsaalooke term, *diakaashe*, is the word for this "determination" and "sincerity of purpose" to which a dancer aspires.

In the state of *diakaashe* a dancer becomes pathetic, powerless, and swept away in the feeling of his or her own helplessness and abandonment. This affective state is termed *akleete*, "one with no possessions," or "an orphan," one with no relatives who can help in this state. In this contemplative state of mental and somatic deprivation, the Apsaalooke believe that cosmological spirits, who possess *maxpe*, may "adopt" the faster and become that person's "Medicine Father" or *Iilaxpe*. This medicine exchange with a spiritual helper is not simply a subjective, individualistic salvation experience. Rather, the Crow understand this religious experience as philanthropic and cosmic. It is "philanthropic" because being adopted by a Medicine Father has a positive effect throughout the Crow community into the ecosystem. It is "cosmic" because what one has accomplished rises out of deeper realms of the cosmos than is apparent to other participants, family, or outsiders. This experience of *maxpe* is directly related to the ecosystem, not as a region apart from the human community but as the source of that sustenance and power which the Apsaalooke believe always has sustained, taught, healed, and guided them.

Cycles of Apsaalooke heroic stories tell of abandoned individuals whose adoption by Medicine Fathers in animal forms enabled them to accomplish something for their people. All the ritual activities undertaken before the *Ashkisshe*, such as sweat baths and personal reflection, perhaps on an isolated vision quest, prepare a person for this experience. Even after the Sun Dance if a dancer has not had a personal experience of *maxpe* he or she joins in the feasts, giveaways, and later sweat lodges for the dancers knowing that the determination assisted the people. Heroic effort is first for community benefit and, second for family, and finally for personal need.

This vision of sincerity is the ideal which is held up to all participants, whether accomplished healers or novice dancers. Thomas Yellowtail described the ongoing dance toward the centering cottonwood tree in the Big Lodge in this way:

> All this time, the dancing will continue. Even before the dancing starts [on the third day of the ceremony], all of the dancers are exhausted from their ordeal. They have not had anything to eat or drink for almost two days, and many of the dancers have been dancing and blowing on their eagle bone whistles almost constantly. Soon it will be time to resume dancing, and each dancer will have the opportunity to give even more of himself. For the Sun Dance allows an outward physical reflection of inner attitudes, and so we must consider what Acbadadea and our Medicine Fathers expect of us. Most of the Indians know that sincere prayer is required, and everyone should realize that there can be no sincere prayer without proper virtue. Humility is probably the most difficult virtue to realize. No person is ever worthy of great rewards on his own account, but only as a receptacle of power from above. If a person expects to receive a special reward for his efforts, then the Medicine Fathers will almost certainly not reward him. The sincere dancer will express his humility by continued dancing so that he cannot continue without aid from above.
>
> Finally, the Medicine Fathers will take pity on a dancer and give him a vision. They are present on the center tree, and they see into the hearts of everyone. This is a great moment for the dancer who receives the vision and also for the entire tribe.[24]

The seasonal celebration of the *Ashkisshe* becomes a part of the liturgical calendar of dancers. They hear the singing in their imagination long before they step forward to vow silently that they will dance. Participants may signal that they will do so at the last of the four "Outside Dances" or at one of the four "Medicine Bundle Openings" that begin at the full moons as much as a full year before the actual Sun Dance. This major ritual undertaking draws together clan assistance and extended family help in sponsoring the Sun Dance, building the Big Lodge, and helping the dancers prepare. Not separate ritual events, these preparatory activities are a part of the larger ritual process which nests the transactions within spiritual power. These transactions, by which a Medicine Father might adopt a faster, are part of larger cosmological forces which maintain human societies and ecosystem balance. When humans accept their cocreative, anthropocosmic, and philanthropic roles the interdependent whole, or integral cosmology, provides blessings and balance.

Additionally, there are overt acts of giving during the last day of the *Ashkisshe* that extend beyond simply honoring individuals such as Clan Uncles who "prayed the dancers out of the Big Lodge." While these are significant activities and should not be downplayed, in order to analyze and understand the cosmological and philanthropic characteristics of giving in the Native American context let us consider the Potlatch among the Kwakiutl, a Northwest Coast Native American people.

THE POTLATCH AMONG THE NORTHWEST COAST KWAKIUTL-KWAKWAKEWAK[25]

Considerations of community giving and mutual support among Native Americans often begin with an investigation of the Northwest Coast ceremonial called "potlatch."[26] This Chinook term, first used in an academic setting by Franz Boas in the 1890s to describe the intense, agonistic giveaways of the Kwakiutl and other Northwest Coast tribal groups in which elites distributed enormous amounts of goods to invited guests, was picked up by Marcel Mauss in his work, *The Gift*, and subsequently popularized as the definitive term for these exchanges. The following remarks present several interpretations of the potlatch from both materialist and ideational positions. The point is that while the Kwakiutl did not practice charity in this ritual exchange, the distribution of goods implemented ancient indigenous cosmological concepts analogous to the conceptions undergirding philanthropy in Western philosophical settings.

Even after Franz Boas's ethnographic studies during the 1890s, undertaken in conjunction with the Tlinglit-Anglo George Hunt, there emerged no clear understanding of these intense exchanges, which Boas called "potlatches." Despite impressive and voluminous descriptive ethnography, Boas made few interpretative observations other than conjecturing that there was a double-return on the initial exchange in the potlatch which he called "interest." Work by Homer Barnett in the 1930s was insightful regarding the potlatch as promoting social identity, but did not receive a wide reading. Then, Helen Codere, a political scientist, framed a new sociomaterialist interpretation which viewed the potlatch as an assimilationist mechanism. Drawing on the metaphor of warfare, Helen Codere, cited such Kwakiutl phrases as "fighting with property," and "wars of property instead of wars of blood" to suggest that the potlatch marked a dramatic shift from older warfare to a new symbolic warfare with goods. She observed that:

> the binding force in Kwakiutl history was their limitless pursuit of a kind of social prestige which required continual proving to be established or maintained against rivals, and that the main shift in Kwakiutl history was from a time when success in warfare and head hunting was significant to the time when nothing counted but successful potlatching.[27]

Codere supported her view with statistical studies of Kwakiutl occupations, wages, and population accounts in agency records. She related this to the history of the potlatch into the reservation period and cited several Kwakiutl statements recorded by Franz Boas during the eighteen-day Winter Ceremonial given at Fort Rupert in 1895. Among these provocative statements was one in which a Kwakiutl said, "When I was young I have seen streams of blood shed in war. But since that time the white man came and stopped up that stream of blood with wealth."[28] Given such a statement one could argue that Kwakiutl accommodation to intrusive American settlement and economic dominance resulted in an amazing altruistic transformation whereby tribal warfare was replaced by the intensive exchange of gifts which carried the expectation of reciprocation with interest.[29]

In 1967 Philip Drucker and Robert Heizer, building on the work of Boas and Codere, but critical of the lack of explanation of the function of the potlatch in those works, developed a further sociomaterialist interpretation of that ceremonial. They defined the potlatch as:

> a festival given by one social unit—the host group—to one or more guest groups, each of which was a recognized societal entity. The host group displayed certain of its traditional hereditary possessions (often called "privileges" in the literature), which might include dances, songs, carvings, and so on, reciting the legends of the origins of these rights and the histories of their recent transmission; presented certain of its members as entitled to use those privileges; bestowed on each of them a new name from the group's hereditary stock (the names were associated with specific levels in social rank, and the higher ranked ones are often compared to titles of nobility in European society); and ended by distributing gifts to the guests. The guests thus were considered to be formal witnesses to the claims of the persons thus presented—that is, the rights to the privileges displayed, to the names bestowed, and to the associated social statuses.[30]

In such a status-driven context the potlatch can hardly be said to be philanthropy. Elites in Kwakiutl society are reported to be exchanging with other aristocratic groups seemingly for the social purposes of identifying privileged members of groups and defining the status of both host and guest groups. Drucker and Heizer concluded that the potlatch was motivated by social integration, the reaffirmation of social positions among peers, and gamesmanship.[31] The potlatch was definitely not philanthropic in their view but a complex of gift exchanges associated with social status and the indigenous wealth system that escalated as the economic system expanded.

In contrast to these sociomaterialist explanations are ideational interpretations of the Kwakiutl potlatch which emphasize the religious character of the symbol system and the cosmological context needed to understand this type of exchange. In these works extensive fieldwork and efforts to understand indigenous concepts and context revealed cosmological motifs suggesting that ritual distribution had definite altruistic orientations. In *The Mouth of Heaven: An Introduction to Kwakiutl Religious Thought*, Irving Goldman raised the question of the meaning of the potlatch in a religious context. He wrote:

> To ignore Kwakiutl meanings in favor of consensus sociological reconstructions is to ignore reality. Surely no science can claim that deeper realities are reached by bypassing the actual phenomenon. Kwakiutl religious thought on such matters as "potlatches," and marriage, and lineage and rank, and property, in fact, defines their basic reality for the anthropologist. In the cultures of tribal societies, the deeper meanings lie not at the sociological or economic but at the religious levels.[32]

Goldman further explored this religious issue, citing the Kwakiutl term for elite chiefs as *paxala* which is the same term for Kwakiutl healers or shamans. He proposed that a shamanistic religion is at the heart of the Northwest Coast ritual exchange called "potlatch." The main components of this shamanic ethos are that persons endowed with power can overcome the devouring death of the universe, that powers have been granted by animal and supernatural agents to founding ancestors reincarnated in the elite chiefs, and the powers once granted establish a permanent alliance between the donor and the recipient which works ritually to benefit both the people and the ecosystem as a whole.

Seeking to establish an interpretative ground that continued Marcel Mauss's description of potlatch as a "total social phenomenon," Goldman rejected the term "potlatch" as hopelessly misleading but suggestive of specific practices whose occasion and distribution were ritualized. He wrote:

> There never were, at least in precontact days, such events as "potlatches." Rather, there were specific ritual occasions commemorating marriage, death, the construction of a house, investiture of an heir, elevation of young people to new positions, the "sale" of coppers, the giving of Winter Ceremonial dances, the giving of oil feasts in connection with the Winter Ceremonial, and the display of supernatural properties shortly after they had been received. These were not mere occasions for "potlatches," they were ritual occasions in their own right, at which properties were distributed.[33]

In emphasizing Kwakiutl religion as the context for understanding ritual distribution, Goldman attempted to introduce the reader into the complex interaction of myths, rituals, symbols, and material reality by which these people bring their communal lifeway into relationship with the larger spiritual forces (*nawalak*) which they observe in the cosmos. The implications of this cosmological perspective have immediate repercussions for understanding such an accepted term as "goods."

> Kwakiutl property was originally a representation of lives and not dead currency, and that value was not in mere quantity but in quality. Quantity is a value, a measure of supernatural powers and of personal force. But it is not, as has been assumed, comparable to a commercial value. Correspondingly, distribution and exchange of such properties reflect a cosmological conception of circulation, a conception that is outside the scope of sociological theory which reduces a complex concept to mechanical motions of mechanical objects.[34]

Goldman focused his analysis of ritual distribution largely on the Winter Ceremonial of the Kwakiutl. This complex ceremonial period still begins in November during which the whole Kwakiutl community is transformed from a human to a spirit enclave. This seasonal period stands outside the normal liturgical-subsistence calendar when Kwakiutl take on spirit names and prepare for lineage-based dramatic performances of the cosmogonic struggle for control over the pervasive appetite that defines the world. Goldman notes that numerous ritual distributions (potlatches) are performed in the context of spirit impersonations by the nobility to which the commoners, those who do not have inherited honored names, are witnesses and limited recipients of goods.

During the Kwakiutl Winter Ceremonial lineages play a central role, especially in transmitting ranks and privileges. Chiefs among the Kwakiutl are leaders of lineages and claim their position by virtue of direct relationship to the founding ancestor. Lineages are formed by complex arrangements of families into which outsiders can be absorbed and recognized as related to the founding ancestors. Within the lineage are a limited number of eternally reincarnating titles, ranks, and names used only by the elite leaders of a lineage to assert prerogatives and status. At the Winter Ceremonial the lineages demonstrate their prowess in their display of masks, songs, names, coppers, and ritual distributions. Sergei Kan, in his study of Tlingit potlatches, saw the symbolic connections between the wealth and food distributed, and the orality of the chiefs. Kan observed that:

> wealth and food distributed in the Tlingit potlatch carried messages about the immediate strategies, concerns, and emotions of the donors as well as such fundamental cultural values and principles as matrilineal continuity, immortality, respect for one's dead matrikin, and love for one's opposites [moiety opposites]. In that sense, artifacts served the same purposes as words; in fact, the two complimented each other, with gift giving requiring as much skill as oratory.[35]

Giving an overview of the Winter Ceremonial Goldman wrote:

> The spirit impersonations are only loosely orchestrated thematically. When the season begins the noble families agree to initiate their chil-

dren. One family challenges another, one lineage another, and one tribe another. In the course of the season, the ritual action shifts from one lineage house to another. Winter Ceremonials observed by Boas were intertribal. No matter how varied the content, the ritual themes they convey remain the same. The impersonation memorializes a mythical encounter, when the animals or supernatural beings gave powers to a human ancestor. The present impersonator is custodian of those powers, which are generally over life and property. The cannibalistic theme as the most awesome and, in Kwakiutl symbolism, the most far-reaching and all-encompassing, is ritually most demanding; the impersonator-to-be of the Man Eater "goes through," as the Kwakiutl say. Symbolically, he leaves the human world to meet Man Eater and to receive his powers. It is up to the shamans to bring him back safely and to restore him to a normal human state. The novice goes into the woods where he lives alone for four months. He returns emaciated, and with a wild and demonic craving for human flesh, of which he is to be cured.[36]

It may seem that we have wandered far from establishing the philanthropic character of the potlatch in Kwakiutl thought but, in fact, Goldman's emphasis on how the Kwakiutl think about the circulation of life in the cosmos during the Winter Ceremonial sets us on firmer ground for understanding the ritual distribution of gifts. In his work Goldman described the importance of Man Eater and the attendant cannibalistic symbolism as the core of the Winter Ceremonial. Different lineages among the Kwakiutl still reenact this thaumaturgy in their own houses, and the ritual drama becomes the interpretive basis for the many potlatches asserting the prerogatives of lineage. Most importantly for our discussion of philanthropy, Goldman asserted that Kwakiutl cosmology, as presented in the Winter Ceremonial symbolisms, provided the key to understanding the antagonistic transactions called "potlatch." That is, the cosmos is a grand circulation of lives and life forces like that of any organism. The Kwakiutl believe this system to be totalizing, eternal, and fully integrated into every aspect of the universe.

In the context of a spiritual struggle for strength between powerful spirits as donors and humans-impersonating-spirits as recipients Kwakiutl leaders negotiate, through ritual distribution, for the return of life to the seas, to the lands, and to the people. Within this indigenous cosmological context it can be said that these ritual distributions have the result of assisting both humans and animals who are, essentially, mirror images of each other. That is, humans are believed to go for a time after death into the animal world, thus, animals are actually waiting to be reborn as humans. The organic circulation of life, celebrated in the complex Winter Ceremonial, served to feed the "mouth" of the universe. As the Man-Eater symbolism indicated, this conception of the cosmos as "mouths" had numinous dimensions. Just as it was terribly frightening to be caught in the jaws of devouring death, so also there was communal attraction, purpose, and material support for one's lineage leader as he ritually distributed to circulate life again.

At the ritual distributions, according to the Kwakiutl, nothing is destroyed, contrary to some Western observers' disgust in the late nineteenth century with the great destruction of skins, coppers, oil, and food at ritual distributions. Rather, oil, blankets, and coppers, which may be burned or thrown into the sea if they are not distributed to guests, are believed to be alive with the dead within them who are collectively returned to spiritual realms so that they might live again as salmon, as hunted animals, and as humans. Thus, ritual distribution for the Kwakiutl enhances the collective welfare by bringing supernatural powers to bear upon the community's vitality and needs.

A significant advance on both Boas's ethnography and Goldman's insightful work was the study of Stanley Walens, *Feasting with Cannibals: An Essay on Kwakiutl Cosmology*. While space prevents an extended discussion, it is helpful to note his exploration of major metaphors in Kwakiutl thought with cosmological and philanthropical implications, namely, food and the carved box. According to Walens in the Kwakiutl cosmogony creation was a food-related act which Kwakiutl rituals reenact.

> Thus, the Kwakiutl moral universe becomes united, not by any vague religious sense but by the fact that the entire universe contains all beings within its bounds, and that all beings are subject to the principle of being both hungry and the food of other beings who are themselves hungry. The Kwakiutl universe is a universe of related beings, all of whom have the moral responsibility to control their eating. Eating is a universal property of the world, and thus it is the basis for morality.[37]

In Walens's reading of Kwakiutl thought, the Man-Eater image of the Winter Ceremonial takes on deeper ethical implications, namely, the Kwakiutl abhorrence of unbridled appetite, which they viewed as a form of cannibalism to be controlled for the good of the whole universe community. This consideration of ritual distribution also involves the Kwakiutl carved box as both a cosmological metaphor and a major Kwakiutl metaphor for all that is bounded, limited, and controlled.

Kwakiutl boxes, often carved on both the interior and exterior, have long been recognized as beautiful works of art. The role of boxes as storage for food, clothing, masks, and other "treasured items" is well known, but their symbolic and ritual mode remains virtually unexplored. Yet, in Kwakiutl cosmology and social thought "boxness" and the nature of boxes are used as organizing ideas. Walens observes:

> Boxness forms the metaphorical basis in Kwakiutl philosophy for ideas of kinship and separateness, space and time, cooperation and competi-

tion, secularity and sacredness, self and other, life and death, and innumerable other dialectic oppositions. Humans are born from boxes, swaddled in boxes, catch, store, and serve their food in boxes, live in boxes, travel in boxes, and when they die are buried in boxes. Even the body itself is a type of box; humans not only live and die in boxes, but are themselves boxes. The universe is envisioned as a set of conjoined boxes. Time is envisioned as self-contained units that are bounded and integral as boxes. Names act as containers for invisible spiritual matter in the way that wooden boxes contain material items. Social units act as boxes to contain people.[38]

Walens suggests that this metaphorization is not one-sided, namely, just as human and cosmic affairs are meaningfully expressed by boxness, so actual carved boxes have anthropocosmic implications. Thus, qualities of the human, the social, and the cosmic are also attributed to the carved box. Carved boxes are alive in the Kwakiutl belief system, and have skin boundaries and interior dimensions. Significant boxes are named, they are eternal, and they pass through the experience of reincarnation.

In the metaphorization of the universe, the box lid holds a special symbolic place. The opening lid of the box, is often the only part of the box which is distributed by a father-in-law to his son-in-law in a potlatch associated with marriage. A completely new box will be carved to give symbolic rebirth to the eternal name embodied in the box lid. Like the layers of the cosmos, the box lid is the sacred place for entering and leaving. This shamanistic transformation, akin to putting on a mask or donning a special Chilkat blanket, serves to control the unbridled hunger of the universe. By means of the relationships of spirit donors and chiefly recipients the public good is maintained against the maw of time and space. This maintenance by means of ritual distribution does not end or displace the cycle of birth and death but places it, instead, within the control of human remembering of the circulation of life and forgetting the ambiguity of death. It is the commemoration of this philanthropic act which the young Tlingit poet celebrated when he wrote:

> As a man stands on earth
> he has only two reasons
> for being here:
> living and dying.
> And whatever comes between
> is just a form of being remembered.[39]

CONCLUSION

The purpose of this essay has been to explore selected Native American lifeways in terms of philanthropy. Instead of projecting Western understandings of philanthropy onto native cultures, this project sought to draw out particular cultural forms which manifest altruistic orientations in an indigenous thought system. To have focused only on the three case studies presented here not only begs the critical charge of the inadequacy of this study but also the need for other, more exacting studies of philanthropy in a Native American context. Indeed, it is woefully inadequate to pass over such major expression of indigenous public-mindedness and social planning as the Hodenosaunee-Iroquois rites of Thanksgiving, the Lakota sense of *mitakuye oyasin*, "all my relatives," the renewing care of the Muskogee Green Corn Dance, the healing concerns of the Dine-Navajo Chantways, the benefit sought from places and derived from place names by Apache, the communal values inherent in Pueblo lifeways and ceremonial calendars which have endured for centuries.

So also I have not explored the range of Native American philanthropic organizations modeled on Western worldviews. Some, such as the Native Brotherhoods of Alaska, have been active since the late nineteenth century assisting native peoples in their acculturation into mainstream America.[40] Important individuals such as William Apess, Pequot, could be cited who, as early as the 1830s gave freely of his rhetorical skills and courage to the Mashpee peoples of Cape Cod in their struggle for sovereignty. There are also contemporary organizations like the American Indian Science and Engineering Society whose philanthropic activities increasingly embody Native American thought and practices in its scientific concerns. Similarly, the National Tekakwitha Conference, a Roman Catholic organization which has moved from Anglo missionary control to native leadership, sees itself as pursuing an altruistic goal in its self-reflection on the relationship of indigenous spirituality and Christianity. So also I need to mention the Seventh Generation Fund, a native philanthropic foundation which financially assists diverse Native American individuals and groups in projects which enhance the quality of life both on reservations and among urban communities.

In this overview of Native American philanthropy using three case studies several compelling observations can be made. First, Native American philanthropy, while it has found Western institutional expression in the twentieth century, continues to be based on the inherent cosmological values of particular peoples. Second, philanthropy is not separated out from the socioeconomic lifeway of the people. Finally, just as major philanthropic acts reflect the ongoing altruism of public-minded individuals, so also major rituals among the First Peoples of the North American continent foreground philanthropic ideals which find daily expression in these communities.

NOTES

1. Simon Ortiz quoted from Laura Coltelli, *Winged Words: American Indian Writers Speak* (Lincoln: University of Nebraska Press, 1990): 110.

2. Particular names of indigenous nations and peoples, such as Apsaalooke, are preferable to English translations (for example, Crow), or more general references such as American Indian, Native American, First Peoples, First Nations, and Indigenous Peoples. As no one English term is preferable, these terms are used here to refer broadly to the indigenous peoples of the Americas.

3. This term "integral cosmology" follows from Thomas Berry's use of the phrase, "functional cosmology," to describe the pervasive functioning of the origin story for a people in determining their values, behavior, and direction. For a discussion of the term "functional cosmology," see Thomas Berry, *The Dream of the Earth* (San Francisco: Sierra Club Books, 1988); and with Brian Swimme, *The Universe Story* (San Francisco: HarperCollins, 1992). I have altered the phrase to read "integral cosmology" to move away from the strictly causalist-functionalist reading of a cosmology which reading is not intended by Thomas Berry.

4. The term "lifeway" is used here to suggest the close interaction of worldview and economy in small-scale societies (a cosmology-cum-economy society). Contemporary reservation communities, as well as Indian urban communities, mirror amazing varieties of lifeway practice. These native groups, while inextricably dependent on the American and global marketplace, still preserve core experiences of lifeways which enable the community to imagine itself in traditional cosmological ways. Such ceremonial acts as "giveaways," "potlatches," and social structures built on clan reciprocity often constellate these core experiences. Rather than having been lost or completely subverted by dominant American market values, these core experiences have been transmitted in changed settings and reinterpreted by creative individuals.

5. The term "anthropocosmic" is drawn from the work of Tu Wei-ming; see *Confucian Thought: Selfhood as Creative Transformation* (Albany: State University of New York Press, 1985): 64, 137–38.

6. For a discussion of the box metaphor as a cosmological symbol, see Stanley Walens, *Feasting with Cannibals: An Essay on Kwakiutl Cosmology* (Princeton: Princeton University Press, 1981): 46–47.

7. See Lynda Shaffer, *Native Americans before 1492: The Mound Building Centers of the Eastern Woodlands* (Armonk, NY: Sharpe, 1992).

8. Basil Johnston, *Ojibway Heritage* (New York: Columbia University Press, 1976): 23.

9. See Marcel Mauss, *The Gift: The Form and Reason for Exchange in Archaic Societies*, trans. W. D. Halls (London: Routledge, 1990): 3.

10. Johnston, pp. 78–79.

11. See Ruth Landes, *Ojibwa Religion and the Midewiwin* (Madison, WI: University of Wisconsin Press, 1968):3–4; also see Johnston, p. 84.

12. For a discussion of Midewiwin and Ojibway shamanism, see John

Grim, *The Shaman: Patterns of Religious Healing among the Ojibway Indians* (Norman: University of Oklahoma Press, 1983).

13. See Selwyn Dewdney, *The Sacred Scrolls of the Southern Ojibway* (Toronto: University of Toronto, 1975).

14. This sense of liminality, and community (*communitas*) is drawn from Victor Turner, *The Ritual Process: Structure and Anti-Structure* (Baltimore: Penguin, 1969).

15. Richard White, *Middle Ground: Indians, Empires, and Republicans in the Great Lakes Region 1650–1815* (New York: Cambridge University Press, 1991).

16. Winona LaDuke, "Minobimaatisiiwin: The Good Life," *Cultural Survival Quarterly* 16, no. 4 (winter 1992): 69.

17. The Apsaalooke people hold approximately 55 percent of a 2,282,000-acre reservation in Montana. Their tribal name is variously spelled as Absaroke, Apsaloke, et al. The author has traveled out to visit Crow families since 1983 especially the families of Adam Birdinground and Violet Medicine Horse, who passed to the other side in the 1980s.

18. One of the most thoughtful and challenging native intellectual statements regarding the act of imaging and thinking in an oral narrative mode is the essay by N. Scott Momaday, "The Man Made of Words," in *The First Convocation of American Indian Scholars*, ed. Rupert Costo (San Francisco: Indian Historian Press, 1970): 49–84.

19. Regarding teasing, readers might want to consult the "Crow Indian Humor" chapter in Joseph Medicine Crow, *From the Heart of the Crow Country: The Crow Indian's Own Stories* (New York: Orion Books, 1992): 124–33.

20. I am using *Ashkisshe* or "temporary lodge" and Sun Dance to refer to the *Ashkisshelissua* "temporary lodge dance." The English translation "imitation lodge" is also used; see *A Dictionary of Everyday Crow* compiled by Ishtaleeschia Baaciia Heeleetaalawe ["Squirrel that Walks among the Pines" / Mary Helen Medicine Horse] (Bilingual Materials Development Center, Crow Agency, MT, 1987).

21. The older traditional Crow Sun Dance, *Baaiichkiisapiliolissua*, or "fringed ankle dance," was lost during the early reservation period through a complex of social, political, and historical factors connected with U.S. Agency prohibitions of such ceremonies, Christian missionary hostility, the end of intertribal raiding and warfare, the radical subsistence shift required of the Crow with the end of buffalo hunting, and the fact that the older Sun Dance was more marginal to Crow religious life. The current Crow-Shoshoni Sun Dance, *Ashkisshelissua*, or "imitation lodge dance," was brought back to the Crow Indian Reservation in 1941 by the Crow-Shoshoni Sun Dance Chief, John Truhujo and several Crow individuals, especially William Big Day. For a comprehensive discussion of these issues see Fred Voget, *The Shoshoni-Crow Sun Dance* (Norman: University of Oklahoma Press, 1984).

22. Thomas Yellowtail, *Yellowtail, Crow Medicine Man and Sun Dance Chief: An Autobiography*, as told to Michael O. Fitzgerald (Norman: University of Oklahoma Press, 1991): 103.

23. Fred Voget, *They Call Me Agnes: A Crow Narrative Based on the Life of Agnes Yellowtail Deernose* (Norman: University of Oklahoma Press, 1995), 6; Voget also cites the following works in his discussion: Edward Curtis, "The

Apsaroke, or Crows," in *The North American Indian*, vol. 4, 1909; Robert Lowie, "Myths and Traditions of the Crow Indians," American Museum of Natural History *Anthropological Papers* 25, 1918; Lowie, "The Religion of the Crow Indians," in *Anthropological Papers* 25, 1922; Lowie, *The Crow Indians* (New York: Farrar & Rinehart, 1935); William Wildschut, *Crow Indian Medicine Bundles* (New York: Museum of the American Indian, Heye Foundation, 1960); and Rodney Frey, *The World of the Crow Indians: As Driftwood Lodges* (Norman: University of Oklahoma Press, 1987).

24. *Yellowtail*, p. 170.

25. I have given the tribal term, Kwakwakewak, in relation to the more widely known name, Kwakiutl (pronounced "Gwa-gae-ul"), which I will use in this section.

26. The most prominent Kwakiutl terms used for ritual distribution, which occurs during the Winter Ceremonial, are *yaxwede* and *maxwede*. The prefix *yax* refers to property which has been vanquished, for example, skins from a slain animal. The prefix *max* is directly related to *maxenox*, the Killer Whale, and refers to that which has been killed. Thus, ritual distribution has the connotations of vanquishing, killing, and by extension in Kwakiutl thought, shaming.

27. Helen Codere, *Fighting with Property: A Study of Kwakiutl Potlatching and Warfare 1792–1930*, Monographs of the American Ethnological Society XVIII (New York: J. J. Augustin Publisher, 1950): 118.

28. See Franz Boas, "The Social Organization and the Secret Societies of the Kwakiutl Indians," *Report of the U.S. National Museum for 1895* (Washington, D.C., 1897), p. 26.

29. It is appropriate to note that Codere did not bring the type of skepticism and contestation to these statements that a Kwakiutl would bring to them, nor did she reflect on the hyperbolic use of such rhetorical statements in the Kwakiutl lifeway, especially during ritual distributions (potlatch). Neither did she present sufficient historical context regarding the incredible death rates the Kwakiutl suffered from foreign-introduced pathogens during the late eighteenth and early nineteenth centuries. All these issues relate to historical adaptations in the Kwakiutl potlatch.

30. Philip Drucker and Robert Heizer, *To Make My Name Good: A Reexamination of the Southern Kwakiutl Potlatch* (Berkeley: University of California Press, 1967), 8.

31. Homer Barnett, "The Nature of the Potlatch," *American Anthropologist* n.s. 40 (1938): 349–58.

32. Irving Goldman, *The Mouth of Heaven: An Introduction to Kwakiutl Religious Thought* (Huntington, NY: Robert E. Krieger Pub. Co., 1981): 8–9.

33. Goldman, p. 131.

34. Ibid., p. 123.

35. Sergei Kan, *Symbolic Immortality: The Tlingit Potlatch of the Nineteenth Century* (Washington, D.C.: Smithsonian Institution Press, 1989): 249.

36. Goldman, p. 24.

37. Stanley Walens, *Feasting with Cannibals: An Essay on Kwakiutl Cosmology* (Princeton: Princeton University Press, 1981): 6.

38. Ibid., p. 46.
39. Kan, p. 302.
40. See Philip Drucker, *The Native Brotherhoods: Modern Intertribal Organizations on the Northwest Coast*, Smithsonian Institution, Bureau of American Ethnology Bulletin 168, Washington, D.C., 1958.

PART TWO
HISTORICAL/TEXTUAL ROOTS

.3.

Contextualizing Philanthropy in South Asia: A Textual Analysis of Sanskrit Sources[1]

LEONA ANDERSON

In almost every culture generosity, however we define it, is an ideal to be striven for, a goal to be achieved. That this holds true in the case of the Indian subcontinent is without question. Each tradition or culture has its own unique characteristics and each its own manner of setting the parameters for the occasion for giving, for what is to be given, who is to give, and who is to receive. South Asia is no exception to this rule. Here, where social organization is complex, generosity is prescribed in a wide range of circumstances and for various purposes. From earliest times giving was considered a virtue conducive to the accumulation of merit. Though largesse is one means by which merit is accrued, it is often prescribed as a required duty rather than understood as an optional action. In the case, for example, of the reception of guests, our sources are clear that there is only one avenue open to a potential host, namely, to offer hospitality. Here generosity is simply mandated. One who refuses such a request risks losing any merit accumulated over an entire lifetime. A further point to consider in South Asia is that liberality is understood contextually, in accordance with circumstance. Caste, for example, is one factor identifying those who are required to give and those who are to receive. Kṣatriyas (members of the second caste) and

57

Vaiśyas (members of the third caste), for example, are enjoined to give generously, while Brahmins are mandated to receive. So, too, *āśrama* or the stage of life that one occupies determines one's duty to generosity; householders emerge here as the primary donors. As giving and receiving gifts are rarely simple transactions, the Indian tradition is also clear that generosity can be dangerous. Giving is to be approached with caution and care and with a clear understanding of the relationships between donor and recipient that result from this exchange.

This chapter examines the above characteristics of generosity in South Asia with specific reference to recipients, donors (particularly kings), and the substance and purpose of the gift. Before embarking on this discussion some comment is necessary regarding geographical boundaries and my primary materials. I use the term "South Asia" to refer to the Indian subcontinent. My materials, further, are drawn from Hinduism, although one should be well aware that there is no small difficulty in determining exactly what this latter term signifies.[2] It is not here my intent to suggest that either the Indian or the Hindu tradition are monolithic in character. The opposite is in fact the case, and there is a great deal of variation temporally, geographically, and culturally in the context of this region. These terms, "Hindu," "Indian subcontinent," and "South Asia" are used exclusively for convenience and should not be otherwise construed.

Given the multiplicity of occasions for giving in South Asia, the first task is to narrow the focus of the discussion. To this end, this essay will be limited to materials drawn primarily from Sanskrit literature, situating generosity in the Hindu textual tradition. A primary understanding of generosity is to be found in the Sanskrit term *dāna* and acts which are so categorized will further restrict our study. *Dāna* is defined as giving, granting, teaching, liberality, and charity. It refers also to a gift, donation, or present.[3] J. Gonda, in his discussion of this term draws attention to the fact that while there is no complete equivalent for *dāna* in the English language, gift, charity, donation, grant, alms, benefice, and prestation are approximate English equivalents.[4] It is further of note that *dāna* is intimately linked with Hindu notions of dharma or duty. *Dāna* appears in lists of dharmic virtues including, for example, truthfulness, honesty, and self-sacrifice. In this context it has much in common with the practice of *dakṣiṇā* or sacrificial fee, though these terms are by no means synonymous. Debate as to the relationship of *dāna* to *dakṣiṇā* is ongoing. On the one hand, *dakṣiṇā* is distinguished from *dāna* on the grounds that the former is payment for services rendered on the ritual occasion of sacrifice; the latter is not. Still, this case is not as simple as it seems. As Vijay Nath points out in her book,[5] there is a certain elasticity in both terms which renders them on occasion interchangeable, sometimes impossible to distinguish.[6]

Suffice it to say that *dāna* is descriptive of many situations. It is considered a religious obligation and has been dealt with as such at length in ancient scriptures, of which there is an abundance. A survey of the religious literature as represented by Sanskrit materials yields numerous instances describing and prescribing this practice.[7] The merits of giving are mentioned repeatedly in the earliest of the Vedic texts, the *Ṛg Veda,* and its appearance there suggests the antiquity of this practice, though the meaning of *dāna* there is not precise.[8] The numerous *dānastutis* or eulogies of gifts praise the generosity of kings and others.[9] *Ṛg Veda* X.117 eulogizes the gift of food and condemns those who do not offer this substance to the gods, acquaintances, or friends. Here we read that those who feed only themselves, eat only sin (*pāpa*). The same idea occurs also in *Manu* (III.118); *Viṣṇudharmasmṛti* (67.43) and the *Gītā* (III.13). According to the latter, "He who prepares food for himself (alone), eats nothing but sin. . . ."[10] The *Ṛg Veda* also tells us in X.107, 2, 7, 8 that "Donors do not die, they reach immortality in heaven, they do not go down to a low goal, they are not harmed, nor do they suffer pain; *dākṣina* renders unto these donors this whole world and also heaven.[11] The attention paid to giving in this early text would indicate its importance and also serves to identify this act as normative.

In that *dāna* is intimately related to dharma or duty, one would expect it to be given serious consideration in texts which deal with matters of law and duty. Indeed, lengthy discussions on giving are contained in treatises which reflect on these questions. The *Manu Smṛti (Laws of Manu)* which dates between 200 B.C.E. and 200 C.E. and *Yājnavalkya Smṛti* (100 C.E. and 300 C.E.) both comment extensively on the tradition of giving. There are countless digests devoted solely to this topic which date between the seventh and the seventeenth centuries including, for example, Hemādri's *Dānakhaṇḍa* (of the *Caturvargacintāmaṇi*), *Dānakriyā-kaumudī* of Govindānanda, the *Dānamayūkha* of Nīlakaṇṭha, the *Dānava-kyāvali* of Vidyāpati, the *Dānasāgara* of Ballālasena, and the *Dānaprakāśa* of Mitramiśra.[12]

References to giving appear also throughout the epics and Purāṇas. A major portion of the *Anuśāsana-parvan* of the *Mahābhārata* is devoted to the various aspects of this topic. The extensive body of popular purānic literature contains numerous verses on *dāna* with the *Agni Purāṇa,* the *Matsya Purāṇa*, and the *Varāha Purāṇa* all containing extensive passages on various questions of generosity.[13]

In these texts *dāna* emerges as an ideal that one is enjoined to strive toward and not necessarily a practical descriptive of action. In an attempt to investigate the manner in which these ideals are operationalized in Sanskrit literature, I look to popular narratives in which acts of giving are contextualized. In this category of texts are the numerous folktales and popular stories contained in the *Pañcatantra* and the *Kathā-*

saritsāgara. The *Pañcatantra,* for example, dates from about the second century B.C.E. and the numerous recensions in which these same stories appear are indicative of their popularity.[14] The *Pañcatantra* tales are rich in variety, humor, and wit. They function as didactic stories aimed, as the frame story tells us, at teaching the dull-witted sons of King Sudarśana of Pāṭaliputra. The style in which these narratives are written is direct, forceful, and smooth-flowing; they are simple and idiomatic.[15] Here *dāna* is not the focus of technical debate but a matter of popular opinion and custom. The stories give us insight on how *dāna* was understood in practical terms.

The *Kathāsaritsāgara,* a collection of stories written by the Kashmiri Brahmin for the amusement of his Queen Sūryamati serves a similar function.[16] By the admission of its author Somadeva, the *Kathāsaritsāgara* is a condensed Sanskrit version of Guṇāḍhya's *Bṛhatkathā.*[17] The longest collection of stories in the *Kathāsaritsāgara* and the one most relevant is contained in Book Twelve, included in which is the *Vetālapancavimśatikā* or the twenty-five tales of a *vetāla.* Both extant versions of the *Bṛhatkathā* (i.e., the *Kathāsritsāgara* and the *Bṛhatkathāmanjarī*) contain these twenty-five tales, but some evidence suggests that they may originally have formed an independent cycle. (These stories are not found, for example, in Buddhasvamin's *Bṛhatkathā Ślokasamgraha.*[18]) The *Vetālapancavimśatikā* does, however, exist independently in a variety of recensions, the most important of which is probably that of Śivadāsa and dates from the fifteenth century C.E.[19] The *Vetālapancavimśatikā*'s general popularity is attested to by its inclusion in the Kashmiri versions, Somadeva's *Kathāsaritsāgara,* the *Bṛhatkathāmanjarī,* and in its numerous independent recensions. Here, traditions of generosity are contextualized in narrative format.

Distinct from these short narratives is Ahobala's *Virupākṣavasantotsavacampū,* a text in prose and verse dating from the fifteenth century C.E. and originating in the Vijayanagara period of Indian history. This text, whose primary purpose is to provide a description of the Spring Festival as celebrated at the Virūpākṣa temple, also contains a biography of a Brahmin, greedy to the extreme, who takes up residence with his wife in the Virūpākṣa temple. The caricature of this Brahmin illustrates the Hindu recognition of the ease in which the designation of a particular group of people as recipients of gifts (i.e., Brahmins) can be employed to their advantage.

The above list of works in which *dāna* figures prominently is by no means exhaustive but serves rather to indicate the enormous attention accorded to this practice. In this context, though giving is important, it is not efficacious without qualification. For example, though it is understood that merit may be accumulated in numerous ways, the present age offers unique circumstances. In estimating the importance of *dāna,* the

Laws of Manu (I.85, 86) and other law books of similar import say that *dāna* is the principal component of religious life for those living in the present age. Hence Manu says:

> 85. One set of duties [is prescribed] for men in the *Kṛta* age, different ones in the *Tretā* and in the *Dvāpara* and [again] another [set] in the *Kāli*, in proportion as [those] ages decrease in length.

> 86. In the *Kṛta* age the chief [virtue] is declared to be performance of austerities, in the *Tretā* [divine] knowledge, in the *Dvāpara* [the performance of] sacrifices, in the *Kāli* liberality alone.

To understand the significance of this dictum one must refer to the traditional Hindu postulation of the existence of four distinct ages or *yugas*, namely, the *Kṛta yuga*, *Tretā yuga*, *Dvāpara yuga*, and *Kāli yuga*. Each age or period of time constitutes a different stage in the movement of the universe from creation to destruction. Each successive age is one of progressive deterioration and an increasing decline in virtue. Hence, as circumstances change in each *yuga* a particular practice is prescribed as especially appropriate and meritorious. In the first three ages, Manu tells us that austerities (*tapas*), metaphysical knowledge, and sacrifice are appropriate avenues of religious expression, each a means of accumulating merit, and each ultimately a pathway to release (*mokṣa*) or salvation. The present era is known as the *Kāli* age, the black age, the age in which social disorder is at its peak. Dharma is weak, the Vedas forgotten, and Brahmins little respected.[20] It is an age in which, like the others, a particular type of religiosity is most efficacious. For the *Kāli* age, Manu prescribes giving (*dāna*) above all other religious duties, indicating its importance in the religious quest of the present day. Indeed, in the *Kāli* age, Manu seems to suggest that *dāna* is one of the only means of gaining merit available to us given the deterioration of the cosmos.

Hindu texts, further, indicate that acts of generosity in themselves do not return rewards. The merit of a gift depends upon the attitude in which it is offered. The manner in which a gift is proffered renders some acts more beneficial than others. In one of the most important texts for Hindu spirituality, the *Bhagavad Gītā*, this hierarchy is defined in terms of the attitude of the donor. Hence:

> 20. The gift which with the mere thought "One must give!"
> Is given to one that does no [return] favor,
> At the proper place and time, to a worthy person,
> That gift is said to be of goodness.
> 21. But what in order to get a return favor,
> Or with a view to the fruit as well,
> Or when it hurts to give is given,
> That gift is said to be of passion.
> 22. What gift at the the wrong place and time

And to unworthy persons is given,
Without [suitable] marks of respect and with contempt,
That is declared to be of darkness.[21]

Here gifts are distinguished by type according to the well-known tripartite characteristics of the *gunas* (*sattva*, *tamas*, and *rajas*). Each *guna* imbues the act of giving with a quality which in turn determines the worth of the gift and the merit attached thereto. *Guna* means quality or attribute. In certain Hindu philosophies the material world is described as composed of three *gunas* or "strands" each with its own qualities and characteristics: *sattva* or purity, brightness; *rajas* or passion; and *tamas* or darkness, inertia, ignorance, or delusion. The three *gunas* operate either in conflict or cooperation with one another and together account for the composition of the physical world. The *Bhagavad Gītā* having categorized *dāna* as *sāttvic*, *rājjasic*, and *tāmasic*, defines them accordingly. A *sāttvic* gift, we are told, is superior, for this type of gift entails no ulterior motives and is offered at both a proper time and proper place. It is a gift given in the spirit of giving requiring no reciprocation. In short, the *sāttvic* gift, though perhaps the most difficult of gifts, the idealized gift, is also the gift with the most value. This same gift is referred to by Devala as *dharmadāna* the gift given in accordance with duty.[22] Generosity characterized by *rajas* is meritorious but qualified by either desire for reward or hardship. This gift is one which is occasioned by passion and attachment. The *tāmasic* gift is both the last mentioned and the least auspicious, given without consideration of time and place and either in a spirit of contempt or disrespect. This gift earns little merit and thus, in this context giving involves a negative return.

These verses from the *Gītā* would imply that to be efficacious, generosity must coincide with a particular attitude. While this is surely praiseworthy, other sources are equally clear in recognizing the infrequency of such situations. It is a rare sight, we are told, to see anyone giving away in charity wealth that he or she has earned. Vedavyāsa states outright that "amongst a hundred men, one may be found to be brave, among thousands a learned man, among hundreds of thousands an orator, but a donor may or may not be found."[23] There is a tension here between the ideal *sāttvic* gift and the recognition that such gifts are singular in the world. A further qualification to the practice of giving is to be found in the distinction between the duties and responsibilities of each caste and those at each stage in life as described in Hindu society. Though generosity is often construed simply as a duty or a religious obligation, it is not imposed equally upon all members of society and under all circumstances. Giving, for example, is the duty especially prescribed for householders (*grhasthas*) or those who have completed their studies, are married and engaged in maintaining a family. Hindu custom distinguishes four stages (*āśrama*) in the life of an individual—the *brahmacarya* (student), *gṛhastha* (householder), *vanaprāstha* (forest dweller), and *sannyāsi* (renouncer). Each stage coincides with different expectations and different responsibilities. The *Laws of Manu* eulogize *gṛhasthas* (householders) as primary donors. The practice of generosity here is especially auspicious because those in the other stages of life (e.g., student, forest dweller, and renouncer) are cherished and fed with Vedic knowledge but also with food provided by the householder. Manu says:

> 77. As all living creatures subsist by receiving support from air, even so [the members of] all orders subsist by receiving support from the householder.
> 78. Because men of the three [other] orders are daily supported by the householder with [gifts of] sacred knowledge and food, therefore [the order of] householders is the most excellent order. (*Manu*, III)

Gifts offered by householders were not only meritorious for householders but also required by those who were engaged in study or devoted solely to the religious quest. Students, forest dwellers, and renouncers depended upon these gifts.

A further example of the idea that different members of the social body are subject to different rules and one which we return to below is to be found in the prescriptions of giving for the different castes. The duty of some, it would seem, is to give, while others are destined to receive.

RECIPIENTS AND DONORS

In the case of recipients and donors of gifts, both must be worthy and the gift must be offered and accepted. Our sources are clear on the first point, submitting potential recipients and donors to intense scrutiny regarding their character and motivations. As to the second, acceptance completes the transaction and ensures the result; it is therefore of primary importance for the recipient to decide whether or not to take possession of a gift. Obviously a gift which is not received or not accepted does not qualify for the reward of merit.

As one would expect, the *Dharmaśāstras* enjoin giving to individuals who are worthy simply if they are in need.[24] One's social status (caste) or personal qualities are here not at issue. The poor, the helpless, and the disadvantaged are obvious objects of generosity. Interestingly, texts like the *Dakṣa Smṛti* place one's parents, guru (teacher), friend, a well-conducted man, one to whom the donor is in debt, and one who is endowed with special excellence in the same category of recipients as the poor and the hungry.[25] Gifts to any of the above are considered meritorious.[26] As noted above, certain castes are identified as particularly appropriate recipients simply by virtue of their birth. In this latter category, the most worthy of all recipients are Brahmins. Manu tells us that it is the duty of Brahmins to accept gifts while Kṣatriyas and Vaiśyas are required to bestow them.[27] Indeed, according to Manu, Brahmins are the only caste whose duties include the acceptance of gifts. The Śataptha Brāhmaṇa tells us that there are two kinds of gods, those in heaven and Brahmins who have studied the Vedas.[28] Both should be honored with gifts accordingly. Later literature as, for example, evidenced in the Purāṇas extends this notion without restraint and elevates even ignorant Brahmins. In some passages Brahmins need not be questioned about their character. Giving even to Brahmins who were unworthy, thus came to be considered meritorious.[29]

One explanation of the identification of Brahmins as primary recipients of gifts lies in the understanding of this caste as the inheritors, preservers, and transmitters of sacred knowledge. It has been argued that in giving to Brahmins one exchanges material goods (the gift) for spiritual goods (merit). Another explanation for the elevation of Brahmins without restriction is that during these times there was no officially sanctioned educational system. Education was the duty and responsibility of Brahmins who were enjoined to transmit knowledge without charge. Hindu society thus deemed it a duty to provide Brahmins with the resources which would enable them to carry out this task. As such, they were to engage in teaching without imposing a fee. Brahmins were, at least ideally, to live by means of gifts alone. Theoretically, only Brahmins who were learned and who upheld the tradition of study and meditation would be recipients of gifts. According to Nath, this was the case in actual practice, i.e., a Brahmin's earnings depended on his reputation for learning.[30]

Despite the declaration that Brahmins must be gifted unilaterally, some of our data would indicate that this prescription is not universal. Brahmins, in order to qualify, are enjoined to live a simple life of comparative poverty and to occupy their time by study and meditation. Giving to Brahmins who are not learned secures nothing. In this way, numerous Brahmins could be excluded as unfit recipients.[31] Even Manu tells us: "A Brahmin who neither performs austerities nor studies the Veda, yet delights in accepting gifts, sinks with the [donor into hell], just as he who attempts to cross over in a boat made of stone [is submerged] in the water" (IV.190).

Brahmins who are covetous, hypocritical, deceitful, cruel, dishonest, thieves, or ignorant of the Veda are to be avoided.[32] Only misery in the next world both for the donor and the recipient results from such a transaction. This latter is an interesting dictum as it places responsibility equally on the donor and the recipient. It is not sufficient, it would seem, to give liberally; one must be cautious of the risk both to oneself as well as the recipient. A gift to an inappropriate person bodes ill for donor and recipient alike.

The power of the gift thus extends beyond the simple transaction, affecting one's fate in this world and the next. Notwithstanding the overwhelming tone of our texts extolling the virtues of giving to Brahmins, other sources suggest that the temptation to solicit gifts for personal gain alone is sometimes too difficult to resist. The potential of Brahmins to overindulge themselves and forget their responsibilities is recognized in a depiction of a particularly greedy Brahmin in the *Virūpākṣavasantotsā-vacampū* of Ahobala. The story, which can only be a parody, opens with the introduction of the Brahmin, Mahālobhin (literally one possessed of great greed or the greedy one):

> There once was a Brahmin named Mahālobhin who was both very greedy and extremely clever. Routinely, he lived by begging and in the process amassed a great deal of money and spent none. Mahālobhin was so greedy that eventually he was driven out of the city and sought refuge at the local Śaiva temple of Vrūpāksa. Each day he dispatched his wife to the city dressed in the oldest of rags to beg for food and money. Much to the distress of Mahālobhin, one day his wife with the supernatural aid of the goddess Pārvati and lord Śiva, became pregnant. Fearing the expense of raising a child, Mahālobhin attempts to induce his wife to abort. His efforts are futile and a son is born. The child is named Paramalobhin (the greediest), in hopes that he would be greedy from birth. Paramalobhin is indeed as avaricious as his father, sometimes even surpassing him in miserliness. The time comes for Paramalobhin to marry and a suitable spouse is found, with great difficulty, in the daughter of an equally greedy Brahmin known as Atilobhin (i.e., quite greedy). The minds of Mahālobhin and Atilobhin conspire to avoid the minutest expenditure for the wedding. Both Brahmins collect money to meet the extra costs of the marriage ceremony with no intention whatsoever of incurring any such expenses. An isolated location for wedding is selected to ensure that potential recipients of gifts, customary on such occasions, be avoided.

> Our attention now shifts to Śiva and Pārvati, who have been cognizant of the wedding preparations from afar and are appraised of the context. Together they resolve to join the wedding ceremony and take part as guests, in the festivities. Śiva disguises himself as a poor and aged Brahmin named Śankarabhatta, and Pārvati as his elderly wife, Bhavāni. Approaching the wedding hall in search of gifts which, by convention are offered, they are sighted by Atilobhin who rushes to wake up Mahālobhin. Fearing the worst (i.e., that some gifts will have to be offered), Atilobhin loses consciousness. Mahālobhin, however, is not so easily intimidated. When the beggarly couple (Śiva and Pārvati) request an offering, customarily their due on these occasions, Mahālobhin advises him that the forest is dangerous and that they should flee

forthwith. Śiva retorts that Brahmins are always afraid of beggars but Mahālobhin is not impressed, defying the couple even a small morsel of food. As Śiva rises to leave, Mahālobhin settles on the idea of cutting the wedding short and slinking away under cover of darkness. When Śiva appears at the new location, Mahālobhin realizes that the beggar must be Śiva and his wife, Pārvati. Still, the greedy Brahmin is unable to bring himself to part with any of the food or money he had worked so hard to accumulate.

Mahālobhin realizes that nothing short of his own death will rid him of this troublesome mendicant. Hoping Śiva will leave him alone, Mahālobhin feigns his own death. Śiva goes along with the ruse and is about to light the funeral pyre when the gods intervene chastising him for cruelty to Brahmins. Even then, Mahālobhin refuses to give an offering. The story ends with Śiva, defeated, offering Mahālobhin a reward of three boons.[33]

This caricature of Brahmins illustrates an obvious perception that not all Brahmins are worthy of receiving gifts. The temptation to take advantage of a social system which requires one group (Brahmins) to be gifted can be difficult to overcome, even by those with best intentions. The story recognizes, in the extreme, the implications of such social advantage. Mahālobhin lives for alms alone, returning nothing to the social body. In the end even Śiva is defeated by the greedy Brahmin, a comment indicating either that Brahmins cannot be defeated even by the gods[34] or in recognition of the potential corruption involved in legitimizing such a group. Regardless, the story seems, on the one hand, to support the status quo (Mahālobhin defeats Śiva), and on the other to ridicule Mahālobhin for excessive greed.

At least one qualification, however, applies to Brahmins who accept gifts. Although entitled to gifts on account of their Vedic learning and austerity or *tapas*, Brahmins desirous of securing the highest world should not accept them.[35] Manu declares that Brahmins should not repeatedly resort to accepting gifts, since in so doing they risked losing the spiritual power acquired by Vedic study. Hence, "Though [by his learning and sanctity] he may be entitled to accept presents, let him not attach himself [too much] to that habit; for through his accepting [many] gifts the divine light in him is soon extinct" (*Manu* IV.186).

The *Padma Purāṇa* (ch. 70) specifically warns that gifts appear sweet like honey but are like poison (that is, deadly) in their effects. The acceptance of a gift, perhaps because of the resultant relationship of dependency between recipient and donor, was to be approached with caution. The element of danger in accepting gifts is illustrated, for example, in the *Pañcatantra* story of the tiger and the greedy traveler:

> Once a tiger stood on the banks of a lake offering anyone who would dare approach him a gold bracelet. One traveler, greedy for the brace-

let, approached the tiger and contemplated accepting it. Though beasts like tigers are notorious for their ferocity, the traveler is convinced of the tiger's sincerity by his declarations that he has repented from all his bloodthirsty acts and is seeking to do penance for his crimes by giving away the bracelet. When the traveler agrees to accept the gift, the tiger tells him to bathe first in accordance with custom. He does and finds himself sinking in the mud of the lake. Thus trapped, the tiger promptly kills and eats him. (*Pañcatantra* III.2. Paraphrased from the Sanskrit text.)

The moral is clear. In accepting a gift from one of dubious character, one risks loss of one's life. A further instance of the potential danger to a recipient of a gift is found in the *Kathāsaritsāgara*. The frame story of this collection is simple:

> King Trivikramasena accepts a fruit from an ascetic every year only to discover that the fruit conceals a gem. In gratitude he summons the ascetic who asks him to go to a cemetery and fetch a corpse hanging there on a tree as the human carcass is requisite for some religious rite. The king is warned that the success of his mission depends on absolute silence. Accordingly, the sovereign proceeds to the cemetery and recovers the corpse which is dangling from a tree there. As he is transporting the cadaver from the cemetery to the ascetic, a *vetāla* [demon or ghoul] which has entered into the lifeless body, tells the king a story. At the close of the tale the *vetāla* puts a question arising from it to the king who, naturally enough, falls into the trap and answers, thereby breaking the requirement of silence essential to the success of the mission. The corpse escapes and returns to the tree. This scenario recurs twenty-five times with the result that King Trivikramasena's task has to be repeated again and again. Finally, in the terminal story, the king is unable to solve the riddle and the *vetāla* reveals that the ascetic is planning to sacrifice the king and usurp his place. The king returns with the corpse and the ascetic bids him to prostrate himself before it. The king innocently asks the ascetic to show him how to perform the prostration. When the ascetic obligingly demonstrates the procedure, the king promptly cuts off his head.

This story illustrates the danger in bestowing gifts (the donor dies). Receiving gifts should also be approached with caution (the purpose of this gift is to depose the king). Though the king emerges unscathed, his acceptance of the precious gem puts him and his kingdom at risk.

More often, however, it is kings who are required to give generously. In these matters, the obligations of the king are especially onerous. Our texts confirm that the mandate of kingship and benefactor coincide. Here a good king is a generous king. Further, kings gain support and allegiance from those upon whom they lavishly bestow their wealth, and the recipients of the gifts have thus a vested interest in maintaining the status quo. The king's standing and power are in turn guaranteed and validated *vis-à-vis* the recipients of his gifts. The generosity of kings thus creates and maintains a bond between ruler and ruled. Granted the king's primary duty is to protect his subjects, but he is also responsible for the maintenance of the welfare of his kingdom.

In South Asia kings are traditionally required to bestow gifts liberally as a duty, not an option. This is documented in the wide variety of occasions which demand kings to act as benefactors. During Vedic sacrifices kings were mandated to bestow gifts generously to all in attendance. In the *Aitareya Brāhmaṇa* (39.6) a king, the moment he is anointed, should make gifts of gold, fields, and cattle. In the *Mahābhārata* it is said that the wealth of kings exists only for their subjects and not at all for their own comfort and enjoyment.[36] Yājñavalkya in his *Smṛti* (I.133) prescribes that the king should daily make gifts to Brahmins. In the *Vikramacarita* the sovereign, King Vikrama, is depicted distributing booty to his subjects in a public display of rather spectacular generosity. Here Vikrama bestows an astronomic sum of eight crores of gold on one not particularly important anonymous Brahmin who happens to offer his daughter in marriage to the king.[37]

In this context, kings were required to bestow their wealth especially on Brahmins. Kings gave to Brahmins on occasions too numerous to mention. The practice of offering a *mahādāna* (great gift), at least ten different types of which are documented in our texts, is a case in point. Of these ten, the *tulāpuruṣa* or distributing to Brahmins one's weight in gold or silver is documented on numerous occasions. It is referred to, for example, in various Purāṇas including, for example, the *Matsya Purāṇa* (ch. 274–289), the *Agni Purāṇa* (ch. 210), and the *Linga Purāṇa* (II.ch. 28ff.).[38] Gifts of *tulāpuruṣa* are also recorded in the Epigraphical records.[39] Kings who performed this gift-giving ceremony include Govinda IV, Indrāraja III, and Krsnrāya of Vijayanagara.[40] We are also told that Devarāya II of Vijayanagara gave a dinner to one lakh of Brahmins at Prayaga in the year *sake* 1350. The procedure for engaging in this gift is elaborate. The *tulāpuruṣa* is worthy of mention if only to illustrate the point that kings tended to give to Brahmins in lavish public displays. There is no mistaking here who is giving, who is receiving and the amount of the gift. A further example of the generosity of kings toward Brahmins especially is to be found in the custom of granting land. Numerous texts recommend the practice of kings giving land to Brahmins, and these sources indicate the value placed on this gift.[41] Kings were enjoined to record gifts of this type in writing for reference of future kings and to ensure that the land was never reclaimed. Commonly inscriptions in this genre tell us that the donor of land enjoys bliss in heaven for sixty thousand years and one who reclaims the land dwells in hell for the same period.[42] Gifts of villages came to be made very early and seem to have been guaranteed in perpetuity, effectively creating a class of landholding Brahmins.[43]

While gifts of land are common, our sources seem to draw the line at gifts of the whole earth. Both the *Aitareya Bhrāmaṇa* and the *Śatapatha Brāhmaṇa* (XIII.7.1.13–15) record the story of Viśvakarma Bhauvana who desired to make a gift of the earth to his priest Kasyapa. The earth, we are told, appeared and sang the following verse to Viśvakarma: "no mortal must give me away as a gift, 0 Viśvakarma Bhauvana, you desired to give me away; I shall plunge into the midst of water, so that this your promise to Kasyapa is fruitless."[44]

Perhaps because the king is essentially the guardian of material wealth and the Brahmin, the guardian of the sacred, Manu says that acceptance of a gift especially from the king is terrible in its consequences. Hence:

> 85. One oil-press is as [bad] as ten slaughter houses, one tavern as [bad as] ten oil-presses, one brothel as [bad as] ten taverns, one king as [bad as] ten brothels.
>
> 86. A king is declared to be equal [in wickedness] to a butcher who keeps a hundred thousand slaughter-houses; to accept presents from him is a terrible [crime].
>
> 87. He who accepts presents from an avaricious king who acts contrary to the institutes [of the sacred law], wilt go in succession to the following twenty one hells. . . .
>
> 91. Learned Brāhmaṇas, who know that, who study the Veda and desire bliss after death, do not accept presents from a king. (*Manu*, IV)

In this context, it should be noted that the king as warrior and protector has an aggressive and destructive side. As Shulman argues, the king is explicitly compared to death itself.[45] The sovereign is stained with evil consequences of *himsā* or harm to living beings, and it is small wonder that the king who accumulates too much of this harm becomes intent upon ridding himself of it through effecting some kind of transfer. Typically pollution accrued during the king's foray into foreign territory and by the blood on his hands from battle is erased by acts of purification which include the giving of gifts.[46] It is the Brahmin who is the natural candidate for the role of recipient. The Brahmin in accepting a gift from a king might be said to transmit the sacred to the king who, in turn, transmits it to the rest of society. Generally a requirement which upholds the religious/social hierarchy, the giving of gifts specifically renews the king's position at the zenith of the political hierarchy. A prosperous kingdom, we might say, extends from a prosperous king.

THE SUBSTANCE OF THE GIFT AND ITS PURPOSE

Sanskrit books of law and tradition enumerate numerous items that are appropriately proffered on notable occasions. Horses, cows, camels, garments, gold, sesame, clarified butter, food, silver, and salt are commonly prescribed. The *Matsya Purāṇa* (93.92) lists corn, salt, jaggery, gold, sesame, cotton, ghee, precious stones, silver, and sugar as suitable gifts.[47] Other texts extol gifts of elephants, horses, umbrellas, water, cows.[48] Yet even considering these meritorious gifts, a hierarchy of sorts emerges; some gifts are clearly superior to others. Hemādri gives lists of the best gifts and those which are only intermediate in worth.[49] While it would be interesting and valuable to embark on an in-depth discussion of the amazing variety of gifts detailed here, I will focus on gifts of hospitality, gifts of self, and gifts of wealth as generally indicative of the manner in which giving is understood in South Asia.

One of the most prominent gifts according to our sources is the gift of food to a guest. All of our texts agree that guests are to be honored with food. Manu tells us: "Let him not eat any (dainty) food which he does not offer to his guest; the hospitable reception of guests procures wealth, fame, long life, and heavenly bliss" (*Manu* III.106).

The *Āpastamba Dharmasūtra* (II.3.6.6) says that heaven and freedom from misfortune are rewards accorded to those who honor guests.[50] The *Vāyu Purāṇa* (71.74) maintains that *yogins* and *siddhas* (those who have attained transcendent powers) wander over this earth in various forms for the benefit of men; therefore one should with folded hands welcome a guest.[51] Perhaps because food is the gift of sustenance, without which we would not be able to live, it is deemed as an appropriate gift on almost every occasion, but particularly to a guest. The *Aitareya* and *Taittiriya Brāhmaṇas* (8.8.3 and 33.1) equate food with *prāṇa* (life), and in the *Baudhāyana Dharmasūtra* (II.3.68) we are told that "all beings depend on food, the Veda says 'food is life,' therefore food should be given [to others], food is the highest offering."[52] Food, particularly food given to a guest, symbolizes the gift of life if it is not literally that same gift. Further, food is a substance that everyone requires in order to survive. To live, one must eat, and eating generally takes place daily and is well known to others.

By the same token, those who do not make offerings of food are condemned. In the *Ṛg Veda* they are described as eating sin, and this sentiment is echoed in *Manu* (III.18), *Viṣṇudharmasmṛti* (67.43), and the *Gītā* (III.13).[53] Of note in the *Ṛg Vedic* passage is the identification of these who do not give to their friends or guests.[54] Our texts would indicate that this injunction to give the gift of food seems to have been followed generally throughout the history of India.

Manu and other texts on dharma warn potential hosts that the risks of not honoring guests with food include the loss of all spiritual merit.[55] One verse that is quoted in the *Viṣṇu Dharma Sūtra* (67.43), *Mahābhārata* (*Śantiparvan* 191.12), *Viṣṇu Purāṇa* (III.9.15), *Mārkaṇḍeya Purāṇa* (29.31), and the *Brahma Purāṇa* (114.36) is as follows: "When a guest returns from the house of a person with his hope of getting food shattered, he [the guest] transfers his own sins to the householder and departs taking with him, the householder's merit (*puṇya*)."[56]

If one has no food, then at the very least water, room, and grass to lie down upon are to be offered. Manu says: "Grass, room [for resting], water, and fourthly a kind word; these [things] never fail in the houses of good men" (*Manu*, III.101). Though these injunctions are not without their limitations as, for example, in the order in which guests might be received and the amount to be given, the rules of hospitality have been widely acknowledged as authoritative.

At the same time, our popular literature would indicate that this custom can, at times, put the host in a position of danger, and caution, even in these meritorious actions, is advised. The *Pañcatantra* story of the flea and the louse calls attention to the dangers of too much hospitality:

> A louse lived in the bed of a king and sustained herself on royal blood. One day a flea drifted in on the wind and dropped on the bed. Though the louse's instincts told her to cast out the flea, he appealed to her sense of morality, quoting the following verse:
>
>> The Brahmin reverences fire,
>> Himself the lower castes' desire;
>> The wife reveres her husband dear;
>> But all the world must guests revere.
>
> The louse is persuaded to host the flea but with specific instructions on when to feed. Rather, however, than wait, as the louse had suggested, until the king was drunk or in a deep sleep, the flea bit him as soon as he dozed off for a nap. The king felt the bite and called his servants who immediately located the louse, exterminating her and her family. The flea, hiding in a crevice, survived the extermination.[57]

Though this is a simplified version of the tale, one moral would seem to imply that caution is necessary even in following the dictum of hospitality toward guests. The dangers of hosting a guest must be weighed against the requirements of duty. The louse made an error in hosting the flea, but did she have a choice?

A further gift of interest is the ultimate gift that one can make: the gift of the self. This gift, in the case of kings, is illustrated in the *Kathāsaritisāgara* story of King Śibi. The tale is a common one in Sanskrit works appearing, for example, in the Southern version of the *Pañcatantra* and three times in the *Mahābhārata*.[58]

> Once there was a king named Śibi who was austere, compassionate, generous, steadfast, and the protector of all creatures. Indra, to deceive him, assumed the form of a wondrous falcon and quickly pursued Dharma who had taken the form of a dove. The dove, pursued by the falcon, appealed to king Śibi for protection. The falcon commanded

the king to release the dove to satiate his hunger, Śibi offered his own flesh in the place of the dove's. Eventually, the king offered his entire body to the falcon whereupon Indra and Dharma revealed their true form, restored Śibi's body to him and offered him boons. (*Kathāsaritisāgara*, XXIV. Paraphrased from the Sanskrit text.)

Though meritorious here, the custom of offering the self for food is not without its dangers, as the story of the camel, the lion, the leopard, the jackal, and the crow would indicate:

> One day a camel, weak from travel, was abandoned by a caravan in the forest. There he made friends with a leopard, a crow, and a jackal who followed a lion as their king. Because of the peculiar look of the camel in contrast to other forest animals, the lion guaranteed the camel's safety in the forest. After so doing, the lion was gored by the tusk of an elephant and fell ill, unable to hunt. Because the leopard, the crow, and the jackal had come to depend on the lion for food, they were now at a loss as to how to survive. Unsuccessful at hunting themselves, they fell upon the idea of eating the camel. The lion reminds them that he has guaranteed the safety of the camel and hence cannot possibly kill and devour it without suffering the consequences of not honoring his word. So it was that a ruse was planned. The lion, the crow, the jackal, the leopard, and the camel had assembled to discuss the crisis, each one offering his own flesh to revive the lion. First the crow offered himself as food for the lion but the others argued that he was too small a meal. Then the jackal offered his body for food but this proposal too was rejected on account of the jackal's size and the prohibition on animals from this family. The leopard offered his own body which was also rejected as prohibited. The camel, meanwhile, noting with admiration the willingness of the others to sacrifice themselves and confident that the offer of his own body would be rejected like the others, offered himself to the lion. With the permission of the lion, the leopard, the jackal, and the crow fell upon him and killed him.[59]

Offering, as the story would imply, renders the donor vulnerable. The camel was tricked by the conspiracy of the lion, the leopard, the jackal, and the crow, but was his self-sacrifice less noble than King Śibi's?

An additional meritorious gift and one equally prevalent is the gift of wealth. Gifts of wealth are regularly mentioned in Sanskrit texts and include gifts of gold, silver, horses, and cows. Gifts of cows are amongst the objects fitted the most prominently for giving and as such are eulogized in the *Ṛg Veda*.[60] According to Manu one who gifts land obtains land, one who gifts gold lives a long life, one who gifts silver, exquisite beauty, one who gifts a cow obtains the world of the sun.[61] These gifts too, are to be approached with caution. The temptation of accepting a gift of gold, for example, is difficult to resist. As the story of the tiger and the traveler from the *Pañcatantra* illustrates, accepting such a gift can have dire consequences.

The primary purposes of giving according to our texts are two: the accumulation of merit (*puṇya*) and purification or penance *(prayaścitta)*. In the first instance, all actions (karma) either yield merit or demerit. One objective of the religious life is to accumulate as much positive karma as possible and, at the same time, to eliminate negative karma. Gifting negates the power of demerits of past action and, at the same time, is conducive to the accumulation of positive karma. One is able, by giving generously, to shift the balance of positive and negative karma in one's favor and hopefully facilitate a better life and ensure a better rebirth. Gifts often function in this way, a fact that is easily verifiable in tradition and text. Donors whose gifts are recorded in inscriptions and copperplate grants of lands or villages often state outright that the grant is made for the increase of merit of himself and of his parents.[62] Here merit accumulates to the donor as well as other family members.

The notion that gift-giving functions as penance or expiation is equally prevalent. To atone for crimes of various types, generosity is often prescribed. Though the substance of the gift varies with the crime, absolution for even the most heinous crime of killing a Brahmin (Brahminicide) can be achieved by giving all one's wealth to a Brahmin who has studied the Veda.[63] The emphasis here upon giving as an atonement for the murder of a Brahmin calls our attention once again to the special position held by Brahmins in Hindu society.

CONCLUSION

The literature dealing with generosity in the Hindu tradition is comprehensive; the above represents only a cursory examination of *dāna* as constituted in selected Sanskrit texts. The countless debates on the specific components of giving indicate its importance in this tradition. The Hindu analysis of gifts is as thorough as it is complex, supplying us with data that account for almost every eventuality. Examples are common, but the specific transactions of giving and receiving are understood in context; the motivation and legitimation of such acts vary according to condition and circumstance. The extent to which we can draw comparisons with Western traditions of philanthropy is a question worthy of further study. Certain concluding observations regarding the components of the gift and gift-giving which distinguish the Hindu context, however, seem in order.

Our sources would indicate that primary to events of giving are the circumstances in which the act takes place. The Indian tradition's acknowledgment of countless eventualities and its in-depth analysis of the varying conditions of largesse is indicative of the complexity in which each such act is approached. Perhaps because magnanimity is not meritorious in and of itself, numerous factors are to be considered. The result is a clear identification of both appropriate and inappropriate circumstances for generosity. Giving in South Asia is thus not universally mandated. Rather, it is contextualized. Caste, stage of life, the character of the recipient and the donor as well as their attitude and motives are here important considerations. Merit is accorded to those who bestow their wealth in an attitude of selflessness. Otherwise merit, the goal of all philanthropy, is negated. In this spirit, everyone should furnish Brahmins and guests with gifts; householders should give to students and renouncers; and, of course, one should always donate to those who are deserving. Brahmins are not required to give; their role is to receive.

The tale of King Śibi, who offers his own body to save the dove and to feed the falcon, illustrates in the extreme the merits of such acts. The same self-sacrifice on the part of the camel leads to his demise. In Western philanthropic conventions, too, giving is not without restriction. Certain causes emerge as worthy, others do not. A certain offering may be appropriate in one context but not in another. A wide range of circumstances must be considered before determining which causes a particular donor considers appropriate and which inappropriate.

The Indian tradition seems, further, to admit a tension between one's duty to give and the reality of a world in which it is difficult to distinguish those who legitimately deserve support from those whose motives are less noble. Our texts render this tension unavoidable when they declare that giving is a duty and not an option. Wealth is here not merely for one's personal enjoyment but, as above, a test of character. Generosity toward Brahmins in particular is the norm, but to guests and others in specific circumstances it is also mandated. The merits of gifting Brahmins include the creation of a world where learning and culture, the domain of Brahmins, are highly valued. A world in which all have enough to survive is surely a commendable goal, but that same world, without culture, art, and education is, the tradition would imply, barely worth sustaining. The power of the gift extends thus beyond the immediate transaction. The importance of Brahmins comes not by virtue of their personal stature or mere social position but rather in light of their responsibility to pass on knowledge. The emphasis on providing for a group of experts, a concentration of knowledge through which to guide social and moral policy is oddly in accord with my reading of the goals of certain philanthropic organizations. The institutionalization of a sector of trained elites (Brahmins) perhaps represents such a sentiment. What happens, though, when one encounters a Brahmin like Mahālobhin whose sole motivation is the accumulation of wealth? Though Mahālobhin is an extreme case, indeed, a caricature, in his portrayal is the recognition that gifting Brahmins does not always facilitate the transmission of knowledge. Yet our texts are clear that to this group one must gift without hesitation.

Here we find an almost fatalistic acceptance of the dictum that those who are destined to assign their wealth to others must do so. Kings must give, regardless of the outcome; so too must hosts. In this connection one might argue that Hinduism effectively institutionalizes opportunities for giving. Similar to the Western custom of gifting relatives, friends, and worthy causes on holidays, gifting learned Brahmins and guests is as customary as it is meritorious. Just as one would not conceive of missing a mother's or father's birthday, so too a king, in ancient and perhaps even modern times, would be ill advised to conceive of not gifting Brahmins.

Perhaps the customary emphasis on giving to Brahmins is evidence of the skill of this group in entrenching social and economic benefits for themselves. Even if this were the case, as it certainly seems to be, at least two factors limit the Brahmins' influence. First, the danger of legitimizing a specific group as recipients of gifts lies in the potential of that group to succumb to the temptation of greed. Our greedy Brahmin, Mahālobhin, is surely a vision of the implications of such a custom. On this account, even our texts on dharma, the *Dharmaśāstras,* call our attention to the dangers of accepting too many gifts and ridicule Brahmins for accepting gifts too often.

Second, the Hindu analysis of giving recognizes that in every transaction of giving, a relationship is established between donor and recipient. Traditionally, the relationship between those who give and those who receive has been construed as a personal, often intimate connection between these two parties. Gifts of hospitality are particularly personal. As noted above, the reception of guests has been articulated from early times as a duty and responsibility. That hosting even a stranger is mandated by the Indian tradition would indicate, at the very least, that everyone is entitled to protection, safety, and nourishment. India has further always been a land well known for its hospitable welcome extended to guests.

In our modern technological world, personal relationships between those who give and those who receive are often impossible to establish or to maintain. Contact between donor and recipient is often discouraged. Many individuals and institutions alike prefer to simply send a check or debit their credit instruments. Too often, one might argue, gifts are institutional and abstract. The teachings of the Hindu tradition, emphasizing as they do the individual's responsibility for the well-being of the world, might prompt us to ponder the implications of personal involvement in, responsibility for, and commitment to the objectives of generosity. The transactional quality in the Hindu comprehension of the gift demands analysis of motives of self-interest as well as an analysis of community. In the milieu of philanthropy in South Asia, although Western motives of self-interest are obvious, the requirement is for a clear articulation of those interests and their implications. Donors as well as recipients are equally accountable for the consequences of such exchanges.

Our data would indicate that though personal involvement is desirable, there is some degree of danger to oneself in such transactions. While the sharing of food with a traveler is obligatory, one must proceed with caution. As the story of the louse would indicate, the reception of guests is not without its dangers. The louse lost her life while fulfilling the mandate of generosity toward the flea. Did she have a choice? The solution to her dilemma seems not to be to withhold hospitality but somehow to accommodate the guest and, at the same time, stay alive. The advice however, that caution is the order of the day, is as wise as it is lucid. This notion is further substantiated in the story of the tiger and the traveler, the camel, the lion, et al., and the King Trivikramasena. The traveler loses his life when he accepts the gift from the tiger; the camel was ill advised to offer himself as food for the lion, and King Trivikramasena risks his kingdom when he accepts the precious gem from the ascetic. The hazards in such transactions result from shifts in power. Donors like the louse, who offers her home, die in the same way as unwary ascetics and dull-witted camels. Our traveler, tempted by the allure of the gold bracelet, fares equally poorly. What are the lessons of these dictums on duty (dharma) and didactic tales for traditions of philanthropic relations between East and West?

NOTES

1. My interest in this topic stems from my participation in the Conference on Philanthropy and Cultural Context at the Rockefeller Archive Center, Tarrytown, New York, Nov. 3–4, 1994. I delivered a paper there entitled "Generosity among Saints, Generosity among Kings: Situating Philanthropy in South Asia." Some of the data from that paper have been incorporated here.

2. See Gunther D. Sontheimer and Hermann Kulke, eds., *Hinduism Reconsidered* (New Delhi: Manohar, 1989), particularly pp. 7–50 and 197–212 for an in-depth discussion of the term "Hindu."

3. V. S. Apte, *Practical Sanskrit-English Dictionary,* three vols. (Poona: Prasad Prakashan, 1957), II, p. 308.

4. J. Gonda, as cited by Vijay Nath, *Dāna: Gift System in Ancient India* (New Delhi: Munshiram Manoharlal, 1987), p. 20.

5. Nath, p. 22f.

6. Though there are numerous contexts in which *dāna* is to be found, this chapter is generally restricted to gifts that are offered to humans rather than, in a ritual context, to deities.

7. See also Nath, p. 9f. for an extensive discussion of textual sources for giving.

8. See, for example, *(The Hymns of the) Ṛg Veda,* trans. Ralph Griffith (New Delhi: Motilal Banarsidass), X.117, I.125, I.126. P. V. Kane, *History of Dharmasastra* (Poona: Bhandarkar Oriental Research Institute, 1958), I.II.412f., and Nath, p. 13f.

9. *Ṛg Veda,* I.125,126; VI. 47.22–25; VII.18.22–25; VII.68.14–19; X. 62.8–11, and Kane, II.II.837.

10. *The Bhagavad Gītā,* trans. Franklin Edgerton (Cambridge, Mass.: Harvard University Press, 1972), III.118; and Kane, II.II.837f.

11. See also Kane, II.II.838–39.

12. Hemādri, *Caturvargacintāmaṇi,* vol. II. *Vratakhanda,* Part I, ed. Pandita Bharatachandra (Calcutta: Asiatic Society of Bengal, 1878); Kane, II.II.841.

13. *Agni Purāṇa,* ch. 208–15; *Matsya Purāṇa,* ch. 82–91; *Varāha Purāṇa,* ch. 99–111; Kane, II.II.841.

14. Hertel has recorded over two hundred different versions in over fifty languages. Krishna Chaitanya, *A New History of the Sanskrit Language,* reprint (Conn.: Greenwood Press, 1975), p. 361.

15. Chaitanya, p. 366.

16. A. Berriedale Keith, *Classical Sanskrit Literature,* 2nd ed. (Calcutta: Association Press, 1927), p. 281. The present text dates from the eleventh century A.D. and contains twenty-one thousand stanzas, divided into eighteen *lambhakas* with one hundred twenty-four *tarantgas.* See also Chaitanya, p. 366f.

17. Although Somadeva's text is late, many of the stories are undoubtedly much older. See M. Krishnamachariar, *History of Classical Sanskrit Literature,* 3rd ed. (Delhi: Motilal Banarsidas, 1974), p. 419.

18. The *Bṛhatkathāślokasaṁgraha* is another text retelling the stories of the *Kathāsaritsāgara* discovered in Nepal in 1893. See the edition edited by F. Lacote (Paris: 1902–29).

19. Śivadāsa, *Vetālapañcaviṅśatikā,* ed. H. Uhle (Leipzig, 1884), cited by Chaitanya, p. 473.

20. Madeleine Biardeau, *Hinduism: The Anthropology of a Civilization* (New Delhi: Oxford University Press, 1989), p. 102.

21. *Bhagavad Gītā,* trans. Franklin Edgerton (New York: Harper and Row, 1964), 17:20–23.

22. Kane, II.II.842–43.

23. *Vedavyāsa Smṛti,* IV.60 and Kane, II.II.845.

24. Kane, II.II.846.

25. *Dakṣa Smṛti,* III.17–18, and Kane, II.II.845.

26. Equal attention is paid to recipients who are not worthy, including, in the same text, gamblers, rogues, thieves, and wrestlers. None of these are suitable recipients (Kane, II.II.844), and no merit is acquired in giving to them.

27. *(The Laws of) Manu SBE,* trans. Georg Bühler, reprint (Delhi: Motilal Banarsidass, 1964), I.88–90.

28. *Manu,* II.2.10.6, and Kane, II.II.840.

29. See Nath, p. 94 and Kane, I.2.412.

30. Nath, p. 92

31. Kane, II.II.846.

32. *Manu*, IV.192–99.

33. Virūpākṣavasantotsavacampū, ch. 43, p. 88f. Paraphrased from the Sanskrit text.

34. One is reminded here of the Hindu mythological tradition in which the gods (particularly Brahmā) have no choice but to offer boons to ascetics (divine or demonic) who practice severe austerities. The world, it seems, is so ordered that the gods must give a boon even to a demon if the latter's behavior warrants it. As the boon is usually some form of world domination, the only hope the gods have of maintaining their position as world rulers is to impose on the boon a condition.

35. *Yajnāvalkya Smṛti*, I.213 and Kane, V.2.936.

36. *Mahābhārata, Udyoga Parvan*, 116.13–14 and Nath, pp. 43–44.

37. *Vikrama's Adventures (Thirty-Two Tales of the Throne)*, ed. and trans. F. Edgerton (Cambridge: 1926), pp. 133–41.

38. See also Kane, II.II.870.

39. Ibid., II.II.869f.

40. Ibid., 870.

41. See Nath, p. 167.

42. Kane, II.II.862–63.

43. Nath, p. 244.

44. Kane, II.II.840.

45. David Dean Shulman, *The King and the Clown in South Indian Myth and Poetry* (Princeton: Princeton University Press, 1986), p. 28f.

46. J. C. Heesterman, *The Ancient Indian Royal Consecration* (Gravenhage: Mouton and Company, 19), p. 45.

47. There are of course many other gifts of food prescribed in the literature outside of the context of hospitality.

48. Kane, II.II.862.

49. Hemādri, p. 16, and Kane, II.II.847.

50. Kane, II.II.754.

51. Ibid.

52. Kane, V.II.934.

53. *Ṛg Veda*, X.117. 6, and above.

54. *Ṛg Veda*, X.11.6.

55. *Manu*, III.100.

56. Quoted in Kane, II.II.754.

57. Paraphrased from *Pañcatantra*, trans. Arthur W. Ryder (Bombay: Jaico Publishing House, 1981), pp. 103–105.

58. This particular story seems to be of distinctly Buddhist origin. See Charles Rockwell Lanman, *A Sanskrit Reader* (Cambridge: Harvard University Press, 1884), pp. 335–36.

59. Paraphrased from *Pañcatantra*, trans. Ryder, pp. 116–21.

60. Ṛg Veda I.125; I.126.3; V.30, 12; VII.5.37.

61. *Manu*, IV.230, 231.

62. *Epigraphia Indica*, Microfilm vol. 1–35 (Delhi: Archaeological Survey of India, 1970), XI.219 and 221, and Kane, II.II.862–63.

63. *Manu*, XI.76,77.

.4.

Generosity and Service in Theravāda Buddhism

ANANDA W. P. GURUGE AND G. D. BOND

Generosity and service to others have central importance in Theravāda Buddhism. An aphoristic verse in the *Dhammapada* epitomizes the Buddhist attitude as follows: "The niggardly do not go to the world of the gods; fools only do not praise liberality. A wise man rejoices in liberality and through it becomes blessed in the other world."[1] The Buddha himself is described in the texts as "the giver of the deathless," and he is said to have instructed his first group of monks to "go forth for the welfare, the benefit and the good of gods and humans."[2] Since that time, practices that we would recognize as philanthropy and service have constituted an important part of Theravāda Buddhism. One of the central concepts in this regard, generosity/giving, *dāna*, is not merely a basic virtue, but serves as a pivotal practice that pertains to both the path and the goal of Buddhism. In Theravāda, generous giving provides a way of cultivating and attaining the twin ideals of the religion: compassion and wisdom.[3]

The act of giving and its psychological concomitant liberality or generosity receive elucidation in Theravāda Buddhism's vast narrative literature with which the main doctrines—especially the Law of Kamma—were introduced to the growing population of adherents or converts. Already included in the Pāli Buddhist Canon, the *Tipitaka*, are *Jātaka, Apadāna, Vimānavatthu*, and *Cariyāpitaka*, where numerous stories highlight the rewards for liberality. While in the *Jātakas* the recipients of one's gift or service range from birds and animals to all kinds of indigents and holy people, a tendency is to be observed in other texts to narrow down the recipients to a Buddha—whether it was the historical Sākya Muni or any of the previous Buddhas or numerous independently enlightened beings, *Pacceka Buddhas*—and to the Sangha, the community of monks and nuns.

A similar tendency is to be observed in the case of philanthropic service. The *Jātakas*, again, covered a wider range. For example, the preeminence of Sakka, the proverbial lord of gods, is presented as due to his devoted public services in a previous life as young Magha.[4] The public services attributed to him are the construction of roads, wells, and other amenities for public use. But in the more parochial tales, even such services are extolled if performed for the benefit of the Sangha and its institutions. Illustrative of this emphasis is the story of a calf who was reborn in Heaven with divine attributes simply as a result of involuntarily clearing a tuft of grass in a temple compound as it ran across!

To understand the implications of *dāna*, giving, and other related ideas in the context of the religion, we can consider some of the cardinal formulations of the *Dhamma* from this literature. *Dāna* represents one of the ten perfections, *pāramitā*, the ten qualities leading to enlightenment which serve as the defining virtues of a Bodhisattva, but also represent virtues that any individual must perfect en route to enlightenment. In this list, generosity comes first, followed by morality, renunciation, wisdom, energy, patience, truth, resolution, loving-kindness, and equanimity. The perfections stand for the path to enlightenment, with its various stages and tasks. The inclusion of *dāna* at the head of this grouping demonstrates the central place that it has in the path and the connection it has to the key goals such as wisdom.[5] The pattern of these perfections also shows that *dāna* is linked with concepts that have to do with both the good of the individual and the welfare of society. By practicing generosity, one develops the qualities that lead to one's own liberation while also fostering the spiritual development of the community.

The social implications of giving, *dāna*, are brought out even more clearly in the list of the four grounds of social harmony or amity, Sangaha Vatthu: generosity, kind speech, service, and equal treatment—*dāna, peyyāvajja, atthacariyā, samānattatā*. In this grouping, generosity, *dāna*, is one of the cardinal principles of social life and has the connotation of sharing what one has for the common welfare. It is related to service, *atthacariyā*, and to the principle of treating all beings equally, *samānattatā*.[6] The texts describe these actions as the linch pins for society;[7] unless these principles were practiced, social life could not be harmonious and the goals of the Buddhist path could not be attained. One textual explanation of these four grounds of social harmony posits a close relation between service and generosity by explaining that the best form of service is instilling in people the virtues of faith, morality, and liberality.[8]

These social virtues can be interpreted as expressions of another formulation of the central principles of the Buddha's *Dhamma* that is called the four *Brahma Vihāras*— loving-kindness, compassion, sympathetic joy, and equanimity (*mettā, karunā, muditā*, and *upekkhā*). These principles are clearly said to have relevance for both individual liberation and social welfare. By meditating on the virtues that compose the *Brahma Vihāras* a meditator could understand his/her interconnectedness to all beings and, by means of this understanding, move closer to wisdom and liberation.[9] These virtues express the logic or rationale behind Buddhist philanthropy and service. The famous Theravāda commentator, Buddhaghosa, explained that enlightened beings practice giving because they are concerned about all beings' welfare, they dislike all beings' suffering, and they desire the success and happiness of all.[10]

One of the most important textual formulations explaining the place of giving is one that links *dāna* with *sīla*, morality, and *bhāvana*, development by meditation. In this triad, generosity is coupled with *sīla*, morality, as a central component of Buddhist ethics. The Buddhist commentators explained *sīla* in this context to mean following the basic precepts, which include "not killing, not stealing, not lying, etc." In this sense *sīla* is understood as the practice of restraint by avoiding doing harm to anyone, and thus as negative morality. But *dāna*, generosity toward others, is understood as positive morality, as doing good so that beings will be happy. *Bhāvanā* or meditation builds upon these two foundation stones of Buddhist morality. This threefold teaching has been understood within Theravāda to apply especially to the laity and is called the Three Bases of Meritorious Action. It is taken as the lay parallel to the monastic path explained as morality (*sīla*), concentration (*samādhi*), and wisdom (*pannā*). A contemporary Theravāda commentator has noted the way in which the delineation of these two threefold paths emphasizes the importance of morality and giving for lay persons: "Thus moral conduct [*sīla*], the single factor of the monks' general social responsibility, is in the lay version split into the explicit and more tangible social acts of giving [*dāna*], and virtuous conduct [*sīla*]."[11] Although, as we have noted, the monastic community was expected to practice certain kinds of *dāna*, such as giving teachings and counsel, *dāna* was interpreted to constitute a more significant element of the path for the laity. This difference in the roles of laity and monks regarding giving derived from the general Indian view of the householders' duty to support ascetics.[12]

A final explanation of the significance of generosity is found in those texts that explain that generosity in its many forms represents a good action because it counteracts the three roots of evil or unprofitable conduct. These three roots are greed or desire (*lobha*), hatred (*dosa*), and ignorance (*moha*). According to Theravāda thought, these represent the roots of all evil karma and the qualities that block a person from attaining wisdom.

Generosity counters the root of greed in those who give generously. The texts say that for one who is greedy, the antidote is to begin practicing generosity. The Buddha taught, "If beings knew as I know the benefit of giving, they would not enjoy the wealth without sharing, nor would the taint of greed obsess their hearts."[13]

Generosity or liberality (*cāga*) is one of the qualities that are called the Wealth of the Buddha and the Treasures of the Noble Disciple. The five virtues are faith (*saddhā*), moral conduct (*sīla*), learning (*suta*), generosity (*cāga*), and wisdom (*pannā*).[14] The noble disciple who practices liberality (*cāga*), is "free from stinginess or avarice" (*macchera*). One who is progressing toward wisdom is described as "living with a heart free of stinginess, liberal, open-handed, rejoicing in giving, ready to give anything asked for, glad to give and share with others."[15]

Generosity or philanthropy also counters the second unprofitable root: hatred or anger (*akusula mūla*). The great commentator, Buddhaghosa, wrote that one way of overcoming anger toward another person is to give a gift to that person. Giving establishes connections and overcomes alienation.[16] Buddhaghosa explains that right giving softens the heart of both the donor and the recipient. The Buddha taught that giving to others purifies one's mind of anger and other negative states so that the mind becomes malleable and is able to begin to grasp the Four Noble Truths.[17]

Generosity counteracts the last unprofitable root, ignorance or delusion, in many ways. The textual explanations of the function of generosity are significant because they indicate the direct connections between generosity and wisdom. Generosity represents one of the meditation practices called the Recollections (*anussati*). The Recollections are six specific topics that a monk can take as subjects for this kind of meditation—Buddha, *Dhamma, Sangha, Sīla, Cāga, Devas.*[18] To meditate on these, a person must focus the mind on the topic and reflect on the many positive aspects of it. Meditating on generosity, a person reflects on the advantages of giving, the benefits to oneself and others, and the kinship with other beings that makes giving a natural action. Recollecting liberality in this way, the text says, "On that occasion, one's mind is not obsessed by greed . . . or hate . . . or delusion; the mind has rectitude on that occasion being inspired by liberality."[19] This meditation represents a definite form of *samādhi* or concentration that can lead to higher stages of wisdom and ultimately to the attainment of Liberation.

THE SANGHA AS CHARITABLE INSTITUTION *PAR EXCELLENCE*

In the Indian subcontinent from time immemorial there was both a priestly class comprising Brahmans and a multitude of recluses and ascetics, usually identified by the term *śramana*. They were recipients of public charity. The Brahmans received a fee or present, called *Dakṣinā* for their priestly services usually in conducting elaborate sacrificial rituals. In addition, the tradition and subsequently their manuals of social law, the *Dharmasūtras* and *Dharmaśāstras*, stipulated generous donations of food and requisites to students of the *Vedas—Brahmacāris—*and their teachers.

Supporting both Brahmans and *śramanas* without discrimination was a social obligation. Richard Gombrich, in analyzing this practice as a part of the royal duties of a ruler, says, "The classical Indian concept—a norm of the communal religion—was that it was the duty of a layman to respect and even materially support all holy men of whatever path who present themselves"[20] As far as kings and aristocrats and the wealthy were concerned, such generous support to religious people in general without sectarian or denominational discrimination constituted a popular notion of *noblesse oblige.*[21]

The Buddha and his disciples were mendicants. They begged for their food in the streets and that is what the terms *Bhikkhu* and *Bhikkhunī* in reference to members of the Buddhist Sangha signify. Even in the capital of his own father's kingdom, the Buddha begged for his food. When an embarrassed monarch remonstrated, the Buddha's reply was that begging was the noble practice of his dynasty, referring not to his royal descent but to the lineage of Buddhas.

The *Vinaya Pitakam* deals with detailed instructions on *Pindapāta* or begging rounds of the monks and nuns.[22] The very plethora of rules suggests that this mode of living on public charity was central to Buddhist monastic life. The most important among these rules was that which demanded a monk or nun to go from house to house "in order, without skipping any" and receiving and consuming whatever was placed in the begging bowl. Originally, this rule served two purposes: first, to underscore in real practice the Buddha's concept of equality and oneness of humanity in which concept there was no room for class or caste discrimination; second, to promote meditation on the unwholesomeness of life for which a flagrantly convincing object was an unseemly mish-mash of food one was obliged to consume for sustenance.

Eventually, as the Sangha became a full-fledged institution, this emphasis on the charitable status of the Sangha was underscored on the principle that giving to the Sangha was a peerless or incomparable opportunity for people to acquire merit. The Buddha and his disciples accepted invitations to lunch and a ceremonial form evolved from this practice. *Anumodanā* grew into a sermon of thanks highlighting *inter alia* the merit of giving and especially giving to the Sangha. The same extended to the acceptance of robes and shelter. If at the beginning the cloth for robes was collected from the cemetery and dustbin, now gifts of new robes were extolled. The Buddha and his disciples, who lived under trees, public halls, empty houses, and workplaces at first, began to accept gardens and buildings. A verse in the *Vinaya Pitakam* enjoins that beautiful monasteries be built.[23]

Expressed in the form of epithets for the Sangha in an oft repeated formula as *dakkhineyya* (worthy of offerings: cf. *Dakśinā* = sacrificial fee or gift for a Brahmanical priest) and *punnakkhettamlokassa* (a field for the world to cultivate the seeds of merit), the Sangha was presented as the charitable institution *par excellence.* "What was given to it brought immense fruit," says another popular poem in daily devotional use in Theravāda.[24]

Thus in the lifetime of the Buddha himself the emphasis on giving to any deserving recipient in general shifted gradually to giving to the Sangha in particular. The Sangha, however, was not to be the exclusive object of charity or philanthropy. Rules of the Vinaya even spell out how food begged in the street could be shared with a disciple's aged parents or any other needy person. The Buddha by both precept and example identified the sick as deserving special care and attention, saying "whoever attends to the sick attends to me."[25] In the *Anguttaranikaya* there occurs a text wherein the relative importance of the recipients is graded from the point of view of the quantum of "merit" (*punna*) accruing to a donor. In ascending order are ordinary human beings, and achievers of the progressive Path (*Magga*) and Fruit (*Phala*) of the four stages of sainthood (*Sotāpanna, Sakadāgāmi, Anāgāmī, Arahant*) culminating in Buddhas (in the plural).[26] On the level of popular belief in Sri Lanka, there is a similar gradation which extends the idea of the worthy recipients found in canonical and commentarial sources. This list of fourteen kinds of alms-giving enumerates the alms given to the Buddha and his community of monks as the most meritorious and those to crows and dogs as the fourteenth in order of the output of merit.

A further concept was developed to highlight the importance of the Sangha as a recipient. The Sangha was said to receive a gift in the name of the entire community for all time. Monks and nuns bequeathed nothing to anyone and even personal articles of use such as their robes, begging bowls, razors, water strainers, and sandals belonged to the community and were to be passed on for use by those who needed them.

An ancient formula accompanying a gift to the Sangha stressed that the recipients were the members of the Sangha in all directions, present and absent or, more literally, of the present and the future. It occurs in numerous Sri Lankan Brahmi inscriptions from at least the second or the first century B.C.E. as *Catudisasa agata anagata sagasa* in Sinhala Prakrit (Pāli: *Catudisassa āgata anāgata sanghassa*).[27]

The long-term, if not permanent, enjoyment by the Sangha gave such a gift special significance. In fact, any gift—even a meal—given even symbolically to the entire Sangha with the presence of a minimum quorum and the use of appropriate formulae (called a *sanghikadāna*) has been considered the most meritorious.

It also assumed an irrevocability. Anyone who reclaims or violates such a gift is believed to suffer the consequence of being reborn a dog or a crow. Again, in Sri Lankan inscriptions recording donations to the Sangha is found a reminder of this belief in the form of graphic representations of dogs and crows at the bottom of the chain of being.[28]

THE INTERACTION OF SANGHA AND
LAITY THROUGH DONATIONS

Reference was made to the *anumodanā* or Thanksgiving sermon at the conclusion of an almsgiving to the Buddha and his disciples. The tradition has persisted in Theravāda countries up to the present date. Naturally, the central theme had to be the praise of liberality. *Dānamsaggassa sopānam* and such other texts purportedly from the Canon are interspersed for authority. Narratives provide illustrations of benefits accruing to generous donors.[29] As the etymology of *anumodanā* suggests, the purpose of the sermon is the generation of a happy and favorable disposition *post facto*. Relevant also as a strategy to win over donors was the Buddha's injunction on how the members of the Sangha should behave in public. The rules stated that monks should behave in ways that were pleasing to the unconverted and exceedingly pleasing to the already converted. Much charity has been attracted according to historical narratives by the external comportment of monks and nuns.

In the list of ten meritorious deeds (*dasapunnakiriya*), two more related actions extend in a further dimension the joy of giving which one experiences with *anumodanā*. *Abbhānumodanā* signifies the vicarious enjoyment of merits gained by others while *Pattānuppadanā* is the act of transferring one's merits to others. This triple concept is the antithesis of the notion that the left hand should not know what the right hand gives. Giving publicity to one's liberality and associating others in one's acts of giving become essential obligations, if not additional acts of merit. One gives in public or gives publicity to one's liberality to enable others to share in one's merits. Similarly one benefits from the publicity given to other's liberality by sharing in their merits. A popular belief in Theravāda Buddhist countries is that people who have friends and supporters and who have the facility of enlisting others' cooperation had involved others in their acts of charity and philanthropy in previous lives.

This process is not limited to the act of giving or liberality. *Veyyāvacca* as the fifth in the list of ten meritorious deeds makes every personal or social service an act of merit. Specially mentioned as producing longevity, personal beauty, physical strength, and happiness are care and homage to the elderly. That merit too can be transferred and shared. Merit-making, giving merit to others and sharing in other's merits, make publicity an indispensable ingredient. It is, therefore, not surprising that the earliest recorded instances of charity whether in epigraphical records or in literature in the Indian subcontinent and elsewhere relate to charity and philanthropy in Buddhist circles. Votive records inscribed in components of the railings and archways in Bharhut and Sanchi enabled the pioneering epigraphist James Prinseps in the 1830s to crack the code of the Brahmi script which had the recurring last word: *dānam.* Many hundreds of early Brahmi inscriptions in Sri Lanka and the Tinnevely District of Tamil Nadu in South India similarly record donations of caves and other requisites to the Sangha. These records and especially their phraseology suggest the chain reaction which was set in motion as each donation was announced with full details of name, family socioprofessional position and extent of generosity of the donor.[30]

Equally efficacious has been the keeping of records of merit gained by individuals. These personal records, called *Punnapotthaka* in Pāli and *Pinpota* in Sinhala, listed one's meritorious deeds, both donations and services, for the specific purpose of being read at one's deathbed. It is believed that the recollection of one's meritorious deeds at the moment of death guaranteed rebirth in a better state. King Dutthagamini of Sri Lanka (second century B.C.E.) is said to have had his record read before death.[31] The chronicle holds that he rejoiced most on recalling two instances when, under trying circumstances, he was still able to offer meals to some monks.

The records of meritorious deeds for both publicity and personal solace at death provided the basic raw material for the historical chronicles which evolved in Sri Lanka. There is little doubt that the Buddhist initiative in historiography as these chronicles reveal was motivated by a need to record and give publicity to gifts and services as a means of promoting further generosity. The historical introductions in the Sinhala commentaries known as *Sīhala-Atthakathā-Mahāvamsa* (from circa third century B.C.E.), the tentative first effort in organized historiography, the *Dīpavamsa* (fourth century C.E.) and the non-stop Sri Lankan

Pāli epic which commenced with *Mahānāma's Mahāvamsa* (sixth century C.E.) listed the services of Sri Lankan monarchs from the inception of the Sinhala Kingdom in regard to (a) charity to the Buddhist Faith, (b) secular services to the people such as the construction of reservoirs and irrigation canals, roads, and hospitals, and (c) steps taken for national security and integrity. The prototype of the Sri Lankan chronicles has inspired equally fascinating counterparts in Myanmar, Thailand, and Cambodia.

RELATION OF *DĀNA* TO THE PATH AND THE GOAL OF BUDDHISM

This discussion of the laity as the givers and the Sangha as the recipients of the gifts brings up the question of whether Theravāda Buddhism comprises two separate paths: one for the laity and another for the monks or nuns. The most influential interpretation along these lines was that of Max Weber. In his analysis of Indian Theravāda Buddhism, Weber described lay Buddhist ethics—of which generosity and the karmic rewards therefrom constitute a central part, as "an insufficiency ethic for the weak who will not seek complete salvation."[32] He also said, "In truth, an insoluble gap yawns between the ethic of action and the technical rules of contemplation and only the latter yields salvation."[33] Other scholars since Weber, most notably the anthropologist Melford Spiro, have developed Weber's ideas and argued that Theravāda has two distinct paths leading to two distinct goals: a karmic path leading to karmic benefits and rebirth, and a Nirvanic path leading to the ultimate goal. On this analysis, philanthropy—with its karmic rewards—would represent the lower path restricted to the lay people. But this is an incorrect interpretation. Theravāda Buddhism does not conceive of two paths or of an "insufficiency ethic"; rather it understands the soteriological path to be a continuum, a long, gradual path leading to the only ultimate goal, *nibbāna*. This gradual path spans the myriad lifetimes through which a person must pass on the way to the ultimate goal, and therefore it comprises various practices and benefits suitable to persons at various spiritual levels. But it is one path with one ultimate goal.

Generosity, *dāna*, is one of the central practices that links the various levels of the path and reveals the connections between karmic benefits and the ultimate goal. As Strong has noted, "Dāna . . . is an act that is kammatic and nibbanic at the same time."[34] Thus, to answer Weber's charge, generosity or philanthropy solves the insoluble and yawning gap because it links the ethic of action to the goal of salvation.

The literature of Theravāda provides many illustrations of the way that giving, *dāna*, serves as one of the pivotal and unitive factors on the Buddhist path. These stories and teachings point out, as Swearer and

Sizemore have noted, that "the concept of *dāna* serves to integrate the layman's striving for a better rebirth and the monk's search for *nibbāna*."[35] The stories of three individuals, in particular, have been celebrated by Theravāda as exemplars of the virtue of giving. These three individuals are Vessantara, Anāthapindika, and Asoka; in their stories we see how the practice of *dāna* both implies and leads to the goal of the religion.

THE STORY OF VESSANTARA

For explaining the significance of *dāna* on the path to enlightenment, the story of Prince Vessantara has also been celebrated historically in Theravāda literature, art, and popular practice. Vessantara, of course, was the Bodhisatta, or the Buddha in his last birth before becoming Gotama. This connection is important because it demonstrates that the perfection of generosity was central to the Bodhisatta's path of purification and liberation.

Prince Vessantara inherited the prosperous and happy kingdom that his father had built. However, because of his complete and unquestioning generosity, Vessantara was besieged by people who requested that he give them assistance. Responding to their requests, Vessantara gave everything away—his possessions, the wealth of the kingdom, the magic, rain-providing elephant, and finally even his children and his wife. In the end he was driven into exile by his subjects who blamed him for destroying the kingdom's prosperity. Clearly Vessantara was generous to a fault. But the point of the story is that he was completely non-attached to wealth and the things of this world. The story shows that this total non-attachment represents both the highest form of generosity and a crucial virtue for the attainment of liberation.

The story of Vessantara blends the ideal of generosity with the ideal of renunciation. Vessantara's voluntary journey into exile from the kingdom represents the logical extension of his total generosity. Indeed, this story confirms what the texts say elsewhere, that the logic of generosity is grounded in the centrality of the ideal of renunciation. The Commentary to the *Brahmajāla Sutta* explains the logic of the path that is related to giving to one who begs from you: "Further when a beggar asks for something, a Bodhisattva should think: 'He is my intimate friend . . . he is my teacher, for he teaches me: When you die you have to abandon all. Going to the world beyond, you cannot even take your own possessions! He is a companion helping me to remove my belongings from this world which, like a blazing house, is blazing with the fire of death'."[36]

Many other *Jātaka* stories also deal with the ways that the Bodhisatta perfected his generosity in his previous lives. Some of them relate that he not only gave his possessions, but on many occasions also gave himself, his life, for the benefit of others.[37]

THE STORY OF ANĀTHAPINDIKA

According to the Theravāda texts, Anāthapindika was a wealthy merchant, who met the Buddha and became his greatest patron. His generosity toward the Buddha and the Sangha was boundless—he gave food, robes, whatever they needed, and he served them night and day. He offered to build the monastery at Jetavana for the Buddha and his monks, and to purchase the appropriate site for it, he blanketed the property with gold coins. The commentarial versions of this legend say that Anāthapindika eroded the family fortune by this ceaseless giving and by not attending to his business. At one point he was reduced to poverty, having nothing but broken rice and sour gruel to eat, but instead of eating it himself, he gave even that to the Buddha and the monks. Then, as a result of the karma from his generosity, his fortune was restored. His philanthropy led to his gaining even greater wealth.[38]

The point made in this story is that although Anāthapindika gained much merit from his generosity, he never made merit or karmic gain the focus of his life. The texts say that he gave generously without any thought of reward. As a result of this detachment, at the end of his life Anāthapindika attains to the higher stages of the path to liberation. The story says that when Anāthapindika was on his deathbed, one of the Buddha's chief monks, Sāriputta, came to visit him. Sāriputta proceeded to give him a *Dhamma* talk or sermon about meditation and the right way of reflecting on the impermanence of life. Anāthapindika's response was to say that he had never heard these matters explained before; whereupon, Sāriputta said that such sermons were usually not given to lay persons. The implication of this incident is that Sāriputta assumed that Anāthapindika had progressed sufficiently on the path that he could benefit from hearing about these forms of meditation just before he died.

After death, Anāthapindika was reborn as a *deva* or god in heaven—a rebirth that signified that he had reached a higher stage of the gradual path to enlightenment. Then as a *deva* he returned to the world and appeared to his friends to tell them that they should not seek wealth or a noble rebirth for its own sake, but should follow the highest moral life and seek *Dhamma* and wisdom.[39] Anāthapindika clearly stands in classical Theravāda as an exemplar to laity, but, in the end, the story reveals that the path and the rewards available to the laity are not separate from the gradual path leading to Nirvana.

THE STORY OF ASOKA

The third exemplar of generosity was the great Indian king, Asoka. His story shares many of the same themes as those of Anāthapindika and Vessantara, but also introduces important new elements. According to the legend and the inscriptions, the third Mauryan Emperor Asoka the Righteous (265–228 B.C.E.) accepted Buddhism as his personal religion and in the tenth year from his coronation began to promulgate Buddhist piety and virtuous conduct. He caused to be inscribed on rock slabs and stone pillars his thoughts and intentions, records of actions and accomplishments and injunctions to officials, subjects, and successors. From these we gain much valuable information on Buddhist principles, particularly his thoughts pertaining to generosity and philanthropy.

First and foremost is his compliance with the Buddha's statement that the gift of *Dharma* (i.e., moral instruction and knowledge of virtue) excelled all other gifts. Besides quoting it twice in Rock Edicts IX and XI, Asoka incorporated this idea in his code of ethical principles, which he propagated through every known method: orally using formal and informal communicators, through audio-visual and dramatic representation, and instructions inscribed on rocks and pillars. Particularly significant are a set of tracts or *Dharma* documents which he termed *Dharmalipi*. These *Dharmalipis* exemplify the ways and means by which the Buddhist concept of *Dharmadāna* was applied in practice.

These *Dharmalipis* as well as several other inscriptions stress the importance of liberality. The most-mentioned recipients for one's liberality are Brahmans and recluses. But several inscriptions also highlight generosity toward friends and acquaintances as well as elders. The emperor engaged himself with the welfare of the elderly. He visited various parts of his empire "visiting Brahmans and recluses and making offerings to them; visiting the aged and making provisions of money for them."[40]

As a patron of communal religion, as defined by Richard Gombrich, Asoka made no distinction among religious personnel of different sects or persuasions.[41] He enjoined that all should be respected and supported alike.[42] In this the emperor was emulating the Buddha whose spirit of tolerance as regards support to rival teachers is best stated in *Upāligahapatisutta*[43] and *Udumbarikasīhanādasutta*.[44]

In the thirteenth year from his coronation Asoka created a new cadre of officials called *dharmamahāmātras*. The main duty assigned to them was the supervision of the charities which the emperor himself and the members of the royal family had instituted.[45] Asoka becomes a subject of a case study because his concept of charity and philanthropy goes far beyond the above preoccupations with *Dharmādana* and charities destined to the welfare of Brahmans and recluses without denominational or sectarian discrimination. Both within his empire and in neighboring countries, he set in motion many welfare services. In a list issued in the thirteenth regnal year, he lists them as follows:

> installed two kinds of medical treatment: one for humans and the other for animals;
>
> medicinal herbs, beneficial to humans and animals, were brought and planted where they were not found;
>
> wherever they did not exist, roots and fruit were brought and planted;
>
> along roads, wells were dug and trees were planted for the use of animals and people.[46]

Fifteen years later a second list was issued:

> on roads, banyan trees were caused to be planted to provide shade for humans and beasts;
>
> mango groves were caused to be planted;
>
> wells were caused to be dug every half (or eight) krosas;
>
> resthouses were constructed;
>
> many watering stations were caused to be erected for the benefit of humans and beasts.[47]

Asoka in his charitable and philanthropic actions shows an equal concern for animals as for human beings. Apart from his services in the provision of medical care, shade and water and healing herbs for animals, he prohibited very early in his reign all forms of animal sacrifice and brought down from many hundreds to just three the animals killed in the royal kitchen.[48] He enjoined humane treatment for animals and issued a unique list of animals to be protected.[49] He has also recorded that in the twenty-six years of his reign he had released prisoners on amnesty as many as twenty-five times.[50]

The story of Asoka emphasizes again the importance that liberality and service had for those who sought to tread the Buddhist path. The legends about Asoka preserved by Mahayana Buddhists even go on to claim that he gave everything he had to the Sangha, including himself. Strong describes this legend by saying that Asoka made "a total gift to the *sangha* of all his belongings as well as his concubines, his advisers, his family and his self."[51] Although no historical evidence exists for this act of total generosity by Asoka, the legend undoubtedly had a powerful effect on lay piety and generosity down through the centuries of Buddhist history. As in the case of Vessantara and, to some extent, that of

Anāthapindika, the example of Asoka shows that the lay path forms a continuum with the monastic path to the goal and that generosity that is based on complete non-attachment provides the crucial link between these levels of the path.

CONCLUSION: CHARITY AND PHILANTHROPY IN THERAVĀDA BUDDHIST SOCIETIES TODAY

Generosity and philanthropy continue to constitute the foundation of religious and spiritual life in Theravāda Buddhist societies. The three-stage path of training comprising *dāna, sīla, bhāvanā*, which was dealt with above, figures prominently as Buddhism finds widespread expression as a lay religion, in terms of not only the numerical ratio between the laity and the Sangha but also the emphasis on secular goals of moral, intellectual, and social development and overall welfare. Merit-making and merit-sharing, in the sense of acquiring *punnakamma* or good and meritorious *kamma*, becomes a pivotal motivation for liberality, and the scope of philanthropy has widened to include all forms of gifts, sacrifice, service, and altruism.

In this context, *dāna* in practice assumes three forms. First, *āmisadāna* or donation of material things consists of almsgivings to the Sangha as well as to the needy. Gifts to the Sangha still represent a ceremonially and socially important act of charity. Included in this form of *dāna* is the provision of requisites, amenities, and services to monasteries, charitable institutions and persons needing assistance. Gifts of time and energy in the service of the poor and the disadvantaged also fall into this category. A significant example is the Sarvodaya Movement of Sri Lanka founded on the principle of voluntary service, called *shramadāna* or the gift of labor. Second, there is the grant of security and sanctuary, *abhayadāna* (literally, the gift of a fear-free status).[52] Symbolically practiced by buying and releasing animals destined for slaughter or birds and fish kept in captivity, this kind of *dāna* comprises all acts of mercy. A recent example of this ceremony took place during 1995 at the ground-breaking ceremonies for the new headquarters for the World Fellowship of Buddhists in Thailand. This ceremony consisted of setting free a cow, a buffalo, and many birds and fish at an expenditure of several thousand dollars. The Second International Conference on the Buddhist Contribution to World Peace, held in Taipei, Taiwan, in December 1995 discussed the concerns expressed by Buddhist environmental preservation workers in South Korea and Thailand in regard to ecological problems created by large-scale release of imported birds and fish in alien environments as a result of the widespread practice of this popular form of giving and merit-making. Third, there is *dharmadāna*, the gift of *dharma*. Wideranging educational activities from teaching to publication, whether related directly to the propagation of the word of the Buddha or not, continue to be recognized as "gifts of *dharma*," which as stated above, were extolled by the Buddha as the highest gift.

The diversity thus brought into charitable and philanthropic activities in Theravāda Buddhist societies has necessitated new structures and procedures for their management. The traditional structures had been dismantled in the process of administrative reform due to either colonization or modernization or both. For example, the Sangha and its monastic institutions had been the beneficiaries of enormous grants of land and revenue made to them by ancient kings and benefactors. They have also continued to receive generous donations. The procedures which existed to manage such temporalities ensured that the monks were free from trials and tribulations of business affairs and money matters. In Sri Lanka, for instance, the temple lands were assigned to lay people according to a land-tenure system which ensured that certain goods and services were rendered to the temple at regular intervals. The breakdown of the system as a result of the land policies of the British continue to hinder the improvement of management and the full utilization of temple properties.

The Buddhists have neither a concept of temporalities similar to the Muslim *waqfs* nor centralized and modern management structures such as those of Catholic and Protestant Christian organizations. In their absence, the task has fallen on the government. In Myanmar and Thailand, the *Ratthaguru* and the *Sangharaja* with centralized ecclesiastical systems, supported by the Ministries or Departments of Religious Affairs, exercise directive and supervisory functions which prove to be adequate and satisfactory. In Sri Lanka, the multiplicity of sects and administrative units of the Sangha has left a blurred picture, and the involvement of the government is restricted to a fraction of the institutions. In Cambodia and Laos, the recent military and political upheavals have created further complications. In India and Bangladesh, the Buddhists form such small minorities as to be left to their own means even though such means are totally inadequate. It would therefore be correct to say that the Theravāda Buddhist societies have the improvement of the management of their charitable and philanthropic activities more or less as a major priority.

In the search for more effective and feasible models, these countries have explored the possibility of adapting such models as foundations, non-profit organizations, and legal corporations. The challenge before them is the evolution of systems which would optimize the cooperation between the Sangha and the laity. Emerging in each of the Theravāda countries is a Sangha with increasingly higher levels of general and higher education. The Buddhist temple has fast become a center of educational and social service, and the monk has proven his capacity as an organizer, purveyor, advocate, and agitator for rural development and education. He has equally demonstrated his ability as a fund-raiser both within and outside the country. It is therefore clear that the Sangha has to play an increasing role in both the promotion and the management of charity and philanthropy in Theravāda Buddhist societies.

NOTES

1. Canonical and non-canonical Pāli texts of the Theravāda tradition are referred to with the following abbreviations:

A   *Anguttaranikāya*
D   *Dīghanikāya*
IT   *Itivuttaka of the Khuddakanikāya*
J   *Jātaka of the Khuddakanikāya* and its commentary *Jātakatthakathā*
M   *Majjhimanikāya*
Sn   *Suttanipāta of the Khuddakanikāya*
Vism. *Visuddhimagga of Buddhaghosa*

Dhammapada v.177. Chapter (Ch.) and verse (v.) in the case of *Dhammapada* and the *Mahāvamsa* refer to any standard edition of these popular texts in Pāli or English translation.

2. D.II.48.

3. Some sources that illustrate the importance of giving in Buddhism are: Richard Gombrich, *Theravada Buddhism: A Social History from Ancient Benares to Modern Colombo* (Oxford: Oxford University Press, 1990); Ananda W. P. Guruge, *Asoka the Righteous: A Definitive Biography* (Colombo: Central Cultural Fund, Ministry of Cultural Affairs and Information, 1993); Guruge, *Mahāvamsa: The Great Chronicle of Sri Lanka* (Colombo: Associated Newspapers of Ceylon Limited, 1989); Nyanatiloka, *Buddhist Dictionary: Manual of Buddhist Terms and Doctrines* (Kandy: Buddhist Publication Society, 1980); Senerat Paranavitana, *Epigraphia Zeylanica: Being Lithic and Other Inscriptions of Ceylon*, vol. IV (London: Oxford University Press, 1943) and *Inscriptions of Ceylon*, vol. I (Colombo: Department of Archaeology, 1970); Russell F. Sizemore and Donald K. Swearer, eds., *Ethics, Wealth, and Salvation: A Study in Buddhist Social Ethics* (Columbia: University of South Carolina Press, 1990); Max Weber, *The Religion of India*, trans. and ed. Hans H. Gerth and Don Martindale (New York: 1921).

4. J.I.207.

5. In the Mahāyāna Buddhist tradition where the number of *Pāramitās* is reduced to six, *dāna* still heads the list.

6. The *Anguttaranikāya* (IV.364) comments on the meaning of the four Sangaha Vatthuni by saying that the best *dāna* is *dhamma dāna*; the best kind speech is teaching the *dhamma*; the best *atthacariyā* is to cause others to attain *saddhā, sīla, cāga, pannā*.

7. A.II.32

8. Ibid.

9. The *Pāramitās* are related to the *Brahma Vihāras* according to Buddhaghosa because the Mahasattas who fulfill the four *Brahma Vihāras* also fulfill the *Pāramitās* toward all beings. For example, one who has compassion gives alms, follows the moral precepts, etc. See Vism.IX.24.

10. Vism.IX.124.

11. Phra Rajavarmuni, "Foundations of Buddhist Social Ethics," in Russell F. Sizemore and Donald K. Swearer, eds., *Ethics, Wealth and Salvation: A Study in Buddhist Social Ethics* (Columbia: University of South Carolina Press, 1990), p. 48. See also A.IV.236–48 on the ethical significance of giving.

12. Cf.*Sigālovāda Sutta*, D.III.191.

13. IT.18.

14. D.III.163, A.III.53.

15. A.III.70; A.II.66.

16. Vism.IX.39–40.

17. Sn.506–507.

18. Vism.VII, A.III.282.

19. Vism.VII.113.

20. Richard Gombrich, *Theravada Buddhism: A Social History from Ancient Benares to Modern Colombo*, (Oxford: Oxford University Press, 1984), p. 29.

21. Cf. Aparihāniyadhammas, D.II.73, and Advice to Sigāla, D.III.191.

22. *Vinaya Pitakam*, V.249, on *pindacārika* and *pindapāta*.

23. *Vinaya Pitakam*, II.147, "*vihāre kāraye ramme.*" This relaxation of severity and austerity was apparently opposed by some of the Buddha's disciples. Ascribed to Devadatta are the five rules requiring austerity. The rejection of these rules by the Buddha is said to have caused the first recorded schism in the Sangha.

24. See *Ratana Sutta, Sutta Nipāta*, 227.

25. *Vinaya Pitakam*, I.302.

26. An identical text is to be found in the Chinese "Sutra in Forty Two Sections" (Section 11) where the highest *dāna* is that given to a Bodhisattva. It is equal to a gift given to ten trillion Buddhas of the three periods.

27. Cf. Vessagiti Cave Inscription, *Epigraphia Zeylanica*, I.18.

28. *Epigraphia Zeylanica*, IV.86.

29. A.IV.236ff.

30. One thousand, two hundred, seventy-six such votive inscriptions in Brahmi Script, dated third century B.C.E. to first century C.E., are deciphered and translated in Senarat Paranavitana, *Inscriptions of Ceylon*, vol. I, (Colombo, Department of Archaeology, 1970).

31. *Mahāvamsa*, xxxii,26ff.

32. Max Weber, *The Religion of India*, p. 215.

33. Ibid., p. 217.

34. John Strong, "Rich Man, Poor Man, *Bhikkhu*, King: Quinquennial Festival and the Nature of Dāna," in Sizemore and Swearer, *Ethics, Wealth, and Salvation*, p. 122.

35. *Ethics, Wealth, and Salvation*, p. 15.

36. *Sumangala-Vilāsinī*, ed. T. W. Rhys Davids and J. Estlin Carpenter, (London: Pali Text Society, 1968), p. 298ff.

37. Leslie Grey, *A Concordance of Buddhist Birth Stories* (Oxford: Pali Text

Society, 1994). This book lists many *Jatākas* whose moral was generosity (e.g., Akitti, Ambara, Bilārikosiya, Cullapaduma, Dasabrahmana, Khanika, Dīghītikosala, Dūta, Godha, Kanakavama, Kadirangāra, Kummasapinda, Mahāsatva, Maitreya, Manicūda, Nigrodhamiga, Sanjīva, Sasa, Simhakapi, Sivi, Supriya). Each describes acts of charity and sacrifice by which the Buddha in a previous birth fulfilled a particular level of *dāna Pāramitā*, the perfection of liberality. The first level involves giving worldly or material possessions, including wives and children as in the Vessantara *Jatāka*. The second level involves the donation of one's flesh or parts of the body (e.g., Sivi *Jatāka*). The highest level is when one's life itself is sacrificed for the good of another as in the Mahāsatva and Sasa *Jatākas*.

38. *Jatāka* 4. See Nancy Auer Falk on these legends of Anāthapindika, "Exemplary Donors of the Pāli Tradition," in *Ethics, Wealth, and Salvation,* p. 124ff.

39. M.III.262

40. Rock Edict VIII. Regarding the citations for the Asokan inscriptions, RE and PE will refer to Rock Edicts and Pillar Edicts respectively.

41. Gombrich, p. 29.

42. RE XII.

43. M.I.371.

44. D.III.36ff.

45. RE VII.

46. PE II.

47. PE VII.

48. RE I and II.

49. PE V.

50. PE V.

51. Strong, "Rich Man, Poor Man," p. 110.

52. The earliest known decree granting sanctuary to specified species and regulating killing, branding, and caponizing of animals is Pillar Edict V of Asoka (third Century B.C.E.). The example of this Buddhist emperor had been followed by other Buddhist kings of South and Southeast Asia, e.g., Amendagāmini Abhaya of Sri Lanka (second Century B.C.E.), who declared the whole island a sanctuary for animals with his *māghāta* ("don't kill") decree.

.5.

The Mahāyāna Buddhist Foundation for Philanthropic Practices

LESLIE S. KAWAMURA

In discussing the topic of philanthropy and culture one of the difficulties faced is the fact that philanthropy, especially the manner in which it is understood and practiced in the North American context, is not a common occurrence in Eastern civilizations. In this chapter, I would like to investigate and to share a few ideas about how philanthropy might be understood from the Mahāyāna Buddhist perspective.

I have already mentioned that philanthropy as we are used to seeing it in the North American context, i.e., through foundations such as the Ford Foundation and the Rockefeller Foundation, is not a common occurrence in the Eastern cultures. This is not to say, however, that philanthropic-like acts do not occur in the East. In discussing an Eastern, and specifically a Buddhist, perspective on philanthropy a comparative approach will be utilized, because an inquiry into the meaning of "philanthropy" and an investigation of how philanthropy is understood in the Western civilizations can provide the basis from which we can interpret philanthropic-like activities within the Buddhist cultures.

I wish to examine how philanthropy is understood in the Western civilization by turning to Demetrios Constantelos, who opens his book *Byzantine Philanthropy and Social Welfare* with the following words:

philanthropia, which is a pure Greek compound word, describes man's love for his near ones, his affection and active concern not only for his kin and friend but for his fellow man in general. Philanthropia as a Byzantine concept is identified with *agape* and underlies an active feeling of benevolence toward any person, independent of that person's identity or actions.[1]

Here we find that philanthropy in the Western civilization is closely related to the idea of altruistic hospitality and charity. Here it is interesting to note that at a conference on the economic aspects of philanthropy, a conference held by the National Bureau of Economic Research in cooperation with the Merrill Center for Economics at the Merrill Center, South Hampton, Long Island, from June 26 through June 30, 1961, "concluded its eighteen sessions without locating the current boundaries of philanthropy."[2] According to Frank G. Dickinson, the inability to locate boundaries of philanthropy indicated that "the basic idea of philanthropy seems to exclude the application of a conventional theory of value and of what is known of ordinary market behavior [and] . . . philanthropy involves a one-sided exchange; that is, there is no *quid pro quo* unless it is extremely remote."[3]

These ideas compel us to raise the following question: Is it possible for humanity to act without seeking any form of reward in return? In other words, can there be a philanthropic-like act wherein there is no *quid pro quo?*

Kenneth E. Boulding of the University of Michigan discussed this very question from the perspective of motivation. That is, he questions whether there is a "rational" philanthropic behavior. In other words, is it possible to have a "genuinely unilateral transfer . . . *a quid* for which there is no *quo,* not now, in the future, nor in the past."[4] He asks whether a blind man should give something in return if one were to drop a dime in his cup. He states, "We feel a certain glow of emotional virtue, and it is this we receive for our dime. Looked at from the point of view of the recipient, we might suppose that the blind man gives out a commodity or service which consists in being pitiable."[5] Thus, granting that the blind man has no intention of returning his "being pitiable" for the gift of the dime from the donor, we can understand how this transaction is one in which there is a "*quid* for which there is no *quo,* not now, in the future, nor in the past."

On the basis of the above discussions, we will have to agree with Kenneth Boulding that this transaction "is clearly a very curious one," but it is exactly this type of philanthropical act that comes closest to the act of benevolence or philanthropy found in the Buddhist tradition. For example, the *Samyukta Nikāya* (I. 105) states:

> Monks, go and travel around for the welfare of the multitudes, for the happiness of the multitudes, out of sympathy for the world, for the

benefit, welfare, and happiness of gods and humans. Two should not go on one [path]. Monks, teach the dhamma that is beneficial in the beginning, beneficial in the middle, and beneficial in the end.

This passage indicates that if we are to speak at all about philanthropy within the Buddhist context, then it would be a one-way transaction wherein there is no *quid pro quo* and wherein a monk works for the benefit and happiness of the many without anticipating any benefits therefrom. The classical Buddhist application of such a transaction is found in a famous anecdotal story in which Anāthapiṇḍada, a wealthy banker, bestows a monastery in a pleasure garden (Jetavanārāma) to Prince Siddārtha who became the historical Buddha, that is, an Enlightened Being. Jetavanārāma, according to Dr. S. Dutt, "Perhaps . . . was the largest and most famous of all *ārāmas* of antiquity and the legends say that the Buddha spent as many as nineteen vassa-periods here."[6] In this account, there is no indication of Anāthapiṇḍada's desire to gain something in return for his act of providing the Buddha the *ārāma*, unless we can deem the fact that he was in high spirits when the Buddha accepted his invitation as a case of *quid pro quo*. This act closely parallels what Kenneth E. Boulding calls a "genuine donation"; that is,

> gifts for which there is no identifiable *quid pro quo* even in the shape of a personal gratification. There is a real moral difference between the gift which is given out of vanity and the desire for self-aggrandizement or the desire to be merely fashionable, and the gift which is given out of a genuine sense of community with the object of the donation. It is this sense of community which is the essence of what I regard as genuine philanthropy.[7]

Had Kenneth Boulding stopped his comments on the idea of a "genuine" donation with the above statements, his view on philanthropy would have concurred closely with philanthropic-like action within the Buddhist tradition. But the statements that follow shift the idea of a "genuine donation" away from *dāna,* the act of giving, found within the Buddhist tradition. He continues with the following information:

> even pity is the manifestation of self-identification with the pitied. It is this capacity for empathy—or putting oneself in another's place, for feeling the joys and the sorrows of another as one's own—which is the source of the genuine gift. It is because "no man is an island," because the very realization of our own identity implies in some sense that there is a common identity in humanity, that we are willing to "socialize" our substance and to share with the afflicted. This is "charity" before the word became corrupted by vanity and fashion.[8]

Without doubt empathy is an important aspect of a "genuine donation" but so long as that feeling of empathy is based upon a feeling of exchange, it does not describe the act of *dāna* (giving) found in the

Buddhist tradition. As one of my colleagues, Dr. J. Yokota has pointed out:

> Mahāyāna Buddhist social ethics is based on the reality of emptiness and specifically on the implications of the reality of no-self and no-possessions. The basis of all ethical theory in Buddhism, especially from the Mahāyāna perspective, is compassion, and this compassion is made possible only through the insight into reality of the non-substantiality of the self and of all objects. . . . This reality of emptiness is the basis for acting for the other, since it is recognizing that there is no other apart from the self and that there is no self apart from the other. To act for one's own benefit is to act for the other's benefit. . . .[9]

Here we see in operation the "logic of illogic" so common in Mahāyāna, especially in the early Mahāyāna traditions established by Nāgārjuna and Asanga. Of course, the difficulty of such a "logic of illogic" lies in the fact that under normal circumstances self and others are understood as separate and unique entities. Thus, normally it is difficult for a person to overcome one's own desire and self-centeredness. This means that "one is caught up in self concern and can never rise above it."[10] In other words, "We love our neighbor, but not quite as ourselves. As he gets more and we get less, we rejoice indeed in his affluence, but at some point our dissatisfaction with our own penury is likely to exceed this vicarious enjoyment."[11]

Although from its inception, the teachings and activities of the historical Siddārtha Gotama, who became a Buddha, always focused on the welfare of the multitude, it should be noted that the manner in which the "welfare of the multitude" was actualized or realized differed from one Buddhist tradition to another. The basis for this difference can be seen in view of the variegated methods or ways that are available for one to become an Enlightened Being. Traditionally, Buddhism has developed along two main streams—that of the Northern, known as the Mahāyāna, and that of the Southern, known as the Theravāda. These two divisions are not homogeneous, for the Mahāyāna has many subschools and even Theravāda has been bifurcated into at least two divisions. According to H. B. Aronson:

> two widely quoted Western writers on South Asian Buddhism, Winston King and Melford Spiro, . . . have bifurcated Theravāda Buddhism, finding one part of the religion devoted to the means for attaining pleasurable rebirth, the other to escape from rebirth altogether. The former has to do with wholesome intentions and activities (kamma) which insure rebirth as a human or in heaven . . . "kammatic Buddhism" and the other [is] "nibbanic Buddhism."[12]

Regarding this "nibbanic Buddhism" Spiro writes:

> There is no point at which any of the doctrines of nibbanic Buddhism articulates with the secular order, either to give it value, on the one

hand, or to provide a fulcrum by which it can be changed on the other. . . . the only emotional state ultimately valued by nibbanic Buddhism— [is] that of detachment (upekkhā). Ultimately, the behavior of the true Buddhist (unlike, say, the true Christian) is governed not only by love but by detachment.[13]

Here, we find a salient difference between philanthropy as discussed above within the Western context based on *agape* and a philanthropic-like activity found in Buddhism based upon love and detachment. The aspect of the "unity of love and detachment" is contextually the same as the Mahāyāna bodhisattva ideal, the defining characteristic of which is detachment from any form of attachments. Although *upekkhā*, as detachment, plays an important role in nibbanic Buddhism, it is questionable in a Mahāyāna Buddhist context whether this term should be interpreted merely as "detachment." This is not the place to argue the point in detail, but simply stated, *upekkhā* (*Sanskrit, upekṣā*), when discussed within the Mahāyāna context especially if it is to be discussed in the light of philanthropic practices, is better understood in view of the Mahāyāna practices of the ten perfections (*pāramitā*), and mainly with the first one, *dāna-pāramitā* (perfection of generosity and charity). In other words, *upekkhā* in the Mahāyāna tradition points to a "tranquil flow of mind" which means "being free from both love and hate towards living beings."[14]

Freedom from love and from hate, in other words, generosity and charity are based upon compassion (*karuṇā*). His Holiness, the Dalai Lama, considered by Tibetan Buddhists to be a human manifestation of Avalokiteśvara, is the perfect manifestation of compassion. According to Achok Rimpoche:

His Holiness, the Dalai Lama, has given all his time and effort to help-ing his suffering people, even undergoing exile, abuse and misunder-standing, as well as hardship and loss, solely to benefit others. . . . His love and compassion are for all people, including the Chinese. He has never abused them, in fact [he] has referred to [m]any (sic) good things they have done, and he always asks his people not to have any harmful thoughts, even towards enemies.[15]

This feeling of compassion demonstrated by His Holiness arises from his practicing the ten perfections beginning with giving (*dāna*) reli-giously. Such activities of compassion may come easily for someone like His Holiness, but we ordinary mortals will encounter difficulties in prac-ticing compassionate acts. For example, in the Eastern religious tradi-tions, one is taught not to kill even an insect, but is it possible for one to watch a swarm of mosquitoes or bees partake of one's body? Is it not more tempting to swat these insects even before they attack us? In other words, it is easier for us to put ourselves ahead of others. Achok Rim-poche correctly points out that:

> The source of fear and suffering for all human beings is exaggerated self-concern, or self-cherishing, and therefore a lack of concern for others. You can not cure this suffering with medicine or weapons. The only cure or opponent is changing one's attitude from self-concern to concern for others or, in other words, to care more about others than about oneself.[16]

Therefore, in order to accomplish philanthropic-like activities within the Buddhist tradition, one would have to change one's attitude "from self-concern to concern for others" no matter how difficult such a change may be. The transformation of one's attitude depends upon one's ability to see reality-as-it-is (i.e., wisdom) and on the basis of that, to act spontaneously and appropriately according to what a situation warrants (i.e., compassion). Thus the transformed person is one who possesses the qualities of wisdom and compassion.

What is clear from the above is that the doing of philanthropic-like acts within the Eastern traditions must go hand in hand with the elevation of a person spiritually, but at the same time, philanthropic acts are not done for the purpose of spiritual elevation. In other words, an act can be considered an act of philanthropy if by virtue of going through the action it integrates one's personality. Consequently, the going out in the four directions by Buddhist monks for the benefit of humankind or the donating of *ārāma* by Anāthapiṇḍada can be understood to be philanthropic-like acts only if the results of these activities are such that a person who does these acts becomes spiritually elevated. Here there is no evaluation as to whether one act of charity is better or worse than another act.

It would be problematic indeed if philanthropic actions produce mediocre results or if the needy were overlooked; hence, generosity must be administered by activities that are most appropriate to a situation. This means, from a Buddhist perspective, that the giver of the gift must stand on a solid foundation of wisdom and compassion. In other words, there can be no sense of "distribution" in philanthropic-like acts. The *Arya-sumatidārakā-paripṛccha-nāma Mahāyānasūtra* states:

> Young lady [Sumati], when a bodhisattva possesses four qualities, then treasures will abound. Which are the four? They are 1) to give timely, 2) to give without regret, 3) to give willingly, and 4) to give without hoping for a reward. Young lady [Sumati], when a bodhisattva possess those four qualities, then treasures will abound.[17]

A bodhisattva gives "timely" in that if the recipient is not ready to receive or if the situation does not warrant an act of giving, then no thing is given. This is an important observation, because we often wish to give with all of the correct intentions, but at the wrong time. We have all heard about the helpful cub scout who insisted on doing his good deed for the day by taking an old lady across the street even though she did not need to cross.

To give without regret is not necessarily limited to the meaning that one does not regret the fact that one gave something away. To give without regrets means also that one appreciates the opportunity to give. In the Japanese Pure Land Buddhist tradition, there are followers of the faith who are called *my ō-kō-nin* or "wonderfully amiable persons." One such person was Seikuro about whom is told the following story:[18]

> While Seikuro was at a service, a thief entered his dwelling by breaking in through a wall. Seven ounces of silver money that Seikuro had left under a straw mat had been taken. Upon hearing about this, people would say, "I am sorry to hear about the theft."
>
> Seikuro replied, "A man who commits theft must be, indeed, short of money. But also, he broke into my house where there is nothing to steal. It was certainly a pity. However, he was able to take seven ounces of silver money. This was the change I had left over from 15 ounces of silver money that I had earned from selling rape seeds. The other 8 ounces had been spent to pay for the laundry bill owing from spring. On any other occasion, I would not have had even 7 ounces of silver money. How joyful I am that the thief came at the right time. He took great pain to break in and did not leave empty-handed! It was only a small amount but I am grateful that it was there for him."
>
> When people heard his reply, they were put out. "What nonsense is this?" they asked. "Joyful after having been robbed!"
>
> Seikuro replied, "Why ought I not be happy? I, the victim of the theft, am likewise an unenlightened fool by nature, quite capable of committing theft. . . . On the contrary, isn't it wonderful that I can be the one from whom someone can steal! . . . To have a thief enter my home is indeed imprudent of me, but this incident brought no disgrace to me or to my fellow practitioners. What could be more joyful?

To give willingly means both "to give" and "not to give." Ordinarily, when we think of giving, we think not about giving voluntarily but in commercial terms—that is, we think that in an act of giving, some commodity must always be exchanged. But often silence is the greatest gift that one can give. In Buddhist history, silence has played an important role as for example when Siddārtha contemplated whether he should impart his insight to others. Also, Kaśyapa's noble silence in the *Avatamsakasūtra* is known. But unlike such acts of silence that show the magnitude of the insight possessed by an Enlightened Being, silence in the form of a gift permits the other to determine a course of action or nonaction in the other's own terms and time. One is not forced into making a decision on the basis of some other person's desire or wish. This kind of charity is difficult to accomplish, because "giving" usually is understood as an instrument of commerce whereby the giver measures one's capacity for charity according to the degree of influence one can have on another. Of course, this is contrary to giving without the desire for reward.

The four qualities discussed above indicate that philanthropic-like acts within a Buddhism context are acts of giving in which there is no gift, no giver of the gift, and no receiver of the gift. This differs from philanthropy as understood in the West, where philanthropy is seen as an affection for mankind, especially, as manifested in donations of money, property, or work to needy persons or to socially useful purposes.

In more recent times, the activities of Dr. Ehan Numata, a Buddhist believer, reflect well the Buddhist philanthropic life.[19] Ehan Numata was born in Hiroshima on April 12, 1898. Soon after graduating Heian High School in Kyoto, he received ordination as a priest of the Nishi Honganji Temple in February, 1917, and in June of that year he crossed the Pacific Ocean to California as a Buddhist missionary. His missionary work was not so successful, and thus he decided to study at the University of California, Berkeley, from which he graduated with a master's degree in June of 1926. During his study, Mr. Numata became very ill, but recovered from his illness, a recovery which he attributes to his faith in the Buddhist teachings. His dream was to publish the complete Buddhist Canon into English and other languages so that the Buddha's teaching would reach every part of the world. He tried to get a few works published, but every time he tried, he ran out of funds. This made him realize that without money, he could not accomplish his dream of having the Buddha's teaching reach every corner of the globe. He decided to put his learning of economic countercycle policy to work, but for him this meant that he had to manufacture something that had never been made before. In October 1934, he established the Mitsutoyo Company to produce special kinds of micrometers, a company that turned out to be the foundation for the fortune that enabled him to undertake philanthropic activities, especially philanthropic activities that advanced the study of Buddhism throughout the world.[20] As pointed out above, his need to acquaint the American public with the Buddha's teachings stemmed from his belief that it was the Buddha's teachings that nourished him back to health from a severe illness he faced while studying in the United States and from his sense of failure as a Buddhist missionary. As a result, once Mitsutoyo began to profit, Mr. Numata systematically put aside 1 to 3 percent of the profits that provided the funds for the book *Bukkyo Seiten* (The Teaching of the Buddha) to be translated first into English and then into thirty-five languages of the world. To date, half a million of these books have been placed in hotels and hospitals throughout those countries. Also, the profits have been the source for the financial aid for establishing ten Chairs of Buddhist Studies in universities throughout the world, for translating into English the one hundred volumes of the Chinese Buddhist Canon, for awarding prizes in Buddhist Literary Works and Buddhist Practices, for building Ekoji (Light-Bestowing) temples-cum-Buddhist-center buildings in the United States and Germany, and for the publication of the journal *The Pacific World*.

In the final edition of Mitsutoyo's newsletter published under the directorship of Ehan Numata, he wrote, "To establish a Mitsutoyo Company anywhere is to establish a Buddhist temple there."[21] In this manner, Mr. Numata's philanthropic activities have aided many students, scholars, and people throughout the world. As the activities of the Chairs of Buddhist Studies expand and more of the Buddhist Canon become available in English there will be greater and everlasting influences that will benefit the world.

In this chapter, I have attempted to show the difference between philanthropic acts done by granting agents and organizations and philanthropic-like activity in Buddhism. In summary, whereas philanthropy in the Western civilization are acts done by granting agents geared to having a *quid pro quo* (something in return for another), in the Eastern civilization, and in particular in the Buddhist act of giving, there is neither a *quid* nor a *quo*.

NOTES

1. Demetrios Constantelos, *Byzantine Philanthropy and Social Welfare* (New Brunswick: Rutgers University Press, 1968), p. 3.

2. Frank G. Dickinson, ed., *Philanthropy and Public Policy* (New York: National Bureau of Economic Research, 1962), p. 111.

3. Ibid., pp. 111–12.

4. Kenneth E. Boulding, in Frank G. Dickinson, ed., *Philanthropy and Public Policy* (New York: National Bureau of Economic Research, 1962), p. 60.

5. Ibid., pp. 57–58.

6. S. Dutt, *Buddhist Monks and Monasteries of India* (London: George Allen and Unwin, 1962), p. 67.

7. Kenneth Boulding, p. 61.

8. Ibid.

9. John Yokota, "Shin Buddhist Ethics," *The Pure Land,* New Series, no. 4, December 1987, pp. 18–19.

10. Ibid., p. 27.

11. Boulding, p. 61.

12. H. B. Aronson, *Love and Sympathy in Theravāda Buddhism* (Delhi: Motilal Banarsidass, 1980), p. 78. It should be noted further here that although the Mahāyāna and the Theravāda represent two different traditions, it is not the case that they are mutually exclusive regarding certain fundamental doctrines such as "benefit to others . . . compassion," and so on.

13. Quoted in ibid., pp. 78–79.

14. G. M. Nagao, *Mādhyamika and Yogācāra,* trans. L. S. Kawamura (New York: SUNY Press, 1993), p. 92.

15. Achok Rimpoche, "The Importance of Love and Compassion in Buddhism," in E. Steinkellner and H. Tauscher, eds., *Contributions on Tibetan and Buddhist Religion and Philosophy* (Vienna: Arbeitskreis für Tibetisch' und Buddhistische Studien Universität Wien, 1983), vol. 2, p. 11.

16. Ibid., pp. 2–3.

17. See *Tibetan Tripitaka Peking Edition* (Tokyo-Kyoto: Tibetan Tripitaka Research Institute, 1961), vol. 24, no. 30, p. 92, folio 225b, lines 1–4.

། དུ་མོ་གུང་རྒྱབ་སེམས་དཔའི་ཚོས་བཞི་དང་ལྡན་ན་ནོར་ཆེ་བར་འགྱུར་ཏེ། ། བཞི་གང་ཞེ་ན། འདི་ལྟ་སྟེ། དུས་སུ་སྦྱིན་པ

དང་། འགྱུད་པ་མེད་པར་སྦྱིན་པ་དང་། ཡིད་དུ་འོང་བ་སྦྱིན་པ་དང་། རྣམ་པར་སྦྱིན་པ་ལ་མི་རེ་བར་སྦྱིན་པ་སྟེ། དུ་མོ་གུང་རྒྱབ

སེམས་དཔའི་ཚོས་བཞི་པོ་དེ་དག་དང་ལྡན་ན་ནོར་ཆེ་བར་འགྱུར་རོ།།

18. For a discussion on the *My ō-kō-nin,* see my book, *The Bodhisattva Doctrine in Buddhism* (Waterloo: Wilfrid Laurier University Press, 1981), pp. 223–38. For the incident described here, see pp. 231–32.

19. The life activities of Mr. Numata can be found in various newspapers in Japan. See, for example, *Mainichi Shinbun* (Everyday Paper: December 16, 1987), *Nippon Keizai Shinbun* (Japan Economics Paper: July 6, 1985), *Asahi Shinbun* (Morning Sun Paper: March 11, 1984), *Asahi Shinbun Yukan* (Morning Sun, Evening Edition: October 21, 1980), and so on. See especially the last-mentioned for a historical sketch of his life.

20. For example, there are Mitsutoyo plants in England, Germany, Singapore, United States of America, Canada, Mexico, and Brazil aside from those in Japan.

21. See the June 1990 edition of *Heisei Gijiku,* p. 201.

PART THREE
PHILANTHROPY IN CONTEXT

.6.

Philanthropy, the Law, and Public Policy in the Islamic World before the Modern Era

SAID AMIR ARJOMAND

A good name remaining for posterity
Is better than a gilded mansion left behind.

—SAʿDĪ OF SHIRAZ

How can the issue of philanthropy be set in a comparative perspective? While culture defines the *motives* for philanthropy distinctive of different civilizations, the legal framework is decisive in determining the respective *mode* of philanthropic activity. As regards the motivation to philanthropy, the epigraph by the great poet Saʿdī of Shiraz (d. 1291) singles out the good name to survive the donor as the chief worldly motive for philanthropy. Charity, hospitality, and philanthropy were the means for acquiring a good name and leaving it for posterity. Within Islam the religious and otherworldly motive for philanthropy is expressed as the desire to approach God, and this motivation is incorporated, in the form of "nearness (*ghurba*) to God," into the legal formula for the constitution of an endowment.[1] The formula leaves the clear mark of Islam as a world religion of salvation on all charitable and philanthropic action. For the second comparative point of reference, it can be said categorically that the Islamic mode of philanthropic activity was distinctively shaped by the institution of *waqf* in Islamic law.

Payton identifies "voluntary giving for public purposes" as a principal form of philanthropy.[2] A comparative approach must also consider the *purpose* of philanthropy. This means addressing the issue of voluntary agency within the framework of the constitution of the respective society. Although philanthropy begins as an act by a private individual or group, its public purpose inevitably brings public authority into the picture in one form or another. The articulation of private agency, public purpose, and public policy can be understood only by comparing various sociopolitical constitutions. The enormous impact of philanthropic foundations on public policy in the United States in the last century, for instance, cannot be understood without reference to its politico-legal context, and especially by the importance of associations in the American polity as highlighted by Tocqueville in the nineteenth century. A constitutional perspective is particularly useful for making the boundary between the public and the private in differing sociopolitical constitutions an object of comparison. In this perspective, what we may call civil society and the state can serve as analytical points of reference.

EVOLUTION OF THE LAW OF *WAQF* AND ITS
CONSTITUTIONAL CONTEXT

It is interesting to note that it was the non-Koranic *waqf*, whose law was elaborated by the Islamic jurists in the eighth century, and not the Koranic norms of charity, *ṣadaqa* and *zakāt*, that became the legal foundation of philanthropy in Islam. The Islamic jurists developed the *zakāt* into a poor-rate incumbent on all believers to be collected by the state. Its collection, however, proved inefficient and corrupt, and fell into desuetude only to be revived as a battle cry by contemporary Islamic fundamentalists. The *ṣadaqa* was considered religiously meritorious, but remained unregulated voluntary charity to the poor. It did, however, affect the development of the law of *waqf*.

The law of *waqf* developed during the formative period of Islamic law—that is, the eighth and ninth centuries of the Common Era. The presumption of the influence of the Roman law on its development has been discarded.[3] No hierocratic control of pious endowments as found in Byzantium was possible, there being no Islamic institution comparable to the Church. The influence of the pre-Islamic Iranian law, on the other hand, has now been incontestably established.[4] The discovery of the Sasanian law book, *Mātakdān-i Hazār Dātastān* (Book of the Thousand Judgments) has enabled us to understand the epigraphic evidence on the institution of private endowments "for the soul" (*pat ruvān*) or "for pious purposes" (*pat ahravdāt*) whose purpose was determined by the founder and set forth in an instrument of endowment. The general supervision of these endowments throughout the Sasanian empire was entrusted to a bureau (*dīvān*) of religious institutions.[5] The inscription on a bridge in Fars, built in the fifth century and funded by one such endowment established by the highest official of the Sasanian state for his soul and those of his sons, reads as follows: "This bridge was built by Mihr-Narseh, the prime minister, for his soul's sake and at his expense. . . . Whoever comes on this road let him give a blessing to Mihr-Narseh and his sons."[6]

The Muslim conquerors found the institution of endowment for the soul in Iraq where the capital of the Sasanian empire was located. The institution was duly recognized and Islamicized by the jurists of the formative period in the form of *waqf.* The literal meaning of the terms for endowment, *waqf* (suspension), or *ḥabs* (confinement), of property, explicitly indicates the immobilization of property and the assignment of its usufruct for a variety of purposes. Foremost among these purposes, and the one that served to justify all others, was the designation of the poor and "the migrants and warriors on the path of God" (as the general beneficiaries of the endowment). Some early jurists did allow temporary immobilization, but the view that a valid *waqf* required the permanent and irreversible alienation of property from the donor prevailed.[7] Furthermore, benefaction to one's own kin was recognized as a form of charity conducive to nearness to God. In any event, in the process of subsequent legal formalization, the desire to approach God on the part of the donor was simply presumed by most schools of law.[8] Despite the persistence of differences among authorities, the regulations concerning charity (*ṣadaqa*) and a form of testamentary disposition of property unrestricted by the Islamic law of inheritance,[9] eventually converged, notably in the work of the great jurist, Muḥammad b. Idrīs al-Shāfiʿī (d. 820), to create the distinctive Islamic law of pious endowment, which he significantly termed *ṣadaqa muḥarrama mawqūfa* (set-apart, suspended charity).[10]

From the beginning, *waqf* appears in two forms that correspond to the original Iranian institution: "family" and "public" endowments.[11] The overwhelming majority of the endowments in the early period, including the one instituted by Shāfiʿī himself,[12] were in fact small private endowments whose beneficiaries were the members of the founder's family and the poor,[13] the type that was subsequently called "family *waqf*" (*waqf ahli*). In this period, mosques were practically the only endowments that could be called public.[14] Nor would the chief Kadi (judge) of Baghdad, Abū Bakr Muḥammad b. ʿAmr al-Shāybanī, known as al-Khassāf (d. 874–75) allow the law of *waqf* to be used as an instrument of public policy. He refused to recognize as valid the institution of a *waqf* for the benefit of the scholars of the Prophetic Traditions and lecturers because they could not be regarded as the poor.[15]

Attempts at the registration and supervision of the *waqf* by the Kadis are recorded as early as the eighth century, and *waqf* had spread widely enough by the latter part of the tenth century for the Fatimid state in

Egypt to establish a bureau for its supervision.[16] By the eleventh century, as we shall see, the possibility of control of public education through the law of *waqf* suggested it as an instrument of public policy to the rulers of eastern Iran. In the second half of the eleventh century under the greater Seljuq empire, Nizam al-Mulk and other Seljuq viziers institutionalized the systematic use of the law of *waqf* as a major instrument of public policy.

In what follows I shall use the term "civil society" with reference to medieval and early modern Islam. This requires some justification. Hegel characterizes civil society as a community of private persons which is formally constituted through the *legal system*, and whose universal principle of freedom rests on the protection of property by law.[17] According to this conception, we may apply the term "civil society" to a sphere of social relations in medieval Islam whose autonomy was in principle guaranteed by Islamic law. We would, however, have to be on guard against Hegel's implicit juxtaposition of civil society as the realm of particular interests and private freedom to the state as the arena of public life and the realization of general freedom. As Hegel would readily have admitted, the stark dichotomy of private/particular and public/general does not fit the premodern world. Far more appropriate as a counterpart to medieval Muslim civil society than Hegel's idealized state is Max Weber's notion of the patrimonial state. Weber's model of patrimonialism has the advantage of not implying any systematic opposition between civil society and the state, and of not invoking the private-public dichotomy anachronistically.[18] On the contrary, the patrimonial state is characterized as a system of authority that is inherently *personal*: where the kingdom is an extension of the household of the ruler and where the modern distinction between the private and personal on the one hand, and the public and the impersonal, on the other, does not apply. In the patrimonial state office is not disengaged from property, and can be appropriated; there are strong hereditary tendencies in tenure of certain offices, and the officials own many of the means of administration.

Our picture of the constitutional context of philanthropy can be completed by the introduction of the Islamic law as the institution that mediates between civil society and the patrimonial state and brings them into partial integration. As Weber also pointed out, the responsibility for the welfare of the subjects is central to the legitimacy of the patrimonial state, and the patrimonial states in medieval Islam are no exception.[19] This responsibility drew the rulers and their viziers into the sphere of philanthropy. As we shall see, in much of the period under study, the Persian viziers at the head of the state bureaucracies, far from being pitted against civil society in inveterate opposition, emerge as its chief protectors against the Turko-Mongolian military ruling class. And to protect civic institutions, they used one of the chief instruments of agency at the disposal of the Islamic civil society: the (civil) law of *waqf.*

PHILANTHROPIC ENDOWMENT AS THE MODE OF AGENCY OF THE IRANIAN CIVIL SOCIETY IN THE TENTH AND ELEVENTH CENTURIES

Within a century and a half after the conversion of northeastern Iran (Khurasan) and Transoxania to Islam, which had begun on a significant scale in the mid-eighth century, a new patrician class that included a significant component of the pre-Islamic landed aristocracy, the *dihqāns*, was firmly established in the cities of the region, creating one of the strongest instances of civic agency found in Islamic history. The dominance of this class over the cities of northeastern Iran remained unchallenged throughout the tenth and most of the eleventh century, and the rulers of the independent dynasties that arose in the region sought their cooperation. The patricians of northeastern Iran resided in the cities and had substantial landholdings in the surrounding countryside. The institution of family *waqfs* among the patricians was very widespread, and served both for holding the family property intact and as a measure of its honor and prestige.[20] Furthermore, the continued dominance of this patrician class rested in no small part on their control of the offices of the Kadis and the Shaykh al-Islams (heads of the religious institutions), which in turn owed much to their creation and control of the *madrasas* as institutions for learning the Islamic sciences, traditions, jurisprudence, and theology.[21] Already by 1025, there were over twenty *madrasas* in Khuttal in a remote corner of our region, all fully endowed with *waqf.*[22] As for the area around the capital of Khurasan, Nishapur, Bulliet counts some thirty *madrasas* founded before the middle of the eleventh century. As he also emphasizes, these *madrasas* were controlled by members of the patrician class as founders and as professors, and served as a powerful mechanism for its reproduction. The *madrasa* education in this period was not an avenue of social mobility for the propertyless classes.[23]

From the end of the tenth century, we have evidence of the endowment of *madrasas* by the rulers and high officials of the state.[24] It is indicative of the vigor and assertiveness of the patrician class that its members competed with the rulers, at times defiantly, in the founding of *madrasas* by *waqf.* In 1023, the Ghaznavid Sultan Maḥmūd had the Shaykh al-Ra'īs, Abū'l-Qāsim 'Alī b. Muḥammad, a rich *dihqān* and a prominent patrician of Baihaq arrested and brought to him in Ghazna because the latter had founded not only a *madrasa* for his own (Hanafite) school of law, which was also the Sultan's, but also two other *madrasas* for two competing schools of law. His influential friends interceded with the

Sultan and he escaped punishment. Four years later, however, the Shaykh al-Ra'īs endowed a fourth *madrasa* for the benefit of yet another group ("the Zaydis and the Mu'tazilites") under the direction of the Koran commentator, Ibn Abī'l-Ṭayyib, a protégé who had been summoned to Ghazna with him in 1023 and beaten by the Sultan's order.[25] When our defiant philanthropist was appointed the *ra'īs* (mayor) of Baihaq in December 1031, the town people wrote "a letter in Arabic" to the government headquarters in Nishapur commending the Shaykh for his good work: "His benefaction is widespread, and his charity extensive, noble *madrasas* testify to his philanthropy and lofty mosques to his excellence, and proud endowments (*waqfs*) establish his honor."[26]

Elsewhere, Badr b. Ḥasanūya (or Ḥasanwayh; d. 1015) who was the Buyid (or Buwayhid) governor of several provinces in western Iran for over thirty years, was making systematic use of *waqf* as an instrument of a vigorous public policy. He built bridges, hostels, and wells and endowed them from *waqf* on his property and assigned state revenues for their maintenance. Above all, he created a large number of endowments for inns that were attached to teaching mosques for students without private means.[27] Badr's extensive endowment of hostels therefore seems to have been an important philanthropic innovation. Makdisi considers the "mosque-inn college of law" it established a major step in the development of the Islamic institutions of learning. The main elements of the mosque-inn complex—a place of learning (the mosque where circles of teaching were held) with an adjacent inn or hostel for students from out of town who, furthermore, received a stipend—were built into the *madrasa* model in the second half of the eleventh century. The *madrasas* were established as charitable trusts for the support of chairs of Islamic law and other subjects, *and* for the support of a small number of students without private means. This innovation made education an avenue for upward social mobility in practice as well as in theory. Although the extent of this mobility in Islamic society should not be exaggerated, stories of the poor student receiving free education in the *madrasas* and moving on to become professors and judges that begin to appear in the literature attest to its reality. Far more spectacular than its opening of the avenue of social mobility, however, was the *madrasas*' tremendous facilitation of geographical mobility among the educated elite of the Islamic world[28] which resulted in the creation of a remarkably uniform Islamic high culture in the late Middle Ages.

Makdisi argues that the college was then imported into Europe in the twelfth century, first by the Knights Templar of the Levant whose headquarters was in England and who founded the Inns of Court in London, which were attached to churches, and later by one John of London, who must have seen *madrasas* in or on the way to Jerusalem, and endowed the Collège des Dix-Huit in Paris for eighteen poor students in 1180. In the mid-thirteenth century, the first three colleges of Oxford were founded as charitable trusts.[29]

From the tenth century, we also have considerable evidence of the use of *waqf* for the building of hospitals, which were also used for the training of physicians, and for other cultural institutions. In the mid-tenth century, the Buyid ruler, 'Aḍud al-Dawla, built hospitals and charitable foundations in Fars, and endowed a famous teaching hospital in Baghdad which reportedly cost him 100,000 dinars.[30] In contrast to the medieval Western Christendom, where hospitals were primarily charitable hospices for feeding and sheltering the poor, and were only incidentally concerned with the provision of medical care,[31] hospitals in the Islamic world were specialized medical institutions that also offered training for future physicians and surgeons. Most notable among the early philanthropic foundations were the libraries, often referred to as the "house of knowledge" (*dār al-'ilm*) that were used for research, lectures, and learned gatherings. A famous *dār al-'ilm* was founded in Baghdad in 991 or 993 by the Buyid vizier, Sābūr (Shāpūr) b. Ardashīr.

PHILANTHROPY AND PUBLIC POLICY UNDER THE GREATER SELJUQ EMPIRE

The Seljuqs were the leaders of the Oghuz Turkic tribes who had recently been converted to Islam and became the masters of Khurasan after the decisive defeat of the Ghaznavid armies in Dandanqan in 1040, and entered Baghdad fifteen years later. In 1071, the Seljuq Sultan, Alp-Arslan, defeated the Byzantine emperor at Manzikert, and brought Anatolia under Muslim rule. He conquered Syria the following year, extending the Seljuq empire from Central Asia to the Mediterranean. Under the Seljuqs, the *madrasas* spread from northeastern Iran to Iraq, Anatolia, Syria, and thence to Egypt. Together with that institution, the Ash'arite theology that had matured in the *madrasas* of Khurasan also spread to the rest of the Muslim world.[32]

Ḥasan b. 'Alī b. Isḥāq al-Ṭūsī, Niẓām al-Mulk, came from a landholding *dihqān* family and served Alp-Arslan as his vizier in Nishapur, when the latter became the governor of Khurasan in 1058. Five years later, in 1063, Alp-Arslan (1063–1072) succeeded his uncle Toghrïl Beg (1037–1063) as Sultan, and Niẓām al-Mulk became the grand vizier of the Seljuq empire, a position he continued to hold under Malik-Shāh (1072–1092) until his dismissal, shortly before his death in 1092. In Nishapur, Niẓām al-Mulk founded a famous hospital and built an observatory, named after Sultan Jalāl al-Dīn Malik-Shāh. The building of the observatory went hand in hand with the correction and establishment, in 1075, of the Persian solar calendar, which was called Jalālī after the

Sultan.[33] Niẓām al-Mulk's friend from his student days at a *madrasa* in Nishapur, Omar Khayyam, the astronomer known for his incidental quatrains (the *Rubaiyyat*), organized the observatory and carried out the calendar reform.[34] Niẓām al-Mulk also founded a *madrasa* for the eminent Shafi'ite jurist and Ash'arite theologian, the Imām al-Ḥaramayn Juvaynī (d. 1085).

In 1065, two years after the accession of Alp-Arslan to the Sultanate, Niẓām al-Mulk ordered his agent in the Caliphal capital, Baghdad, to build a *madrasa* for the Shafi'ite school of law like the one in Nishapur. The construction was completed in two years, and the new *madrasa* was inaugurated in 1067. The deed of *waqf* was read out at a special gathering of the Chief Kadi and other dignitaries of Baghdad on 14 April 1070.[35] During his last visit to Baghdad in 1091, Niẓām al-Mulk himself held a session for dictating Traditions in the library of the Niẓāmiyya.[36]

Meanwhile, the Sultan and the Hanafite high officials of the Seljuq state would not refrain from patronizing their own school of law. The head of the Sultan's tax bureau, Abū Sa'd Muḥammad b. Manṣūr al-Khwārazmī Sharaf al-Mulk, who had been sent on a mission to the Caliph in Baghdad in 1065, saw what Niẓām al-Mulk's agents were doing and began building a shrine and a *madrasa* on the location of the tomb of Abū Ḥanīfa, the founder of the Hanafite school of law.[37] The shrine and *madrasa* of Abū Ḥanīfa was built speedily and inaugurated in the same year as Niẓām al-Mulk's (1067). This must have been done with the approval of the Sultan and as an official act. Niẓām al-Mulk himself embarked on a systematic policy of building *madrasas* in major cities reserving their administration for himself, while appointing deputies to manage them, and maintaining a tight personal control over the appointment of the professors. A recent study confirms the founding of Niẓāmiyyas in eleven cities.[38] The total annual revenue from the endowments for the *madrasas* and other philanthropic and religious foundations of Niẓām al-Mulk is given as 600,000 dinars, whose main source had been the one-tenth of the state revenue that accrued to the vizier.[39]

Under the Seljuqs, the women of the royal house were powerful, had their own viziers and at times ruled as regents or even independently. Toward the end of his long career, Taj al-Mulk Abū'l-Ghanā'im, the vizier of one of Malik-Shāh's wives, Terken Khātūn, emerged as one of his major rivals. In rivalry with Niẓām al-Mulk, he built a dome to the congregational mosque of Isfahan and endowed a rival *madrasa* in Baghdad inaugurated in 1089.[40] The Niẓāmiyya *madrasa* of Baghdad, however, remained the most prestigious institution of learning until and beyond the fall of Baghdad to the Mongols in 1258.

I have parted company with Makdisi, Bulliet, and other scholars in presenting the endowments by the high officials of the state as public acts. These views can be seen as anachronistic in the light of our medieval constitutional model. From the strictly legal point of view, *waqf* is an institution of private law, as are virtually all institutions of Islamic law (*sharī'a*). As Schacht points out, *waqf*, "in its technical function, is strictly individualistic, in so far as the provisions laid down by the founder have the force of law."[41] This does not, however, mean that it cannot be used as an instrument of public policy by the rulers and the high officials of the state. Makdisi is overly emphatic on the private character of the act of endowment, and insists fastidiously that Niẓām al-Mulk and other founders of *madrasas* were acting as private individuals.[42] This is misleading, especially if we bear in mind Max Weber's definition of patrimonialism as a personal system of authority. The personal nature of delegated authority under patrimonial monarchy meant that the significant acts of the vizier always had a public character, and, more importantly, that there was no real distinction between the private property of a vizier and the public funds at his disposal. There can be no doubt whatsoever that Niẓām al-Mulk and the viziers of the subsequent centuries were assigning the fiscal resources of the state for endowing mosques, shrines, and institutions of learning, and for their patronage of culture by other means. Furthermore, amassing enormous property holdings was inseparable from their extensive procurement of the means of administration, and a part of that property could be expected to be used in pursuit of state policy. In short, there can be no doubt that acts of endowment by viziers should be seen as policy measures and therefore public acts.

Furthermore, Schacht's abstract statement can be misread, as it ignores some very real limits to the donor's control over public space, especially beyond his/her own lifetime. The Kadi had the right to order unstipulated changes, including exchange or sale of *waqf* property without the stipulation of the founder (*istibdāl*), in the general interest (*maṣlaḥa*) (of the foundation or the public).[43] In practice, furthermore, the deed of endowment was with the administrator, may or may not have been registered in the Kadi's record, and could be tampered with or lost, especially with the passage of generations. All this made the Kadi's power of supervision and intervention in the general interest a matter of great practical consequence. It can therefore be said that "the state is an acknowledged party to the legal operation of waqf."[44]

Niẓām al-Mulk had nine mature sons, most of whom served as subordinate viziers under him, and some became viziers and grand viziers after his death, as did some of his grandchildren. The administration of the Niẓāmiyya *madrasas* seems to have remained with Niẓām al-Mulk's sons and grandsons. Nevertheless, there was no doubt that they were public institutions, and the most important appointments were made by the Sultan's decrees.

Seljuqid women became more active with the division of the empire into appanages of the Seljuq princes and their Atabegs (tutors) in the twelfth century, and created many endowments in the regions under their control. Zāhida Khatun, who ruled Fars for over twenty years after the death of her husband, Boz Aba, in 1146–47, made several estates and orchards and large villages acquired by sale of her jewels and treasures into *waqf* for the *madrasa* she built in Shiraz. Zaitūn Khatun, the wife of the Seljuq ruler of Kirman, similarly built many *madrasas* and constituted *waqfs* for them.[45] Gaining independence as Seljuq governors (Atabegs), Zangī b. Mawdūd (d. 1175–76), Sa'd b. Zangī (d. 1226), and Abū Bakr b. Sa'd (d. 1260) continued the tradition of philanthropy and created extensive *waqfs* from estates and villages in the surrounding countryside for charitable and religious foundations.[46] Terken Khatun (d. 1264), the wife of Sa'd b. Abū Bakr who became the effective ruler of Fars when her husband died two weeks after his father in 1260, founded a *madrasa* whose enormous endowment was producing a revenue of 200,000 dinars in 1326, when Fars was being governed by her granddaughter through her daughter, Abīsh Khatun (d. 1286), who had reigned in her infancy as the last Sulghurid Atabeg in 1264–65 and married the son of the Īl-Khānid Sultan Hülegü.[47] Terken Khatun's granddaughter, Princess Kūrdūjin (d. 1338), who was the offspring of this marriage and in turn married a string of five Turko-Mongolian emirs, beginning with the ruler of Kirman, Soyūrghātmish, governed Fars for the Īl-Khānid Sultan Abū Sa'īd from 1319 onward for at least a decade, and not only rectified the proper use of the enormous revenue from her grandmother's *waqfs*, but also in turn founded hospitals, *madrasas*, mosques, and irrigation dams with her own *waqfs*.[48]

Madrasas began to appear in Syria after the Seljuq conquest. During the last quarter of the eleventh and the first half of the twelfth century, Seljuq governors, women of the ruling house and high officials established *waqfs* for five Shafi'ite and five Hanafite *madrasas* and a Sufi convent. In the second half of the twelfth century, the Zangid Atabeg of Mosul and Syria, Nūr al-Dīn, extended his rule to Syria and, like the Atabegs of Fars, established extensive endowments that included two Shafi'ite and one Hanafite *madrasas* in addition to the first *dār al-ḥadīth* (college for the study of Traditions) and the first two Malikite *madrasas*.[49] Nūr al-Dīn's successor Saladin (Ṣalāḥ al-Dīn al-Ayyūbī) followed the same policy, and the Ayyubid state he founded in Syria and Egypt established a number of important *madrasas*. In Damascus alone, Gilbert counts 85 *madrasas* between 1076 and 1260.[50]

WAQF, CIVIL SOCIETY, AND THE ĪL-KHĀNID STATE (1256–1335)

The Mongol invasion under Chingiz Khan (d. 1227) that began in 1219 introduces three and a half decades of direct rule from Mongolia about which we have little information other than the utter devastation of the cities.[51] The strong civil society of northeastern Iran, already exhibiting alarming self-destructive factional tendencies by the twelfth century, was destroyed, never to be reconstituted. The second major invasion in 1256 marks the beginning of a brighter period. Hülegü, the brother of the great Khan, led the Mongol army on an expedition whose goal was to destroy the Ismāʿīlī state that controlled Alamut and some 150 other mountain fortresses, and to subjugate or overthrow the ʿAbbasid Caliphate in Baghdad. He did not return to Mongolia after these missions were accomplished but instead chose northwestern Iran as the center of his empire, and founded the Īl-Khānid state. The Īl-Khānid state was served by a series of remarkable Persian viziers who emerged as protectors of civil society in western and central Iran and extended their authority to Fars and Yazd, whose civil society had, under Atabeg successor states, avoided depredation and destruction by peacefully accepting Mongol suzerainty.

Throughout the thirteenth century, Sufism gathered momentum as a popular movement and spread from the cities to the countryside. In the northeast, where the cities never recovered, it became the unmistakably dominant form of Islam. However, even in Fars, whose cities had remained intact, Sufi convents appear alongside the *madrasas* as objects of philanthropic endowment. Our poet Shaykh Muṣliḥ al-Dīn Saʿdī (d. 1292) was a frequenter of both. As far as charitable foundations in general are concerned, there is a notable increase in the foundation of Sufi convents, and of hostels outside of cities (*ribāṭs*) which were originally associated with Sufi orders.

Although the Mongol rule disestablished Islam, it did not affect the status of *waqf* property, which the Mongol rulers even exempted from taxation.[52] However, the centralized supervision of the *waqf* appears to have increased in comparison with the situation under the Seljuq empire and the successor states, and we find a central bureau of *waqf*. This made the use of *waqf* as an instrument of public policy all the more attractive to the viziers and the high officials of the Īl-Khānid state who assumed the patronage of the debilitated civil society and sought to foster its cultural institutions in the second half of the thirteenth century.

Hülegü's chief vizier, Shams al-Dīn Juvaynī (d. 1284), the *ṣāḥib dīvān*, whose father had entered the service of the Mongols in the 1230s and whose brother, ʿAṭā-Malik, held the governorship of the newly conquered Iraq and southwestern Iran for over twenty years, used his extensive holdings to create charitable foundations. In 1272–73, to advertise his patronage of cultural institutions, he held a teaching session at the Niẓāmiyya college of Baghdad in the presence of his brother, the governor of the province, and a bevy of poets and publicists who eulogized him for the occasion.[53] During the reign of Abaqa (1265–1282), Juvaynī ordered his agent in Yazd to build a hospital. When the agent presented the plan, it appeared too modest to him, and the final project was a complex that included a mosque, a *madrasa*, a hospital, a pharmacy, and a madhouse, and was completed in 1267–68. The dignitaries of Yazd who attended its inauguration ceremony contributed five hundred barrels of water (annually) to its endowment.[54]

The idea of building a charitable complex must have become fashionable by the time of Juvaynī, and we come across many such charitable complexes in the early fourteenth century. Then, a typical charitable complex had come to include a mosque, a *madrasa* (with a library), a teaching hospital, a Sufi convent and, often, an observatory or elaborate mechanical clock, and a hostel for travelers. An important feature of what I will call fourteenth-century educational-charitable complexes is the conjunction of the *madrasa* and the hospital in the same complex.

The man who used *waqf* as an instrument of public cultural policy much more systematically than Juvaynī was the philosopher and astronomer Khwāja Naṣīr al-Dīn Ṭūsī (d. 1274). Ṭūsī had been instrumental in the surrender of the last Ismāʿīlī ruler whom he was serving as a vizier and became one of the chief advisors in the capture of Baghdad. In 1259, Hülegü put him in charge of building an observatory in his capital, Maragheh, and appointed him the head of the *waqf* bureau of the empire, a position he held for fifteen years. Naṣīr al-Dīn appointed officials in each district responsible for remitting one-tenth of the revenues of the endowments (the usual administration fee) to the treasury, mainly for expenditure on the observatory.[55] The building of the observatory was completed under Hülegü's successor, Abaqa. Naṣīr al-Dīn also brought the books captured in Khurasan (from the Ismāʿīlī fortresses), Mosul, and Baghdad, and housed them in the library of the observatory which is said to have contained 400,000 volumes. He traveled to Iraq to collect more books in 1264, and died in Baghdad while inspecting the accounts of its *waqf* department in June 1274. His son, Ṣadr al-Dīn ʿAlī, succeeded him as the director of the observatory and administrator of its endowment.[56]

After the conversion of Ghazan Khan (1295–1304) to Islam, the Īl-Khānid rulers themselves began to use *waqf* for the founding of charitable-educational complexes. Ghazan Khan had been impressed by the mausoleum of the Seljuq Sultan Sanjar in Marv, and decided to build one as magnificent for himself in his capital, Tabriz. The idea of an educational-charitable complex around the dome of the mausoleum to perpetuate his good name must have suggested itself to Ghazan Khan. In his history of Ghāzān's reign, his vizier, Rashīd al-Dīn Faḍl Allāh Hamadānī,[57] whom he appointed its administrator, gives us a summary of the *waqf* instrument. The sumptuous royal complex consisted of a congregational mosque, two *madrasas*, one Shafiʿite and one Hanafite, a Sufi convent, a house for the descendants of the Prophet (*dār al-siyāda*), an observatory, a hospital, a library, an office for registration of laws (*bayt al-qānūn*), a bath and a pool house, a public kitchen, and an orphanage school for one hundred orphans. Provisions were also made for burial assistance for the poor, distribution of water to townspeople, repair of roads, ration of cotton for five hundred poor widows, and food for birds during the winter months. Ghazan also created other *waqfs* for Sufi convents, houses for the descendants of the prophet, and other foundations whose administration he entrusted to Rashīd al-Dīn. Ghazan's successor, Öljeitü (1304–1316), followed his example in constituting *waqfs*, and set up a charitable-educational complex that included a congregational mosque, a *madrasa*, a Sufi convent, and a house for the descendants of the Prophet in Sulṭāniyya, where he built his own mausoleum. The complex was endowed with estates that produced one million dinars.[58]

Both Ghazan and Öljeitü were, however, outdone by their vizier, Rashīd al-Dīn Faḍl Allāh (d. 1318), of whose stupendously extensive endowments we have ample record. As a physician, Rashīd al-Dīn took a keen interest in founding teaching hospitals and pharmacies. He founded a hospital and a pharmacy in his native city of Hamadan.[59] He also appointed another physician, Maḥmūd b. Ilyās, who had composed a book and named it after him, the administrator of a hospital founded by the Atabegs of Fars.[60] Rashīd al-Dīn charged his protégé with reorganizing the endowment property, which had suffered from neglect, and upgraded his salary by a draft on the state revenue of Shiraz.[61] Furthermore, Rashīd al-Dīn reportedly sent a decree appointing Sharaf al-Dīn ‘Alī, a physician with whom he had studied medicine in his youth, to a high office in Yazd and ordered him to build an educational-charitable complex for him in that city. The order arrived after Sharaf al-Dīn's death, but his sons built the complex that included a *madrasa* that became known as the Rashīdiyya in 1315.[62]

We are fortunate to have an extant copy of the deed of *waqf* for the educational-charitable complex around his mausoleum that Rashīd al-Dīn constituted in 1314. In its printed version, it covers over 250 large pages and contains a mine of information about the social history of fourteenth-century Iran, much of which is corroborated by another extant deed of *waqf* from the 1330s by one of Rashīd al-Dīn's sons-in-law and the latter's father in Yazd.[63] For instance, we have evidence of very minute and elaborate division of the watershares in the connected underground wells (*qanāts*) which constituted valuable property and were made the object of *waqf* alongside rural estates, villages, shops, and urban property. Here I will describe only the general features of the complex, and especially its college and library.

Rashīd al-Dīn built a new quarter in the west of Tabriz for his philanthropic complex that comprised his mausoleum, mosques, a Sufi convent, a school for ten orphans, a hospice for travelers with a lavish refectory,[64] a poor house with a public kitchen, a library, a *madrasa*, and a teaching hospital. Two hundred and twenty slaves were made *waqf* for the maintenance of the complex and provision of services such as baking. The slaves included twenty Turks, some of whom manned the police force of thirteen set up for the quarter. The new quarter, named Rab'-e Rashīdī by the founder after himself, prospered well beyond the provisions of the deed of endowment, and in a later letter to one of his sons, Rashīd al-Dīn brags that the quarter includes twenty-four caravanserais, fifteen hundred shops, thirty thousand houses, textile, paper, and other factories, four hundred scholars of Islamic sciences, residing in a street that had become known as the *'Ulamā'* Street, a thousand students, with six thousand students who had been attracted from all over the world having to be settled elsewhere in Tabriz, fifty medical professors with ten students each, and two hundred Koranic cantors (*ḥāfiẓs*).[65] He had appointed twenty-four at his mausoleum in the *waqf* instrument.[66]

Both with his own *waqf* and those he instituted for Ghazan Khan, Rashīd al-Dīn put a great deal of emphasis on the registration of the *waqf* instruments and their confirmation and subsequent reconfirmation by each Chief Kadi of Tabriz and Baghdad, and in the former case, had the signature of the Chief Kadi witnessed by forty notaries and made registration and confirmation of the instrument by incoming Kadis of Tabriz the duty of the administrator.[67] He also took great care in disseminating information about the terms of all his *waqfs*, and a special prefatory book on them was to be appended to the deeds available at all major foundations.[68]

Rashīd al-Dīn has left us copious evidence of the twin motivation of perpetuating a good name and reaping otherworldly reward for philanthropic deeds. Like virtually all the great Seljuq and Īl-Khānid viziers before and after him and many lesser ones whom we have not mentioned,[69] Rashīd al-Dīn was executed by the order of Sultan Abū Sa'īd (1316–1335). A man of his intelligence could not have been unaware of the great peril as well as the great power of his position at the head of the imperial bureaucracy. He was obsessed with being remembered, and required all funded students to make copies of his books (which would become their own property), and laid down that his name, "Faḍl Allāh b. Abī'l-Khayr b. 'Alī known as Rashīd the physician" be noted as the benefactor of all the books copied at the scriptorium and made *waqf* for the Muslims of the city to which it was being sent.[70] In a letter, he admonished one of the many sons he had appointed a provincial governor that the key to the domination of the world was the removal of illegitimate dues from the endowments for shrines, mosques, and hostels, and the investment of the surplus state revenue on mosques, *madrasas*, Sufi convents, and the like.[71] By explicit instruction in the *waqfs* he himself constituted, and by order as the administrator of those of Ghazan Khan, Rashīd al-Dīn prescribed regular prayer in his name as the founder, or the one instrumental in the foundation of the endowment.[72]

Rashīd al-Dīn's rival vizier, Tāj 'Alī Shāh, also built a rival complex that contained the congregational mosque of Tabriz with a *madrasa*.[73] Rashīd al-Dīn's son, Ghiyāth al-Dīn Muḥammad, the last of the great Īl-Khānid viziers whose execution in 1336 marked the disintegration of the empire, founded his own college, the Ghiyāthiyya, in Tabriz.[74]

Among the high officials who served under Ghiyāth al-Dīn was his brother-in-law, Shams al-Dīn Muḥammad (d. 1333), his deputy-vizier at the financial bureau. Shams al-Dīn came from a patrician family of Yazd who claimed descent from the Prophet and 'Alī, and had served as judges. Rashīd al-Dīn knew the family well, and had appointed one of them, Niẓām al-Dīn 'Alī, a protégé, who later edited a collection of his "Questions and Answers," the Chief Mufti (jurisconsult) in the first decade of the fourteenth century. The young Shams al-Dīn impressed the vizier by presenting a book on Seljuq history to him in 1311–12, and became his agent in Yazd, and later married his daughter.[75] Shams al-Dīn's father, Rukn al-Dīn Muḥammad (d. 1331–32), was a Kadi in Yazd, and at some point secured appointment as the chief Kadi. Rukn al-Dīn created some twenty-three *waqfs* in the region of Yazd, the instrument for which was drawn up toward the end of his life, together with some twenty-two *waqfs* of his son, Shams al-Dīn Muḥammad.[76] The most important *waqfs* were two educational-charitable complexes where the founders were to be buried. Rukn al-Dīn's was near the congregational mosque of Yazd, which he endowed with *waqf* properties, and consisted of his mausoleum and mosque, a Shafi'ite *madrasa* (the Rukniyya) for ten students, an elaborate mechanical clock with astronomical tables, a library with three thousand books, a Sufi convent, a teaching hospital, and a pharmacy. A list of the *waqfs* were inscribed on glazed tiles on the wall of the *madrasa*.[77] The blueprint for Shams al-Dīn Muḥammad's complex, the Shamsiyya, was designed in Tabriz and sent to builders in Yazd, and consisted of:

> four minarets, a house for the descendants of the Prophet, a Sufi convent, a bazaar, a bath . . . and two *madrasas* opposite each other. . . . The building was completed in the year 733 (1333) when Amīr Shams al-Dīn died in Tabriz. His body was brought to Tabriz and buried in his *madrasa*. . . . He inscribed all the *waqfs* . . . in the quadrangle of his *madrasa* and added a litany of curses (*la'natnāma*) on anyone who would tamper with them.[78]

Shams al-Dīn's endowments included a set of properties for the benefit of fifty-six manumitted Turkish, Mongolian, Indian, Ethiopian, and black slaves, and another set of properties for his children.[79] Outside of the city of Yazd, our patrician father and son founded the ʿIṣmatiyya *madrasa* in Isfahan, a college for the study of Traditions in Kazerun, fourteen Sufi convents and eleven hostels on various roads throughout the region of Yazd and Abarquh.[80]

Yazd, it will be recalled, had remained under the rule of an Atabeg successor state, and its strong civil society was not destroyed by the Mongol invasion. Furthermore, the patrician class in fact survived the disintegration of the Īl-Khānid empire in 1336, and the Muẓaffarids, a patrician house from Maybud, created their own state in Yazd, Kirman, and Fars. The acts of foundation by the viziers and the Chief Kadi in the late thirteenth and early fourteenth centuries were matched and imitated by the patricians of Yazd who, throughout the fourteenth century, constituted *waqfs* for numerous philanthropic foundations, including tens of *madrasas* that are described in two fifteenth-century histories of the city we possess.[81]

Rural areas and regions without a notable civil society, too, were affected by philanthropy. Sufi convents, the new beneficiaries of *waqf* in the Mongol era, were enriched by endowments, made by officials and women of the ruling stratum, at times by the conversion of conditionally held state land with the Sultan's permission[82] became the institutional base for the emergence of a new elite that controlled the religious life of the masses: the Sufi Shaykhs. Perhaps one of the most notable Sufi Shaykhs who gained enormous political influence was the founder of the Safavid order and ancestor of the future dynasty, was Shaykh Ṣafī al-Dīn Isḥāq (d. 1334). Ṣafī al-Dīn, who owned twelve sheep and one goat in 1300, accepted numerous endowments from his followers for the benefit of his order, himself, and his descendants, and consolidated his own holdings in Azerbaijan and elsewhere constituting them into an enormous *waqf* in 1333, the year before his death.[83] It is a telling indication of the legitimacy of legal property that, to make his holdings licit, Ṣafī al-Dīn "repurchased" the lands converted into *waqf* from the vast estate of the great vizier, Juvaynī, which had been confiscated for the state upon his execution in 1284, from Juvaynī's descendants who had refused to give up their claim and retained the deeds of original royal grants.[84]

The impact of the pious endowment of the educational-charitable complexes on the civil society of Iran can be gauged from a late-fourteenth-century manual on the craft of the secretaries in the proper modes of address and "the ordering of ranks." The first eleven ranks of the elite of civil society (*ashrāf al-nās*) are products and functionaries of the educational-charitable *waqf* complexes. In order, they are as follows: the law professors, the jurisconsults, the Koran commentators, the Traditionists, the preachers, the deliverers of the Friday sermons (*khaṭībs*), the physicians, the assistant professors, the mosque prayer leaders, law students and graduates (*faqīhs*), and the Koran cantor/memorizers. Astronomers are mentioned in the fifteenth place. The next two ranks, the Sufi Shaykhs (*arbāb-e futuvvat*) and hermits, found institutional supports in the endowed Sufi convents and *ribāṭs*.[85]

In concluding this survey of the early-thirteenth-century philanthropic foundations, I would like to emphasize one dimension of their public character shown clearly by our better documentation for the period. Rashīd al-Dīn showed no hesitation whatsoever in mixing state revenues and state land with the estates and property he insisted had been his own or Ghazan Khan's legally acquired private property, and frequently issued drafts on state revenue to be regularly added to the endowments of *waqfs*. Nor did he have any qualms about the matter. In an annex to the deed of *waqf* for the Rab'-i Rashīdī, he mentions conveying the large grants on state land generously given him by Sultan Öljeitü, and considers himself a mere "intermediary and builder" for the good deed for which God's rewards will go to the Sultan.[86] Likewise, the deputy-vizier Shams al-Dīn Muḥammad made benefices he held from the state revenues of Tabriz and Kazerun *waqf* on his father-in-law's Rab'-i Rashīdī and his own college in Kazerun.[87]

SOME LATER DEVELOPMENTS IN THE OTTOMAN AND SAFAVID EMPIRES

The disintegration of the Īl-Khānid empire coincided with the rise of the Ottomans further west, who imported the idea of a charitable-educational complex founded by *waqf*. Within a decade of the death of the Īl-Khānid vizier, Ghiyāth al-Dīn Muḥammad, his contemporary Orkhan Ghazi (1326–1359) had modified the use of the *waqf* complex into an instrument of urban development, and had built a *bedestān* at the center of the Ottoman capital, Bursa. In the *bedestāns*, or more generally the *'imāret* complex the Ottomans set up as *waqf* at the commercial centers in their cities, they made increasing use of new urban property, mostly shops, in addition to rural estates that had constituted the bulk of the Īl-Khānid endowments. *Waqf* was similarly used throughout the next century of Ottoman conquests as an instrument of state policy for the development of the cities of Edirne and Istanbul.[88] Creation of *'imārets* as public *waqfs* by Ottoman officials, or by Sultans with high officials acting as endowment administrators, in the fifteenth and sixteenth centuries was an important means for urban development in Edirne. It is estimated that the public kitchens of these *'imārets* at some point fed over 10 percent of the population of Edirne.[89] Similarly, for half a century after the conquest of Cyprus in 1571, Ottoman military governors (Pashas) created the overwhelming majority of *waqfs* for the establishment of mosques and the spread of Islam, while four complexes were established by the other of the Sultans and a Sultan's mother.[90] Once more, there was no doubt about the public character of the *waqfs* founded by the officials, and the Sultan could even issue an imperial order concerning the important ones.[91] Public endowment continued to be made by Ottoman governors down to the nineteenth century, although by then the majority of the *waqfs* had for some time been private.[92]

The Ottoman uses of the *waqf* clearly disproves the commonly held view on its alleged inflexibility. Ottoman civil society made two innovative uses of the institution. The use of the law of *waqf* was extended for the creation of pious foundations by non-Muslims and more significantly, for the creation of cash endowments which loaned money at interest rates, typically, between 10 and 20 percent.[93] This last innovation gave rise to a major controversy, as it required the circumvention of the categorical prohibition of usury in the Koran.[94] Nevertheless, expediency prevailed and cash *waqf*, already practiced in the fifteenth century, was justified by the great Kurdish Shaykh al-Islam of Istanbul, Abū'l-Suʿūd (d. 1576), and became a major credit institution in the Ottoman empire, especially attractive to men and women with more modest means.[95]

In Iran, Shah ʿAbbās I (1587–1629) used the law of *waqf* as an instrument of urban policy in developing his new capital, Isfahan. In 1614, jointly with the royal tutor who became the administrator, he constituted a *waqf* for the creation of a major educational-charitable complex around the royal mosque (*masjid-e shāh*), where a *madrasa* with thirty-seven students set the pattern for many more colleges that gave rise to the revival of Islamic philosophy by the "School of Isfahan" in the seventeenth and early eighteenth centuries.[96] He also made very effective use of *waqfs* for the propagation of Shiʿism, and of the cult of the Shiʿite Infallible Imams in whose names he created endowments with administrators who acted as their deputies and used seal rings bearing their names.[97] Farther east, Shah ʿAbbās's contemporary Allāh Yār, a leading Qataghan emir, was building a *madrasa* in Balkh (circa 1610–15), which he endowed with *waqf*. Some fifty years later, Subḥān Qulī, the governor of Balkh, began building a much larger educational-charitable complex for a mausoleum for himself and his wife, for which the *waqf* instrument was drawn up around 1690, when he had become the emir of Bukhara. Its *madrasa* had four professors and seventy-five rooms for resident students.[98]

CONCLUSION

Legal reforms and modernization of the state in the Islamic world have made the law of *waqf* as an instrument of public policy obsolete, and have drastically reduced the public purpose of endowments. The process first occurred in British India, where the "Permanent Settlement" of Bengal in 1793, systematically distorting pertinent titles and concepts in translation, converted a variety of conditional and primarily political grants into private property.[99] It is interesting to note that in India, the "private" element in the *waqf* came to predominate over the public once more.[100] This appears as a curious reversion to the earliest, legally unsettled period when, as we have seen, the immobilization of property for the benefit of one's designated heirs was interwoven with the charitable public purpose of assignment of the usufruct from a property for the benefit of the poor. Pending further research, it can be said tentatively that where a similar conversion of conditional tenures to private property did not occur until the twentieth century, as in Iran, the private aspect of the *waqf* remained unimportant and secondary to its public purpose. This hypothesis finds some support in the evidence from Iran where this legal change occurred only in the twentieth century. An analytical survey of the *waqf* in the city of Yazd in 1971 shows four-fifths of the *waqf* shops in the bazaar to support a mosque or a *madrasa*. Only some 3 percent (8 out of 237) of endowed shops, producing under 3 percent of the total *waqf* revenue were family *waqfs*.[101] In this century, however, modernization and legal reforms put an end to the use of *waqf* as an instrument of public policy in Iran. It is interesting to note that the establishment of the Islamic republic has not changed the situation. The foundations (*bunyāds*) that were created out of confiscated property after the Islamic revolution and have become powerful baronies beyond control of the central government are, from the legal point of view, modern corporations, and have not drawn upon the Islamic law of *waqf*.

The current vogue of the advocacy of civil society and its promotion by philanthropic foundations seems to rest on a mistaken assumption of inveterate opposition between civil society and the state.[102] This study, by contrast, has shown the complex and at times complementary relationship between the state and civil society in the Islamic world before the modern era. In the contemporary Muslim world, the law of *waqf* has generally been superseded by the modern law of corporations as patrimonial monarchy has been replaced by the bureaucratic state. The traditional civil society depicted in this chapter has long been destroyed, and the modern civil society that has emerged in its place has, by common scholarly consent, little institutional support vis-à-vis the all-pervasive state. For this reason alone, it would be foolish to neglect the historical tradition of the involvement of public authorities in philanthropy. Such involvement should be viewed as complementary to the indubitably desirable measures to empower civil society directly, and to strengthen its autonomous agency.

NOTES

1. G. Makdisi, *The Rise of Colleges: Institutions of Learning in Islam and the West* (Edinburgh: Edinburgh University Press, 1981), 39.

2. R. Payton, "Philanthropy in Action," in *Philanthropy: Four Views* (Transaction Publishers, 1988), 1.

3. C. Cahen, "Réflexions sur le waqf ancien," *Studia Islamica* 14 (1961): 37–56.

4. As A. Perikhanian points out in his "Iranian Society and Law," in E. Yarshater, ed., *The Cambridge History of Iran*, vol. 3 (2): *The Seleucid, Parthian and Sasanian Periods* (Cambridge: Cambridge University Press, 1983), 664–65, "the resemblance in legal régime between Iranian endowments for a fixed purpose and *waqf* properties is striking." In both cases, the act of foundation is irrevocable, the administrator is nominated by the founder, and there are the two "family" and "public" forms of endowment. The distinction between the "principal" and the "income" to be used for fixed purposes, the distribution of income, and tax obligations are also the same. "Such a coincidence in both real and formal aspects can hardly be accidental."

5. Ibid., 664.

6. Ibid., 661–62.

7. Ch. Décobert, *Le Mendiant et le Combattant: L'Institution de l'Islam* (Paris: Seuil, 1991).

8. J. N. D. Anderson, "The Religious Element in Waqf Endowments," *Journal of the Royal Central Asian Society* 38, (1951): 292–99.

9. The Islamic law of inheritance restricted testamentary bequests to a maximum of one-third of the estate, and provided for automatic division of the rest among the male and female heirs in fixed proportions.

10. The conception of *waqf* as ṣadaqa is attested in a papyrus deed of endowment for a house in Fayyum from the mid-ninth century, Y. Ragib, *Marchands d'Étoffes du Fayyum au IIIe/IXe Siècle*, vol. 1: *Les Actes des Banū 'Abd al-Mu'min* (Cairo: C.N.R.S., 1982), 41–43, and in an inscription on an inn made into *waqf* in Ramlah dated 913 (301), M. Sharon, "A *Waqf* Inscription from Ramlah," *Arabica* 12 (1966): 77–78. See also Décobert, 301–302.

11. Perikhanian, 664–65.

12. W. Heffening, "Wakf," *Encyclopedia of Islam* (Leiden: Brill, 1934).

13. Cahen, 47–49.

14. Décobert, 351.

15. Cahen, 48.

16. Heffening, 1098.

17. G. W. F. Hegel, *Philosophy of Right*, T. M. Knox, trans., (New York: Oxford University Press, 1953 [1820]), 110, 126.

18. Max Weber, *Economy and Society*, G. Roth & C. Wittich, eds., (Berkeley: University of California press, 1968), vol. 2, ch. 12.

19. S. A. Arjomand, *The Shadow of God and the Hidden Imam: Religion, Political Order and Societal Change in Shi'ite Iran from the Beginning to 1890* (Chicago: The University of Chicago Press, 1984), ch. 3.

20. 'Alī b. Zayd Baihaqī, known as Ibn Funduq, *Tārīkh-e Baihaq*, ed. A. Bahmanyār (Tehran: n.p., 1938), 117–18, 129, 172, 195.

21. R. W. Bulliet, *The Patricians of Nishapur: A Study in Medieval Islamic Social History* (Cambridge, Mass.: Harvard University Press, 1972), 64–67.

22. C. E. Bosworth, *The Gaznavids: Their Empire in Afghanistan and Eastern Iran*, 2nd ed (Beirut: Librairie de Liban, 1973), 175.

23. Bulliet, *Patricians of Nishapur*, 56, 249–54.

24. Ibid., 250.

25. Baihaqī, 185, 194.

26. Ibid., 195.

27. G. Makdisi, *The Rise of Humanism in Classical Islam and the Christian West* (Edinburgh: Edinburgh University Press, 1990), 25.

28. J. E. Gilbert, "Institutionalization of Muslim Scholarship and Professionalization of the *'ulamā'* in Medieval Damascus," *Studia Islamica* 52 (1980): 105–34.

29. Makdisi, *Rise of Colleges*, 224–30; *Rise of Humanism*, 311–17.

30. N. Kasā'ī, *Madāris-e niẓāmiyya va ta'thīrāt-e ijtimā'ī-ye ān* (Tehran: Amīr Kabīr, 1984), 108.

31. S. F. Roberts, "Contexts of Charity in the Middle Ages: Religious, Social, and Civic," in J. B. Schneewind, ed., *Giving: Western Ideas of Philanthropy* (Bloomington: Indiana University Press, 1996).

32. R. W. Bulliet, *Islam: The View from the Edge* (New York: Columbia University Press, 1994), 147–56.

33. Kasā'ī, 83.

34. Ibid., 33, 57.

35. G. Makdisi, "Muslim Institutions of Learning in Eleventh-Century Baghdad," *Bulletin of the School of Oriental and African Studies* 24, 1 (1961): 37.

36. Kasā'ī, 118.

37. Makdisi, "Muslim Institutions of Learning," 19.

38. Kasā'ī, 70–71, 249.

39. Ibid., 71–72.

40. Makdisi, "Muslim Institutions of Learning," 25, 41; Kasā'ī, 37, 143–44.

41. J. Schacht, *An Introduction to Islamic Law* (Oxford: The Clarendon Press, 1964), 209.

42. Makdisi, "Muslim Institutions of Learning," 19, 30.

43. This discretion of course did generate some unease, as can be seen in the following statement by a mid-fourteenth-century dissenting jurist: "The tyranny of the Kadi has made [*istibdāl*] a device for invalidating the majority of the waqfs of the Muslims." Cited in R. D. McChesney, *Waqf in Central Asia: Four Hundred Years in the History of a Muslim Shrine, 1480–1889* (Princeton University Press, 1991), 13, n. 39.

44. Ibid., 14.

45. A. K. S. Lambton, *Continuity and Change in Medieval Persia* (New York: Bibliotheca Persica, 1988), 150–51.

46. Ibid., 150.

47. Ibid., 120, 272, 275.

48. G. Ghanī, *Baḥth dar āthār va afkār va aḥvāl-e ḥāfiẓ* (Tehran: Zavvār, 1933), 1, 3–4.

49. Gilbert, 127–29.

50. Ibid., 115, 119.

51. Sources from the second half of the thirteenth century give the incredible figures of 1,300,000 for those killed in Marv, 1,747,000 for Nishapur, and nearly 700,000 for Herat, while Marco Polo in the same period reports Balkh to be deserted and derelict. See Lambton, 19–20.

52. Lambton, 151.

53. Kasā'ī, 156.

54. Aḥmad b. Ḥusayn b. 'Alī Kātib, *Tārīkh-e Jadīd-e Yazd*, ed. I. Afshār (Tehran: Farhang-e Īrān-Zamīn, 1966), 131–33; Lambton, 65–66.

55. Lambton, 151–52; M. T. Mudarris Raḍavī, *Aḥvāl va Āthār-e Khwāja Naṣīr al-Dīn Ṭūsī*, 2nd ed. (Tehran: Asāṭīr, 1991), 41, 49.

56. Mudarris Raḍavī, 41–71.

57. Rashīd al-Dīn Faḍl Allāh Hamadānī, *Tārīkh-e Mubārak-e Ghāzānī*, ed. K. Jahn (London: E. J. W. Gibb Memorial Series, 1940), 209–17.

58. Lambton, 155.

59. Rashīd al-Dīn Faḍl Allāh Hamadānī, *Savāniḥ al-Afkār-e Rashīdī*, ed. M. T. Dānishpazhūh (Tehran: Central Library of Tehran University, 1979), 235–36.

60. Annual clothing for the same physician was provided for in the vizier's endowments in Yazd. I. Afshār, "Rashīd al-Dīn Faḍl Allāh va Yazd," *Īrānshināshī*, vol. 2 (1970): 27.

61. Rashīd al-Dīn, *Savāniḥ al-Afkār-e Rashīdī*, 231–34.

62. Aḥmad b. Ḥusayn b. 'Alī Kātib, 134–35.

63. I. Afshār, *Yādgārhā-ye Yazd*, 2 vols. (Tehran: n.p., 1975), 2: 391–557.

64. Guests could stay for three days free of charge.

65. The last item is interesting and merits a comment. While the number of chairs and students at *madrasas* appears to have been set on the basis of strictly functional criteria, the number of Koranic cantors selected to perform at a founder's tomb was sumptuary, and often became a matter of extravagance. As pointed out, Rashīd al-Dīn appointed twenty-four cantors or memorizers of the Koran for the benefit of the future visitors to his tomb, and rulers, royal women, and other officials and dignitaries apparently competed in this regard. In the fourteenth century, consequently, we find a distinct professional class of Koran memorizer/cantors (*ḥāfiẓs*), of which the great poet, Hafiz of Shiraz, is only one member.

66. Rashīd al-Dīn Faḍl Allāh al-Hamadānī, *Vaqfnāma-ye Rab'-e Rashīdī*, M. Mīnuvī and I. Afshār, eds., Tehran: Anjumane-e Athāre-e Millī, 1977, 135; Rashīd al-Dīn, *Savāniḥ al-Afkār-e Rashīdī*, 289–90.

67. Rashīd al-Dīn, *Tārīkh-e Mubārak-e Ghāzānī*, 215; Rashīd al-Dīn, *Vaqfnāma-ye Rab'-e Rashīdi*, 25–30, 235.

68. Rashīd al-Dīn, *Vaqfnāma-ye Rab'-e Rashīdī*, 241.

69. The one apparent exception is Niẓām al-Mulk, who was assassinated by an Ismā'īlī terrorist after his dismissal. But in this case, too, Malik-Shāh, who died shortly afterward, was widely believed to have instigated his assassination. As the poet Amīr Mu'izzī put it, "many a heart would have been

broken by the death of the king of kings, had the killing of the vizier (*dastūr*) not preceded it." Cited in Kasā'ī, 44, n. 80.

70. Rashīd al-Dīn, *Vaqfnāma-ye Rab'-e Rashīdī*, 133–34, 240.

71. Rashīd al-Dīn, *Savāniḥ al-Afkār-e Rashīdī*, 34–35.

72. Rashīd al-Dīn, *Vaqfnāma-ye Rab'-e Rashīdī; Savāniḥ al-Afkār-e Rashīdī*, 51.

73. S. S. Blair, "Īl-Khānid Architecture and Society: An Analysis of the Endowment Deed of the Rab'-i Rashīdī," *Iran* 22 (1984): 77, 83.

74. Dānishpazhūh's introduction to Rashīd al-Dīn, *Savāniḥ al-Afkār-e Rashīdī*, 33.

75. J. Aubin, "Le Patronage culturel en Iran sous les Īlkhāns: Une grande famille de Yazd," *Le Monde iranien et l'Islam* 3 (1975): 111–12.

76. Afshār, *Yādqārhā-ye Yazd*, vol. 2, 393, 396.

77. Afshār, vol. 2, 559–61; Aubin, "Le Patronage culturel," 115.

78. Cited in Afshār, *Yādqārhā-ye Yazd*, vol. 2, 591–92.

79. Afshār, vol. 2, 506–16, 546–52.

80. Aubin, "Le Patronage culturel," 116–17.

81. See Aḥmad b. Ḥusayn, *Tārīkh-e Jadīd-e Yazd*, and Ja'far b. Muḥammad, *Tārīkh-e Yazd*, I. Afshār, ed., Teharan, 1960.

82. Aubin, "La Propriété foncière en Azerbaydjan sous les Mongols," *Le Monde iranien et l'Islam* 4 (1976–1977): 93–101.

83. Ibid., 114–25.

84. Ibid., 99.

85. Other occupations mentioned are the market constables, the poets, the guild masters, the merchants, the strong men of the city quarters, the police, and finally, the architects and builders. Muḥammad b. Hindūshāh Nakhjavānī, *Dastūr al-Kātib fī Ta'yīn al-Marātib*, ed. A. A. Alizade (Moscow: n.p., 1971), vol. 1, pt. 2, 291–332, 267–90, 300.

86. Rashīd al-Dīn, *Vaqfnāma Rab'-e Rashīdī*, 245.

87. Afshār, *Yādgārha-ye Yazd*, vol. 2, 505; Aubin, "Le Patronage culturel," 114. For examples of conversion of state land into *waqf*, see Aubin, "Le Propriété foncière," 97–99.

88. H. Inalcik, *The Ottoman Empire: The Classical Age 1300–1600*, trans. N. Itzkowitz and C. Imber (New York: Praeger, 1973), 142–44.

89. H. Gerber, "The Waqf Institution in Early Ottoman Edirne," *Asian and African Studies* 17 (1983): 44.

90. R. C. Jennings, *Christians and Muslims in Ottoman Cyprus and the Mediterranean World, 1571–1640* (New York: New York University Press, 1993), ch. 2.

91. Ibid., 48.

92. G. Baer, "Women and Waqf: An Analysis of the Istanbul *Taḥrīr* of 1546," *Asian and African Studies* 17 (1983): 27. An important consequence of the creation of *waqf* by the officials of the state by mixing urban private property with state land, or the revenue from the land assigned to them by the state, was the conversion of conditional tenures into endowment property, part of the revenue from which could be assigned to the officials' descendants as beneficiaries in perpetuity. The consent of the Sultan was therefore required for this kind of endowment, and difficult to withhold,

given the philanthropic purposes of the *waqf*. The officials could thus protect themselves against future withdrawal or confiscation of conditionally held land, while providing for their offspring and securing for them a respectable public role as administrators of the *waqf* foundations. This seems to explain the motivation behind some endowments by officials in the eighteenth century. F. M. Göcek, *Rise of the Bourgeoisie, Demise of Empire: Ottoman Westernization and Social Change* (New York: Oxford University Press, 1996), but the motive was largely absent in fifteenth- and sixteenth-century Edirne. H. Gerber, "The Waqf Institution in Early Ottoman Edirne," *Asian and African Studies* 17 (1983): 35.

93. R. C. Jennings, "Zimmīs (Non-Muslims) in Early 17th Century Ottoman Judicial Records—The Sharī'a Court of Anatolian Kayseri," *Journal of the Economic and Social History of the Orient* 21 (1978): pp. 225–93.

94. J. E. Mandaville, "Usurious Piety: The Cash Waqf Controversy in the Ottoman Empire," *International Journal of Middle East Studies* 10 (1979): 289–308.

95. R. C. Jennings, "Loans and Credit in Early 17th Century Ottoman Judicial Records—The Sharī'a Court of Anatolian Kayseri," *Journal of the Economic and Social History of the Orient* 16 (1973): 168–216; Jennings, *Christians and Muslims in Cyprus*, 44–45.

96. R. D. McChesney, "Waqf and Public Policy: The Waqfs of Shah 'Abbās: 1011–1023/1602–1614," *Asian and African Studies* 15 (1981): 189.

97. Ibid., 175.

98. McChesney, *Waqf in Central Asia*, 130–37.

99. G. Kozlowski, *Muslim Endowments and Society in British India* (Cambridge: Cambridge University Press, 1985), 32–49, 127–28.

100. This is the case with the one example offered by Kozlowski (ibid., 60–61) as typical, where the proportion of revenue assigned to the public and private (support of the founder's family) purposes respectively is roughly one to two and a half.

101. M. E. Bonine, "Islam and Commerce: Waqf and the Bazaar of Yazd, Iran," *Erdkunde. Archiv für wissenschaftliche Geographie*, 41 (1987): 187–88.

102. S. N. Katz, "Philanthropy and Democracy: Which Comes First?" *Advancing Philanthropy* 2, 2 (summer 1994): 34–39.

.7.

Chinese Philanthropy As Seen through a Case of Famine Relief in the 1640s

JOANNA F. HANDLIN SMITH

In 1912 one slim volume documented Chinese charitable traditions for English readers and then dropped nearly out of sight.[1] Western scholars of China have sometimes consulted it, but not as a stepping stone toward further work. They assumed that the subject of Chinese charity was a curiosity, an anomaly pertaining only to a few towns in a predominantly agrarian society—towns that had by and large been influenced by Western ideas and missionary activities. If scholars noticed Chinese acts of benevolence at all, they dismissed them:[2] Chinese benevolence, they thought, served the self-interest of the elite, lacked piety, and was not altogether voluntary. Consider, for example, the small burial societies that contributed funds to inter the corpses of the poor: the Chinese themselves praised these associations for their generosity, yet one American scholar has argued that they were motivated not by charity, but by necessity, that is, by the need to rid streets and ditches of disease-carrying corpses.[3]

Consider, too, the huge famine relief operations, which Chinese texts commend for having saved thousands, even hundreds of thousands of lives. According to many Western accounts, such relief efforts were not charitable either; they were techniques of social control whereby local elites fended off rice riots; they were tools of propaganda whereby local elites advertised their beneficence in order to validate their privileged positions; or they were strategies whereby the local elites created opportunities to unload their grain hoards while collecting interest at exorbitant rates.[4]

Westerners failed to take a good look at Chinese charitable traditions because they had simplistic notions about philanthropy (as voluntary, selfless, and independent of the state).[5] They were also simply incredulous. In the early decades of the twentieth century Westerners, self-confidently enjoying the benefits of industrialized society, observed a China that was torn apart by civil war and foreign invasion, a China that suffered overpopulation and food shortages. They also observed the rise of an authoritarian regime that crowded out all individual, voluntary initiatives for the public good. China's deplorable conditions, captured in photographs, were vividly brought home to Westerners. One photograph showed poorly fed laborers harnessed like draft animals to a huge ship that they were tracking up the Yangtze River. Who among the viewers of such a scene could pay heed to talk of Chinese benevolence? Or could see back to a time when Chinese society had been guided by—and sometimes even lived up to—a more humane and life-nurturing rhetoric? That most Chinese themselves turned against their past culture and society as creations of a self-serving elite has, moreover, reinforced Western myopia.[6] Thus it was as recently as 1989 that an op-ed piece in the *New York Times,* taking a cue from Teng Hsiao-p'ing's son, made a statement that should stun anyone who is familiar with the centrality of the concept of humaneness (*jen*) in Confucian thought.[7] Wrote the journalist: "The restraining philosophy of humanitarianism is absent or nearly absent in Chinese tradition," and then he added, "China developed no great philosophy of charity, aid to the downtrodden or an obligation to help the less fortunate."[8]

Yet, for those who are willing to search through the historical record, evidence is abundant for a vast array of philanthropic activities: benefactors paid for the construction of bridges, maintained free ferry services across dangerous waters, and planted trees alongside roads so that travelers would have shade. They distributed alms to beggars, provided winter shelters for the homeless, sponsored community schools for penniless village boys, set up soup kitchens to feed the starving poor, and gave medicines to the needy.

A list of charitable activities in Chinese history could be drawn up at great length but in itself would have little meaning. It might serve as a faint signal that, yes, the Chinese have had their traditions of charity, but it would do only that. Items on a list, when left dangling at random, are like lights in pitch blackness, each looking alike and impossible to measure and locate.

The problem of weighing the facts and determining their significance is exacerbated by the length of China's history and the complexity of her culture. Inevitably for a territory as vast and regionally diverse as China, it is often unclear just how representative a particular case of charitable practice was for China as a whole. Inevitably for a society that has repeatedly legitimized new activities by citing old texts, thereby masking innovation, it is difficult to assess change. Even so, historians over the past two decades have made much progress in putting the facts about Chinese charity in chronological order and relating them to specific social contexts. In light of recent work, certain turning points in the Chinese practice of charity are now evident.

The shift most heavily documented—and therefore most visible—occurred toward the end of the Ming dynasty (1368–1644). From around the 1580s down to the fall of the dynasty, members of the scholarly elite wrote more extensively than ever before about their charitable deeds. Unlike their predecessors, they also focused on philanthropy as a discrete subject.

Before the late Ming, especially from the Sung dynasty (960–1279) on, Chinese rulers and the bureaucratic elite had sponsored a host of welfare activities—poorhouses, foundling homes, and burial plots for the poor.[9] Mention of pre-Ming projects was scant, however, and generally made only in such impersonal sources as state regulations (the *hui-yao*), administrative handbooks, and ethical guides. These texts outlined the ideals of welfare for the needy and exhorted readers to be humane or share their wealth with others (*fen-ts'ai, ch'üan-fen*). But they associated charity more closely with the paternalistic responsibility that office-holders should bear for the welfare of the people than with questions of personal piety. Occasionally one reads of a philanthropist who took personal responsibility for the needy: the retired official Liu Tsai (1165–1238) set up soup kitchens that enabled thousands of people to survive a famine.[10] But Liu's generosity was considered unusual in his day. In the twelfth and thirteenth centuries, the subject of charity rarely engaged those men who wrote the vast majority of documents that are now extant, the bureaucratic-scholarly elite.

Before the late Ming, most charity was carried out through institutions whose main purpose was something other than charity. Buddhist monasteries provided shelters, medicines, and soup kitchens for the poor, but these undertakings occupied only a small part of the complex monastic organization.[11] Lineages sometimes used income from land trusts called "charitable estates" to aid their poor members—as well as poor folk outside their kinship group. Such aid, however, was incidental to the main function of the charitable estates, which was to relieve kin of burdensome ritual and educational expenses in order to foster lineage prosperity and longevity.

From the late sixteenth century on, there appeared several new types of charitable institutions and organizations. These included clubs that released animals from captivity; benevolent societies, which buried the poor, managed soup kitchens, and distributed medicine; orphanages for abandoned infants; and lodgings for widows. Even while taking up causes that had concerned previous generations, these institutions were new in character. Unlike Buddhist monasteries and lineages, they were wholly dedicated to philanthropy. Unlike state-sponsored institutions, they were set up and managed by members of the local elite (which this chapter defines broadly to include retired officials, scholars, and wealthy residents).

Before the late Ming, individual benefactors valued doing good in secret.[12] They feared that public displays of philanthropy might be seen as having nefarious political ambitions. So it was with the eleventh-century poet-statesman Su Shih: when he raised funds for a public hospital, bridge construction, and a program to discourage infanticide, he shoved the credit onto religious figures and friends, and begged intimates to keep his role secret. Men were reluctant to take credit for charitable acts because there was a lack of consensus about what such acts meant.[13] From the late Ming on, the ethicalness of charity was widely understood and accepted; with no compunction whatsoever, benefactors made a great show of their good deeds.

The subject of philanthropy, which had been peripheral to elite concerns in earlier times, cropped up in numerous late-Ming genres and became unprecedentedly salient. Local gazetteers (which each district, or *hsien,* periodically published to celebrate regional lore and commemorate worthy residents) devoted whole chapters to the biographies of persons who had performed good deeds. Popular didactic works dwelled on the virtues of aiding the poor and distressed. Essays and diaries showed scholars and officials turning their thoughts to philanthropy; doing good, or being charitable, had become important to how they thought about themselves.

FAMINE RELIEF IN SHAN-YIN *HSIEN,* 1640–1642

Much of the information about philanthropy provided by district gazetteers and didactic works is in the form of brief biographies of individuals who responded to specific cases of need—whether by giving alms to the poor, constructing a tea pavilion for travelers, or canceling a crippling debt.[14] The accounts are so sparse as to frustrate the historian. They barely identify who the benevolent men were, where they stood in their community, or what moved them to generosity. For such data we might storm the pages with an arsenal of questions, but in vain. With few exceptions, the biographies merely name the person, define the cause he served, and applaud his benevolent response to that cause. Between the statement, "There was a great famine," and the resolution, "Ten thousand lives were saved," the biographers take the shortest route possible, admitting just enough details to particularize each account.

Yet the very paucity of information is in itself telling: the aim of the biographies was not to spin a yarn or to entertain, but to commemorate local worthies and to display, for the edification of future generations, fine models of beneficence. What the records sought to explain was not why these men did good, but why they deserved celebration. Elaborations on motivation, social standing, and private resources were therefore superfluous. Explanations of behavior held no interest. The securing of a reputation, or name, in lasting print was the goal.

Eagerness to leave behind a good image is especially evident in reference to the case of the famine that struck Shan-yin *hsien* (in Shao-hsing perfecture) during the period 1640–1642—a crisis that affected much of the population and elicited comment from many members of the elite.

Historians have usually explained the famines that perturbed China in the 1640s in terms of the paradigm of the dynastic cycle: as the Ming state declined, the infrastructure crumbled. Organizations that had kept granaries stocked and society stable ceased to function. Officials failed to act; members of the local elites stepped in, but did so reluctantly; thus the responsibility for social order and welfare shifted from an imperial government that was ailing to local residents who were rapacious and self-serving. This paradigm is so familiar, so comfortable, that historians of China easily revert to it. Yet, for the famine that struck Shao-hsing during the years 1640 to 1642, it will not hold. Inclement weather did present the threat of food shortages, and residents were cognizant that China's borders were being besieged. Nonetheless, grain was available, representatives of imperial authority commanded respect, and townsmen showed dedication to serving their community. What the residents of Shao-hsing faced was not an absolute food shortage stemming from a crumbling infrastructure, but problems of distribution that had been created by changed economic and social conditions.[15]

Members of the Shan-yin local elite took responsibility for relief activities willingly and energetically because they harbored an image of themselves as benevolent and dedicated men—an image that must have developed not just in response to one emergency but over some time.[16] A result of this self-image is that several actors in this famine left behind accounts. One record was by a residing official, the statecraft thinker Ch'en Tzu-lung (1608–1647).[17] Looking back on the crisis, Ch'en testified that grain was available and that the famine relief operation ran smoothly and uneventfully to a successful outcome. He tells how, after a brief sojourn in the capital celebrating the New Year, he returned to his post as police magistrate (*t'ui-kuan*) in Shao-hsing. As he approached the area he felt a sense of urgency in the air. It had been snowing heavily for over ten days and the mountain roads were impassible.

As Ch'en recollected: "I hastened ahead; along the roadside I saw thousands of starving people forming mobs; with knives outstretched they carried [empty] sacks and crowded around so that carts could not get through. A report came in saying: 'The people are on the verge of dying; they must be going to plunder so-and-so's house.' " Ch'en next described how he brought order to the area; and along the way he mentioned his foresight the previous year, when, anticipating a food shortage, he had encouraged the local residents to compile records of their grain-holdings so that price-stabilizing sales would later be feasible.

By letting someone else's report corroborate his own impression of urgency, Ch'en communicated, without seeming self-serving, the magnitude of the crisis; and by thus establishing the severity of the crisis—of the test that he was to pass—he displayed his talent for leadership.

According to Ch'en, the preparations he had made the previous year for the provision of grain now facilitated the relief efforts: "I walked through the snow to ask the wealthy households to issue grain, and they were all moved: some reduced prices by thirty percent out of kindness to the villagers; and others contributed twenty percent for the formation of soup kitchens to save the poorest households. The wards (*fang*), townships (*shih*), and rural areas (*hsiang*) all commissioned the young graduates and various students to oversee [the project]. In addition, they transferred several thousand taels [ounces of silver] of public funds to merchants . . . who were to go to buy grain from the neighboring prefecture (*chün*)."[18]

Ch'en Tzu-lung concluded his account with the usual round of clichés: order was restored; thousands of lives were saved. He also extended glowing praise to all those who had responded to the emergency so unhesitatingly and harmoniously. He commended the residing officials for their cooperation, the local gentry (that is, retired officials) for their compassion, on down to the young graduates and various students, who, Ch'en noted, "had also been very worthy and helpful in managing [the relief operations]."[19]

As told by Ch'en Tzu-lung, the harrowing events surrounding the famine of 1641 assumed the shape of a good story. Writing with hindsight, Ch'en knew exactly where his tale would go. He organized the elements to have a clear beginning, middle, and end: his confrontation with a crisis, his dealing with that crisis, and his celebration of the happy solution. His narrative progressed, smoothly and directly, from the ominous encounter with the hungry mobs in the snow to the achievement of beneficence. What had meaning for Ch'en were those elements that fitted into a comprehensible and familiar pattern, namely, the successful restitution of order.

An entirely different view of the same famine is provided by one of the local gentry whom Ch'en Tzu-lung had singled out as having been particularly helpful, a former official, Ch'i Piao-chia (1602–1645), who was then living in Shan-yin district, his hometown, and who kept a diary.[20] Where Ch'en's account is short, retrospective, and tidy, Ch'i's record of the famine years sprawls on for nearly two hundred pages; it captures a daily, nearsighted perspective of the crisis; and it lays bare the randomness of events and openendedness of negotiations, the false starts and the rude awakenings. Along the way Ch'i tells us that the nephew on whom he had placed managerial responsibility was found to have been lining his own pockets, that the people were losing their trust in Ch'i,[21] that wrongdoers were smuggling rice out of the area to be sold elsewhere,[22] and that some friends thought Ch'i self-serving.[23] When entering each installment into his journal, Ch'i could not prejudge which matters would assume weight over the long run; nor could he anticipate whether the squabbles of one day would boil over or cool down by the next. As Ch'i observed midway through the crisis, "Everyone was anxious, truly not knowing how it would end."[24]

Above all, Ch'i's *Diary* documents disagreements that divided members of the local elite on just about every imaginable issue concerning famine relief: What form should aid take? Should relief be extended by selling rice to stabilize prices, or, as one person insisted, only by giving "outright aid" (*chen*)?[25] Should one set up soup kitchens, or should one give out rice? Should the soup kitchens be free of charge, or should persons in the category of "next poorest" be asked to pay a small amount per bowl?

How should grain be obtained? Should it be stored in local granaries, or imported from neighboring areas? Should purchase-and-sale programs for the stabilization of prices be forced (*ch'iang-ti*), or should they be simply encouraged (*ch'üan-t'iao*)?

How should the distributions be timed? Should soup kitchens be started in the third month, as one resident proposed, or in the fifth and sixth months, as Ch'i argued?[26]

Should grain be given out all at once so that the needy, debilitated as they were from starvation, could avoid having to make repeated trips to the depots, or should distributions be made on a daily basis so as to pace the consumption of grain?

How—if at all—should grain prices be regulated?[27] Should charitable granaries (*i-tsang*) be set up, and, if so, how should they be stocked? By taxing landowners on the basis of the size of their landholdings, or through some other means?[28]

A broad range of strategies was thus known to and represented by members of a tiny elite who occupied a narrow social stratum and shared the same general assumption: that, during food shortages, the haves had some moral responsibility for the have-nots. Some policies favored certain groups or locales over others, but it is virtually impossible to identify any particular policy with an elite class interest.[29]

A few gentry types grew so fed up with the protracted debates that they detached themselves from the larger community of elite to set up their own programs. Among them was Chang Pi, member of a prosperous family (and the half-brother of the famous essayist Chang Tai), who took care to write up his own account.[30] Chang was skeptical that all the debating would lead to a resolution. Should one, he asked, hold up the process of feeding the starving until after some "marvelous plan" had been found? Diplomatically, he conceded that the "theories of the various [other] gentlemen were excellent," but he also argued that each of the strategies under consideration had certain shortcomings. He particularly feared that "poor scholars, widows, orphans, and cripples who are suffering hunger but are housebound"—that is, the genteel poor who were ashamed to leave their homes to line up for handouts—would be overlooked. To carry out the program of his choice, he assembled a few friends (for "private discussions") and turned to his mother's lineage for funds.[31]

Nonetheless, much of the elite community gravitated toward a united effort, toward the wide-scale cooperation that in the end justified Ch'en Tzu-lung's high praise. As Ch'i reported, "thirty to forty friends gathered together" at one meeting, the upshot of which was that fifty to sixty people took on managerial responsibilities.[32] On another occasion over one hundred people congregated at Ch'i's home, compelling him to move the discussion to the more public Yung-fu Shrine.[33]

Given the enormous differences of opinion among members of the local elite, how was it possible to achieve the massive coordination of relief? Given that each of the men who were inclined to do good was intent on doing it in his own idiosyncratic way, how did they come to be united in a common effort? Answers to these questions may be found by looking at Ch'i Piao-chia. On the subject of relief strategies, Ch'i was just as opinionated as his peers, but rather than detaching himself from the community of elite, he rose to the position of key coordinator.

As Ch'i presented himself in his *Diary*, he wished to take responsibility for the relief operations. At times he claimed that he had been called to the task, as when he noted that local officials had asked him to stay behind after a large meeting had dispersed. But in subtle ways Ch'i also set himself apart from other members of the gentry and set himself up, as it were, for a special role. He did so, for example, by arriving to that meeting late, and again by campaigning after the meeting for a strategy different from the one the attendees had agreed upon.[34]

One ingredient of Ch'i's success as a leader was that he worked hard to build consensus among his peers and made it his business to be informed. He pored over famine relief handbooks, combed letters and the Capital Gazette (*ti-pao*) for famine news, and grilled visitors on grain prices elsewhere.[35] He also made a point of disseminating information: he wrote up and circulated proposals and tracts; and when he received letters commenting on famine relief, he forwarded them to his peers. As he once asserted in his *Diary*, "Each matter must be discussed in detail before a decision can be reached. Even if we are enthusiastic, we must not put [strategies] into effect lightly."[36] Indeed, it was because Ch'i took the issues seriously and was discomforted by conflicts among his peers that he so often noted the debates in his *Diary*.

Ch'i labored hard on the relief activities. He attended meetings, made arrangements for grain loans, organized the management of soup kitchens, made out food tickets for the poor, and supervised the stringing of cash for distribution. The chores often kept Ch'i up deep into the night, exhausted his energies, and shook his nerves. Yet, instead of skipping days in his *Diary* or perfunctorily jotting down something along the lines of "too busy to write anything today," he sayed up late night after night precisely so that he might leave behind a record of just how much those labors had drained him. It was already "by candlelight," he wrote, when he "finished a draft of 'Arrangements for Giving out Rice.'"[37] It was "under lamplight" that he "drafted some 'ten items on distributing gruel'" with the result that by bedtime, he was "extremely exhausted."[38] He was kept up "halfway through the night" filling out ration tickets, he noted, and then added: "The cold wind pierced my bones; I was extremely tired and only then went to bed."[39]

Just when Ch'i was most harried and rundown, his diary entries stretched out explicitly to underscore his busyness, as when he described a day packed with such tasks as negotiating with grain brokers, filling out food vouchers, visiting the homes of the starving to distribute those vouchers, and responding to letters that asked for loans or discussed relief. "All very busy" is how Ch'i summarized that day, and then, so that no one would miss the point, he added, "It was about the third watch [11 P.M. to 1 A.M.] when I went to bed."[40]

Taking pride in his hard work, Ch'i made sure to report how he strained to juggle numerous conflicting demands. In reference to "the matter of soup kitchens," he wrote: "For the past ten days, . . . sometimes the starving complained that they had nothing to eat; sometimes the prosperous households complained that the exactions were unfair; or the persons overseeing the collections said that the wealthy households refused to cough up [funds]; or the managers said that the starving were irascible. Some [made their complaints] by letters; some visited in person. I estimate that there were at least five or six crises a day. Today I again received [numerous] letters from . . . [all sorts of people] and responded to them all, with the result that I have scarcely had any rest."[41]

In displaying his efforts, Ch'i was not alone. Ch'en Tzu-lung mentioned that, for an inspection tour of the soup kitchens, he had "penetrated the poor rural areas *(hsiang)* and deep valleys," and had "for months trod by foot through brush and raced by horse through woods."[42] Chang Pi left his own account of what he "had personally been through," informing us how he had "rushed about day and night, without acknowledging [his] fatigue," to the point that he had become "emaciated and weak." Chang then commented on the "various friends" who had "from beginning to end . . . toiled and rushed about, . . . and who had gone from door to door making inquiries and not shirked work . . . and had entered records in their notebooks and filled out the printed [ration] tickets, to the point that their wrists had almost dropped off."[43]

The picture of the worthy official who endured hardship while personally inspecting the scene of a disaster was commonplace in Chinese writings.[44] But two features differentiate the Shao-hsing accounts from earlier ones. First, participants in this relief operation appropriated for themselves an image that earlier writings had most frequently associated with officials. Second, rather than entrusting the painting of their portraits to later hagiographers, they assumed the task themselves, so conscious was their wish for a reputation of beneficence. Consequently, one remarkable feature of the famine of 1640–42 is its extensive documentation.

This consciousness of establishing a good name is evident in Ch'en Tzu-lung, who, by the time of compiling his account, could declare that "the affair [of the famine] was clear in the *history of relief*," because, he explained, a memorial of praise had been sent up to high authorities and the accomplishments had been accordingly recorded by imperial decree.[45] The consciousness is again evident in Chang Pi, who stated of his various helpers, "I have here recorded their names to make their generosity/goodness *(hao-i)* known."[46] And for whom if not for some imagined audience did Ch'i comment in his diary that, when he organized various friends to aid vagrants, he first distributed 1200 cash *(wen)* to set an example?[47] And to what end if not to enhance his own image did Ch'i state with a touch of feigned modesty, "[Alas], I sighed, 'Those who wish to take on responsibility for the world must certainly have talent and insight' "?[48] The value of secret merit *(yin-te)* so cherished in earlier dynasties, had given way to outright competition in displaying one's dedication to doing good.

The do-gooders of late-Ming Shao-hsing perceived that an image of kindness would enhance their reputation and stature, and hence their authority in the community. But in living up to this image, they did not specifically strive for control over local affairs. When a local magistrate (Chou) requested that Ch'i Piao-chia take on the task of judging disorderly people, Ch'i refused.[49] This was not because Ch'i lacked the needed talent, but because, in his mind, the exercise of law was a matter for officials. As a resident in his hometown, he wanted to associate himself with the extension of kindness.

Ch'i was no lackey of the local officials either. Keeping his own sense of purpose and self-definition intact, he often disagreed with their suggestions and seized the initiative in forming policy.[50] Sometimes gentle pressures to act did come from official quarters; the pressure to act also came from the threat of social disorder. But Ch'i and his fellow do-gooders had already been socialized to respond to the famine with alacrity and to take matters into their own hands. If Ch'i turned to local officials for help, he did so to put into effect relief policies that he favored and helped to shape.

Ch'i respected official authority and the social hierarchy. Whenever he listed attendees at some policy meeting or rewards ceremony, he listed them in hierarchical order, always starting with the officials, descending down the social scale, and ending with the nameless students.[51] For virtually every decision he made regarding the relief efforts, Ch'i sought the stamp of approval from local officials. For him, official authority, coming from above and following clear hierarchical lines, had a special value, as is suggested by his frequent diary entries about officials rewarding and disciplining the participants in the famine relief operations and about his own role as intermediary in the proceedings. When he accompanied Ch'en Tzu-lung on an inspection tour of the rural soup kitchens, upon finding that the people at one depot were not getting their allotted food, it was Ch'en, in his capacity as an official, who chastised the managers (who lamely tried to excuse themselves by claiming that the "hungry people were ashamed to eat gruel").[52] When Ch'i wished to reward the students for "having taken on responsibility," he sent a letter praising them to Ch'en Tzu-lung.[53] After supervising relief work for a famine and the plague that followed, Ch'i Piao-chia broached "the matter of rewarding those who had managed the relief efforts" with the residing official before assembling the doctors (who had distributed medicines) for a vegetarian feast.[54] Official presence, he comprehended, would honor the banquet and legitimize the rewards.

Ch'i understood that official authority complemented informal leadership and that he might himself draw upon it to coordinate relief activities on a wide scale. He occasionally took pains to note that local officials had placed the responsibility for relief on him; and when dealing with merchants or the young student managers, he often armed himself with the calling cards or letters of officials. If on one occasion two local officials "sat and watched" while Ch'i called out the names of the starving residents and distributed tiny monetary handouts, official presence added to his sense of importance. Carrying out his responsibilities under official eyes, with his status elevated and activities legitimized by official witness, Ch'i felt his image as benefactor grow, as he mused—so his diary tells us—upon how pitiable the starving appeared, just like the suffering figures in a Buddhist painting.[55]

Ch'i recognized that, to accomplish certain ends, official cooperation was essential and advantageous. He turned to officials to make loans of public funds, to sanction the purchase of grain from the outside, to prohibit the export of grain to other areas, and to back up these policies with their legal authority. Ch'i knew that the borders of China were under siege, was anxious about the fate of his dynasty, and understood that, with famine, came the "sprouts of disorder."[56] When discussing famine relief in general, Ch'i once opined that "nowadays, officials sit ceremoniously, tending only to tax collection and criminal investigations."[57] However, in this particular famine in Shan-yin, there is no evidence that imperial authority, as extended through local officials, was deteriorating.

This still leaves unanswered the question: Given that some of Ch'i's peers were so much like Ch'i—in that they, too, were retired officials, came from eminent households, harbored images of themselves as generous, were eager to display their merit, worked hard on relief activities, and forged helpful contacts with officials—given all these similarities, what differentiated Ch'i from the others? Why was it he who rose to the role of chief coordinator of the relief activities? Was it simply that he worked harder than the others or had some special diplomatic skills?

A key to Ch'i's success as a leader may have been that he favored policies that suited the conditions of his time. New social and economic networks were, more than ever before, crisscrossing administrative boundaries, with the result that members of the elite had grown uncertain about the geographic scope of their responsibility. This uncertainty was evident when the residents of Ch'i's hometown became involved in the plight of a neighboring district (Sheng *hsien*) to the point of contributing aid to that district.[58] The uncertainty about the scope of responsibility also accounts for many of the debates among the local elite. It accounts for a debate between Ni Yüan-lu (1594–1644) and Ch'i Piao-chia—where Ni proposed that "each ward (*fang*) take care of that ward,"[59] but Ch'i insisted on a more inclusive view. It accounts for a debate between Liu Tsung-chou and Ch'i Piao-chia—where Liu wanted subscription records to be compiled on a neighborhood-by-neighborhood basis, but Ch'i insisted that the records be "*united*" in one place."[60]

It also accounts for numerous debates concerning the responsibility of city dwellers for villagers.[61] These debates could not be easily resolved among the local elite, for the boundaries defining who should be in on the discussion and who should be cared for had turned fuzzy.

In each of these debates, Ch'i pressed for the more inclusive approach and opposed any tidy compartmentalization based on arbitrary administrative boundaries. He understood that the arable land of his district was insufficient to support its population;[62] that the area had become economically dependent on producing crops and goods for export; that interregional trade and economic interdependence, in other words, were inescapable, even beneficial. He also recognized, as he put it, that the affluence of his region (Yüeh) "was certainly enough to take care of the famine";[63] and that, if left unaided, the needy in neighboring districts would be driven to roving into his own district, where they would surely stir up trouble.[64] With this expanded perspective, Ch'i favored relying on merchants to import grain during crises over keeping granaries stocked,[65] and insisted that wealthy locales must come to the aid of poor areas.

Thus Ch'i resolved conflicts, not by disengaging himself, as Chang Pi had done, and not through some voting process, as we might do (and which, in any case, assumes a bounded community) but by reaching for a higher authority, namely official authority, to back his expansive view. When he made that reach, it was his good fortune that there just happened to be in place Ch'en Tzu-lung, a worthy official of like mind.

Much has been said elsewhere about the breakdown of community during the late Ming, but usually in reference to the deterioration of relations between landlords and tenants.[66] What the case of the Shao-hsing famine points to is how the weakening of community boundaries also altered relations within the local elite; it increased competition among them, prompting them to display their goodness ever more vociferously through a variety of means, including an outpouring of personal records; and it moved them to seek to resolve their differences and strengthen their activities at home by securing the sanction of those in authority above.

LESSONS FROM THE CASE STUDY OF THE FAMINE OF SHAN-YIN

In his diary Ch'i commented on the same riot that Ch'en Tzu-lung had observed, and like Ch'en, he did so tersely: visiting the city on the day of the disturbance, he learned that no fewer than ten households had been raided and one household completely demolished; "gentry households had decidedly not been spared"; when wealthy residents distributed rice and money, the troublemakers "grew even more arrogant and demanding"; throughout the city businesses were shut down, and scarcely anyone was to be seen.[67] Ch'i thus took note of the riot, but the format of the diary quickly drew his attention to the fresh events of each day and his role in the relief activities. Although he was cognizant of the threat of social disintegration, his immediate preoccupations crowded out attempts to analyze it.

The constructive response to the Shan-yin famine of the 1640s represents but one of several scenarios allowed by the social relations, political structure, and beliefs of the late Ming. The residents of Shan-yin *hsien* themselves could look back with shame on a famine of 1588, when, as Liu Tsung-chou put it, "The rich kept to themselves [with the result that] many [people] died."[68] What distinguished the two responses— was it some change in attitude, or a fluke in leadership?—is impossible to say for lack of material. Outstanding writers had resided in Shan-yin district during the 1580s, but on the topic of the crisis of 1588, they had remained hushed. What may be surely said is that the case of Shan-yin in the 1640s shows relief efforts at their best.

Other areas fared less well. One should consider in particular the deeply pessimistic and sensational account concerning how the famine of the 1640s affected the city of Su-chou, roughly 180 miles north of Shao-hsing prefecture. There, following a rapid rise in grain prices in 1637, troubles perturbed the area for several years: tenants burned down the country residence of their landlord; several thousand townsmen rioted against a magistrate; grain transport soldiers mutineed, plundered, and murdered; and prisoners broke out of jail. In 1640, a neighboring prefecture, having itself suffered floods and drought, failed to export its rice to Su-chou. Thousands of poor people, ridden with anxiety, led a riot in the city center. In the eastern section of the city some residents, upon learning that a neighbor had bought grain from an Anhwei merchant, instantly relieved him of one thousand piculs *(tou)* of his hoard; in the western section, someone known for his wealth and well-stocked granaries was also plundered—not only of his grain, but also of treasures from his ancestors and money valued at several tens of thousands of ounces of silver.[69] Rioting escalated. The Grand Coordinator immediately had the leaders beaten to death as a warning to the masses, but this failed to pacify them. High officials distributed tickets enabling poor households to purchase rice at reduced prices, but these measures were inadequate. In 1641, grain prices shot up further, whereupon officials, fearing that the poor people would start a rebellion, set up food kitchens at six locations. Some people thus "received kindness," but many continued to go hungry, and it was difficult to distribute the grain thoroughly. The older generation recalled the big famine of 1589, which back then they had thought to be an extraordinary event. But now, asks the author of this account, "with the price of rice up to

2.5 taels . . . is this [famine] not more extraordinary?" and then he laments, "How can the people bear it?"[70]

Splattered with such phrases as "is it not strange?" this account emphasizes the sensational aspects of the crisis in Su-chou. Judging the relief efforts as inadequate, it wastes no ink celebrating charitable deeds, reserves no space commemorating do-gooders.[71] Completed after the fall of the Ming dynasty, its outlook conforms to the model of dynastic decline, with disorder spreading out from the center of the city to the eastern and western districts. Reporting on "things heard about the T'ien-ch'i and Ch'ung-chen reigns," that is, about the last two reigns of the dynasty, it draws attention to the inadequacies of government and the failure of a state that had callously insisted on raising taxes in the area precisely when local officials most urgently requested that taxes be remitted.[72]

THE HERITAGE OF WRITINGS ABOUT FAMINE RELIEF

Such dark counterexamples found in the Su-chou account and other writings notwithstanding, Ch'i Piao-chia's forthright *Diary* lends veracity to that sincerity of purpose and depth of commitment to welfare activities claimed by authors of abstract handbooks, didactic works, and self-congratulatory retrospective reports. Undoubtedly some members of the elite coldly ignored the needy, or they exploited the ideals of welfare simply to mitigate tensions between rich and poor while advancing their own selfish interests. But under the right circumstances, the ideals did motivate genuine feelings of beneficence. Where did those ideals come from?

Chi'i's concern for and approach to famine relief were shaped by a vast and varied body of literature. Among these were the practical handbooks on famine relief and agronomy, each of which built on the offerings of its predecessors. By rearranging, making extracts from, and adding to the contents of previous handbooks, compilers both accumulated wisdom from the past and updated discussion for their own time.

Thus a handbook of the early thirteenth century by Tung Wei (d. 1217)—*Chiu-huang huo-min shu* (A book on relieving famine and keeping the people alive)—was supplemented in the fifteenth century by Chu Hsiung and consulted (along with many other writings) in the early seventeenth century by Hsü Kuang-ch'i (1562–1633), the compiler of a massive compendium in sixty sections (*chüan*), *Nung-cheng ch'üan-shu* (The complete book of agriculture).[73] Hsü died before finishing his masterpiece, but his draft manuscript was rescued from Hsü's grandson—by Ch'en Tzu-lung. Ch'en edited the manuscript, added sections to fill in lacunae, and brought it into print in 1639,[74] shortly before taking up his post as police magistrate of Shao-hsing. In its published form, Hsü's work is a veritable storehouse of information on husbandry, farming equipment, irrigation techniques, sericulture, and the like; it also assembles materials on famine relief—excerpts by ancient political theorists, and proposals, memorials, and outlines of strategies by eminent predecessors.

Ch'en gave a copy of Hsü Kuang-ch'i's work to Ch'i Piao-chia, who then consulted it while dealing with the famine crisis.[75] At the same time Ch'i labored to draft his own definitive magnum opus—a work he planned to entitle *Chiu-huang ch'üan-shu* (The complete book of famine relief).[76] In like spirit, if far less ambitiously, Chang Pi made a small contribution to famine relief literature, in the form of his *Chiu-huang shih-i.*

As shown by their writings, Ch'i Piao-chia, Chang Pi, and Ch'en Tzu-lung were familiar with past wisdom about famine relief. They understood the strengths and weaknesses of the various (that is, charitable, community, and ever-normal) types of granaries; the pitfalls of lowering grain prices (which simply encouraged merchants to hoard supplies);[77] the methods of preventing hungry masses from rioting at the soup kitchens; and the challenges of triaging the population according to levels of need so as to use limited resources fairly and effectively. They were conversant with strategies for mobilizing farmers to defend crops against locust attacks, and with therapies for the sorts of illnesses that accompanied hunger. They thus joined a long line of worthies who had, in action and writing alike, concerned themselves with famine relief. They participated in a tradition that derived authority from past luminaries, inspired aid to the starving, and promised enduring reputations to beneficent men. One towering figure with whom they were all familiar was the twelfth-century thinker Chu Hsi, who was famous both for having advanced the learning of the Way and for having sponsored community granaries. This fact wedded in the minds of later men an interest in famine relief with what in the West is commonly thought of as "Confucian values."

The tradition of famine relief cannot, however, be reduced to a particular system of belief. Enriched and altered over time, it appropriated diverse strands of thought.[78] To be sure, it accorded with what may be counted as keystones in the thought of Confucius and his followers—the value of humaneness and the concern for the well-being of the common people. But, especially in Hsü Kuang-ch'i's hands, it also embodied the interests of those Legalist writers who had coldly striven, largely through the manipulation of rewards and punishments, to strengthen and enrich the state.[79]

Ch'i Piao-chia cited ancient Confucian texts[80] and acted in accord with their teachings. Recognizing the interdependence of Heaven and man, he appreciated that self-cultivation—in particular, examining one's own faults—was essential to protecting society against natural disaster.[81] Nevertheless, Ch'i himself warned against getting bogged down in ancient texts.[82] He questioned the feasibility of implementing Chu Hsi's community granary in his own day;[83] and he argued that ignoring contemporary conditions was especially misguided in the matter of famine relief, because, as he noted, soil types varied with place and crop yields with the times.[84] Thus responsive to his era, Ch'i did not cleave to the position of so many of his predecessors—that one solution to dearth was to encourage artisans and merchants to return to agriculture. Instead he accepted the realities of his irreversibly commercialized environment: in his crowded region, not everyone could own or rent land to till; making a living through handicraft industries (and, by implication, buying grain with one's earnings) was therefore an acceptable way of "averting famine."[85]

Inspiration for Ch'i's charitable activity came also from Buddhist teachings, which affected many aspects of his life. Ch'i socialized with and sponsored Ch'an monks, even crossing paths "with a priest from India," whom his friend Yen Mao-yu had questioned about the principles of causation.[86] During the vexatious famine years Ch'i occasionally pored over and recited the *Śūraṅgama sutra*, and one day suddenly determined that every night he would bow to the Buddha and call out his name 150 times.[87]

Buddhist sentiment likewise touched many of Ch'i's fellow philanthropists.[88] Chang Pi succeeded in persuading members of his mother's lineage to make funds available for his own, independent relief effort by appealing to their Buddhist beliefs. As Chang explained: "My mother's lineage worship the Buddha and have long kept vegetarian diets; throughout their lives they have practiced a charity as bountiful as the sands of the Ganges River, and they have long been concerned that we achieve enlightenment." By selling off a parcel of poor land to raise funds, he argued, they would "create merit for my mother."[89] Ni Yüan-lu, too, drew on Buddhist beliefs to mobilize donors to organize a supplementary relief program.[90] Although he was active as a leader in the group efforts commended by Ch'en Tzu-lung,[91] Ni worried that the main relief program neglected those famine victims who dwelled in remote areas or whose names had been left off the "registers of hungry people."[92] He therefore took it upon himself to circulate subscription charts shaped like a pagoda, each floor of which represented one life to be saved.[93] According to Ni's guidelines, donors could sign on individually or in groups for one floor (one life) and were then responsible for making grain contributions every ten days between the third and seventh months, that is, until the next harvest. In the seventh month, the manager of the society would circulate a pamphlet verifying the names of the people whom each person had saved, and the participants would make vows to the Buddha. A fortnight later, the society would hold a ceremony for the "transfer of merit," at which six Buddhist monks would chant six sections of the *Lien-hua ching* (Lotus flower sutra). The names of donors and recipients alike would be listed, and everyone who had assembled would burn incense. At this point in his guidelines, Ni asked, "If there is anyone who is not wholehearted in doing this, won't the Buddha know about it?"

Buddhist ideas thus permeated philanthropic activities, but their precise role in motivating beneficence is impossible to pin down. Some philanthropists eschewed Buddhism altogether; others drew on the vocabulary of both Buddhist and Confucian traditions. Ni Yüan-lu had the results of his fund-raising simultaneously "announced to Heaven and made clear to the Buddha" (*kao-t'ien pai-fo*).[94] Many benefactors used Buddhist and Confucian terms interchangeably, speaking of both "good deeds" (*shan-chü*) and "just acts" (*i-hsing*).[95]

Ch'i's philanthropy was compatible but not altogether congruent with what might be called Confucian and Buddhist values; for it did not express those values exclusively, and it extended beyond famine relief to areas about which earlier writers had paid only a little heed. Moved by compassion, he ransomed a wife about to be sold as prostitute, rescued animals from slaughter, dispensed alms, paid for the burial of abandoned corpses, supervised a medical dispensary for the poor, and sponsored a bureau for foundlings.[96] In these activities Ch'i was guided less by bureaucratic handbooks or Buddhist prescriptions than by the sentiments of popular didactic works, a genre that was informed by both Buddhist and Confucian ideas but had acquired a distinct late-Ming coloring when it blossomed just before Ch'i's own lifetime.

These books promoted that idea that, through a law of "cause and effect" (*yin-kuo*),[97] or "influence and response" (*kan-ying*), a divine mechanism distributed rewards and retribution for good and bad deeds, respectively. This idea of cosmic retribution had, by the fourth century A.D., become entangled with the Buddhist idea of karma. However, it is not exclusively Buddhist, for it can also be traced back to ancient concepts, in particular, to the concept of "repayment" (*pao*), which predated the introduction of Buddhism to China.[98] Moreover, during the late Ming, it became tied up with teachings that were not essentially Buddhist, placing the responsibility for one's own fortune (or the fortune of one's descendants) squarely on the individual. This was a period of rapid social mobility, economic change, social unrest, and spiritual anxiety; the emphasis on personal responsibility for one's fate offered a much needed moral explanation for sudden reversals in social status and wealth.[99]

Late-Ming popular didactic works assembled biographies of good and bad people to illustrate the principles of reward and retribution. At the same time, they tried to uphold the view that good deeds would earn merit only if performed with genuine feelings of goodness and without thought of rewards. An ambivalence thus crept into their message, for these same writings both promoted a notion of a pure goodness free of ulterior motives and profusely illustrated that charitable men did in fact win long life, prosperity, male progeny, and success in the civil service examinations.[100] One account first dictated, "Instead of craving for your own good fortune, you should commiserate with the suffering of all living things," but it then concluded, "Then . . . your good fortune will of its own accord be doubled."[101] Another account told of a benefactor who was so virtuous as to turn down a pearl he had been rewarded for his benevolence; but the account then went on: because he was upstanding, he ended up receiving two pearls.[102]

One such popular morality book was *Ti-chi lu* (Records of right behavior and good fortune), written by the *chin-shih* degree holder and official Yen Mao-yu, whom Ch'i personally knew and held in high respect. When suffering from illness and mental anxiety in 1631, Ch'i sought Yen's counsel, after which he had cause to remark, "One evening of discussion with Yen is more beneficial than ten years of studying books."[103] A few months after making that remark, Ch'i endorsed *Ti-chi lu* by gracing it with a preface.[104]

Anecdotes in Yen's book exhort readers to bury abandoned corpses, rescue animals from slaughter, and the like—in short, the sorts of good deeds that Ch'i performed. In reading Yen's book Ch'i must have encountered all the materials about relief strategies and generous benefactors organized under the rubric "Recompenses for providing famine relief."[105] He also must have read the cautionary historical accounts in the companion section, entitled "Recompenses for failing to provide relief." One entry showed how easily an inhumane official could lose legitimacy: toward the end of one dynasty, starving people, angry at a magistrate for his callousness, killed him, broke into the granaries to make distributions to the poor, and let the city fall to rebel troops. Another entry told of a wealthy man who refused to make his grain available for price-stabilizing sales: one day, just as he was discussing price fluctuations, lightning killed him and ignited his grain stocks.[106]

Ch'i no doubt also read a section of *Ti-chi lu* on making charitable donations. There Yen exhorted his readers to consider that a small monetary contribution might revive people who are dying of hunger and disease in the ditches, that what the rich spend during the course of one night is enough to save ten lives, that contributions of 10 percent of one's grain and clothing would suffice to save a thousand lives, and that the rich could easily save the homeless by forming small clubs to set up empty rooms piled up with straw matting. Yen rhetorically asked the rich how they would feel to be in the place of the poor, and how they could, under the circumstances, be so lacking in compassion as to begrudge contributing a little grain from their huge granaries. "We are all people," Yen stated, and then added that one never knows when fire, banditry, illness, and other disasters will clean out one's own family. Would it not be best to accumulate merit, inviting protection from heaven? "This principle is very clear," Yen concluded, and then observed: "Those who reek of copper [coins] simply have not thought about this."[107]

REWARDS AND INCENTIVES

The belief that beneficent deeds were rewarded by Heaven was sustained by—and may even have originally been shaped by—social realities; for, in actuality, local officials made a point of distributing rewards to those who performed good deeds. The rewards for charitable acts were sometimes substantial, as when benefactors were exempted from land taxes.[108] More often, the rewards were honorary: benefactors received inscribed tablets or banners for their front gates; or they were invited to special wine-drinking ceremonies; or they were granted "caps and belts" with the insignia of low-ranking officials.[109] Sometimes their names were preserved in local records, such as the district gazetteers, or, as Ch'en Tzu-lung noted, names were sent in a report up to the highest echelons and recorded by imperial decree.[110] If official honors failed to come, late-Ming do-gooders took it upon themselves to advertise their fine deeds. They circulated lists of donors. Or, like Chang Pi, they published pamphlets, ostensibly to describe relief strategies for future reference, but along the way displaying the importance of their own participation.[111]

In an agrarian society where, generation after generation, the vast majority of households were tied to their native places, a good reputation had real currency. Philanthropists who earned the trust and respect of their community found that they could easily obtain credit for financial transactions.[112] They commonly believed that they were protected from extortion and banditry; possibly thieves, fearing the ire of officials, did in fact avoid those worthy households with which a magistrate, through his dispersal of rewards, had associated himself.

Above all, through charitable activities do-gooders could forge advantageous social connections. Hoping to consort with residents of high status, young students and licentiates[113] scrambled to assume the onerous responsibility of administering relief efforts. Those who contributed their labor and resources could, at the very least, hope to attend a banquet, which customarily followed the successful completion of a philanthropic project. One example was a vegetarian feast Ch'i Piao-chia held for doctors who had treated patients suffering from the outbreak of disease following the famine. As Ch'i recorded in his diary, he "bowed to them all around to thank them" and everyone who had helped out, down to the lowly runners, "were all pleased."[114]

Ch'i, though already prominent in his community and deeply committed to doing good, appreciated as much as everyone else that doing good would bring him personal benefits. When Ch'i made the extended inspection tour of soup kitchens in Ch'en Tzu-lung's company, it was with pride and a touch of exhilaration that he recorded in his diary how they had ridden around together, "laughing and talking," and what they had discussed—not just the business at hand, but poetry and scenic splendors, topics conducive to a cultured friendship.[115]

When it worked well, the system of rewards, linked with symbols of status, encouraged charitable behavior. However, this "system"—as envisioned by the writers discussed here—depended on a respect for the existing social hierarchy. Ch'i Piao-chia and Ch'en Tzu-lung assumed that students, aspiring to pass the civil service examinations and form ties with officialdom, would scramble to aid local officials or gentry who had access to those officials—just as Ch'i welcomed the opportunities created by the relief efforts to hobnob with the high-ranking Ch'en Tzu-lung.

Late-Ming philanthropic practices were shaped by and enmeshed in particular social and economic conditions, and they were expressed in terms of the accumulation of merit—an amalgam of Buddhist, Confucian, Taoist, and even Legalist thinking that acquired its distinct features during the late Ming. Neither Confucian nor Buddhist teachings can help to explain the huge changes that took place over the centuries—such as the shift from keeping merit secret to publicizing it, or the shift of sponsorship from the imperial court and bureaucratic officials to members of the local elites. Where continuities appear to exist, usually it is because the writers of each era dredged up precedents from the past and reinterpreted them to legitimize their own activities. At best the search for any essential or enduring cultural traits must be done with utmost care; at worst, it may be entirely misguided.

The heightened visibility of philanthropy in late-Ming Shan-yin district may best be understood in terms of how members of the local elite expanded their interests within the confines of the existing political structure. Here we should keep in mind that, in the administration of welfare, distinctions between state and society, and between what in the West are considered private and public spheres of activity, were often blurred. The realm of formal administration, overseen by the emperor, overlapped considerably with the realm of informal good works carried out by members of the local elite and the most common of people. As the official Ch'en Tzu-lung stated, contributions totaling 75,000 units of grain for financing famine relief, medical care, and a foundling home came from official coffers *and* wealthy households, and the merit (*kung*) belonged to "superior officials *and* worthies and elders."[116]

Though having clearly specified duties, officials were far more than bureaucrats responsible for performing specific tasks. They were scholars trained in the Confucian classics and presumably equipped to exercise moral judgment and leadership in all sorts of contingencies. It was in this informal capacity that an official initiated and organized philanthropic projects. He did so at his own discretion, often stressing that his contributions came, not from the public coffers, but out of his own salary.[117] Official status lent authority to his good example, but what made that authority effective, what moved the residents to emulate him, was that he acted as a man of compassion. His financial contributions and those of the residents then mingled in a common fund, a fund that was often managed by the local inhabitants.

The official role, defined by tasks and the obligation to perform those tasks, was fused with the personal role, guided by individual judgment, compassion, and general resourcefulness. Thus officials were defined as parents of the people. This was particularly true of the magistrates, who of all officials dealt most often with the local populace. Posted far from their home districts, they had no special ties to the households under their jurisdiction;[118] nonetheless they were nicknamed "father-and-mother officials" and interpreted their duties in parental terms. Facing an outbreak of disease in his district, one magistrate explained: "The people are my children; I am the parent of the people. Where has there [ever] been an ailing child whom a parent has failed to nurture and cure?" and he then commanded that medical clinics be set up and doctors be engaged night and day to look after the sick so as to reduce the number of untimely deaths among the destitute poor.[119] A counterexample is found in the cautionary account cited above about how a local official's callousness precipitated a rebellion: in that case, the magistrate lost legitimacy because he had failed to fulfill his parental responsibilities to the people. As the text commented, "How could he be called a father-and-mother of the people?"[120]

Officials were clearly distinguished by titles and insignia. In terms of education and culture, however, little separated the police magistrate Ch'en Tzu-lung from gentry like Ch'i Piao-chia and Ni Yüan-lu; both parties had earned their positions by mastering the Confucian classics. Lines between young scholars and their superiors were also blurred, especially because honored gentry and mere student often belonged to the same family, and because, however finely stratified the local elite may have been, all its members were clearly set apart in wealth and education from the vast majority of the population.

Late-Ming prosperity furthered the eclipsing of official and elite spheres. Especially in the affluent Yangtze delta area (where Shan-yin district was located), there resided ex-officials who had found excuses to retire early to the comforts of their gardens; educated men who pursued lucrative alternatives to stressful bureaucratic careers;[121] and numerous scholars who, because the spread of literacy had produced a glut of candidates for the bureaucracy, remained stuck and frustrated as perpetual students and men of leisure. Thus the ranks of those whose culture overlapped with that of officialdom greatly expanded. Shan-yin district became packed with its Janus-faced residents who, when thinking about their future prosperity and career success, looked for approval from both officials and fellow townsmen, or who, when thinking about the well-being of their hometown, felt free to press both local officials and local residents into action. Most influential among those occupying such pivotal positions, were, of course, members of the gentry, who had easiest access to officials and greatest authority in the local community. As Yen Mao-yu put it when opening the section on "Recompense for virtuous deeds done by gentry residing at home": "The gentry are the hope of the state. The good they do while living at home can affect the prefecture and district and transform the customs of the subprefectures and villages."[122]

Pressures upon members of the local elite to do good at home came from many directions. From below came the threat that the mass of small peasants would, if desperate for food, disrupt the social order. As the records about Shan-yin and Su-chou districts make clear, one riot, one raid against a wealthy household, was often sufficient to mobilize grain hoarders to organize famine relief. From above came harassment by officials, often in the form of menacing rumors that wealthy households who failed to distribute their grain would be forced to sell it at below-market prices.[123] Thus threatened, the well-to-do hastened to pursue the alternate route: by seizing the initiative in giving, by showing that they "liked to make donations" (*hao shih*), or "took pleasure in doing good" (*le shan*), they could at least earn merit, stand high in the community, and take some personal satisfaction in their own goodness.

Also important—but more subtle than the pressures emanating from either end of the social hierarchy—was the burden felt by Ch'i Piao-chia and other highly educated men of his district to live up to the general lessons about being humane and serving society that they had internalized from their years of study. Challenging them to shoulder huge responsibilities was the weighty heritage of famine relief knowledge and precedent associated with great worthies of the past, worthies whose own achievements and renown demonstrated the validity of that heritage. Reinforcing this sense of responsibility was surely the presence in Shan-yin district of Liu Tsung-chou, who had earned wide admiration for his learning and moral integrity. Evidence for his genuine attractiveness can be found in the fact that numerous educated residents of Shan-yin and neighboring districts acknowledged Liu as their teacher and formed bonds among themselves on the basis of having this mentor in common.[124] Ch'i's writings reveal a deep respect for Liu Tsung-chou. Though strongly differing with Liu on many issues, Ch'i repeatedly looked to him for approval or (on the subject of famine relief, at least) sought to bring him around to his own views.[125] Often in his diary—as when he noted, "Formerly Mr. Liu had urged me to manage the administration of famine relief"[126]—Ch'i derived authority from and took pride in his relationship with Liu. With so high a regard for Liu, Ch'i, even when in sharp disagreement, must have countered Liu's position by tapping his own mental and spiritual resources, his conscience, for worthy justifications.

But all these above-mentioned pressures on the scholarly elite had been endemic throughout the course of China's late imperial history; late-Ming circumstances simply made them more visible. What was new to the late Ming were pressures that came from within the ranks of the elite themselves. As their numbers expanded, members of the local elite grew competitive. Doing good offered opportunities to stand out in the community and to influence the course of local affairs. This Ch'i Piao-chia understood well when, drawing attention to the grand implications of his actions, he observed, "Whether the [crisis-stricken] live or die, breathe or not, completely depends on their rescuers," or noted, "The lives of thousands of people hang on the one or two people who manage the affairs."[127] In an increasingly cramped social space, doing good, saving lives, enlarged and elevated those men who would be benefactors.

NOTES

1. Tsu Yu-Yue, *The Spirit of Chinese Philanthropy: A Study in Mutual Aid* (1912; rpt., New York: AMS Press, 1968). Previous versions of this paper were presented as "Chinese Philanthropy in its Historical Context," for the meeting on "Philanthopy and Cultural Context: Western Philanthopy in South, East, and Southeast Asia in the Twentieth Century," Rockefeller Archive Center, Tarrytown, New York, November 3–4, 1994; and as "From Dissension to Cooperation: Local Leadership in a Famine of the Early 1640s," for the panel, "Changing Patterns of Famine Relief," Annual Meeting of the Association for Asian Studies, Washington, D.C., April 8, 1995. I should like to thank the panelists at these sessions, particularly Pierre-Étienne Will. I should also like to thank Vivienne Shue for her comments on a draft of this article.

2. One exception is a fine article concerning a charitable estate that Fan Chung-yen set up in the mid-eleventh century for the benefit of members of his lineage; but that article reinforced a common Western view that,

if the Chinese were at all inclined toward benevolence, it was in ways that enhanced their families. See Denis Twitchett, "The Fan Clan's Charitable Estate, 1050–1760," in *Confucianism in Action,* ed. Davis S. Nivison and Arthur F. Wright (Stanford: Stanford University Press, 1959), pp. 97–133. On a debate concerning whether charitable estates were truly charitable or whether they were basically corporations, the benefits of which were to be divided in fixed shares among lineage members, see James L. Watson, "Chinese Kinship Reconsidered: Anthropological Perspectives on Historical Research," *China Quarterly* 92 (Dec. 1982): 589–622, and "Comment" by Denis Twitchett, ibid., 623–27. (I should note here that lineages, though composed of kin, were not necessarily intimate organizations; they often included hundreds of members of greatly varying social statuses and economic means. They should not, in other words, be confused with extended households.) Some local gazetteers (defined, p. 136) specifically praise as "charitable" or "just" (*i*) those men who made donations to their lineages. See, for example, the section, "charitable deeds" (*i-hsing*), in *An-fu-hsien chih* (1872), where one man is praised for assisting in the wedding expenses of the poor members of his lineage (12.47), and another is praised for having singlehandedly contributed 150 taels to repair the ancestral shrine (12.55b–56a).

The perceptions of China changed in the 1980s, when several scholars simultaneously started working on philanthropy in China. See, for example, Fuma Susumu, "Dōzenkai shōshi: Chūgoku shakai fukushi shijō ni okeru Minmatsu Shinsho no ichizuke no tame ni" [A brief history of benevolent societies: on the place of the late Ming and early Ch'ing in the history of Chinese social welfare], *Shirin* 65.4 (1982): 37–76; and "Zenkai, zendō no shuppatsu" [The emergence of benevolent societies and benevolent halls], in *Min Shin jidai no seiji to shakai* [Government and society in the Ming and Ch'ing periods], ed. Ono Kazuko (Kyoto: Kyōto daigaku jimbun kagaku kenkyūjo, 1983); Angela K. Leung, "L'Accueil des enfants abandonnés dans la Chine du bas-Yangzi aux xviie et xviiie siècles," *Études chinoises* 4.1 (spring, 1985): 15–54; Liang Ch'i-tzu [Angela K. Leung], "Ming-mo Ch'ing-ch'u min-chien tz'u-shan huo-tung te hsing-ch'i—i Chiang Che ti-cu'ü wei li" [The rise of charitable activities among the common people during the late Ming and early Ch'ing—with examples taken from the areas of Kiangsi and Chekiang], *Shih-huo yüeh k'an, fu k'an* 15.7 (1986): 52–79; Angela Ki Che Leung, "To Chasten Society: The Development of Widow Homes in the Qing, 1773–1911," *Late Imperial China* 14.2 (1993): 1–32; Raymond David Lum, "Philanthropy and Public Welfare in Late Imperial China" (Ph.D. diss., Harvard University, 1985); and Joanna F. Handlin Smith, "Benevolent Societies: The Reshaping of Charity During the Late Ming and Early Ch'ing," *Journal of Asian Studies* 46.2 (1987): 309–37; and "Opening and Closing a Dispensary in Shan-yin County: Some Thoughts about Charitable Associations, Organizations, and Institutions in Late Ming China," *Journal of the Economic and Social History of the Orient* 38.3 (1995): 371–92.

On philanthropy in the Sung dynasty, see James T. C. Liu, "Liu Tsai (1165–1238): His Philanthropy and Neo-Confucian Limitations," *Oriens Extremus* 25.1 (1978): 1–29; Hugh Scogin, "Poor Relief in Northern Sung

China," ibid., pp. 30–46; Richard von Glahn, "Community and Welfare: Chu Hsi's Community Granary in Theory and Practice," in *Ordering the World: Approaches to State and Society in Sung Dynasty China,* ed. Robert P. Hymes and Conrad Schirokauer (Berkeley and Los Angeles: University of California Press, 1993), pp. 221–354; and Robert P. Hymes, "Moral Duty and Self-Regulating Process in Southern Sung Views of Famine Relief," in ibid., pp. 280–309.

Future studies of Chinese philanthropy will want to consult a massive, landmark study that appeared after this article was completed: Fuma Susumu, *Chūgoku zenkai zendō shi kenkyū* [A study of benevolent societies and benevolent halls in China], Oriental Research Series no. 53 (Kyoto: Dōhōsha shuppan, 1997).

3. See James L. Watson, "Chinese Kinship Reconsidered," pp. 601–2.

4. For some of these views, see Kung-chuan Hsiao, *Rural China: Imperial Control in the Nineteenth Century* (1960; rpt., Seattle: Washington University Press, 1967), esp. chapter 5.

5. For a critique of these "myths" about the non-profit sector, see Lester M. Salamon, "The Rise of the Nonprofit Sector," *Foreign Affairs* 74.4 (July/Aug. 1994): 109–22.

6. Photograph of trackers by Dmitri Kessel, *Life Magazine,* 1956. Reproduced in Lyman P. Van Slyke, *Yangtze: Nature, History, and the River* (Reading, MA: Addison-Wesley, 1988), p. 122.

7. The notion of "Confucian thought" is problematical, since there is no term in Chinese that exactly corresponds to it. Rather the notion refers to a cluster of ideas found in ancient texts (in English sometimes called "the Confucian classics") that Chinese scholars believed to have been written or transmitted by Confucius. Over the centuries scholars reinterpreted and elaborated on these ideas and, especially from the twelfth century on, began to talk of "the learning of the Way" (*tao-hsüeh*), which is often translated as "Neo-Confucianism." Officials in late imperial China are often called "Confucian officials" because they were recruited into the bureaucracy through an elaborate sequence of civil service examinations that tested their knowledge of the ancient ("Confucian") classics. Although I try to avoid these loose terms, for convenience' sake I sometimes inevitably revert to them, hoping nonetheless that readers will understand the problems involved.

8. Harrison E. Salisbury, "In China, 'A Little Blood,' " op-ed piece, *New York Times,* 13 June 1989.

9. Wang Te-i, *Sung-tai tsai-huang te chiu-chi cheng-ts'e* [Policies for disaster and famine relief during the Sung dynasty] (Taipei: Shang-wu yin-shu kuan, 1970), esp. pp. 86–131.

10. James T. C. Liu, "Liu Tsai." References are also available on state sponsorship of welfare institutions (in particular, poorhouses) during the Sung dynasty (960–1279). See, for example, Hugh Scogin, "Poor Relief in Northern Sung China."

11. The relationship between Buddhism and Chinese philanthropy is complex, and documents for the period predating the twelfth century are scarce. Early Chinese Buddhist donors generally made gifts to the mon-

asteries rather than to the poor in the society at large; and critics accused monasteries of impoverishing the people by draining their resources. Subsequently monasteries, probably in response to such attacks, expanded their philanthropic activities so as to appear socially useful; and the imperial government increasingly relied on monasteries, which had the buildings and a work force (in the form of monks) to administer welfare activities. As it evolved in China, Buddhism was molded by the state and native Chinese traditions, and its social functions were coopted (apart from its beliefs) by the rulers and Confucian officials. On Buddhism and charity, see Ryōshū Michihata, *Chūgoku bukkyō to shakai fukushi jigyō* [Chinese Buddhism and social welfare activities] (Kyoto: Hōsokan, 1967). See also the important work by Jacques Gernet, *Les Aspects Économiques du Bouddhisme dans la Société Chinoise du Vᶜ au Xᶜ Siècle* (Saigon: École Française d'Extrême-Orient, 1956). On the misery the large Buddhist constructions brought to the peasants, see Gernet, p. 13. On the paucity of information of early Buddhist charitable institutions see ibid., p. 217. For one example of imperial cooptation, see ibid.: Empress Wu (early eighth century) had lay commissioners oversee all "fields of compassion" activities of the Buddhist monasteries, that is, care for orphans, indigents, the infirm, and the old (citing *T'ang hui yao* [Statutes of the T'ang dynasty], 49.9b). Note also Gernet's comment that it was by penetrating existing cultural groupings or creating new ones based on these models that Buddhism spread rapidly in China—in urban and rural communities, which often used the gate of a monastery or some chapel for their reunion centers (ibid., p. 263). Gernet's work has recently been translated into English by Franciscus Verellen, with some revisions, under the title *Buddhism in Chinese Society: An Economic History from the Fifth to the Tenth Centuries* (New York: Columbia University Press, 1995).

12. The notion of secret merit (*yin-te*)—that is, merit known to the self but not to others—goes back at least to the *Shih chi* [Historical records] by Ssu-ma Ch'ien (B.C. 145?–90?) on the Former Han dynasty and thus predates the first known reference to Buddhism in China (A.D. 65). See Morohashi Tetsuji, *Dai Kan-Wa jiten* [Great Sino-Japanese dictionary], 13 vols., s.v. *yin-te* (no. 41691.235).

13. On Su's philanthropy and fears of political reprisals, see Ronald C. Egan, *Word, Image, and Deed in the Life of Su Shi* (Cambridge: Harvard Council on East Asian Studies, Harvard University, 1994), chapter 5. On the "uncertainty" during the Sung dynasty concerning the "ethical basis . . . of charity," see Robert Hymes, *Statesmen and Gentlemen: The Elite of Fu-Chou, Chiang-Hsi, in Northern and Southern Sung* (Cambridge: Cambridge University Press, 1986), pp. 162–63.

14. Typically a section on charitable deeds (*i-hsing*) in a local gazetteer might report on the following among other deeds done during the late Ming dynasty: when a disastrous flood washed several thousand corpses ashore, one man paid Buddhist and Taoist priests to perform the funeral rituals; when desperate poverty forced fathers and husbands to sell their wives and daughters into servitude or concubinage, another resident, whose "family was not that rich, but who was charitable by nature," redeemed the women—four in all (*Shan-yin-hsien chih* [1803], 14.88b); one do-gooder

aided travelers (*Shan-yin-hsien chih* [1724], 33.7b); and another provided medicine for the sick. The Shan-yin gazetteer of 1724 pays particular attention to the late-Ming benefactors who provided aid during the famine of 1641. It tells, for example, of a Chu Chiung, whose donations in 1641 enabled many to survive the famine of 1641 (ibid., 33.7a); of Chang Yao-fang and his son Chang Pi (ibid., 33.6a–7a); of a Ni Fu, who, when the price of rice reached three hundred *ch'ien* (three taels), aided the starving with two hundred piculs (*shih*) of grain (ibid., 33.7b); and of a Shan Mao-yung, who sold his property in order to provide relief, thus keeping numerous persons alive (ibid., 33.26a). With the exception of Chang Yao-fang and Chang Pi, these men are known to us only because their good deeds were commemorated in the local gazetteer.

15. That the problem might not be availability of grain but involves definitions of entitlement should be clear to anyone familiar with Amartya Sen, *Poverty and Famines: An Essay on Entitlement and Deprivation* (1981; rpt., Oxford: Oxford University Press, 1991). For the role of politics and cultural assumptions in grain distribution, see also Cecil Woodham-Smith, *The Great Hunger, Ireland 1845–1849* (1962; rpt., London: Penguin Books, 1991).

16. Consider, for example, the reward mentality that, from roughly the 1580s, spread among the elite, a theme I discuss on p. 150. See Cynthia J. Brokaw, *The Ledgers of Merit and Demerit: Social Change and Moral Order in Late Imperial China* (Princeton: Princeton University Press, 1984).

17. See his *Ch'en Chung-yü kung tzu-hsü nien-p'u* [A chronological biography of Mr. Ch'en Chung-yü as told by himself], in *Ch'en Wo-tzu hsien-sheng shih-wen ch'üan-chi* [The complete prose and poetry of Mr. Ch'en Wo-tzu] (1802). For a brief biography of Ch'en, see Arthur W. Hummel, *Eminent Chinese of the Ch'ing Period* [hereafter *ECCP*] (Washington, D.C.: United States Government Printing Office, 1943–44), pp. 102–3.

18. Ch'en added that "the fluctuations in price were used partly to benefit the people and partly to benefit the merchants; within ten days, the money reverted to the treasury, and the people began to have the hope of survival"; *Ch'en Chung-yü kung tzu-hsü nien-p'u,* 1.17a. Like Ch'i Piao-chia, Ch'en favored reliance on merchants (rather than grain storage) as a solution to grain shortages.

19. Ch'en Tzu-lung, *Ch'en Chung-yü kung tzu-hsü nien-p'u,* 1.17b.

20. On Ch'i see *ECCP*, p. 126, and information included as part of the biography of his father, Ch'i Ch'eng-han, in L. Carrington Goodrich and Chaoying Fang, eds., *Dictionary of Ming Biography, 1368–1644* (New York: Columbia University Press, 1976), pp. 216–20. On Ch'i's social milieu and the challenge that his wealth posed to his social consciousness, see Joanna F. Handlin Smith, "Gardens in Ch'i Piao-chia's Social World: Wealth and Values in Late-Ming Kiangnan," *The Journal of Asian Studies* 51.1 (1992): 55–81.

21. Ch'i Piao-chia, *Ch'i Chung-min kung jih chi* [The diary of Mr. Ch'i Chung-min] (rpt., Shao-hsing, 1937) [hereafter *Diary*], 1641 (3/5).18b. Each year of the diary bears a separate title and has independent pagination. I designate the titles by the closest corresponding year in the Western calendar, even though I understand that the Western and Chinese calendars

are not exactly matched. In parentheses I give the month and day from the Chinese lunar calendar by which Ch'i marked each diary entry. The parts of the diary cited in this article are:

Diary 1631. *She-pei ch'eng yen* [Words on my journey to the north].

Diary 1635. *Kuei nan k'uai lu* [A record in joy on returning south].

Diary 1636. *Chu-lin shih pi* [Jottings on chance, while residing in the woods].

Diary 1637. *Shan-chu cho lu* [A record of stupidity, while living in the mountains].

Diary 1638. *Tzu-chien lu* [A record of self-reflection].

Diary 1639. *Ch'i lu* [A record of giving up].

Diary 1640. *Kan-mu lu* [A record of longing].

Diary 1641. *Hsiao chiu lu* [A record of my modest relief efforts].

22. *Diary* 1641 (2/25).15b.

23. *Diary* 1641 (6/22).44a–b.

24. *Diary* 1641 (5/8).34a.

25. *Diary* 1640 (5/11).16b.

26. *Diary* 1641 (3/1).16b-17a; esp. debate with Yü Huang.

27. Cf. *Diary* 1641 (4/21).29b, where Liu Tsung-chou: "proposed that prices be lowered" and Ch'i wrote a letter "forcefully arguing that it could not be done."

28. *Diary* 1640 (10/30).36b.

29. One consequence of the protracted debates was that action was postponed, thereby allowing the participants time to stake out their roles in the relief efforts. Given that some residents genuinely wished to do good, they must have wanted to do so in ways that would bring them full credit. This may be what motivated Chang Pi (discussed on p. 140) to strike out on his own. Rather than letting his contributions simply enhance Ch'i's leadership role and reputation, he managed to organize a program that in the end built up his own reputation (with endorsements by Liu Tsung-chou and another Shan-yin resident, Wang Ssu-jen [1576–1646], and notices in the local gazetteers). Likewise, Ni Yüan-lu, though cooperating with Ch'i, also organized his own "Life-Saving Pagoda" ("I-ming-fu-t'u hui") campaign, which I discuss on p. 149. If one purpose of Ni's small campaign was "to aid those left out of the relief efforts and to broaden the art of doing good," as he explained, another surely was to establish his merit in the community. Indeed, his reputation was thus secured because his guidelines for the fund-raising effort have survived and his role in it was recorded for posterity in his chronological biography. See Ni Hui-ting, *Ni Wen-cheng kung nien-p'u* [Chronological biography of Mister Ni Wen-cheng], in *Yüeh-ya t'ang ts'ung-shu* [Collectanea of Yüeh-ya Library] (1853; facs. rpt., Taipei: Hua-wen shu-chü, 1965) 3.8a–b. On Ni Yüan-lu, see n. 59.

30. For Chang Tai (1597–1684?), see *ECCP*, pp. 53–54. Little information is available on Chang Pi. See *Shan-yin-hsien chih* (1724), 33.6a–b, 22b.

31. Chang Pi, *Chiu-huang shih-i* [The organization of famine relief], Hsüeh-hai lei-pien edition (rpt., Taipei: T'ai-lien kuo-feng ch'u-pan-she, 1977). Other residents responded independently to the crisis, but details of

their generosity are obscure except for brief notices in the Shan-yin gazetteers. See n. 14.

32. *Diary* 1641 (3/23).22b. On another occasion twenty "scholars and elders" assembled; see *Diary* 1641 (3/8).19a.

33. *Diary* 1641 (6/12).42a.

34. *Diary* 1640 (5/11).16b–17a.

35. Cf., for example, *Diary* 1641 (3/9).19b, (3/12).20b. Ch'i often mentioned letters on specific topics related to famine. For mention of letter discussing aid to vagrants, see *Diary* 1641 (3/13).21a. On Ch'i's reading famine relief handbooks, see *Diary* 1641 (2/23).15a, (3/5).18b, (4/8).26b, (10/3).59b. For discussion of these handbooks, see pp. 147–48.

36. *Diary* 1641 (3/11).20a. This was in reference to the "clinic" (*ping-fang*) organized to take care of those debilitated by the famine, but this activity was definitely seen as an extension of the famine relief activities. See Ch'en Tzu-lung's account of *Ch'en Chung-yü kung tzu-hsü nien-p'u*, 1.18a.

37. *Diary* 1640 (5/21).18a, on "Kei-mi shih-i."

38. *Diary* 1641 (3/24).23a. See also: "On my return, already by candlelight" (*Diary* 1641 [4/19].29a); "I had almost no time to breathe. . . . Only in the middle of the night did I get to sleep" (*Diary* 1641 [7/20].49a); and "It was the second watch [9–11 P.M.] before I got home" (*Diary* 1641 [8/3].51a). Cf. also: after one emotionally draining day that began with visiting soup kitchens and ended up with consultations on how to quiet his broken nerves, Ch'i observed that, although it was "already dusk" when he reached his boat, he nonetheless used the time on the boat ride home to edit *A Book on City Defense*, and "reached home at night"; *Diary* 1641 (1/5).1b. And numerous other instances: *Diary* 1641 (5/12).36a, (3/13).20b, (8/3).51a.

39. *Diary* 1641 (1/20).5b.

40. *Diary* 1641 (1/19).5a. See also *Diary* 1641 (5/10).35b.

41. *Diary* 1641 (5/24).38b.

42. Ch'en Tzu-lung, *Ch'en Chung-yü kung tzu-hsü nien-p'u*, 1.17b.

43. Chang Pi, *Chiu-huang shih-i*, 9a.

44. Cf., for example, the account of Chung Hua-min riding on horseback . . . (drawn from *Huangzheng congshu*, compiled by Yu Sen; 1690) in Pierre-Étienne Will, *Bureaucracy and Famine in Eighteenth-Century China*, tr. E. Forster (Stanford: Stanford University Press), p. 93.

45. Ch'en, like Ch'i, did not leave to chance that his role would later be remembered: the source for this report, which is sometimes unabashedly self-congratulatory, is Ch'en's self-narrated chronological biography, *Ch'en Chung-yü kung tzu-hsü nien-p'u*, 18a.

46. Chang Pi, *Chiu-huang shih-i*, 9a.

47. *Diary* 1641 (3/15).20b.

48. *Diary* 1641 (3/11).20a.

49. *Diary* 1641 (1/22).6b. Note also that, in response to the mob riots, Ch'i conceded that it was "fitting to arrest and punish," but he also stressed that one must be kind no less than strict; see *Diary* 1641 (1/16).3a.

50. Cf., for example, his disagreement about the handling of vagrants; *Diary* 1641 (3/1).17a, (3/9).19b.

51. See, for example, *Diary* 1641 (5/8).16a.

52. *Diary* 1641 (5/8).33b; see also, on imposing fines, 1641 (4/9).26b.

53. *Diary* 1641 (4/9).26b.

54. *Diary* 1641 (8/3).51a.

55. *Diary* 1641 (5/7).33a.

56. See, for example, *Diary* 1640 (9/6).29b–30a; 1641 (1/28).10a.

57. Ch'i Piao-chia, *Ch'i Piao-chia chi* [Collected writings of Ch'i Piao-chia] (Shanghai: Chung-hua shu-chü, 1960), p. 116. Hereafter cited as *CPCC*.

58. See, for example, *Diary* 1637 (3/9).7b–16b.

59. Cf. when Ch'i first heard Ni's proposal, he was skeptical, for that policy would encourage vagrants to mass together and riot; *Diary* 1641 (1/19).5a. On visiting the rural area of T'ien-le, Ch'i further observed, "In that village area *(hsiang)*, there were many who were poor and few who were rich, so it was not fitting completely to use the policy of 'using the subdivision *(t'u)* to save the subdivision and the village to save the village' "; *Diary* 1641 (3/18).22a. For a brief biography of Ni (1594–1644), see *ECCP*, p. 587. See also Ray Huang, "Ni Yüan-lu: 'Realism' in a Neo-Confucian Scholar-Statesman," in *Self and Society in Ming Thought*, ed. Wm. Theodore de Bary (New York: Columbia University Press, 1970), pp. 415–82.

60. *Diary* 1640 (5/18).17b. For a brief biography of the influential thinker, Liu Tsung-chou (1578–1645), see *ECCP*, pp. 532–33.

61. *Diary* 1641 (3/1).17a, for example.

62. Ch'i calculated: Shan-yin had scarcely more than 62,000 *mou* of land while the population exceeded 1,240,000. With two people eating from each *mou*, the yield will only last half a year, even though the land is fertile. See *CPCC*, p. 116.

63. *Diary* 1641 (1/6).1b.

64. *Diary* 1641 (1/19).5a.

65. Of course, this policy was eminently sound for the southern area, where the warm climate presented enormous challenges to effective grain storage; see discussion of grain preservation in Pierre-Étienne Will and R. Bin Wong, *Nourish the People: The State Civilian Granary System in China, 1650–1850* (Ann Arbor: Michigan monographs in Chinese studies, no. 60, 1991), pp. 103–40. But the difficulties of storing grain did not deter Liu Tsung-chou, much inspired by Chu Hsi, from steadfastly proposing some sort of community granary system for the area and debating this issue with Ch'i Piao-chia.

66. Cf. Will, *Bureaucracy and Famine*, p. 73; See also Mi Chu Wiens, "Socioeconomic Change during the Ming Dynasty in the Kiangnan Area" (Ph.D. diss., Harvard University, 1973).

67. *Diary* 1641 (1/16).3a.

68. Liu Tsung-chou, preface to Chang Pi, *Chiu-huang shih-i*, 2a.

69. See Yeh Shao-yüan (1589–1648) et al., *Ch'i Chen chi wen lu* [A record of things heard during the T'ien-ch'i and Ch'ung-chen reigns], in *T'ung-shih* [Histories of distress], ed. Le-t'ien Chü-shih (Shanghai: Shang-wu yin-shu-kuan, 1911–17), esp. 2.3a–11a. I thank Pierre-Étienne Will for bringing this text to my attention. (Authorship of this work is unclear: Yeh's preface is dated 1638; but much material in this work concerns matters that postdate

the preface and Yeh's death.) For Will's discussion of this account as a description of social breakdown, see his *Bureaucracy and Famine*, pp. 73–74.

70. Yeh Shao-yüan, *Ch'i Chen chi wen lu*, 2.7a–8a.

71. The account does mention one "beautiful deed" (*mei chü*), namely the commissioning of monks in three shrines to pray for the souls of the dead who had no one to care for their graves—this after reporting that, since the community had failed to bury the corpses of vagrants found along the streets, starving people, under the cover of night, hacked up the bodies for food; see Yeh Shao-yüan, *Ch'i Chen chi wen lu*, 2.11b.

72. Yeh Shao-yüan, *Ch'i Chen chi wen lu*, 2.9b–10a.

73. For a brief biography of Hsü, see *ECCP*, pp. 316–19.

74. Ch'en Tzu-lung, *Ch'en Chung-yü kung tzu-hsü nien-p'u*, 1.13b.

75. On Ch'i's receiving a copy from Ch'en, see *Diary* 1641 (2/23).15a; on his reading it, see, for example, *Diary* 1642 (1/1).1a. Another work Ch'i read that contained much on agriculture was *Huang-Ming ching-shih wen-pien* [Writings on statecraft from the Ming dynasty], compiled by Ch'en Tzu-lung et al.; see *Diary* 1641 (4/28).31a, (3/17).21b–22a. Ch'i in addition had access to volumes on agriculture and famine relief in his father's enormous library; see Ch'i Ch'eng-han, *Tan-sheng t'ang ts'ang shu mu* [Catalogue of books stored in the Library of Tranquil Living], in *Shao-hsing hsien-cheng i-shu* [Works left by former worthies of Shao-hsing], ed. Hsü Yu-lan (Kuang-hsü reign), 8.1a–2a.

76. This work was not published, but is available in a draft manuscript in the Pei-ching t'u-shu kuan, China. I have seen only copies of a few pages, which Fuma Susumu was kind enough to give me. The "Chiu-huang ch'üan-shu hsiao-hsü" [Brief Prefaces to the Complete Book on Famine Relief], which I guess to be essays introducing the sections of the projected work, are published in *CPCC*, pp. 76–143. Six of the eight "Brief Prefaces" correspond in name to the six sections that, according to Ch'i's diary, constituted the completed work; see *Diary* 1642 (2/27).6b. For a later note that Ch'i divided the work into eighteen *chüan*, see *Diary* 1642 (8/1).21a.

77. *Chiu-huang shih-i*, p. 3b. Citing the thirteenth-century Huang Chen.

78. Note, for example, that Ch'i Piao-chia cites the Legalist text, the *Kuan tzu*, as an authority (*CPCC*, p. 76).

79. Ch'i specifically cites Hsü in reference to this theme; *CPCC*, p. 79.

80. *CPCC*, pp. 77–78.

81. *CPCC*, p. 77.

82. *CPCC*, p. 77.

83. *CPCC*, p. 83.

84. *CPCC*, p. 77.

85. *CPCC*, p. 78.

86. *Diary* 1631 (12/12).18a. On Yen, see n. 104.

87. For his decision to call out the Buddha's name, see *Diary* 1640 (10/8).34a. Ch'i's reference to Buddhism and his relations with Buddhist monks are too numerous to list here. See, for example, *CPCC*, pp. 61–62 (on his regard for two Ch'an monks) and *Diary* 1641 (3/11).20a (on his coordinating monks to manage soup kitchens for vagrants).

88. Among these were Ch'i's own father and the influential lecturer

T'ao Shih-liang. The widespread interest among members of the elite in Buddhism during this period can be traced to the compelling proselytizing of the monk Yün-ch'i Chu-hung. See Chün-fang Yü, *The Renewal of Buddhism in China: Chu-hung and the Late Ming Synthesis* (New York: Columbia University Press, 1981).

89. Chang Pi, *Chiu-huang shih-i*, 2a–b.

90. Ni Hui-ting, *Ni Wen-cheng kung nien-p'u*, 3.8b–9b. For other references to Ni's interest in Buddhism, see ibid., 3.9a–b (on Ni's keeping to a vegetarian diet), and 1.20a (on a dream Ni had about the importance of writing out sutras). Ni Yüan-lu was a native of Shang-yü hsien, but in 1637, upon retiring from office, he chose to settle in Shan-yin so that he might avail himself of the area's fine scenery for the purpose of building himself a garden; ibid., 3.2b.

91. See, for example, Ch'en Tzu-lung, *Ch'en Chung-yü kung tzu-hsü nien-p'u*, 1.17b.

92. Ni Yüan-lu, "I ming fu-t'u hui shu" [An announcement about the pagoda-chart association], in Ni Yüan-lu, *Hung-pao ying-pen* ([Ni] Hung-pao's volume of responses) (1642; facs. rpt., Taipei: Tai-wan hsüeh-sheng shu-chü, 1970), 27.24a. See also *Ni Wen-kung nien-p'u*, 3.8.

93. For a similar document, cf. Ch'ien Su-le, "I-ming fu-tu hui ts'e ch'üan tz'u" [An exhortation for the One-life-pagoda-chart Society], in his *Ch'ien Chung-chieh kung chi* [Collected writings of Mr. Ch'ien] (Ssu-ming ts'ung-shu edition), 4.17a–19b. For an illustration of a pagoda charts, see Yü Chih (Wu Yün), *Te-i lu* [Records of having obtained what is good] (1869; facs. rpt., Taipei: Hua-wen shu-chü, 1969), 2.44a. Though published in the nineteenth century, this work includes much material from the Ming dynasty.

94. Ni Yüan-lu, "I ming fu-t'u hui shu," in *Hung-pao ying-pen*, 27.25b.

95. Pierre-Étienne Will makes this point in his *Bureaucracy and Famine in Eighteenth-Century China*, p. 138.

96. For the ransom, see *Diary* 1640 (8/9).30a. For distributing alms, see *Diary* 1631 (12/10).18a, (12/28).20b. For Ch'i's sponsorship of medical aid, see Joanna F. Handlin Smith, "Opening and Closing a Dispensary in Shan-yin County." On the topic of saving animals much can be gleaned from Fuma Susumu, "Zenkai, zentō no shuppatsu"; see also "Saving Animal Lives in Ming-Ch'ing China: Buddhist Inspiration and Elite Imagination," paper presented to East Asian Studies, Princeton University (November 15, 1995), and elsewhere. On burying the poor, see, for example, *Diary* 1637 (4/22).12b, (10/3, 10/5, 10/10).33a–34a; 1638 (1/24).4a, (6/6).18a; 1639 (9/22).9a.

97. Ch'i occasionally mentioned discussions about the subject of "cause and effect." See, for example, *Diary* 1635 (12/4).28b and 1636 (10/8).27b. Yet, Ch'i seems to have been ambivalent about such thinking because it diminished true moral self-cultivation. At least once he distanced himself from the "theory of cause and effect," saying that this was not the reason for "encouraging good"; see *Diary* 1640 (5/2).15a. See also *CPCC*, p. 114. His ambivalence may have been stirred up by Liu Tsung-chou, who sharply criticized the practice of calculating merit.

98. For an excellent summary of these concepts, see Brokaw, *The Ledgers of Merit and Demerit: Social Change and Moral Order in Late Imperial China*, pp. 28–31. See also Lien-sheng Yang, "The Concept of *Pao* as a Basis for Social Relations in China," in *Chinese Thought and Institutions*, ed. John K. Fairbank (1957; rpt., Chicago: The University of Chicago Press, 1967), pp. 291–309. On the belief in cosmic retribution being common to all the major Chinese schools of thought, see Brokaw, p. 31.

99. Brokaw persuasively shows that, although these concepts may be traced back to ancient texts, merit accumulation as a system that could be manipulated by human beings was new to the late Ming; see chapter 2, esp., p. 31. See also Tadao Sakai, "Confucianism and Popular Educational Works," in *Self and Society in Ming Thought*, ed. Wm. Theodore de Bary, pp. 331–66.

100. Note, for example, that for his good deeds, Chang Pi's father, Chang Yao-fang, lived to a ripe old age; see *Shan-yin-hsien chih* (1724), 33.7a.

101. Yü Chih, *Te-i lu*, 7.3b; "Fang-sheng yüan kuei t'iao" [Regulations for a yard for saving animals].

102. Chu-hung, "Fang-sheng wen" [Essays on releasing animals], p. 13b, in *Yün-ch'i fa-hui* [Collected works of Master Yün-ch'i] (Nanking: Ching-ling k'e-ching ch'u, 1897). On Chu-hung's influential piece, see Chün-fang Yü, *The Renewal of Buddhism in China*, pp. 76–87.

103. *Diary* 1631 (9/3).5a.

104. *Diary* 1631 (12/20).19a, (12/23).19b. For the preface, see Yen Mao-yu, *Ti-chi lu* (edition in Harvard-Yenching library, n.d.). Tadao Sakai, "Gan Moyu no shisō ni tsuite" [On the thought of Yen Mao-yu], in *Kamada Hakushi kanreiki kinen rekishigaku ronsō* [Essays in history commemorating the anniversary of Professor Kamada] (Tokyo: Tōtsūsha shuppanbu, 1969), pp. 259–73. On an association for moral reform, which Yen organized in 1624 and which had as one entrance requirement the accumulation of good deeds, see ibid., pp. 266–69. See also Terada Takanobu, "Ki Hyōka to Gan Moyu—*Tekikichiroku jo* no kakaretagoru" [Ch'i Piao-chia and Yen Mao-yu: on the writing of the preface to *Ti-chi lu*], in *Dōkyō to shukyō bunka* [Taoism and Religious Culture], ed. Akizuki Ken'ei (Tokyo: Hirakawa shuppansha, 1987), pp. 471–88.

105. Yen Mao-yu, *Ti-chi lu*, "Tu chi," 37a–50b.

106. Yen Mao-yu, *Ti-chi lu*, "Tu chi," 51a–53a.

107. Yen Mao-yu, *Ti-chi lu*, "T'ai chi," 13a–14a.

108. See, for example, the statement by Ch'en Chi-ju (1558–1639), a friend of Ch'i's father: "Those who contributed 150 *shih* of rice would avoid taxes on 500 *mou* of land for three years, and those who contributed 300 *shih* of rice would avoid taxes on 1000 *mou*"; see Ch'en, "Chu-chou t'iao i" [Regulations for soup kitchens] (Hsüeh-hai lei-pien edition), p. 3b. On Ch'en, see *ECCP*, pp. 83–84.

109. See, for example, *CPCC*, pp. 113–14, 138, and *Diary* 1641 (8/29).54b. See also Ch'i's recommendation of various rewards, including letting students take the civil service examinations at the prefectural level (*CPCC*, p. 47).

110. Ch'en Tzu-lung, *Ch'en Chung-yü kung tzu-hsü nien-p'u,* 1.18a.

111. Cf. Chang Pi, "Chiu-huang shih-i," 9a. In actuality Chang Pi's generosity was made known to the court, and he was duly honored with insignia. See Chang Lü-hsiang, *Yen-hsing chien-wen lu* [Records of words and deeds seen and heard], 31.6b, in *Yang-yüan hsien-sheng ch'üan-chi* [The complete works of Mr. Yang-yüan] (preface, 1644; 1871).

112. Wang Tsung-p'ei makes the point that members of small communities built up trust through good deeds. See his *Chung-kuo ho-hui* [Chinese mutual aid societies] (1931; rpt., Nanking: Chung-kuo ho-tso hsüeh she, 1935), p. 2.

113. That is, *sheng-yüan,* who have already passed the lowest rung of the civil service examinations, thus earning the privilege to prepare for the next level.

114. *Diary* 1641 (8/3).51a.

115. *Diary* 1641 (5/9).34b; 1641 (5/7).33b.

116. See Ch'en Tzu-lung, *Ch'en Chung-yü kung tzu-hsü nien-p'u,* 1.18a.

117. On the importance of officials setting a good example in this manner, see *CPCC,* p. 96–97. Ch'en Chi-ju, contributed his salary "to take the lead"—that is, to set a good example. See his "Chu-chou t'iao-i," p. 3a.

118. Officials were recruited nationally through the civil service examination system and then assigned (by the Bureau of Personnel, which was supervised by the Emperor) to posts throughout the empire—usually in accordance with the law of avoidance (that no official should serve in his own county) and the rule of rotation (whereby an official was transferred to a new post at least once every three years) so as to discourage officials from forming strong bonds with local elites, that is, men of wealth and informal power.

119. Tai Chao-tso, *Yü kung Te cheng lu* [Mr. Yü's Records of virtuous government], Ming-Ch'ing shih-liao hui-pien edition, 1st series (facsimile rpt., Taipei: Wen-hai ch'u-pan-she, 1967), 7:18b.

120. Yen Mao-yu, *Ti-chi lu,* "T'ai-chi," 51a.

121. For example, Ch'en Chi-ju, desisted from taking the upper levels of the civil service examinations, pursuing instead a successful career in publishing; see *ECCP,* pp. 83–84.

122. Yen Mao-yu, *Ti-chi lu,* "Tu-chi," 54a. Interpretations of the term translated as "gentry" *(hsiang-shen)* are various, sometimes including scholars who have never served as officials. See Mori Masao, "The Gentry in the Ming: An Outline of the Relations between the *Shih-ta-fu* and Local Society," in *Acta Asiatica* 38 (March 1980): 31–53. I generally follow Ch'i Piao-chia's strict definition of *hsiang-shen* as retired officials, and use the term "local elite" to include scholars, students, and cultured merchants.

123. On Ch'i's opposition to the forced sale of grain to equalize prices, see *Diary* 1641 (1/10).2a; (1/18).4a.

124. See "Ti-tzu p'u" [Register of disciples], in *Liu tzu ch'üan shu* [The complete works of Master Liu], (Photorpt. of Tao-kuang ed., Taipei: Hua-wen shu-chü, 1968). One of the followers listed was the great intellectual

historian Huang Tsung-hsi, whose *Ming-ju hsüeh-an* [Records of Ming scholars] lauded Liu's towering accomplishments.

125. See, for example, "Liu Tsung-chou very much agreed with what I said"; *Diary* 1641 (1/20).5b.

126. *Diary,* 1641 (1/10).2a.

127. *CPCC,* p. 89.

.8.

A View of Philanthropy in Japan: Confucian Ethics and Education

MARY EVELYN TUCKER

INTRODUCTION

Robert Payton has defined philanthropy as involving three related activities: voluntary service, voluntary association, and voluntary giving for public purposes. He goes on to note that the purposes of philanthropy can be roughly divided into acts of mercy to relieve suffering and acts of community to enhance the quality of life.[1]

When we apply these definitions to the case of Japan the key terms for further exploration are "voluntary" and "public purposes." In both the premodern and modern period in Japan there are certainly examples of philanthropy as defined above. However, some of the central differences between cultures involve the motivations for philanthropy and acceptable recipients. In other words, the questions of why philanthropy and for whom are important elements in cross-cultural comparisons. In exploring these themes religion becomes a significant factor to consider.

In the case of East Asia, Confucianism traditionally has played a major role in shaping worldviews and ethics that result in social patterns of familialism, educational systems of moral cultivation and public service, and political arrangements of benevolent government. Many of these traditional ideas have carried over into the present both consciously and unconsciously. As the contemporary Confucian scholar, Tu Wei-ming, has observed, Confucianism is the cultural DNA of East Asian societies.

The deep undercurrent of the Confucian worldview in East Asia becomes manifest as it spread through ethics taught in the family, in schools, and by the government. Although Confucianism did not form "churches," its pervasive moral, social, and political influence in East Asia is undisputed. Moreover, through the work of Wm. Theodore de Bary, Tu Wei-ming, and Rodney Taylor, the religious dimensions of Confucianism are now more widely understood. This paper will thus explore some of the ethical assumptions of the Confucian worldview, give an example of "Confucian philanthropy" with regard to education in premodern Japan, and comment briefly on aspects of philanthropy in contemporary Japan.

While one hesitates to make generalizations about complex terms used in other cultures, it is clear that in Japan the notion of public and private spheres deserves some careful exploration. In discussing public and private we need to examine certain Confucian notions of virtue as well as various Japanese adaptations of those ideas. To explore the spheres of public and private we will look at the ideas of particularized love, benevolent government, and humaneness as developed in the Confucian tradition.

CONFUCIAN VALUES OF PARTICULARIZED LOVE AND BENEVOLENT GOVERNMENT

In early China there arose an intense debate between the idea of universal love as developed by Mo Tzu (ff. 479–438 B.C.E.) and particularized love as explicated by Mencius (371–289 B.C.E.?). Mo Tzu advocated a universal love toward all that would bring mutual benefit. He urged people to "regard other people's countries as one's own. Regard other people's families as one's own. Regard other people's person as one's own." Mo Tzu's idea of universal love was bitterly opposed by the Confucians, especially Mencius, who argued for the need to have love with distinctions. The Confucians also disagreed with Mo Tzu's motivation of mutual benefit as being too utilitarian, saying that one should be motivated by righteousness, not by personal gain.

Mencius argued that love without distinctions would cause people to forget their special obligations to their family and to lose a sense of appropriate order in their concerns and obligations (*Mencius* 3A:5, 3B:9). It was Mencius's notion of love with gradations that became dominant in Confucian ethics in East Asia. Furthermore, Mencius's idea of "humane or benevolent government" that would care for the needs of all people was adopted as a Confucian ideal. It was the government that was supposed to assist in promoting agriculture or in providing relief efforts when crops failed or floods intervened.

Thus the paternalistic involvement of "benevolent government" frequently superseded the need for certain kinds of philanthropic activities in East Asia. Likewise, the particularization of love did not necessarily support public philanthropy from private citizens. Rather, the idea of particularized love tended to encourage specific efforts of philanthropy directed to known individuals or groups rather than anonymous giving to unknown or unrelated people. Both of these ideas are true in Japan today where the government tries to provide most social services and where loyalty and support for one's family and one's group takes precedence over concern for the "anonymous other." This is in part because of a hesitation to become entangled in the many obligations and responsibilities involved in giving and receiving assistance.

JAPANESE ETIQUETTE OF GIVING AND RECEIVING

In Japan particularized love has been expressed, traditionally and currently, in elaborate patterns of exchange embedded in language and ritual interaction. The notion of reciprocal obligations and responsibilities involved in human relations, particularly in giving and receiving, has created an elaborate hierarchy of exchange etiquette in Japan. This has been well documented by anthropologists such as Chie Nakane, Harumi Befu, Robert Smith, and Ruth Benedict.

A complex web of relationships defined by rules of *on* (obligation or indebtedness) and *giri* (duty) existed in premodern Japan and still affects human relations today. Central to these human relations are the obligations one incurs to one's parents which should be repaid by filial piety, respect, loyalty, and obedience. Underlying many of these interpersonal exchanges are various Confucian values, in particular the virtue of humaneness (Ch. *jen*; Jp. *jin*).

These Confucian obligations and virtues extend outward to teachers, relatives, close neighbors, and business associates. All are reciprocal relations involving mutual care and concern for people with clearly established lines of connection. This is intended to create a familialism of behavior patterns reinforcing group harmony. It also underscores the particularity of relationships and the expectation of some kind of return. For example, presents are exchanged at certain times of the year to cement these relationships. It is understood that they should be presents of equal value and similar kind. All of this creates a kind of social glue binding individuals to one another, often for life.

Anonymous gift-giving to people to whom one has no clear line of relationship is almost unheard of in Japan. Similarly, one hesitates to become involved outside one's sphere of obligations and duties for fear of not knowing what will be expected or due to concern of becoming overly committed beyond one's immediate group. Thus, philanthropy that is not directed toward a known group is rare. Grass-roots organizations for philanthropic purposes are similarly rather unusual in Japan.

THE VIRTUE OF "HUMANENESS" IN CONFUCIAN SOCIETIES

The above comments are not to suggest that philanthropy has not existed in premodern Japan or that it is weak in contemporary Japan. Rather, it is to note that the motivations are derived from specific ethical patterns and that the relational structures of the society and the role of government must be taken into account when examining philanthropic efforts. To more fully appreciate the religious, social, and political dimensions of the patterns of human interaction in Confucian-influenced societies such as Japan, it is necessary to understand the meaning of the virtue of humaneness (Ch. *jen*; Jp. *jin*). This has been translated as love, benevolence, human-heartedness, goodness, etc.[2] It is generally comparable to the Judeo-Christian virtues of love and charity. Thus, it is important to examine humaneness more deeply in this context of trying to understand the nature of "giving" in East Asian societies. While Buddhism also has notions of benevolence and compassion and has contributed significantly to certain kinds of charitable efforts to relieve suffering in East Asian societies, this paper will concentrate on Confucianism because of its broad historical and contemporary impact on social and political structures in East Asia. In particular, we will analyze the ideas of Confucius and Mencius on humaneness as these have helped to create a worldview which has significantly shaped social and political structures and is reflected in human relations of giving and receiving.

The two most important figures of early Confucianism are Confucius (551–479 B.C.E.) and Mencius (371–289 B.C.E.).[3] Both were born in the area of eastern China currently known as the Shantung peninsula. They made their living by teaching during periods of intense political and social upheaval. Each had a deep sense of his mission to bring peace to a world divided by conflict and dissension. Their teachings aimed at creating a viable social and political order based on harmony in the family and the practice of humaneness between individuals. In its simplest terms, humaneness might be described as the activation of the depths of reciprocity implicit in human relationships.[4]

HUMANENESS FOR CONFUCIUS

For Confucius, the practice of humaneness has the effect of ripples in a pond, extending first to one's family, and then to teachers, friends, and acquaintances, and finally, to all within the larger region and state where one lives. Humaneness is thus particularized; it must have priorities along with expansiveness. It is not to be practiced in an indiscriminate manner by a variety of altruistic actions which exhaust the individual. In the second line of the *Analects* we are told that humaneness is rooted in proper behavior toward one's family members. To know this essential root of humaneness is to understand the branching and flowering of humaneness in the larger social and political order. Without the proper beginnings of humaneness, further extension could be misplaced. Confucius reemphasizes this when he says a person must first be filial and then extend humaneness to others (1:6). Above all he urges people to "seek the intimacy of the good" (1:6) as something which is not remote but, on the contrary, is close at hand (7:29).

In the *Analects*, humaneness emerges as a virtue on which all other particular virtues or ritual practices depend. Without the inherent quality of humaneness, culture, learning, and religious rituals themselves become empty ornaments. Confucius asks, what can a person who lacks humaneness have to do with ritual or with music?

The practice of humaneness becomes an essential source of personal strength and balance. Indeed, it is a necessary condition for enduring the extremes of hardship and for delighting in the moments of good fortune. As Confucius says, "Without humaneness a person cannot for long endure adversity and cannot for long enjoy prosperity" (4:2). Humaneness, then, is a virtue which is both comprehensive and particular. It is seen as the basis for religious, cultural, and scholarly activities and as a primary source for maintaining social and personal equilibrium in the midst of the extremes of life.

Perseverance and Practice

Confucius does not hesitate to stress the need for the constant practice of humaneness. Indeed he asks, "If a superior person abandons humaneness, how can he make a name for himself?" (4:5). Confucius points out that a person ought not to be so preoccupied that reciprocity is forgotten. Nor should one lose the will to persist in this process of cultivation. Confucius doubts whether anyone has managed to "do good with his whole might even as long as the space of a single day" (4:6). He points out this is due to lack of will, not lack of strength.

This perseverance in the path of humaneness is something one continues until death. Confucius does not underplay the difficulty and challenge of humaneness. Indeed, he speaks of its practice as a burden which is heavy to bear. Yet he notes that a person who aspires to realize perfect virtue makes this "difficulty to be overcome his first business and success only a subsequent consideration" (6:20).

Although Confucius is often reluctant to say whether a certain person is virtuous or not (5:18), he gives many examples of the characteristics of humaneness. He describes a person who is closest to humaneness as persevering, simple, and modest (13:27). He notes that humaneness means being courteous in private life, diligent in public life, and loyal in relationships. This holds true regardless of where a person lives, whether he is in the capital or amidst barbarian tribes (13:19).

Ritual and Relationship

One of the key aspects of humaneness is its connection to ritual and propriety for a person who can sincerely engage in ritual is a humane person (12:1). Indeed, to practice ritual with a sense of decorum reflects an inner breadth of spirit in the individual. This same spirit allows a person to enter into events or human relationships with appropriate behavior and a sincere manner. Rituals are not done simply for outer ceremony but to celebrate the inner dynamics of human relationships.[5] At the root of this ritual relatedness is humaneness.

Through the practice of a genuine ritual reciprocity in human relations Confucius believes a peaceful society and a just political order will emerge. If the ruler is a person of humaneness and encourages such virtue among people, the state will be regulated in a proper manner. Confucius points out that the norm for both the citizen and the ruler is that "wishing to establish himself, he seeks also to establish others; wishing to enlarge himself he seeks also to enlarge others" (6:28). Indeed, Confucius urges people to take their feelings as a guide so as to practice humaneness fully. As he points out, humaneness for the Confucian means not doing to others what one would not like done to oneself (12:2).

Knowledge and Humaneness

Confucius emphasizes the need to combine knowledge and humaneness in government and in private life. Without both virtues "full excellence is not reached" (15:32). Confucius points out how wisdom and virtue complete each other: "Love of humaneness without love of learning degenerates into silliness. Love of wisdom without love of learning degenerates into utter lack of principle" (2:15). Thus, the dual aspects of the practice of inner virtue and outer investigation is well established by Confucius. It remained for Chu Hsi, the twelfth-century Sung Neo-Confucian, to revive this as a central axis for the pursuit of sagehood.

One of the flowers of scholarship in the Confucian tradition is humaneness. In the *Analects* humaneness is established as a distinguishing mark of the scholar and the sage: "One who studies widely and with set purpose, who questions earnestly and then thinks for himself about what he has heard—such a one will achieve humaneness" (19:6). These directives for study remain central to the Confucian tradition and are later singled out and elaborated upon by Chu Hsi in his five precepts for study, namely study widely, question thoroughly, think carefully, judge clearly, and act seriously.

SUMMARY OF CONFUCIUS'S VIEWS ON HUMANENESS

For Confucius, then, humaneness was strengthened by continual personal effort, dynamized in active human relationships, and nourished by study. These three aspects of personal perseverance, social expression, and spiritual wisdom were also essential to the understanding and elaboration of humaneness by later Confucian writers.

Confucius summarizes this activation of humaneness as the constant practice of five qualities: "Courtesy, generosity of soul, sincerity, earnestness and kindness" (17:6). He describes the result of these five aspects of humaneness as follows: "If you are courteous you will not be treated with disrespect. If you are generous you will win all. If you are sincere, people will repose trust in you. If you are earnest you will accomplish much. If you are kind this will enable you to employ the services of others" (17:6). Accordingly, humaneness is based on personal sincerity and authenticity in plumbing one's own nature which results in the trust of other people and the transformation of the larger social order.

As one of Confucius's disciples has said, the heart of humaneness and the central thread which runs through all his teaching is simply "Loyalty and reciprocity" (4:15). As more elaborately translated by James Legge, that thread is "being true to the principles of our nature and the benevolent exercise of them toward others—this and nothing more." This might be seen as an appropriate expression of the inner substance and outer function of humaneness. Thus, a person of humaneness is one who authentically understands the principles of his or her own humanity and activates them in relationship to others. He or she is then able to function as a pebble tossed in a pond, sending ripples across it and evoking from others a similar response of humaneness.

Humaneness is the root of a life of personal responsiveness and public responsibility for it seeks to bring moral principles to bear on practical concerns. It is, then, a virtue which is humanistic in effecting integration of the individual, social in activating the deepest bonds of human relationships, and spiritual in its moral power of reciprocity and transformation. It has clear implications for how individuals conceive their role in a society and how acts of humaneness are seen as part of a larger web of social obligations and political responsibilities. In this worldview, individual duties rather than rights are emphasized and care for harmony and order in the whole society is a task for each participant in that society. In such a situation philanthropy to unknown individuals or groups clearly has a secondary function. Yet a different form of "Confucian philanthropy" emerged that combined the public and private spheres. In theory at least (and often in practice) benevolent government and responsible citizens created the humane grounds for communal societies.

MENCIUS ON HUMANENESS IN PERSONS AND IN POLITICS

For Mencius the doctrine of humaneness was developed specifically with regard to its application to government and to the individual. These are the two complementary poles of Confucian thought, and Mencius wished to describe how humaneness operates in both these spheres. In doing so he expanded upon the ideas already evident in Confucius's teaching. With regard to government and humaneness he elaborated the first comprehensive plan for practical reforms. With respect to the individual and humaneness, he stressed the importance of balancing the virtue of righteousness as a corrective to Mo-tzu's idea of universal love for utilitarian ends.[6] Righteousness in this sense simply means behavior appropriate to circumstances and within specific spheres, beginning with the family and leading outward to the society and state.

Benevolent Government

Throughout his work Mencius advocates the establishment of "benevolent or humane government." This is government *for* the people rather than *by* or *of* the people. Such a public-minded paternalistic government virtually supersedes the need for private-sector philanthropy. Mencius notes how the ruler should share his pleasures with the people and the people will, in turn, respect him (1:A:2). By seeing himself as a parent overseeing the people (1:B:7) the ruler will act in a way that is responsive to their needs. Even more concretely, however, a benevolent government can be established through the public responsibility of the ruler in carrying out practical social and economic programs. Mencius suggested measures to be taken for productive, yet ecologically sound, farming, fishing, hunting, animal husbandry, and sericulture (1:A:3,4,7/2:A:5). Similarly, specific plans were devised by him for irrigation, taxation, labor, education, and land distribution. Mencius uses numerous examples of the early sage kings in setting forth programs by which government can operate both effectively and benevolently.

Mencius points out how these programs and laws are incomplete unless humaneness is practiced by the ruler. He writes that while "Goodness alone is not sufficient for government; the law unaided cannot make itself effective" (4:A:1). Thus, a balance of virtue and law is necessary, for when a ruler is indeed a person of humaneness, "people will flow to him like water flowing downward with tremendous force" (1:A:6). Furthermore, they will respond to his virtuous nature which they would not do to coercive measures or by surrendering their individual integrity. Rather "when people submit to the transforming influence of morality they do so sincerely, with admiration in their hearts" (2:A:3).[7]

Humaneness in the Person

Mencius believed that a person of humaneness was one who had retained the heart of a newborn babe and, in a ruler, this would evoke the favorable response mentioned above (4:B:12). For the ruler, or for any citizen to practice humaneness is to strive for a purity of spirit like one's original, unblemished mind. Such practice means, primarily, the elimination of all intentions of personal aggrandizement or profit. Mencius opens his work with a passage condemning motives for human action that are measured simply in terms of profit. He stresses that, instead, both the state and the individual should be governed by the principles of humaneness and righteousness. He writes, "Benevolence is a man's peaceful abode and righteousness his proper path" (4:A:10).

Mencius elevates righteousness to a virtue comparable to humaneness for a number of reasons. First, he wishes to establish a moral principle which will provide a foundation for the operation of humaneness that would be an appropriate contrast to the utilitarianism and universal love taught by Mo-tzu. In so doing he formulated a compelling directive to purify one's intentions and discriminate in one's actions. Thus, to practice humaneness for the sake of what is right means that one can set aside egotistical preoccupations which interfere with sincerity of the will. As Mencius writes of the result of such sincerity, "There has never been a man totally true to himself who fails to move others" (4:A:12).

Moreover, by linking humaneness and righteousness Mencius provides an alternative to Mo-tzu's idea of universal love without distinctions. Mencius feels universal love is impractical and may lead to unfilial behavior through neglect of immediate family members. So, by stressing righteousness as a part of humaneness, he reaffirms Confucius's teaching that humaneness is rooted in the family and extends outward. For Mencius these kinds of distinctions are important to the cohesion and coherence of the social fabric. For him a discriminating sense of duty is an indispensable counterpart to the practice of humaneness.

Self-Cultivation Nourishing Innate Goodness

Mencius's particular development of humaneness can be seen in his view of human nature as essentially tending toward the good. He says, "The tendency of human nature to do good is like that of water to flow downward. There is no man who does not tend to do good; there is no water that does not flow downward" (6:A:2).

Mencius speaks of the innate compassion of the human: "No person is devoid of a heart sensitive to the suffering of others" (2:A:6). This is the seed which flowers into the virtue of humaneness. Mencius sees this as the beginning of all virtues and points to three other seeds which are also innate in the human. The second is shame which leads to righteousness. The third is a sense of courtesy and modesty which leads to the observance of ritual, and the fourth is the consciousness of right and wrong which leads to wisdom. Mencius assures us that if a person is able to develop these seeds they will grow organically within a person "like a fire starting up or a spring coming through" (2:A:6).

The way to nourish these tendencies is by neither needlessly neglecting nor artificially assisting them. Instead, one must cultivate them without force but with constant effort. This balanced care is illustrated by Mencius through the contrast of the story of the man from Sung who pulled up all his rice plants in trying to weed the field. Such mindless action is not what cultivating virtue implies (2:A:2). Elsewhere Mencius observes that human nature is not originally barren or devoid of the possibility of growth. To illustrate this he uses the example of Ox Mountain where the trees were chopped down and, although new shoots arise, they are eaten by cattle and sheep grazing on the mountain. Thus, the mountain remains bald although it wasn't always like this. He concludes that in nature and in the human person, "Given the right nourishment there is nothing that will not grow and deprived of it there is nothing that will not wither" (6:A:8).

For Mencius, every human being instinctively feels compassion toward others' sufferings and shame toward one's own failings. These are the beginnings of the two great virtues of humaneness and righteousness on which rest effective government, the cultivation of the individual, and social harmony.

This can be seen as a continuity and a development of Confucius's idea of humaneness. Mencius makes explicit the doctrine of the innate goodness of the human. He feels the goal of all learning is to recover our original mind which inclines toward the good. Mencius stresses that effort is needed to activate the supreme virtue of humaneness, yet ultimately "all things are complete within oneself" (7:A:4). Like Confucius he believes the essential component for governing both the state and the individual is the practice of humaneness or the activation of innate virtue. He describes the results of this process in discussing the "good person":

> The desirable is called "good." To have it in oneself is called "true." To possess it fully in oneself is called "beautiful," but to shine forth with this full possession is called "great." To be great and be transformed by this greatness is called "sage"; to be sage and to transcend the understanding is called "divine." (7:B:25)

For both Confucius and Mencius, humaneness is the primary goal of the sage. Their teachings have been developed in even richer forms by the later Neo-Confucian thinkers who expanded on the metaphysical and cosmological aspects of humaneness.

This virtue, then, of humaneness has had and continues to have a significant impact on East Asian thought and society. It has helped to form a worldview based on the cultivation of the individual in relation to others where particularized love is encouraged over universal love and where public responsibility for a harmonious society is highly valued both by individuals and by government officials at large. With this kind of worldview and ethics a rather different sense of philanthropy has emerged in East Asian societies. In short, public philanthropy is seen as the government's responsibility, and private philanthropy is seen as individual responsibility to care for the needs of family members.[8] In the area of education a combination of public sponsorship and private initiatives had some remarkable results in the premodern period in Japan. It is to this period that we will now turn as an example of "Confucian philanthropy" in the field of education. What is fascinating to note is the various mixtures of provincial leadership, individual Confucian scholarship, and agricultural support that emerged, particularly in a school like the Shizutani gakko.

EDUCATION IN TOKUGAWA JAPAN: THE FIRST PUBLIC SCHOOL

It is now commonplace in Japanese studies to note the drive toward education that was characteristic of the Tokugawa period (1600–1868). Within a span of a little more than two and a half centuries Japan moved from a largely illiterate society to a highly literate one. The impact of this on the so-called "modernization" process, while debated in some of the particulars, has no doubt been considerable. The work of Ronald Dore, Herbert Passin, Richard Rubinger, and Tetsuo Najita[9] has contributed significantly to a better understanding in the West of the role of education during this premodern era in Japan.

It is evident that modern civil societies have been shaped in large part by the quality of their educational systems and these have often depended on public and private philanthropy. Whether in providing a literate and informed citizenry for political participation, or an educated class of merchants for economic transactions, or a cultivated group of artists for aesthetic expression, the contribution of education has been significant. Moreover, it is clear that in the transmission of ethical ideas and political ideals education has played a leading role. This is especially true in the dissemination of Confucianism during the Tokugawa era, for without schools in this period Confucianism might have remained a purely textual tradition.

In examining the establishment of a public school in seventeenth-century Japan, we can see a kind of collaborative public philanthropy in action. In this case it required the combined efforts of a local lord (Ikeda Mitsumasa) for sponsoring, Confucian scholars (such as Kumazawa Banzan) for teaching, and local farmers for financing. The school that was established, the Shizutani gakko, is the oldest public school open to commoners in Japan and surely one of the oldest public schools in the world as well.

HISTORICAL CONTEXT AND EDUCATIONAL SIGNIFICANCE OF THE SHIZUTANI GAKKO

The closed country (*sakoku*) of Tokugawa Japan was a period of internal peace characterized by educational advance, economic growth, and relative political stability. Although the later part of the era saw a rise in peasant rebellions along with the breakdown of Bakufu authority, the earlier part saw an attempt, albeit imperfect, at balancing the centralized authority of the Bakufu with regional control by the local *daimyo*. One of the means for individual provinces (*han*) to maintain some kind of regional autonomy was through the establishment of schools. This provided a group of literate individuals from various classes who could be utilized by the *han* to promote political, economic, and social agendas. Moreover, the dissemination of Confucian thought through the schools gave rise to a common intellectual discourse for the discussion of both ideas and practical learning (*jitsugaku*) in Tokugawa Japan.[10] Indeed, the further study of particular regional schools such as the Shizutani gakko would give us greater insight into the intersection of ideas, institutions, society, and public philanthropy that could be helpful for both intellectual and social historians of the period.

We know more about the temple schools and private schools of this period than we do about the public schools. Indeed, Ronald Dore's study of temple schools (*terakoya*) in Tokugawa Japan served to demonstrate the growth of literacy in premodern Japan, while Richard Rubinger's study of private schools (*shijuku*) suggested the variety and independence of curriculum in these schools. A lacuna in our knowledge in the West about education in this period concerns the public prefectural schools (*hanko*) and local schools (*goko*) established by *han* governments. Here we will give a case study documenting the founding of one such local school, the Shizutani gakko, in Okayama province.[11] Moreover, we will explore the educational philosophies of its founder Ikeda Mitsumasa (1609–1682) and his advisor the renowned Confucian scholar Kumazawa Banzan (1619–1691). In doing so, we will see how Confucian ideas of benevolent government, practical learning, and moral education were put into practice. This illustrates a kind of Confucian public philanthropy in action.

Our discussion of the founding and early development of the Shizutani gakko occurs in the context of broader contemporary discussions of the role of education in helping to shape premodern civil societies. In light of this and against the background of the spread of education in premodern Japan, the Shizutani gakko, established in Okayama *han*, is noteworthy in several respects: 1) Inspired by Confucian educational ideals it promoted a strong Confucian curriculum along with efforts at practical learning (*jitsugaku*). As such it provides us with a model of the method and routine of Confucian studies carried out in a provincial school. 2) It represents the determined effort of the Okayama *daimyo*, Ikeda Mitsumasa, to put his Confucian ideas into practice by founding and maintaining a school despite considerable financial difficulties in the *han*. 3) It was supported economically by a unique system of bringing in farming families to live and work in the surrounding fields. This was intended to provide income to maintain the school which would be independent of the vagaries of *han* finances. 4) The school was important because of whom it served both in terms of class and geography. It was intended to educate commoners for local leadership. Its popularity spread so that it attracted students from all over Okayama *han* and from other provinces. 5) It is remarkable for its longevity and endurance. It functioned as a school almost continuously, although with changed form, from its founding in 1670 until the end of World War II, some 275 years. The majority of its buildings, although rebuilt, are still standing and it is now a prefectural educational center in Okayama.

TYPES OF SCHOOLS IN TOKUGAWA JAPAN

During the Tokugawa period both public and private schools were founded to promote education, particularly in the Confucian classics. The public schools included official government schools (*kangakko*), prefectural schools (*hanko*), and local schools (*goko*). The *kangakko* were established by the Bakufu government to educate those who served under the Shogunate. The *hanko* were set up by individual prefectures usually in the provincial capital to instruct the local samurai who served in the *han* governments. The *goko* were established regionally by individual prefectural governments to encourage the education of commoners. The Shizutani gakko established by Ikeda Mitsumasa is an example of this last type. In addition, there were the private schools (*shijuku*) of individual teachers and the Buddhist temples (*terakoya*).[12] Merchants also contributed to educational efforts. One of the most notable examples was the Kaitokudo Merchant's Academy in Osaka which was supported by wealthy merchants.[13]

IKEDA MITSUMASA'S PHILOSOPHY OF
"BENEVOLENT GOVERNMENT"

In this climate of education, promoted both by the Bakufu and by the individual prefectures, local schools (*goko*) arose in an attempt to extend learning to the commoners. These local schools played a significant role in enhancing regional culture. Okayama was one of the first prefectures to emphasize the importance of education for the commoners.

Ikeda Mitsumasa was the prefectural lord (*daimyo*) of Okayama province for more than forty years from 1632 to 1672. Even after he resigned from office he continued for the last ten years of his life to participate actively in *han* government affairs. Known as a *meikun*, or "wise ruler," he was recognized as a model administrator who used Confucian principles to govern. The keynote of his political philosophy was the Confucian idea of benevolent government. To establish such a government he believed firmly in the importance of education. A special love of learning pervaded his life and he aimed as a prefectural ruler to maintain a unity between politics and learning. Because of this he strongly promoted the discipline of study and training for his retainers and heirs. He urged them to avoid selfishness, favoritism, self-conceit, and contempt and encouraged the cultivation of Confucian virtues, especially humaneness. He felt that education was important not only for the samurai but also for the commoners so they could take leadership responsibilities for local affairs. As a result, he concentrated a significant amount of energy on promoting general education for commoners.

Through studying and practicing the Confucian discipline of the mind-and-heart (*shingaku*), Mitsumasa himself made a tireless effort to actualize benevolent government. Indeed, it is said that Mitsumasa set his mind on learning at an early age and that he frequently denied himself sleep so as to continue his studies. When he was asked at age fourteen about the secret of good government he replied that by the virtue of the ruler the people could be led and peace established in the state. He also was aware at this early age of the difference between a petty person and a noble person (*kunshi*). The noble person, he acknowledged, cultivates virtue for its own sake while the petty person does so to be recognized by others. Moreover, most importantly for Mitsumasa was the idea that the noble person does not learn only for oneself, but for helping the country as well. These ideals became the guiding principles of his own Confucian political philosophy.

Mitsumasa attached great importance to the three threads of the Confucian text, *The Great Learning* which emphasized cultivating luminous virtue, renewing the people, and attaining the highest good. He saw these as a means to actualize benevolent government as explicated by Mencius. Mitsumasa authored several texts giving essential explanations and vocabulary lists for *The Great Learning* and *The Doctrine of the Mean.* He copied many other Confucian texts like *The Classic of Filial Piety.* He continued to value learning throughout his life and even on the obligatory alternate attendance journey to Edo (*sankin kotai*) he brought along the thirteen classics and some of the Sung Confucian texts. (His traveling library was so large that it was said to have weighed some forty kilograms.) The learning of Mitsumasa centered on Confucianism, but also included a wide selection of Japanese and Chinese books such as Japanese poetry and Chinese histories.

The foundation of Mitsumasa's educational philosophy was Confucian political theory and personal self-cultivation, both of which he saw as more appropriate for the needs of his era than Buddhism. Indeed, his zeal for Confucianism caused him to close more than half of Okayama's Buddhist temples and to expel many of the Buddhist priests from the province. His anti-Buddhist sentiment was so strong that instead of registering people at Buddhist temples he required them to register at Shinto shrines.

KUMUZAWA BANZAN'S PHILOSOPHY OF "PRACTICAL LEARNING"

To accomplish his goals as provincial ruler, Mitsumasa invited the Confucian scholar, Kumuzawa Banzan, to Okayama to act as an advisor to the *han* on practical affairs and to help spread Confucian studies in the schools. Banzan first served as a youthful retainer for Mitsumasa from 1634 to 1639 between ages fifteen and twenty-one. During these years he practiced the martial arts and at age twenty-one was introduced to the Confucian classics. For a brief period he left Mitsumasa's service to study with the Confucian scholar Nakae Toju (1608–1648) for several years. Banzan returned to Okayama in 1645 and served the Okayama province for over a decade.

There is no doubt that Banzan's profound influence on Confucian learning in Okayama prefecture dates from this time of service (1645–

1656) as a chief scholar-official of the *han*. As an advocate of practical learning (*jitsugaku*) he believed in the adaptation of Confucian ideas to time, place, and circumstances for practical ends. He was deeply committed to the implementation of humane government through proper administrative policies, careful management of finances, and sound agricultural and irrigation practices. James McMullen speaks of him as a pragmatic man "concerned primarily with the social and political utility of New-Confucian ideas."[14] Indeed he launched a highly successful reform movement in Okayama.

Banzan believed in benevolent government that combined moral suasion from the officials in charge with pragmatic action and practical knowledge. The following quotation from one of his writings reflects this combination of idealism and realism that lay behind a kind of Confucian philanthropy. It also reflects the Confucian continuum of the moral and natural spheres where a virtuous person was thought to affect "the transforming and nourishing [creating and annihilating] powers of Heaven and Earth" (*The Doctrine of the Mean*):

> Assisting the creating and annihilating processes by means of virtue is a matter for sages and worthies. It involves harmonizing the ether of Heaven-and-earth on a grand scale through a sage-ruler and his worthy ministers. But there are times when this assisting is achieved by talent and knowledge and a man, even though he is not a sage or worthy, may, if he has some slight aspiration to morality, assist the creating and annihilating processes. Heaven and earth produce and grow things in an unregulated manner. In some years there are good harvests, in others, poor. It is the responsibility of human talent to extend the harvests of years of good crops to supplement years of crop failure. Here the creating and annihilating processes may be greatly assisted even if one does not possess the virtue of a worthy or superior man, by being unashamed of questioning one's inferiors, and by using the knowledge available in the land.[15]

PROMOTING EDUCATION IN OKAYAMA PROVINCE

Ikeda Mitsumasa's commitment to Confucianism led him to establish in 1641 the *Hanabatakekyojo*, considered to be one of the first domain schools (*hanko*) in Japan. In 1666 this *han* school was superseded by a new academy for samurai called *Kagakkan* established by Mitsumasa within the castle. This academy was so popular that it attracted students from beyond Okayama. To spread Confucian learning even further, in 1668 Mitsumasa embarked on an ambitious educational effort in the Okayama *han*. He set up over one hundred local schools (*goko*), known as writing schools (*tenaraijo*) for commoners throughout the province. The instructions for setting up one of these schools in 1671 suggest that children of village leaders should be trained in writing and arithmetic so as to be able to carry on local affairs and in morals so as to be effective community leaders.[16] By 1674 there were as many as 124 such schools in Okayama province. This was the first such major prefectural attempt in Japan to establish a public school system for commoners. It later became a model for similar efforts in other domains. It represents a kind of Confucian public philanthropy which brought together the cooperative efforts of government officials, teachers, artisans, and farmers.

THE ESTABLISHMENT AND CONTINUATION
OF THE SHIZUTANI SCHOOL

In 1668, as part of his innovative plan to promote education for commoners, Ikeda Mitsumasa established one of these small schools in a particularly remote and peaceful location in *Kitani* village about forty-five minutes outside of present-day Okayama city. Two years later he renamed this area "Shizutani" to reflect the quiet nature of the mountain valley in which the school was situated. With the help of a samurai scholar, Tsuda Nagatada, the school was expanded in 1670 to include a lecture hall, dining hall, and study hall. From 1673 Tsuda lived in a small house at Shizutani. He became the chief administrator and an overseer of the school and its property which included sizable rice fields, farming land, and woods. In 1672 Mitsumasa had retired, but he continued to be deeply involved with promoting education in the *han*, especially at the Shizutani school. Until his death in 1682 Mitsumasa supported Tsuda's efforts as chief administrator of the school.

In 1674 Mitsumasa's son and successor as *daimyo*, Tsunamasa, wrote three rules for the Shizutani school which still hang on a wooden board in the lecture hall. In 1674 Tsunamasa had consulted with the Tairo Sakai Tadakiyo as to how to manage the *han's* financial difficulties. As a result of this consultation, in the summer of 1675 Tsunamasa wrote to his father Mitsumasa requesting permission to close the schools. Mitsumasa wrote back a strong letter admonishing his son not to close the schools and offering some of his own income to help support the schools. He criticized those who think learning only wastes money as well as those who are overly eager to see its achievements immediately. He stated clearly his belief that learning is important for the people of all classes—upper, middle, or lower. He was particularly concerned that once the schools were closed, reopening them would be very difficult. He conceded, however, that if Tsunamasa must close the writing schools (*tenairaijo*), the officially designated Shizutani school should at least remain open.

Ikeda Mitsumasa's plan to set up numerous local schools in the province proved to be overly ambitious. In most cases it was understood that the domain would provide the initial capital to start these schools and support them for several years. Then it was hoped the local people would be able to take over the operating expenses. This proved to be impossible because of floods, loss of food crops, and near starvation, which occurred in 1673 and 1674.

Thus, in 1675 all the writing schools (*tenaraijo*) which had been established by Mitsumasa seven years earlier had to be closed. Due to the financial difficulties of maintaining them, they were consolidated in the Shizutani school. The books from these other local schools were collected together at Shizutani and in 1677 a library (*bunko*) was complete to house them. In the same year, a building was erected for the prefectural lord to use during his visits to the school. A loose affiliation grew up with the *han* school, although the conscious effort to include commoners at the Shizutani school distinguished it from the largely samurai student base of the *han* school.

Mitsumasa hoped to ensure the longevity of the Shizutani school by devising a long-range financial plan to maintain it. To this end, farming families were hired to live in the area and care for the fields. The income from these fields was intended to provide a sound financial resource to support the school. Mitsumasa established the school's land separately from the prefectural property so as to ensure an independent economic base should anything happen to the feudal system or to the local *daimyo* family in power.

After Ikeda Mitsumasa's death in 1682 a hall was built in his honor and named *Higashi Mido*. Tsuda Nagatada was a tireless administrator for the school and two years after Mitsumasa's death he drafted a proposal to the *han* officials to continue Mitsumasa's educational vision. He wrote:

> The late Lord [Mitsumasa] said that Confucianism which is based on the way of loyalty and filial piety is the way of rectifying one's mind and cultivating one's self which leads to the way of regulating the family, the state, and the universe. He deeply wished for the people of all four classes to learn these principles. Those who worked to achieve his wishes have had many difficulties to overcome in fulfilling his wishes. He hoped that at least one school should continue into the future as a place of learning.[17]

Tsuda requested official documentation to protect the lands and income supporting the Shizutani school. Realizing that Mitsumasa's son Tsunemasa was far less committed than his father to education Tsuda wanted to ensure the continuity of the school after his own death.

With the death of Tsuda Nagatada in 1707 the school seemed to go into a temporary decline. Later in the eighteenth century with the help of the Confucian scholar, Takemoto Kimitachi, the school experienced a revival. Its reputation spread so that people from different provinces were urged to seek a similar school or to attend this school. During the Meiji period (1868–1912), it was converted into a private school (*shijuku*) and then a private junior high school and finally a prefectural junior high. After World War II it became a public high school, and it is now a prefectural educational center. Its buildings, repaired during the 1960s, are still in remarkably good condition.

SUMMARY OF THE SHIZUTANI GAKKO'S CONTRIBUTIONS

The Shizutani gakko is clearly an important example of the first public school for commoners established in Japan. Recognizing the need for educated commoners to carry on local affairs, Mitsumasa launched one of the most ambitious public school efforts in Japanese history by setting up over one hundred local schools. While this was short-lived due to financial difficulties in maintaining the schools, it became a model for other provinces in setting up regional public schools.

From this large plan of Mitsumasa the Shizutani gakko was born. Enduring from the seventeenth down to the twentieth century, it provided a Confucian-based education for those who were not traditionally destined to be educated, as samurai children were. Various classes, including commoners, thus benefited in terms of receiving basic literary, moral teachings, and practical learning which would allow them to participate in the growing cultural and intellectual life of Tokugawa Japan. In terms of both its longevity and the population it served, the Shizutani gakko achieved a place of distinction in Japanese educational history. More research needs to be done on this and other local schools in Tokugawa Japan as we recognize increasingly the importance of education as a basis for creating civil societies. The Shizutani gakko is an example of Confucian public philanthropy bringing together the initiative of a local governor, the commitment of Confucian teachers, and the financial support of farmers and government. It is a useful indication of some of the limits and possibilities of philanthropic efforts in a Confucian-based society as complex and intricately linked as Japan. We will highlight some of these limits and possibilities in the final section, which will provide a brief overview of the principle currents of philanthropy in Japan both historically and at present.

JAPANESE PHILANTHROPY PAST AND PRESENT: A BRIEF OVERVIEW

It is evident that certain Confucian values in relation to politics, society, and education have been important in Japan both in its premodern and its modern phases. With strong Confucian roots, the social, political, and educational organizations in Japan have had very different structures and emphases. In particular, the strong role of "benevolent government," the importance of humaneness as expressed in differentiated social relations, and the emphasis on moral and practical education as a means of contributing to the social order have helped to shape Japan historically and currently. Because of this, philanthropy in Japan has taken very different forms than in the United States and in the West.[18]

These Confucian values continue to play an important role in Japan. One indicator of this is the fact that human relations is central to all activities and that reciprocity in these relations is often the grounds for giving. Thus anonymous giving, purely altruistic giving, or giving to strangers is unusual in this framework. In this respect, the need for philanthropy to the needy is greatly reduced by sustained attention to the educational system, by long-range economic planning of government and business, and by strong family and kin support systems.

This has been true in both the premodern and modern period. It is not to suggest that there have not been peasant rebellions in the premodern period and labor problems in the modern period. However, Japan has been able to achieve a modicum of income distribution that has almost eliminated the need for philanthropic efforts of private groups. The family, the school, or the state is meant to care for and educate the individual in this context.

Thus it is of great interest that schools were established at such an early period in Japanese history. The effort toward education that blossomed in the Tokugawa period laid a firm foundation for creating an educated workforce and energetic citizenry which was prepared for the task of modernization. The ingenuity and drive of a leader such as Mitsumasa and the commitment of local people such as in Okayama was replicated throughout the country. Thus for nearly three hundred years Japan was able to form a basis of an educated public equipped to build new economic and political structures after Japan was opened to the West in the 1860s. While not without its cost in the social and environmental spheres, this has been the key to much of Japan's excesses and successes in the twentieth century. An educated citizenry combined with paternalistic government can be mobilized for either nationalistic excesses as in World War II or for economic success as in the postwar period. This dual heritage is something Japan is still dealing with as it searches for the means to establish itself in the contemporary global situation. We will conclude this paper, then, with a brief overview of some of the main currents of philanthropic activities in Japan in the premodern period with an eye toward future possibilities and priorities.

Premodern Period

Confucianism helped to create a vibrant educational system in the premodern period, as well as to provide for certain social and economic needs. Clearly this was not always successful, as peasant uprisings well attest. Historically it is also clear that Buddhism did encourage giving, especially for temple building and for charitable works associated with the temples. Sumo matches and Noh performances were held to raise money. In the nineteenth century, at the end of the Tokugawa period, several voluntary associations arose inspired by the idea of paying back blessings received (*ho-on*). Gratitude, reciprocity, and mutual aid became hallmarks of these groups largely designed to help farmers in need. One of the principal leaders in this movement was Ninomiya Sontoku (1787–1856), who wrote extensively on agriculture and the need for long-range planning and budgeting. He established credit unions under the name, "Society for the Repayment of Virtues" (*Hotokushu*).[19] These associations spread throughout Japan in the nineteenth and twentieth centuries. Nonetheless, in the premodern period philanthropy has largely remained a function of "benevolent government."

Modernization Period

With the rise of industry during the modernization period of the last one hundred years after Japan was opened to the West, new forms of philanthropy arose in Japan. In 1911 the Imperial Relief Association (*On-shi Zaidan Saisei Kai*) was established by the Meiji Emperor who contributed ten million yen in seed money. The aim was to provide medical assistance to the poor and to encourage contributions from provincial governors and industrialists.

While this had a strong government involvement, the *Morimura Homei Kai* established in 1913 was more of a private effort at philanthropy for education and charitable purposes. Other leading industrialists or corporations (*zaibatsu*) also began to set up foundations. One of the largest of these was set up by the Mitsui corporation and called *Mitsui Ho-on Kai*, after Ninomiya Sontoku's voluntary associations for repaying virtues. This was established in 1934 with a sizable endowment of 30 million yen. It continued until the end of World War II and aided public works and social welfare projects. However, because this was set up during the war, it is generally believed that it was an effort to demonstrate nationalist loyalty and patriotism.

Postwar Japan to the Present

Postwar Japan witnessed the rise of various foundations set up for scientific and technological research to help "catch up" with Western developments. In contemporary postindustrial Japan, philanthropy is beginning to take other forms due to the rise of personal and corporate wealth and to pressures within and outside the country. Domestically Japan is changing rapidly and on an international scale Japan is being asked to contribute more to global needs.

Since World War II, it has been noted that there are certain similarities between Japan and Europe in terms of fund-raising for philanthropic causes. For example, in Japan (as in Europe), "the government is more involved in social, scientific, and educational issues; foundations have closer ties to the government; tax incentives are less generous; individual wealth is less important; fund-raising professionalism is less developed; and the tradition of volunteerism is less practiced."[20] In addition, there are restrictions on corporate giving in Japan due both to cultural customs and lack of tax incentives.[21] Policies for corporate giving exist in only a few firms, and tax structures generally do not reward philanthropic gifts.

Some of this is changing in an attempt to understand and imitate American-style philanthropy, especially with Japan's growing corporate presence in the United States. Moreover, Japan has recognized the increasing importance of its playing a role in world affairs. Indeed, one of the primary concerns in Japan for the last several years has been how to become more internationally minded and less insular in outlook. It is having an impact on foreign aid, foundations, and corporate philanthropy.

Foreign Aid: The need to contribute to global affairs has been one factor pushing Japan to give extensively to overseas development projects and foreign aid, especially in Southeast Asia. Indeed, Japan is currently the largest donor of foreign aid in the world.[22] The availability of surplus capital and trade have contributed to this, as has Japan's desire to enhance its image abroad. One of the most noticeable changes in Japan's growing foreign aid ventures is the fact that Japan sent troops overseas for the first time since World War II to assist the United Nations peace-keeping forces in Cambodia. In addition, it made sizable financial contributions to those efforts, which were the largest ever for the United Nations (over $5 million in total).

Foundation Philanthropy: There are over 20,000 private foundations in Japan, but only some 2,000 give grants, and only 250 have assets over $500,000. The assets of these 250 make up only 60 percent of the Ford Foundation assets. Grant-giving is thus rather modest.[23] Other drawbacks include the following: Japanese foundations often lack trained professional staff to process a large volume of grant proposals, foundation guidelines are frequently too narrowly defined, and the review process is often rather subjective or too dependent on personal connections.[24] Nonetheless, in the educational field, foundation support has been crucial for scholarly exchanges and research projects.

Corporate Philanthropy: Traditionally individual corporations in Japan have had rather circumscribed views of their responsibilities to society. This has involved producing goods and making returns on investments, but giving away corporate profits has not been considered a high priority or responsibility. Nor have tax structures encouraged giving. Moreover, if "charitable" funds are given, there is usually some expectation of receiving thanks or something in exchange.

However, under the umbrella of the Japan Federation of Economic Organizations (*Keidanren*) Japanese corporations have been active in philanthropy for several decades. With nearly 1,000 corporations as members representing virtually all branches of economic activity in Japan, some $50 million was distributed between 1970 and 1989. In November 1990 a One Percent Club was established whereby corporate executives agreed to give to charity 1 percent of their pretax profits and 10 percent of their own salaries. (This was modeled after similar clubs in the United States.) There are now some 150 individual members and over 300 corporate members.[25]

SUMMARY

Because of the strong role of the government in assuming responsibility for public service and social welfare, philanthropy in Japan will probably grow at a somewhat modest rate. It can be argued, however, that although Japan is far from a utopian society, it has done an excellent job in providing health care and other social services and in ensuring a more equitable distribution of wealth than many other countries. While poverty is almost unknown, there are increasing problems of the homeless and of the so-called "guest workers" from abroad. Moreover, corporate and foundation giving overseas is beginning to increase with Japanese concern to improve its image abroad. Educational institutions and the arts in the United States have already been the beneficiaries of this concern. As Japan begins to deal with diversity within its borders and internationalizing pressures, philanthropic efforts will, no doubt, respond and expand accordingly. There are numerous signs this is already underway.

NOTES

1. Robert Payton, *Philanthropy: Voluntary Action for the Public Good* (New York: American Council on Education/Macmillan, 1988), p. 32.

2. See also Wing-tsit Chan's article "The Evolution of the Confucian Concept *Jen*," *Philosophy East and West* 4 (1955), 295–319.

3. Some secondary sources in English on Confucius are: H. G. Creel, *Confucius and the Chinese Way* (New York: Harper, 1960); Herbert Fingarette, *Confucius: The Secular as Sacred* (New York: Harper and Row, 1972); Raymond Dawson, *Confucius* (New York: Hill and Wang, 1981). Confucius's sayings in the *Analects* appear in a number of English translations including those by: James Legge (Dover Publications, 1971, from the original 1893 translation); Arthur Waley (Vintage Books, 1938); D. C. Lau (Penguin Books, 1979). Mencius's teachings appear in James Legge's translation (Dover Publications, 1970), from the original 1895 translation, and in D. C. Lau's translation (Penguin Books, 1970).

4. It should be noted that the Chinese character for *jen* consists of two parts, a person and two, conveying the meaning of a person in relation to another. This sense of relationship is central to the idea of humaneness and, indeed, to Chinese thought in general.

5. For a more developed discussion of the importance of ritual in Confucianism see Herbert Fingarette, *Confucius: The Secular as Sacred* (New York: Harper and Row, 1972).

6. See *Mo Tzu: Basic Writings*, trans. Burton Watson (New York: Columbus University Press, 1963), 39–51.

7. This is an important distinction between Confucians who felt that moral influence and education would be more effective in establishing a harmonious social-political order than the laws and punishments approach advocated by the Legalists.

8. Definitions and understandings of family, kin, and clan in East Asia have taken different forms and these need further study to appreciate "philanthropy" in different national contexts in East Asia.

9. Ronald Dore, *Education in Tokugawa Japan* (Berkeley: University of California Press, 1965); Herbert Passin, *Society and Education in Japan* (New York: Teachers College and East Asian Institute with Columbia University Press, 1965); Richard Rubinger, *Private Academies of Tokugawa Japan* (Princeton: Princeton University Press, 1982); Tetsuo Najita, *Visions of Virtue in Tokugawa Japan: The Kaitokudo Merchant Academy of Osaka* (Chicago: University of Chicago Press, 1987).

10. See Wm. Theodore de Bary and Irene Bloom, eds., *Principle and Practicality* (New York: Columbia University Press, 1979).

11. The sources I have relied on are: Nakamura Saihachi, *Shizutani gakko* (Okayama: Fukutake Shoten, 1988), and Kido Hisashi, *Shizutani gakko* (Tokyo: Chuokoron Bijitsushuppan, 1968).

12. See Rubinger, *Private Academies*, and Dore, *Education*, respectively.

13. Tetsuo Najita, *Visions*.

14. James McMullen, "Kumazawa Banzan and *Jitsugaku*: Toward Pragmatic Action" in Wm. Theodore de Bary and Irene Bloom, eds., *Principle and Practicality* (New York: Columbia University Press, 1979).

15. Masamune Atsuo, ed., *Banzan Zenshu* (Tokyo: Banzan zenshu kankokai, 1940–43), vol. 2, pp. 174–75. Quoted by James McMullen, *op. cit.*, p. 358.

16. Passin, *Society and Education*, p. 38.

17. *Okayama Ken Kyoikushi* (Okayama: Sanyo Shimbunsha, 1981), p. 55.

18. A useful resource is Barnett Baron, ed., *Philanthropy and the Dynamics of Change in East and Southeast Asia* (New York: East Asia Institute, Columbia University, 1991).

19. See R. Tsunoda, W. T. deBorg, and D. Keene, eds., *Sources of Japanese Tradition* (New York: Columbia University Press, 1958), pp. 73–83.

20. Katherine Jankowski, ed., *Inside Japan Support*, (Rockville, MD: The Taft Group, 1992), p. xiv.

21. See Nancy R. London, "The Regulatory and Cultural Context of Philanthropy in Japan," in Barnett Baron, ed., *Philanthropy and the Dynamics of Change in East and Southeast Asia* (New York: East Asian Institute, Columbia University, 1991); also Nancy R. London, *Japanese Corporate Philanthropy* (New York: Oxford University Press, 1991.)

22. Robert M. Orr, Jr., *The Emergence of Japan's Aid Power* (New York: Columbia University Press, 1990).

23. Some $30–40 million was distributed in 1989. The information in this section is from Jankowski, *Inside Japan Support*, p. xxiii.

24. Ibid.

25. Ibid., pp. xxi–xxvi.

PART FOUR
PHILANTHROPY AND SOCIAL CHANGE

.9.

The Origins of Modern Jewish Philanthropy

DEREK J. PENSLAR

Until recently, studies of Jewish philanthropy tended to be more apologetic and celebratory than analytical. The subject attests to the difficulty in accurately assessing the relationship between religious prescriptions and cultural practices. Much writing on Jewish philanthropy sets forth what I could call an "essentialist" approach to the subject. Essentialist analyses of Jewish philanthropy claim that Jewish civilization was the first to conceive of charity as a religious obligation. From antiquity to the present, so the essentialist argument goes, Jewish philanthropy has been characterized by exceeding compassion, generosity of spirit, and communal solidarity. Jewish philanthropy is also claimed to have always featured a preventive as opposed to a merely palliative approach and a desire to foster the economic independence of the poor. Jewish writings making this sort of argument focus on ancient Israelite social legislation, ostensibly for its function as a preventive against pauperization. Talmudic sources as well are combed for appropriate citations demonstrating rabbinical solicitude for the poor and respect for their dignity. These arguments tend to be as anachronistic as they are apologetic. For example, Ephraim Frisch's classic *Historical Survey of Jewish Philanthropy* (1924) depicted the medieval *gabbai* (beadle) as a modern-day social worker, employing "enlightened and wide-awake measures of treatment, with rehabilitation as the constant goal in view."[1]

Underlying the essentialist approach to the study of Jewish philanthropy is a heavy reliance on the Hebrew Bible and halakhic literature as explanatory sources for the Jews' remarkable levels of charitable action and philanthropic cohesion over time. Yet I would urge caution in drawing direct causal links between the charitable practices of the Jews in a particular time and place and the exhortations to care for the needy found in the Jews' textual canon. For one thing, the corpus of biblical and halakhic literature, composed over a period of more than two millennia, contains widely different dicta on charity and directives for their implementation. Moreover, throughout the long period from the completion of the Talmud to the seventeenth century—a period that we can call the "Jewish middle ages"—it was not so much the Jews' textual heritage as the specific conditions of the Jews' social, legal, and economic status that shaped the practice of Jewish charity.

Medieval Jewry was primarily urban and mercantile. The Jews lived in tightly knit communities, in close physical proximity. Prosperous Jews were unable to translate their wealth into landed property, and so retained large amounts of liquid capital, much of which went to tax payments and poor care for the community. Lacking the characteristics of the gentile nobility, wealthy Jews lived cheek by jowl with their poorer brethren. The gentile authorities demanded that this elite care for the Jewish poor, and, due to both compulsion and a sense of obligation, the Jewish elite fulfilled this demand. The Jews had to care for their poor because the two principal sources of medieval charity, the Church and the guilds, were closed to Jews. As a sign of the hostile environment in which medieval Jewry lived, among the most vital philanthropic services provided by the medieval communities was the ransoming of Jews taken captive in wars and acts of brigandage.[2]

What does this picture of medieval Jewish charity have to do with its modern manifestation? There have indeed been some lines of vertical, diachronic transmission of Jewish philanthropic sensibility across the centuries, but influences from the surrounding environment and culture have been at least as strong. Any understanding, therefore, of modern Jewish philanthropy is impossible without a contextualist approach that places the practice of *tsedakah* (charity) within the framework of the modernization of philanthropy on the European continent as a whole. At the same time, a contextual analysis should not reduce Jewish philanthropy to a mere echoing of gentile practices. If the philanthropic strategies of the Jewish leadership elite frequently resembled those of their gentile counterparts, the reason is not that the former were mimicking the latter, but rather that the two shared similar problems and a common pool of resources, technological and intellectual, with which to solve them. Moreover, although the social problems affecting Jews and gentiles in modern Europe occasionally overlapped, as did the solutions they set forth, the problems and solutions often diverged as well. Thus the approach I would like to offer here is best described as comparative rather than contextual.[3]

JEWISH PHILANTHROPY AND EUROPEAN SOCIETY
IN THE EARLY MODERN PERIOD

There was a dramatic shift in attitudes toward poverty and the poor in Europe beginning in the sixteenth century. Due to both a real increase in the number of poor and the rise of a more activist way of thinking about poverty and its treatment, municipalities throughout Western Europe attempted, from the middle of the 1500s, to centralize and rationalize the distribution of alms. This process quickened in the eighteenth century with the rise of Enlightenment concepts about the eudaemonistic value of work and mercantilist policies to productivize the poor as a means of maximizing the wealth of the nation.[4]

The demographic increase and geographic diffusion of European Jewry during the early modern period promoted a notable increase in philanthropic activity. There was an expansion of traditional private charities for dowering poor brides, redeeming captives, and sending money to the Holy Land. The *hevrah kadishah,* a burial society consisting of communal notables who receive no compensation for their services, came into existence in the sixteenth century. In addition to these charities, which had no exact parallels in the gentile world, there was a growth of institutional relief, taking the form of almshouses and hospitals (that is, shelters for the itinerant as well as the ill), similar to those administered by and for gentiles. The first Jewish orphanage appeared in Amsterdam in 1648.[5] Along with this material increase came sporadic attempts to rationalize poor-care along lines similar to those found on the continent as a whole. A statute issued by the Avignon Jewish community in 1558 requested individuals to give the poor only small amounts of aid and instituted a certificate system for the receipt of communal alms. In Poland, a synod of the Council of the Four Lands in 1623 sought to divide the Polish-Lithuanian kingdom into districts for the regulation of itinerant begging.[6]

The major turning point marking the beginning of modern Jewish philanthropy came in the mid-seventeenth century, with the formation in the German lands of a sizable class of Jewish vagrants, who came to be known in the 1700s as *Betteljuden.* The *Betteljuden* were the product of many social forces. They first emerged during the chaos and violence of the Thirty Years' War in central Europe, and their numbers increased dramatically following the 1648 Chmielnitski massacres and and the Russo-Polish-Cossack wars that ravaged the Jewish communities of the Ukraine. In the following century, demographic increase and strict residence requirements in the German lands, coupled with a new influx of Jewish refugees from the Ukraine in the wake of the Haidamack uprisings, placed an enormous burden on the central and Western European communities.[7] The wave of vagrants aroused fear, lest they commit crimes against gentiles and thereby bring the wrath of the authorities down upon the entire Jewish community. A *takkana* (communal regulation) from Moravia of 1649 referred to "vagabonds, worthless people, robbers, and cut-throats who endanger the entire Jewish community" and who must be either expelled or handed over to the gentile authorities.[8] A regulation of the Portuguese community of Amsterdam branded the refugees from Poland "dangerous people" who are to be encouraged to return to their homes; and if they are arrested by the gentile authorities, the Sephardim are not to intervene on their behalf.[9] But fear alone does not account for the devotion to and rationalization of poor-care, which occurred in the Sephardic diaspora communities in the seventeenth century.

The impoverishment of Ashkenazic Jewry occurred simultaneously with the establishment or reestablishment of communities in Western Europe by prosperous Sephardic merchants. As a result, the Western communities had the means as well as the motive to expand their philanthropic activity. Moreover, fear of gentile wrath was not the only motive prompting the Sephardic elites to care for the poor among them. In part, the Sephardim were perpetuating those characteristics of the traditional autonomous community that were still available to them. That is, although the Sephardim in France were organized as merchant guilds, and not as legally autonomous communities, they took care of many of their own needs, including not only religious affairs and education, but also poor-care. Although the practice of autonomous poor-care reached deep into the Jewish past, the methods employed by the Sephardim were new. From the mid-seventeenth century, the almoners of the Bordeaux Jewish community had a central poor-register, regularly inspected the recipients of aid, and made efforts to locate gainful employment and interest free loans for the poor.[10] A similar striving for efficiency characterized the Portuguese community in Amsterdam. A regulation of 1664 forbade, under pain of excommunication, all private donations to the "Ashkenazic" (that is, of German origin) and Polish poor.

Although, as we said above, fear of the Jewish poor as potential criminals was one motive behind such actions, there was also a strong element of ethnic prejudice, in that Ashkenazim were singled out from the resident Sephardic poor and accused of "vices, foreign to the morality and ways of Judaism."[11] The language employed by the Sephardic leadership in Amsterdam is significant for its emphasis on the alleged moral degradation of the poor Ashkenazim, who were said to be as impious as they are dangerous. Conceiving of poverty as a moral as well as an economic problem, the *Ma'amad* of the Portuguese community shared in the contemporary general currents of thought about poverty. Since morality, in the social thinking of the era, was closely associated with productivity, it is not surprising that the Sephardic elite sought to moralize the Ashkenazic poor by teaching them a useful trade. The society "Avodat Hesed," founded in Amsterdam in 1642, emphasized vocational training for the poor, but only so long as its purview was the Ashkenazim. When, after 1670, its focus switched to the Sephardic poor, the work requirements dropped from its agenda.[12]

Thus the modernization of Jewish philanthropy, like so many other aspects of Jewish life, occurred first among the Western Sephardim. This modernization was the result of both an external stimulus, that is, the economic dislocation of large segments of Ashkenazic Jewry, and changes in sensibility among the Sephardim about poverty, labor, and charity. In the Ashkenazic communities of Western and Central Europe, this change in sensibility began in the late eighteenth century. Confronted by their impoverished brethren, communal leaders in England, Alsace, the German lands, and Bohemia sought to rationalize poor-care by stanching the flow of Jewish vagrants, centralizing the distribution of alms, and forming strict criteria for the receipt thereof.

The rationalization of Jewish philanthropy in Europe was predicated on mixed feelings by the Jewish economic elite about their poor brethren. On the one hand, there was an undeniable humanitarianism and an acknowledgment that the Christian character of most public charity forced the Jews to care for their own. On the other hand, there was a common assumption that the poor, particularly the foreign poor, were parasitic and noxious. The most hostile views tended to come from progressively minded Jews championing educational reform and social integration. Such Jews accepted the connection, made first during the Enlightenment and then transmitted to nineteenth-century liberalism, between poverty, on the one hand, and unproductivity and immorality, on the other. Jews of a more traditional bent criticized the new Jewish philanthropic practices as inhumane; they saw the poor as deserving unfortunates and charity as a religious commandment to be practiced ungrudgingly. These distinctions between the purviews of Jewish and gentile charity, between the domestic and the foreign Jewish poor, and between progressive and traditionalist forces in the Jewish communities, all emerge clearly when we examine the modernization of Jewish philanthropy in Germany.

ENLIGHTENMENT, REVOLUTION, AND THE REGENERATION OF
THE JEWISH POOR: THE CASE OF GERMANY

With the growth of the *Haskalah*, or Jewish Enlightenment, in late eighteenth-century Prussia, came a bifurcation between progressive and traditional Jewish forces regarding poverty and poor-care. The radical reformer David Friedländer (1750–1834) compared foreign Jewish beggars to ill, and thus presumably dangerous, vagrants. He urged that "all foreign incoming beggars be held back, by the strongest means, already at the border of the Prussian state."[13] In 1809, the board of elders of the Berlin community, dominated by Friedländer and other supporters of the *Haskalah*, claimed that pregnant unmarried women were "an extraordinary burden on the community and its charitable institutions," and thus urged the chief of police to prevent poor pregnant Jewish women from entering the city. Four years later, Friedländer attempted to eliminate the subsidies paid to bastard children, who received aid from the Talmud Torah society, which provided a traditional education for poor children. The relatively lenient Orthodox Jews, who ran the Talmud Torah, however, refused to hand over the names of the recipients of their services.[14]

The rationalist spirit motivating the modernizers among the Berlin Jewish leadership was present throughout Germany during the first half of the nineteenth century. The German-Jewish press was filled with hostile depictions of the Jewish poor as cheeky beggars and con artists, a "cancer," as one correspondent put it, that requires radical treatment.[15] A particularly grim example of the new Jewish philanthropic ethos comes from proposals, published in 1840, to establish Jewish "industrial schools," which would combine military discipline, spartan living conditions, and rigorous labor. Beginning with five-year-olds, children should be kept in school from five in the morning until seven in the evening, taught a useful craft, which they will practice upon completion of their education. Uniform clothing, extended periods outside in cold and inclement weather, simple food, savings funds, and moral instruction would, the author proclaimed, bring about a far-reaching transformation of the Jewish lower orders.[16]

Although this Dickensian vision was never realized, a recent study of Jewish poor-care in Fürth has shown that the treatment of the Jewish poor could be harsh indeed. From the mid-1820s until German unification, the community provided very limited aid to strangers and vagabonds, and strove to keep non-resident Jews out altogether. Poor Jews were sent to the gentile communal workhouse, although kosher food and sabbath rest were not available to the inmates. Moreover, poor Jewish suicides were sent to the local hospital's dissecting theater despite

Jewish religious prohibitions against autopsies. Seeking to prevent the poor from bearing children, the community prohibited marriages if the groom was deemed unable to support a family, expelled pregnant unmarried women, and did not allow bastards into the communal orphanage.[17]

Harsh though they were, these policies were in keeping with the general tone of policies toward the poor in mid-nineteenth-century Bavaria, which featured the most stringent anti-pauper legislation in Germany. Not only among the Jews of Fürth, but in Bavaria as a whole, the receipt of charity was predicated on *Heimatsrecht*, a legal status that could only be acquired by birth in the municipality in question or by legislative decree therefrom. (This was an even stricter requirement than the three-years' residency required for the receipt of public charity in post-Napoleonic Prussia).[18] One should also take into consideration the precarious economic condition of Bavarian Jewry during the first half of the nineteenth century. Under these circumstances, the harshness of Jewish philanthropy in Fürth was the product of both real economic needs as well as a sharing in popular bourgeois prejudices regarding the poor.

The rationalizing philanthropic spirit had undeniable positive as well as negative manifestations. In Berlin, a poor-care commission, which brought together representatives from all the Jewish charitable associations, was created in 1837. The commission, one of its champions explained, was a necessary product of the age of occupational freedom, in which those capable of work can and must be found employment, and the truly invalid can be cared for separately. An applicant for aid from the poor-care commission was visited and examined by two of the commission's members. Whenever possible, the commission located work for those capable of it. Within a year of its establishment, out of 192 recipients of aid, almost half had been put to work, many in a communal laundry subsidized by the commission, and others in cottage-industry weaving, for which the commission supplied the materials.[19] In Hamburg, the move toward modern Jewish philanthropy began as early as 1788, in the wake of the creation by the municipality of a unifying institution for the gentile poor (*Allgemeine Armenanstalt*) and a ban against indiscriminate charity. The city compelled the Jewish community to assess its members for a monthly contribution for charity. The Jews, beset by beggars demanding direct payment, refused to make the contribution, which was thus transformed, during the first decade of the nineteenth century, into an obligatory poor-tax. In the wake of the French conquest of Hamburg in 1813, the community developed a wideranging philanthropic system with an emphasis on preventive measures, especially loans. Cash and in-kind benefits did not, however, go down, but steadily increased.[20]

The Berlin poor-care commission's public-works projects, and the steady climb in Jewish philanthropic spending in Hamburg, point to an important economic change affecting German Jewry during the first half of the 1800s. Although there were substantial numbers of paupers and vagrants, as an aggregate German Jewry was gradually becoming more affluent. The enormous gap between the handful of very rich court factors and the Jewish masses, which existed in the eighteenth century, slowly narrowed due to the creation of a German-Jewish commercial bourgeoisie. It was the growing wealth of the Jewish communities, as much as the poverty within them, which stimulated the growth of Jewish philanthropy throughout Germany.[21] In this sense, Ashkenazic Jewry in the nineteenth century replicated the experience of Western Sephardic Jewry in the seventeenth. The stark opposition of poverty and affluence, combined with rationalist and utilitarian sensibilities about the poor, provided Jews with the means as well as the motive to revolutionize the way they thought about and cared for the poor among them.

For some communal activists in Germany, the centralization of charity on the local level was not sufficient. In 1849, a long article in the progressive *Allgemeine Zeitung des Judentums* explained that the problem of Jewish vagrancy was too great for individual communities to solve on their own. In order to achieve *"Festhaltung und Fesselung"* of the poor, that is, to effectively deny them freedom of movement and enroot them in their home communities, there must be a coordination of local Jewish charitable associations on the district and regional level. The regional bodies would elect representatives, who would in turn be attached to the provincial diets. Although nothing came of this proposal at the time, some twenty years later came the formal establishment of the first national German Jewish organization, the *Deutsch-Israelitischer Gemeindebund* (German-Israelite Communal Federation), which considered the problem of the vagrant poor to be one of its principal concerns.

Underlying the growth of modern Jewish philanthropy in Germany was a complex, and at times contradictory, relationship with charity offered by gentiles. Until the middle of the nineteenth century, Jewish leaders assumed that they had to take care of their poor because no one else would. In the late 1780s, David Friedländer remarked that Prussian Jews received no benefit from public charitable institutions and were not admitted to the royal hospitals although they were required to contribute to them.[22] In Munich, beginning in the 1820s, if not earlier, the Jewish community contributed to general charity while shouldering the burden of supporting its own poor. During the Revolution of 1848, opposition to Jewish emancipation by municipal officials throughout Germany stemmed at least in part from a fear that emancipated Jews would demand public charity.[23] After mid-century, Jews began to be allowed access to public charity, but its availability varied from one locality to another.[24]

The uneven availability of public charity, however, was not the only factor maintaining the independence of Jewish philanthropy. The confessional quality of so much of what passed for "public" charity in nineteenth-century Germany, as in Europe as a whole, provided an additional reason for the maintenance of this independent network. Anger over missionary activity is well known to have stimulated modern Jewish political activity. The Mortara Affair of 1858, in which the Vatican did not allow for the return of a Jewish child who had been kidnapped by the child's Catholic maid, led to the creation, two years later, of world Jewry's first international political lobbying organization, the Alliance Israélite Universelle.[25] Similarly, the desire to keep vulnerable Jewish orphans and invalids out of Christian institutions strengthened the resolve to maintain and establish separate Jewish orphanages and hospitals.[26] In addition to suspecting the gentile authorities of harboring ulterior motives, Jewish leaders also felt at times that they simply could do a better job at caring for their poor. When Hamburg Jewry was formally emancipated in 1864, and the community's legal status was redefined, the majority of the communal leadership wanted to maintain control over poor-care rather than cede it to the municipality. The members of the Jewish poor-care commission claimed that they could provide more effective preventive welfare services than the state.[27]

For Ludwig Philippson, a prominent liberal rabbi and editor of the *Allgemeine Zeitung des Judentums*, the preservation of a separate Jewish philanthropy was essential not merely for instrumental reasons but for substantive ones as well. Protesting a call by an extreme liberal to dissolve all separate Jewish charity and meld it with public institutions, Philippson argued that Jewish charity must continue, partly because general charity does not suffice, but even more so because the Jews require an outlet for their charitable spirit and sense of obligation to their coreligionists.[28] In an article of 1847 on "The Essence of the Jewish Community," Philippson defined the community as a "corporation," which takes charge of not only its religious and educational life, but also its poor-care, which he described as a border zone "where religion and society adjoin." Although the philanthropic spirit is universal, Philippson wrote, it carries a confessional stamp; Jews operate in this spirit no less than Roman Catholics or Protestants. Stressing the "unity of religion and society," Philippson claimed that "[t]he mission of Judaism is therefore: not merely to teach the unity of God, but also the unity of religion and society, the idea and life." Until now, he wrote, the religious reform of Judaism and the social reform of the Jews have gone along separate tracks, but the time has come to combine the two. The *Gemeinde* (Jewish community), argues Philippson, is responsible for changing the poor economically and morally, that is, altering their entire way of life, including all their customs and habits. And the centerpiece of this philanthropic project, for Philippson, is vocational training that will promote occupational restructuring (*Berufsumschichtung*). Vocational training has a religious base in that it morally and spiritually improves the poor, allowing them to attain a truly "bourgeois existence."[29]

Philippson's association of philanthropy with economic regeneration was typical of an era obsessed with the social upheaval caused by peasant emancipation, the introduction of capitalist agriculture, and early industrialization. The notion that Jews had an ethical responsibility to solve the "social question" gained currency in the second half of the nineteenth century. Editorials in the *Allgemeine Zeitung* attest to this sentiment, be it in Philippson's statement of 1867 that "the social question is the religious idea of our time," or a later editor's proclamation in 1905 of the existence of a "social Judaism" akin to "social Christianity."[30] The general prescriptions offered by Jewish activists differed little from those coming from the German churches and municipal authorities. One encounters a universal assault against traditional charitable practices and a striving for efficiency. One also finds in Jewish philanthropic methods the same sort of evolution from a rationalized but purely reactive approach at the beginning of the empire to a more elaborate system of preventive social welfare after the turn of the century.[31]

The most important stimulus behind the development of Jewish social welfare in imperial Germany was the flood, beginning at the end of the 1860s and intensifying in the 1880s and following decades, of itinerant, impoverished Jews from the East. The *Deutsch-Israelitischer Gemeindebund* (DIGB), formally established in 1872, considered the problem of care for the vagrant poor to be one of its principal concerns. From 1899, the DIGB began to seek a national policy on care for the itinerant poor; the result was the establishment in 1910 of a central agency for the Jewish vagrant poor, consisting of representatives from major communities and several national and international Jewish organizations.[32]

The DIGB's actions represent only a small part of the phenomenal growth of Jewish philanthropic institutions during the Wilhelmine period. In 1889 there were twenty Jewish hospitals and sanitoria, ten retirement homes, and twenty-five orphanages in Germany. By 1913 there were 109 Jewish institutions for children, seventy-one hospitals and sanitoria, fifty-six retirement homes, thirty-four institutions for women's education, and twenty-two labor exchanges and workhouses.[33] These institutions, combined with the provisions for outdoor relief made by local poor commissions in virtually every German Jewish community, formed an intricate philanthropic network which scholars have tended to depict as denser and more generous than its non-Jewish counterparts. This may be so, but it is important to point out that no less a figure than Louis Maretzki, president of the German B'nai B'rith organization between 1887 and 1897 and an indefatigable Jewish philanthropist, worked under the assumption that Jewish organizations trailed the churches in the development of modern social welfare.[34] (I will refer to Maretzki frequently henceforth, because he is representative of a sizable number of Jewish philanthropists whom I have studied.)

The prewar development of Jewish social welfare in Germany would have been inconceivable without the B'nai B'rith. When first constituted in 1882, the B'nai B'rith's lodges contented themselves with the promotion of good fellowship, solidarity, and mutual aid among their brethren. Within a decade, however, a group of activists had started to push the Order away from its original philanthropic purview toward national social work. These activists defined social work as the very essence of the Order.[35] In many communities, B'nai B'rith lodges took the lead in providing social services such as labor exchanges, workshops, kindergartens, and holiday camps. The Order's women's societies played an indispensable role in the development of these services, particularly those that directly affected women and children. This concentration resulted at least in part from the attitudes of the B'nai B'rith's male executives, who accorded women a vital but highly circumscribed role in the solution of the social problem. Nonetheless, men in the B'nai B'rith leadership offered women only limited operational independence.[36] The Order's philanthropic activities on behalf of women were often initiated by men, and men held the highest positions therein. Notably, however, women were expected to manage matters on the local level.[37]

The B'nai B'rith epitomized nineteenth-century "associational Judaism," that is, a Jewish identity expressed through activity in sub- or extra-communal, voluntary social organizations. European historians have long emphasized the importance of associational life as the expression of a maturing bourgeois consciousness. One historian has documented the importance of what he called *Vereinskatholicismus* ("associational Catholicism") as a source of secular Catholic identity in Imperial Germany.[38] A *Vereinsjudentum* among Imperial German Jewry was equally strong. The attraction of associational Judaism in the decades before World War I is revealed by a study of Berlin Jewry carried out in 1909. It found that out of a population of 122,000, 20,141 belonged to at least one Jewish association, 1,090 to three associations, and 250 to six or more.[39] Throughout the 1800s, philanthropy had figured prominently among the activities of these associations, and toward the end of the century, their engagement with philanthropy deepened considerably.

To be sure, in the Jewish case the synchronic adoption of the bourgeois association coexisted with the diachronic retention of traditional notions of the sacred association, an integral component of the early modern Jewish community. Associational Judaism represented in part a secularized expression of group solidarity, wherein, for example, involvement in a local hospital association created a sense of communal sympathy akin to that gained by practicing the rabbinic commandments of ministering unto the sick and dead. As mentioned above, such associational identity was common enough in Christian society, but it was of particular importance to the leaders of Germany's small Jewish minority. For Maretzki, only social work, salutary both for the empathy its practice instills into the agent and for its healing effects on the social body, could revive the Jewish spirit.[40]

For some Jewish activists, however, philanthropic activity did not merely affirm Jewish identity but actually defined it. Just as the churches proclaimed that Christian ethics provided the answer to the social question, and interpreted Christian doctrine to support their views, so did Jews state that theirs was an inherently social-activist faith whose biblical and talmudic texts foreshadowed advanced policies of social welfare. The idea of a "Jewish mission" to embody rational religion in its purest form originated in the late eighteenth century, and during the decades before 1848 the mission assumed a specifically political connotation, calling upon Jews to fulfill their religious obligations by being exemplary citizens.[41] Under the empire, Jewish activists expressly associated their creed with an imperative to resolve social tensions. Statements to this effect abounded in the periodical and pamphlet literature of the time. Rabbinic sources were mined for appropriate citations, and no speech on "social Judaism" could refrain from piously invoking Moses Maimonides' celebrated medieval compilation of talmudic dicta on charity.[42] In keeping with general trends of modern Jewish secularization, Maimonides' statements about charity, which represent only the smallest fragment of his vast code of Jewish Law, were wrenched out of context and placed in the center of a new form of Jewish identity focusing on social action.

The discussion thus far has pointed to the many similarities between the Jewish philanthropic network in imperial Germany and its gentile counterparts. Except for their clientele, Jewish vocational programs and institutions of indoor relief, such as hospitals, orphanages, sanitoria, were not easily distinguishable from church-sponsored ones. Yet it is precisely the differences in clientele that point to significant structural differences between the Jewish and non-Jewish philanthropies. Throughout the nineteenth century, as German Jews gained ostensibly equal juridical and political rights, the Jewish community remained a legal entity with taxation powers and considerable responsibilities, including the welfare of its members. The emancipation of Frankfurt Jewry in 1864 came with the expectation that the Jewish community would continue to educate and succor its poor and ill members. Although the 1869 Industrial Ordinance of the North German Confederation technically permitted German Jews and foreign Jews on German soil to receive aid from non-Jewish charities, these charities were not forthcoming. The 1909 statutes of the Berlin Poor Commission, for example, explicitly required charities to send Jewish applicants to Jewish institutions.[43] Besides, itinerant Jews from Eastern Europe preferred Jewish instead of gentile charities, partly out of fear of gentile authority, and partly because Jewish charities provided higher levels of aid.[44]

The continuing distinctiveness of the Jewish community and the realization that it alone would provide essential social services furnished Jewish activists with an identity based on the notion of common struggle against a hostile environment. The Jews have been left on their own, wrote Maretzki, to fight the "struggle for existence" which modern capitalism and urban life have engendered. Moreover, wrote Maretzki, the B'nai B'rith must correct "defects which have nested in our national body" through "internal Enlightenment."[45] Jewish welfare work, then, was more than the latest manifestation of the Jewish charitable tradition or the assertion of Jewish identity through social action. It was also a response to what was perceived as a very real problem, a uniquely Jewish variant of the "social problem" that so worried the citizens of imperial Germany.

The aspect of the "Jewish social problem" most visible to German Jewish philanthropists was the plight of Eastern European Jewry. Jewish philanthropic efforts were directed primarily toward the two million Jews who entered Germany from the East during the Second Reich. These philanthropies did their utmost to expedite the movement of foreign Jews through the Reich, onto steamships and off to distant lands. The organization of the transatlantic migration of Eastern European Jews, along with the provision of services for those immigrants who stayed in Germany, produced not only a great expansion of philanthropic activity, but also an unprecedented degree of intercommunal, and indeed, international, coordination.[46] That is, the "Jewish social problem," which was a subset of the general problem of the laboring poor at the *fin de siècle*, stimulated the formation of a Jewish social policy, which at times imitated, and at times adumbrated, the social welfare policies of European states in the early twentieth century.

Jews, the saying goes, are just like everyone else, but more so. Our comparative approach to the study of modern Jewish philanthropy as a whole, and that of Germany's Jews in particular, has certainly pointed to a number of similarities between Jewish charitable activity and that of the gentile majorities in the Jews' host societies. We have observed a high degree of consonance between the methods of gentile and Jewish philanthropies, on the one hand, and between the socioeconomic sensibilities of their directors, on the other. At the same time, it is precisely a comparative study of the German case that makes us aware of the profound differences between the Jewish and gentile philanthropic spheres. We have noted the legal and social isolation endured by the Jews, even after Jewish emancipation, and the resulting precociousness of Jewish social welfare: the product of an enormous responsibility, placed on a community of some half-million souls, to succor millions of Eastern European immigrants with limited German governmental assistance. Finally, although philanthropic activity provided an important source of social identity to the middle classes in Germany as a whole, it was particularly important to an ethnoreligious minority struggling to maintain its identity in a frequently hostile environment. Such is the significance of Jewish philanthropy, not only in nineteenth-century Germany, but in the modern world as a whole: it seeks to solve the Jews' often overwhelming material problems, while, often unconsciously, addressing the Jews' identity problems, stimulating feelings of fellowship and solidarity that Jewish religious culture alone no longer provides.

NOTES

1. Ephraim Frisch, *An Historical Survey of Jewish Philanthropy from the Earliest Times to the Nineteenth Century* (New York, 1924), 118. For a similar tone, see the early chapters to Boris Bogen, *Jewish Philanthropy* (New York, 1917). For a more recent example of an essentialist and celebratory account of Jewish charity, see the entry "Charity" in the *Encyclopedia Judaica*, and in particular the section on medieval and modern charity by Isaac Levitats.

2. For an overall survey of early modern Jewish society, see Jacob Katz, *Tradition and Crisis: Jewish Society at the End of the Middle Ages* (New York, 1993); on the redemption of captives, see Selwyn Ilan Troen, "Organizing the Rescue of Jews in the Modern Period," Selwyn Ilan Troen and Benjamin Pinkus, eds., *Organizing Rescue: National Jewish Solidarity in the Modern Period* (London, 1992), 3–19.

3. The distinction between contextualist and comparative approaches to the study of modern Jewish history has been made by David Sorkin, "From Context to Comparison: The German Haskalah and Reform Catholicism," *Tel Aviver Jahrbuch für Deutsche Geschichte* XXI (1991), 23–58; and "The Case for Comparison—Moses Mendelssohn and the Religious Enlightenment," *Modern Judaism* XIV, 2 (1994), 121–38. Sorkin's analysis appears to indicate the beginning of a historiographical paradigm shift away from the highly contextualized quality of Jewish social historiography and toward a rethinking of the boundaries between Jewish and gentile culture. See David Biale, "Confessions of a Historian of Jewish Culture," *Jewish Social Studies*, n.s., I, 1 (1994), 43–45, and Amos Funkenstein, "The Dialectics of Assimilation," *Jewish Social Studies*, n.s., I, 2 (1995), 1–14.

4. Stuart Woolf, *The Poor in Western Europe in the Eighteenth and Nineteenth*

Centuries (London and New York, 1986); Thomas McStay Adams, *Bureaucrats and Beggars: French Social Policy in the Age of the Enlightenment* (New York, 1990); Bronislaw Geremek, *Poverty: A History* (Oxford, 1994).

5. Frisch, *Historical Survey*, 137–64; Bogen, *Jewish Philanthropy*, 25; "Hevra Kaddisha," *Encyclopedia Judaica* VIII, 442–46.

6. Frisch, *Historical Survey*, 127–28.

7. "Begging and Beggars," *Encyclopedia Judaica* IV, 387–91.

8. Jacob Katz, *Exclusiveness and Tolerance: Jewish-Gentile Relations in Medieval and Modern Times* (New York, 1961), 160–61.

9. Yosef Kaplan, "The Portuguese Community in Seventeenth-Century Amsterdam and the Ashkenazic World," *Dutch Jewish History* II (1989): 29–30, 37.

10. Arthur Hertzberg, *The French Enlightenment and the Jews* (New York, 1968), 155–57.

11. The language is from a document of 1639, cited in Kaplan, "The Portuguese Community," 30.

12. Kaplan, "Portuguese Community," 32–33.

13. David Friedländer, *Akten-stücke, die Reform der jüdischen Kolonien in den Preussischen Staaten betreffend* (Berlin, 1793), 147.

14. Steven M. Lowenstein, *The Berlin Jewish Community: Enlightenment, Family and Crisis, 1770–1830* (New York, 1994), 111–19.

15. *Der Orient* V, No. 19 (7 May 1844): 150. For another example of this type of writing about the Jewish poor, see the series of articles entitled "Jüdisch-soziale Fragen," by an anonymous author from Aachen, in the *Allgemeine Zeitung des Judentums* (hereafter, *AZdJ*) XIII, Nos. 8, 9 and 10 (19 February, 26 February, and 5 March 1849), 110–13, 118–20, 133–35.

16. *AZdJ* IV (1840): No. 22 (30 March), 322–24; No. 32 (1 August), 465–67; No. 33 (15 August), 475–77.

17. Claudia Prestel, "Zwischen Tradition und Moderne—Die Armenpolitik der Gemeinde zu Fürth (1826–1870)," *Tel Aviver Jahrbuch für Deutsche Geschichte* XXI (1991), 135–62.

18. Hermann Beck, "The Social Policies of Prussian Officials: The Bureaucracy in a New Light," *Journal of Modern History* 64 (June 1992), 279.

19. *AZdJ* II, No. 65 (31 May 1838), 261–63.

20. Arno Herzig, ed., "Die Juden in Hamburg 1780–1860," *Die Juden in Hamburg 1590 bis 1990* (Hamburg, 1991), 64–65; Anke Richter, "Das jüdische Armenwesen in Hamburg in der 1. Hälfte des 19. Jahrhunderts," *Die Hamburger Juden in der Emanzipationsphase (1780–1870)* (Hamburg, 1990), 234–54; Rainer Liedtke, *Jewish Charitable and Self-Help Organizations in Hamburg and Manchester, c. 1850–1914*, Ph.D. diss., St. Anthony's College, Oxford, 1995, 60–61, 92.

21. Jacob Toury, "Der Eintritt der Juden ins deutsche Bürgertum," in Hans Liebeschütz and Arnold Paucker, eds., *Das Judentum in der Deutschen Umwelt 1800–1850* (Tübingen, 1977), 224 ff.; Henry Wasserman, *Jews, "Buergertum," and "Buergerliche Gesellschaft" in a Liberal Era (1840–1880)*, (Ph.D. diss., Hebrew University, 1979), 85–87; David Sorkin, *The Transformation of German Jewry, 1780–1840* (New York, 1987), 114.

22. Friedländer, *Akten-Stücke*, 71.

23. Hendrikje Kilian, *Die Jüdische Gemeinde in München 1813–1871: eine Grossstadtgemeinde im Zeitalter der Emanzipation* (Munich, 1989), 168–69; Dieter Langewiesche, "Liberalismus und Judenemanzipation im 19. Jahrhundert," in Peter Freimark, Alice Jankowksi, and Ina Lorenz, eds., *Juden in Deutschland: Emanzipation, Integration, Verfolgung und Vernichtung, 25 Jahre Institut für die Geschichte der deutschen Juden, Hamburg* (Hamburg, 1991), 156.

24. In the *AZdJ* XVIII, No. 10 (6 March 1854), 115–16, we are told that Jews were now allowed access to general poor-care in Prussia and paid for its upkeep. In Magdeburg, for example, the Jewish poor receive public charity, and the city hospital is open to all. A retrospective piece on "Die jüdische Armenpflege" in the *AZdJ* XXXIX, No. 46 (9 November 1875), 739–40, notes that for decades Jews in some communities have had access to general charity, but in others, such as Berlin, they have not. In 1858, the Munich *Armenpflegschaftsrat* claimed that Jews were not excluded in principle from receiving general poor-care, but that they did not need it, as only one Jew was currently receiving a regular monthly allowance from the city. Kilian, *Die Jüdische Gemeinde in München*, 143.

25. On the impact of the Mortara affair on the founders of the Alliance Israélite Universelle, see Aron Rodrigue, *French Jewish, Turkish Jews: The Alliance Israélite and the Politics of Jewish Schooling in Turkey, 1860–1925* (Bloomington, Ind., 1990), 21.

26. On the fear of proselytism as one of the motives behind the founding of the Paris Jewish hospital in 1842, see Christine Piette, *Les juifs de Paris (1808–1840)* (Québec, 1983), 33. See also the Vienna Jewish newspaper *Die Neuzeit* of 25 October 1861, 91, for descriptions of Jewish children being proselytized in a gentile orphanage and hospital. The problem of proselytism was most grave in Palestine; the heavy Christian presence in Jerusalem stimulated Diaspora Jews to contribute vast sums to build Jewish workshops and hospitals so that destitute, sick, or otherwise vulnerable Jews would not fall into the clutches of the Church. See Mordechai Eliav, *Erets-Yisra'el ve-yishuvah ba-me'ah ha-yod-tet* [The Jewish Community in the Land of Israel in the Nineteenth Century] (Jerusalem, 1978), 232–38; and David Ellenson, *Rabbi Esriel Hildesheimer and the Creation of a Modern Jewish Orthodoxy* (Tuscaloosa, Ala., 1990), 110–13.

27. Over the protests of the Jewish leaders, the Hamburg Senate did, in fact, shift responsibility for poor-care from the Jewish community to the municipality. But the community was allowed to, and did, impose a voluntary annual levy so it could maintain its philanthropic network. Helga Krohn, *Die Juden in Hamburg, 1848–1918* (Hamburg, 1974), 58–60; Ina Lorenz, "Zehn Jahre Kampf um das Hamburger System (1864–1873)," *Die Hamburger Juden in der Emanzipationsphase 1780–1870*, Peter Freimark and Arno Herzig, eds. (Hamburg, 1989), 50–51; idem, "Die jüdische Gemeinde Hamburg 1860–1943," in *Die Juden in Hamburg*, ed. Arno Herzig, 78.

28. *AZdJ* XXXIX, No. 46 (9 November 1875), 739–40.

29. *AZdJ* XI, Nos. 21 and 22 (10 and 17 May 1847), 293–96 and 309–11.

30. Ludwig Philippson, cited in Jacob Toury, *Die politischen Orientierungen der Juden in Deutschland*, Tübingen, 1966, 161; Gustav Karpeles, editorial in the *AZdJ* LXIX, No. 41 (13 October 1905).

31. On the development of German philanthropy in the later 1800s, see C. Sachsse and F. Tennstedt, *Geschichte der Armenfürsorge in Deutschland,* Stuttgart, 1980; Rolf Landwehr and Rüdiger Baron, *Geschichte der Sozialarbeit: Hauptlinien ihrer Entwicklung im 19. und 20. Jahrhundert* (Weinheim and Basel, 1983); and Rüdiger vom Bruch, "Bürgerliche Sozialreform im deutschen Kaiserreich," *Weder Kommunismus noch Kapitalismus: Bürgerliche Sozialreform in Deutschland vom Vormärz bis zur Aera Adenauer,* Rüdiger vom Bruch, ed. (Munich, 1985); for parallels to Jewish philanthropy, see, for example, the comments of B'nai B'rith activist Benjamin Auerbach, "Die Aufgaben und Bestrebungen der Logen auf dem Gebiete der Wohlfahrtspflege und Fürsorgethätigkeit," *Festschrift zur Feier des zwanzigjährigen Bestehens des U.O.B.B. Herausgegeben von der Gross-Loge für Deutschland. 20. März 1902. Redigiert von San.-Rath. Dr. Maretzki* (Berlin, 1902), 52, 69. See also Aharon Bornstein, *Ha-kabtsanim: Perek be-toldot yehudei Germaniya* [The Beggars: A Chapter in the History of German Jewry] (Tel Aviv, 1992), which argues that the German-Jewish image of the Eastern Jewish immigrant changed over the period of the Second Reich from that of a shiftless vagabond to one of an unemployed laborer in need of social services.

32. *Mitteilungen vom DIGB,* No. 51, 1899, 14–15; No. 75, 1910, 1–2; No. 76, 1910, 19; No. 80, 1912, 39–40.

33. *Statistisches Jahrbuch des Deutsch-Israelitischen Gemeindebundes* (Berlin: 1889), 90–91; 1913, 238–39.

34. Compare Giora Lotan, "The *Zentralwohlfahrtsstelle,*" *LBIYB* IV (1959), 185–207; Bornstein, *Ha-kabtsanim,* Ch. 6 passim; and Stefi Jersch-Wenzel, "Minderheiten in der bürgerlichen Gesellschaft: Juden in Amsterdam, Frankfurt und Posen," *Bürgertum im 19. Jarhundert. Deutschland im europäischen Vergleich,* Jürgen Kocka, ed. (Munich, 1988), II, 404–405 n. 22; with Louis Maretzki, *Geschichte des Ordens Bnei Briss in Deutschland, 1882–1907* (Berlin, 1907), 182–83. Cf. the comments of a Dr. Rahmer, speaking at a DIGB *Gemeindetag,* that German Jews are behind their Christian neighbors in the development of a confessionally based health-care system. *Mitteilungen vom DIGB,* No. 10 (1882), 31.

35. Maretzki, *Geschichte,* 183–87. A similar development occurred simultaneously in the American B'nai B'rith. Leo Levi, the Order's president from 1899 to 1904, formalized and gave an ideological base to this turn. Deborah Dash Moore, *B'nai B'rith and the Challenge of Ethnic Leadership* (Albany, NY, 1981), 64.

36. For a full treatment of this issue, see Claudia Prestel, "Weibliche Rollenzuweisung in jüdischen Organisationen: Das Beispiel des Bnei Briss," *Bulletin des Leo Baeck Instituts* 85 (1990): 51–80.

37. Maretzki, "Die Frauen und der Orden," *Festschrift . . . des U.O.B.B.,* 81, 86–87.

38. Thomas Nipperdey, *Religion im Umbruch: Deutschland 1870–1918* (Munich, 1988).

39. "Jüdische Wohlfahrtspflege in Berlin," *Zeitschrift für Demographie und Statistik der Juden* V (1909): 75–78.

40. Maretzki, *Geschichte,* 186–87. On the relationship between philanthropy and modern Jewish identity, see Moore, *B'nai B'rith;* Phyllis Cohen

Albert, "Ethnicity and Jewish Solidarity in 19th-Century France," *Mystics, Philosophers, and Politicians: Essays in Jewish Intellectual History in Honor of Alexander Atmann,* Jehuda Reinharz and Daniel Swetschinksi, eds. (Durham, NC, 1982), 266; Nancy L. Green, "To Give and to Receive: Philanthropy and Collective Responsibility among Jews in Paris, 1880–1914," *The Uses of Charity: The Poor on Relief in the Nineteenth-Century Metropolis,* Peter Mandler, ed. (Philadelphia, 1990), 197–226; Sorkin, *Transformation of German Jewry;* and Marsha L. Rozenblit, *The Jews of Vienna, 1867–1914: Assimilation and Identity* (Albany, 1983), 148–50.

41. Cf. Max Wiener, "The Concept of Mission in Traditional and Modern Judaism," *YIVO Annual of Jewish Social Science,* 2–3 (1947/1948): 9–24; Uriel Tal, "German-Jewish Social Thought in the Mid-Nineteenth Century," *Revolution and Evolution: 1848 in German-Jewish History* (Tuebingen, 1981), 299–328; Sorkin, *Transformation of German Jewry,* 103–104.

42. Friedrich Wachtel, *Das Judenthum und seine Aufgabe im neuen deutschen Reich* (Leipzig, 1871); Adolf Kurrein, *Die sociale Frage im Judenthume* (Mülheim am Rhein, 1890); Benjamin Auerbach, "Die Aufgaben und Bestrebungen der Logen auf dem Gebiete der Wohlfahrtspflege und Fürsorgethätigkeit," *Festschrift . . . des U.O.B.B.*

43. Aharon Bornstein, *Mi-kabtsanim le-dorshei 'avoda: Yehudim navadim be-germania 1869–1914* [From Beggars to Seekers of Work: Jewish Migratory Poor in Germany, 1869–1914], (Ph.D. diss., Tel Aviv University, 1987), 181, 192–93, 222; Robert Liberles, "Emancipation and the Structure of the Jewish Community in the Nineteenth Century," *LBIYB* XXXI (1986), 63.

44. Bornstein, *Mi-kabtsanim le-dorshei 'avodah,* 194, 275–76. The case was similar, though not identical, in France; see Green, "To Give and to Receive," 197–98.

45. Maretzki, "Die Leistungen des Ordens," 20, 28; also *Geschichte,* 183. See also Auerbach, "Aufgaben und Bestrebungen," 69.

46. See Michael Just, *Ost- und sudosteuropäischen Amerikawanderung 1881–1914: Transitprobleme in Deutschland und Aufnahme in den Vereinigten Staaten* (Stuttgart, 1988); and Jack Wertheimer, *Unwelcome Strangers: East European Jews in Imperial Germany* (New York, 1987).

.10.

Mount Holyoke Missionaries and Non-Western Women: The Motivations and Consequences of Nineteenth-Century American Missionary Philanthropy

AMANDA PORTERFIELD

Before the Civil War, many of the American women who became involved in foreign missions believed that they shared a common future with non-Western women. The American women envisioned a worldwide sisterhood upon whose benevolent teachings a just and enlightened world would be built. One of the spokespersons for this vision was Mary Lyon, who founded Mount Holyoke Female Seminary in 1837. By making Mount Holyoke a national center of women's missionary education,[1] Lyon institutionalized the widespread New England belief that Protestant Christianity and women's education were interdependent. She believed that educated Protestant women would be the cornerstones of God's work of redemption, which she envisioned as an amiable, universal society rising over creation like a grand and harmonious building.

These closely linked commitments to Protestant conversion and women's education contributed significantly to the outburst of philanthropic activity that characterized New England culture in the mid-nineteenth century and helped shape the course of American philanthropy for decades to come. Among the principal causes of this extraordinary cultural investment in philanthropy were the opportunities for leadership and service that missionary activism offered women. Before 1860, men dominated the governance of the American Board of Commissioners for Foreign Missions and other organizations through which New Englanders funneled missionary time and money. Although women missionaries were listed only as wives or "Assistant Missionaries," women generated much of the work involved in missionary philanthropy and much of the enthusiasm behind it. Even as missionary women bowed to male authority, and missionary men often failed to acknowledge the extent of women's influence, women found opportunities for intellectual development, management training, and social activism in missionary work that were not easily obtained elsewhere.

In addition to enabling the philanthropic leadership and philanthropic service of women, missionary work brought New Englanders of both sexes into various forms of engagement with non-Western cultures. However poorly they may have understood these cultures, missionaries played important roles in processes of cross-cultural interchange and negotiation. These processes generated new forms of cultural identity and expression, involving new opportunities and new problems for non-Western peoples. This chapter examines some of these processes of cross-cultural interchange and negotiation by focusing on three locales—northwest Persia, western India, and southeast Africa—where Mary Lyon's students were active, and where the effects of American missionary intervention in the nineteenth century have played a role in shaping the world today.

In each instance, the response to missionary intervention was determined both by distinctive qualities within each culture and by the degree of stress to which each culture was subjected by external forces. In northwest Persia, the religious beliefs that Nestorian Christians shared with American missionaries drew Nestorians toward the Americans and away from the Muslim Persians, Turks, and Kurds who surrounded and dominated their culture. This affinity with missionary religion, together with the weakness of Nestorian culture, contributed to the erosion of Nestorian culture under missionary influence. In western India, long-standing tendencies to religious and cultural syncretism, along with a relatively high degree of cultural security and stability, enabled many Hindus to dismiss conversion to Christianity while assimilating missionary ideas about women's education and other aspects of social reform. In southeast Africa, pride in the spiritual strength of Zulu lineage, along with brutal military domination by Western powers, led many Zulu to resist missionary racism while accepting missionary protection.

In all three non-Western situations as well as in New England, women played important roles as mediators of new cultures. In these roles, women's identification with philanthropy was significant. Whether as American missionaries bringing change from outside, or as indigenous actors bringing change or working for stability from inside, women often acted out of concern and compassion for others. And whether as outsiders or insiders, women's philanthropic activity often bent or broke traditional rules for women's behavior, even when undertaken to conserve or re-cover cultural purity. Thus nineteenth-century women who engaged in new forms of philanthropic activity often became objects of controversy as well as mediators of new cultures.

Both Lyon's students and the women they tried to serve were caught up in dramatic forces of social change, and each group contributed to the creation of new cultures that combined missionary and traditional ideals. But non-Western women were also besieged, in varying degrees, by forces external to their own cultures that limited their opportunities to seize the momentum of social change. Lyon's students were far less bothered by forces external to their culture, and unlike their non-West-ern counterparts, they were committed to aggressive programs of evan-gelization. New England women also exerted more control over the momentum and direction of social change within their own culture than many of the other women discussed here. They enjoyed special advan-tages as beneficiaries of education and new developments in trans-portation, communication, and industry, all of which facilitated the dissemination of their evangelical worldview.

But all four groups of women shared concerns about improving their own lives and the lives of other women. Largely as a result of their expo-sure to missionary work, women in all four cultures developed new forms of commitment to the education and welfare of women within their own cultures, and new relationships with, and new knowledge about, women outside their own cultures.[2] These women also shared a similar allegiance to male authority and to idealized conceptions of reli-gious tradition and cultural stability through which that authority was defined. This allegiance to male authority offered respectability, sup-port, and a means of expressing loyalty to the religious traditions and cultural stability of their historic communities. It also limited women's awareness of the oppression they and other women faced, and under-mined many women's efforts to reach across cultures and identify with the needs of others.

THE AMERICAN MISSIONARY MOVEMENT AND THE PLACE OF MOUNT HOLYOKE WITHIN IT

Before the Civil War, American enthusiasm for foreign missions ema-nated principally from New England, where the American Board of Commissioners for Foreign Missions sent idealistic young people to es-tablish Protestant communities beyond Western Europe. While other

New Englanders traveled west along the Erie Canal and Ohio River to establish themselves in territories sparsely populated by Anglo Americans, missionaries booked passage eastward on Yankee merchant ships to what they hoped were the darkest corners of the heathen world. This mobility in both directions from New England occurred as new forms of industry, communication, and transportation developed, and as traditional village lifestyles characterized by self-sufficient economies, ministerial authority, and face-to-face consensus began to disappear. Hoping to combine the best of modern and traditional worlds by establishing a global network of tightly knit religious communities, missionaries laid plans for the universal implementation of traditional Puritan principles on which they believed the best elements of New England culture and the American republic were founded.

Missionary work held special appeal for New England women in a declining rural economy where new forms of economic production were replacing women's traditional domestic roles as makers of cloth, candles, soap, butter, and cheese, and where young women often faced the prospect of becoming economic burdens on their families. The missionary movement enabled such women to find useful work without descending into factory employment, and to elevate their social status by acquiring advanced education and professional competence as teachers. In their work as teachers, missionary women shared in the widespread concern for education that had been stimulated by early-nineteenth-century efforts to implement laws passed at the end of the eighteenth century that mandated public support for schools. The implementation of these laws improved the education of New England girls dramatically, created significant new demands for women teachers, and led to the establishment of new schools of higher learning, like Mount Holyoke, where women teachers could be trained.[3]

Mary Lyon understood the new opportunities for women teachers in early-nineteenth-century America as a highly significant example of God's work of redemption. "Without this wide and increasing field of usefulness," she wrote in 1837, "that would be a dark providence, which, by manufacturing establishments, has taken from families so much domestic labor, which had its influence in forming the character of our maternal ancestors." But "all the labor-saving machinery of the present day"[4] opened a brighter providence for women by freeing them for teaching, and for the personal development and service toward others that teaching offered. As a spokesperson for the connection between missionary work and female education, Lyon linked her efforts to provide advanced education to women of modest means to the religious goal of nurturing a spirit of missionary benevolence in her students that would enable them to contribute to the welfare of other women.

Lyon viewed teaching as one of the most important means of service to other women, and she understood service to others in the context of a long-standing Christian tradition of self-mortification. Although she did not mortify her body as some earlier Christian saints had, she strove to destroy her own pride and the pride of her students, and found service to others a means to that end. A missionary willingness to risk life, health, and comfort for the salvation of others exemplified the self-renunciation that characterized genuine love to God. Lyon's commitment to monetary support of missionary work also offered opportunities to experience the pain she associated with Christian virtue. She endorsed the "Bible standard of giving," which she defined as giving beyond "the point of poverty."[5] This self-sacrificial service to others was finally a means to the Christian's own salvation, but it also involved concern for others. Thus Lyon's program of strenuous giving led her students and teachers to identify with the poverty of other women, and missionary work enabled them to become committed to other women's well-being.

The unending nature of the missionary's own conversion added an element of equality to the process of converting others. With spiraling expectations and self-criticisms expected of Christian life, conversion was the work of a lifetime, in which moments of satisfaction prompted ever greater effort to deserve them. Missionaries had little tolerance for the "Egyptian darkness" in which non-Christians lived, and condemned the beliefs and rituals of all who did not share their theology. They were no less sanguine about the darkness of their own souls, and often criticized themselves for wickedness and idolatry. In addition to this equality of shared sinfulness that missionaries perceived between themselves and other women, the missionary desire to help women victimized by cruelty and superstition had an important referent in the efforts that missionary women made to strengthen their own lives. As some scholars have suggested, preconceived images of impoverished and degraded heathen women may have functioned for American missionary women as unacknowledged images of themselves—symbols both of their fears about their own vulnerabilities and just deserts, and of their hopes for their own relief and elevation.[6] While presumptuous and often uninformed, this identification with other women did carry an implicit call for equality, community, and compassion that stirred hopes for social justice both in missionaries and in many of the people with whom they worked.

NESTORIAN WOMEN IN PERSIA AND THE PROBLEM OF CHRISTIAN UNIVERSALISM

Soon after her arrival in the city of Urmiyah in northwest Persia in 1843, Lyon's protégée and one of the seminary's most popular teachers,

Fidelia Fiske, opened a Girls' Seminary modeled after Mount Holyoke. Fiske instituted a remedial version of the curriculum at Mount Holyoke, and special days were set aside for the two schools to join together in prayers. Teachers and students from Mount Holyoke sent gifts of various kinds to the Girls' Seminary in Urmiyah, and emotional letters flowed back and forth between the two schools. This correspondence figured importantly in the religious revivals Fiske generated among her students, as well as in the perpetuation of missionary fervor at Mount Holyoke. The revivals at Fiske Seminary spread to other sectors of the Nestorian community and helped forge a strong alliance between American missionaries and the Nestorian community. Defined by its deliberate concern for women's roles and attendant animosity to Islam, this alliance led not only to innovations in Nestorian culture, but also to tensions between the Nestorian community and the surrounding Muslim population. These tensions contributed in turn to Muslim animosity toward the United States and to widespread tensions between Christians and Muslims in the Middle East.

Americans educated in church history at the turn of the nineteenth century were familiar with Nestorius, the founder of the Old Church of the East, who was condemned as a heretic by Western bishops in 430 for his defense of the dual nature of Christ, and with the reputation of his followers as early missionaries to India and China. But until scouts for the American Board discovered them in 1810, Americans were unaware of the continued existence of Christians identified with his name and were delighted by the prospect of facilitating their spiritual renovation. American missionaries linked their own religious history to that of the Nestorians, dubbing them the "Protestants of Asia," and hoping to enable them in resuming their missionary role in the conversion of the East. Situated in a geographical crux between the Sunni Kurds and Turks to the west and the Shi'a Persians to the south and southeast, the Nestorians seemed providentially positioned to conquer the Islamic world with Christian knowledge and benevolence. Thus missionaries described the Nestorians as the "prop, upon which to rest the lever that will overturn the whole system of Muhammadan delusion."[7]

When the first contingent of permanent missionaries arrived in 1835, the Nestorians were living rather precariously as a subjugated religious minority. Under Islamic law, the Nestorians' right to exist and enjoy limited forms of self-government was recognized, but they were discriminated against through special taxes, restrictions against selling wares and produce in the bazaars, and prohibitions against engaging in forms of artistry other than carpentry or masonry. They were also subject to periodic attacks from the Kurds. But their vulnerability increased dramatically as their self-perceptions changed under American influence, and as Persians and Turks became alarmed at the political and social implications of American favoritism. The degree of security the Nestorians had enjoyed in the region disappeared. After the outbreak of violence against them in 1843, the Nestorians became more open to new religious attitudes from the West, and this further angered Persians and Turks.[8]

In their initial encounters with the Nestorian community, Fiske and her Holyoke assistant, Mary Rice, were shocked that parents celebrated the births only of sons, and that when asked how many children they had, parents did not include daughters in their count. This reticence about daughters was partly a matter of protecting them from exposure to men, especially from Muslim men, who under Persian law acquired rights to the wealth of a Christian family if a member of the family converted to Islam. But the absence of public enthusiasm at the birth of a daughter also reflected a belief in female inferiority widespread in Middle Eastern culture, as did the expectation that women should serve men and work for them, preparing food, but never eating until men were finished, and laboring long hours in the fields. When the first permanent American missionaries arrived in Urmiyah in 1835, the only Nestorian woman known to be literate was Heleneh, the sister of the Nestorian Church Patriarch Mar Shimon. The Nestorian women first approached by the missionaries had no interest in reading, which they considered outside the sphere of female activity. At least one woman turned down a missionary invitation to learn with the reply, "I am a woman."[9] But missionaries did not fully understand how the limited respect enjoyed by Middle Eastern women was tied to their adherence to foreign systems of male dominance, or fully appreciate the danger into which they led their converts by criticizing Middle Eastern culture.

Moreover, while American missionaries objected to notions of female inferiority prevalent in Middle Eastern culture, they had no intention of freeing women from subjugation to male authority. Emphasizing the Christian virtue of humility as a model for women's behavior, Fiske argued that a wife's submission to her husband should be based in affection rather than coercion. To women who came reviling their husbands and complaining of being beaten, she insisted, "I did not come to deliver you from your husbands, but to show you how to be so good that you can be happy with them." Appalled by the angry outbursts of Nestorian women, Fiske was critical of what she perceived to be the desire for mastery of men expressed by Nestorian women, and regarded their displays of passion as sorry evidence of what women were like without the gospel. She recalled one "virago, who often, single-handed, faced down and drove off Moslem tax-gatherers when the men fled in terror." Recognizing in this woman's "stinging shrillness" and "frenzied gestures" the reason "why the ancients painted the Furies in the form of women," Fiske was thankful for a gospel powerful enough to transform even a woman like that into a model of evangelical humility.[10]

In its replication of the religious and educational system at Mount Holyoke, Fidelia Fiske's seminary became a center for religious revivals in the Nestorian community, an outpost of American Protestant orthodoxy, and a staging ground for the implementation of ideas about the role of women in society that challenged traditional conventions of marriage and gender differentiation in Persia. Fiske Seminary played an important role in fueling what one scholar identified as "the single greatest source of conflict" between Christians and Muslims in Persia, namely, "attitudes toward women."[11] The growing distance of Nestorian attitudes toward women from traditional Middle Eastern attitudes associated with the dominant Muslim population came to symbolize the peculiarity of the Nestorians' community. Because of their special relationship to America, and their willingness to exchange some Middle Eastern concepts of womanhood for American ones, the Nestorians became objects of envy and hatred, and many in the community died violently. Many others fled or eventually emigrated to Europe and America.

One of the signs of the growing difference between Nestorians and Muslims was the change in the use of the veil as a marker of group difference. Before American intervention, Muslim women wore the veil far more often than Nestorian women. However, the veil seems to have been more a marker of social status than religion, since Muslim peasant women worked in the fields bareheaded,[12] and since, in the first years of American involvement, some Nestorian women veiled their faces in mixed company. Thus on the day of annual examination at the Female Seminary in 1850, missionaries arranged for men and women to eat together, and the women suffered through an awkward, transitional moment trying to get lamb and cake behind their veils and into their mouths.[13] Nestorian women who followed the Americans gave up the veil entirely and became more used to participating with men in conversation and eating. Once a sign of protected womanhood shared by Muslims and Nestorians, the veil in Urmiyah came to be an exclusive mark of the religious identity of Muslim women.

Actual hostility between Christians and Muslims developed in the related phenomenon of female sequestering. While polite social interchange between Nestorian men and women became more common, this new sociability did not extend to Muslims. As a result of American influence, Christian girls were freer to socialize with Christian boys, but Christian parents were still careful to restrict their daughters from contact with Muslim boys, warning them that any sign of friendliness might be interpreted as flirtation, and frightening them with stories of Christian girls who were captured and forced to marry Muslims. While the Nestorian concern to protect daughters from Muslim men predated the arrival of missionaries, the missionaries exacerbated this tension by facilitating increased socialization between the sexes in Nestorian culture, and by providing schools and events that catered primarily to Christians.[14]

Nineteenth-century missionary intervention in northwest Persia centered on a rejection of Middle Eastern attitudes toward women that was symbolized in terms of the alleged superiority of Protestant Christianity over Islam. This American disdain for Islam limited the salutary effect of American missionary philanthropy rather significantly. While the grievances suffered by women in Persia were indeed considerable, missionary responses to those grievances were confused by ignorance about Islam, fraught with peril for missionary converts, and instrumental in the construction of Islamic resentment of American culture.

WOMEN'S ROLES IN THE PROTESTANT REFORM OF HINDUISM

Missionary intervention in Maharashtra also produced a Protestant-inspired, reform-minded culture, but one with a very different historical outcome. Of all the missionary endeavors in which Lyon's students participated, their promotion of social reform in Maharashtra had perhaps the greatest benefit for non-Western women. In contrast to the Persian situation, where the weakness of Nestorian culture left the Nestorian people highly vulnerable to intellectual domination by missionaries, the strength of Hindu culture in Maharashtra enabled Hindu reformers to exploit missionary influence to an extraordinary degree. Thus missionary efforts in Maharashtra functioned as a catalyst for Hindu reforms in female education and other forms of social welfare, but also coincided with a significant degree of missionary failure to convert Hindus to Christianity.[15]

India had special appeal for American missionaries as "the place of Satan's seat." As the site of America's first foreign missionary venture in 1813, the Bombay mission occupied a distinctive place in American mission history. Despite meager success in securing conversions, the American Board expanded this mission in 1834, establishing an affiliated mission in Ahmadnagar, 120 miles west of Bombay. By 1854, the number of missionaries sponsored by the American Board in this region had risen to seventy-one. These evangelists disseminated millions of pieces of Christian literature, but out of a population of eight million Marathas, only "a few hundreds of men and women" had converted to Christianity.[16]

While they were relatively unsuccessful in facilitating conversions to Christianity during this period, American missionaries in Maharashtra established educational institutions and offered social services that became models for Hindu reformers, and posed moral challenges to Hinduism regarding the status of women, the morality of the caste system, and the abuses of priestly authority that stimulated Hindu movements of religious and social reform. "The fear of the Christian missionary," remarked the editor of the *Indian Social Reformer*, "has been the beginning of much social wisdom among us." Referring to the reform movement in Maharashtra as a new "school of 'Hindu Protestantism'" in a speech delivered in the 1890s, N. G. Chandravarkar credited the missionaries with bringing the "light" that brought about the "awakening among us on the subject of religion and society." According to Chandravarkar, this awakening was a renewal rather than a repudiation of Hinduism. In its authentic spirit, Chandravarkar believed, Hinduism embraced the best aspects of Christianity. "Christ, too, was a Bhakta," he asserted, referring to the Hindu concept of the saint, "and the law of love which he preached has been the cardinal principle of the Bhakti School."[17]

Mary Lyon's students had no more knowledge or appreciation of the Hindu religion than their male counterparts, but their demeanor conformed more closely to Hindu expectations of religious piety. Their respect for the authority of their husbands dovetailed with Hindu expectations of female piety, and their renunciation of worldly gain in order to find salvation for themselves and others was consonant with the well-respected Hindu state of *samnaysa,* in which pious individuals renounced their worldly life in order to devote themselves completely to religious life. While *samnaysins* typically left home to make pilgrimages or wander the countryside teaching about religious life, household *samnaysins* stayed married and owned property while fixing their minds on God. Lyon's students were pious women who owned few personal possessions and dedicated their lives to purifying themselves and teaching others, while affectionately respecting the dominant authority of their husbands. Thus the students conformed to Hindu expectations of a wife's devotion to her husband, as well as to certain Hindu notions of piety. This conformity helped to make their promotion of female education acceptable, even though it challenged Hindu custom.

The earliest American efforts to teach Hindu girls were greeted with incredulity. In Bombay in the early 1830s, Caroline Read's "efforts to get up a girls' school, were treated by the natives as a perfect absurdity, and by some scoffed at." According to her husband Hollis, "She was asked if she supposed a *donkey* could be taught to read!" As a last resort, Hollis admitted, his wife had paid her students ten pice a week to attend school. The activities in the schools Caroline supervised "were narrowly watched" by Brahmins, who almost succeeded in destroying the schools by circulating the story that Caroline planned to sell some of the girls as slaves. In 1839, the idea of female education still had not made much headway. Sendol B. Munger expressed little optimism with regard to his wife Maria's efforts to introduce reading among the women of Jalna: "The subject of female education is so novel a thing in this place, that she cannot expect to proceed very rapidly."[18]

During the 1840s and early 1850s a sea change in Hindu opinion occurred. In 1850, Robert Hume reported from Bombay that "One of the most encouraging signs of the times in India, is the change which is gradually taking place, in the feelings of the people, in regard to female education." The following year, missionaries in Ahmadnagar reported that "Female education is becoming more and more popular." By 1854, the journal of the American Board could report that in Maharashtra, "a great change has taken place in the sentiments of the people regarding female education. When the missionaries began this work, they encountered great and general opposition. But now the most influential natives subscribe for the support of female schools, attend the examinations, and even send their own daughters to receive instruction."[19] However, the expectations of missionaries differed considerably from those of Hindu students and their families who were involved in mission schools. While missionaries viewed education as laying the groundwork for conversion, many Hindus prized the knowledge and skills imparted in mission schools, but were firmly resistant to conversion. As one historian of this situation noted, Marathas who were interested in social change "quietly exploited" the skills of missionary women.[20] Thus the hope cherished by Lyon's students that education would enable upper-caste Maratha women to play a foundational role in the Christianization of India never materialized, but the impact of American missionaries on women's education was significant. As one Indian scholar claimed, "The credit for pioneering the cause of female education in the early-nineteenth century goes to Christian missionaries."[21]

Missionary arguments for women's literacy were appropriated by Maratha Hindus proud of a regional culture in which widow burning and female infanticide were rarities. Furthermore, the *zenanas* that secluded women from public life in the Punjab and Bengal did not exist. Galvanized by missionary efforts, scholars at the Hindu College in Poona, the traditional seat of religious learning in Maharashtra, appropriated and recast Western ideas in a Hindu context, and became leaders of a national movement for Hindu reform. Among the religious thinkers at Poona, a Hindu "school of thought developed with a constructive program for social and political advancement" that, as one historian put it, "dominated the course of the nationalist movement for several years."[22]

The Hindu reform movement in Maharashtra included a number of prominent women in the late nineteenth and early twentieth centuries—such as Lakshmibai Tilak, Pandita Ramabai, Anandibai Karve, Parvati Athavale, and Leelabai Patwardhan. The most well-known of these women reformers was Pandita Ramabai, who founded the Arya Mahila

Samaj in Poona in the early 1880s to improve the condition of women. Although Ramabai converted to Christianity after a visit to the United States in the late 1880s, she had been educated by reformist teachers concerned to make female education part of Hindu tradition, and by the time she was twelve, she could "recite twenty thousand Sanskrit verses by Heart." Branches of the Arya Mahila Samaj were established in various parts of Maharashtra, and contributed to the region's leadership in the movement for national reform and freedom.[23]

Although the gains for women were considerable, the personal writings of Ramabai and other Maratha women reformers reveal the emergence of a new kind of difficulty as well. According to one historian, the reforms in women's education and marriage stimulated by missionaries led to "the recognition of a woman's individuality," but also weakened extended family ties and "made the husband the centre of the woman's world." As a result, women associated with reform were more isolated from extended family networks than conservative Hindu women, and more dependent on their husbands. Thus, even though they stimulated improvements in women's education, individuality, and freedom, American missionary women in Maharashtra generated new problems of isolation and alienation for women, whose traditional culture revolved around large joint families, a network of female companionship, and domestic community.

THE DILEMMAS OF CHANGE FOR ZULU WOMEN

This double-edged effect of missionary intervention was even more clearly pronounced for Zulu women in Natal. As in Maharashtra, the missionary emphasis on women's education and companionate marriage held forth the possibility of freeing women from some of the difficulties under which they labored in traditional culture, while distancing them from customary networks of social support. But in Natal, the difficulty of this situation was exacerbated by the instability of Zulu culture, and by destructive military, political, and economic forces that challenged every effort the Zulu people made either to preserve their culture or to embrace Christianity and Western forms of social progress. In this often desperate situation, Zulu women were torn between loyalty to traditional culture and hope for social progress. Their choices included shoring up traditional culture against disintegration or fending off the grinding poverty, racial discrimination, and breakdown of family life that accompanied efforts to participate in Westernization. A new culture did emerge to meet these challenges, and this culture drew on both Protestant Christianity and Western education. But its leaders often distanced themselves from American missionaries, who responded too little and too late to the problems that Africans faced.

When American Protestant missionaries first entered Zululand and Natal in the 1830s, the Zulu people were in a state of considerable stress. Amidst ecological crises caused by drought and competition for scarce resources and fear of European traders seeking ivory, skins, and slaves, Zulu kings exerted unprecedented authority, and organized dozens of clans and chieftainships into a Zulu state. The Zulu monarchy held sway in southeast Africa until 1837, when the Dutch Voortrekkers, or Boers, invaded Natal in a quest for free land and free African labor. Although shocked, weakened, and dependent on the menacing authority of the Voortrekkers, the Zulu state was not completely broken when the Americans began their work, and many social and religious customs remained intact.[24]

Under the protection of the British, who assumed control of Natal in 1842, emissaries of the American Board were the first, and for several decades, most dominant missionaries in Natal. In 1850, they had twelve stations, more than thirty missionaries, a number of churches and schools, and several published texts in the Zulu language. In the 1840s, refugees and renegades from the Zulu state flocked to the American mission stations in Natal in considerable numbers. But in the 1850s, the crowds at missionary services dwindled as Africans learned how hostile the missionaries were to their tribal customs. As the spokesman for one group of men put it to Lewis Grout in 1852, "we black people do not like the news which you bring us. . . . You trouble us—you oppose our customs, you induce our children to abandon our practices, you break up our kraals and eat up our cattle, you will be the ruin of our tribe."[25]

Issues concerning the behavior and appearance of women were central to encounters between missionaries and African traditionalists, and both sides insisted on the moral rightness of their own culture's view of women's roles. The letters of Lydia Bates Grout, one of four of Mary Lyon's students in Natal, describe the missionaries' preoccupation with women's conformity to New England concepts of womanhood. Grout treated the traditional custom of going about barebreasted as a barrier to both conversion and education, and spent much of her time with Zulu women teaching them how to sew New England–style clothes. Moreover, she insisted that her students learn to sew in straight lines, even though this procedure was difficult and unpleasant for them, and even though she was aware that curved lines were omnipresent in Zulu culture and fundamental to the Zulu aesthetic.[26] Grout and other American missionaries also required conformity to Protestant expectations for women's role in marriage, and regarded Zulu marriage customs, which included polygamy and cattle exchange, as the epitome of heathenism's degradation of women. While the liberal Anglican Bishop Coenso defended the practice of baptizing polygamists in Natal, American missionaries made the relinquishment of traditional marriage customs an absolute prerequisite for baptism.

American missionaries interpreted the exchange of cattle at marriage as evidence that the Zulu treated women as chattel, purchased from their fathers and sold to the highest bidder at the time of marriage. But the Zulu custom of *lobolo* was in fact a complex ritual of fundamental religious and social importance in which the actual exchange of cattle was only a part. The people regarded their ancestral shades as the real owners of cattle, and invested the cattle dedicated to the shades with spiritual significance; their milk was imbued with the power of the shades, and they could be sacrificed to the shades only in times of need or thanksgiving. The exchange of cattle in *lobolo* compensated the shades of the bride's family for the loss of the bride's future children, who would now grow up as scions of the husband's shades. The cattle also served as an insurance policy for the bride's mother, compensated her for the pain she suffered in bringing children into the world, and enabled her to establish a hut for herself when the time came for one of her husband's sons to become head of the lineage and its kraal.[27]

The Zulu were no less offended by sexual promiscuity than American missionaries; traditional Zulu custom imposed a standard of morality and sexual purity on men and women that ensured women's respectability, provided a certain degree of safety, and established the basis for children's well-being. Sexual propriety and discipline were so obvious in traditional society that even missionaries acknowledged it. Thus one missionary observed that, with the exception of polygamy, which he viewed as a system of male licentiousness, "the Zulus have not their equal . . . for purity in any nation upon the globe, pagan or Christian."[28]

For the Zulu, the sexual act was a religious event in which the husband carried out the desires of ancestral shades by "working with his wife" to conceive a new offspring. As a twentieth-century traditionalist explained, "it is their (the shades') work the man is doing when he is hot." With the shades at work and the ancestral lineage and its future incarnation at stake, sex was serious business. Opportunities did exist for unmarried people to engage in sexual play, but this was supposed to stop short of coitus, and young women who became pregnant without the proper rituals of marriage were regarded as spoiled. The sympathy that missionaries extended to the numerous girls who ran away to mission stations seeking escape from prospective marriages offended many people's sense of religious propriety, and the suspension of traditional sexual behavior at mission stations contributed to the reputation of these places as dens of vice and witchcraft.[29]

Most Zulu women who came into contact with the first generation of American missionaries resisted missionary ideas and asserted their loyalty to ancestral shades and to the complex ritual of *lobolo*, but some were drawn to Christianity. Young women escaping bad marriages or unwelcome prospects of marriage fled to mission stations, and violence was often a factor in their lives. The missionaries' first converts were often women, and Christianity continued to appeal to women in greater numbers than men. In a society that was decidedly patriarchal, the Gospel's egalitarian ring appealed especially to women. Although missionary society was also patriarchal, the language of Christian grace and redemption held forth a possibility of freedom of expression and gender equality that transcended missionary interpretation. According to Jean and John Comaroff, "the egalitarian rhetoric of the gospel" in all parts of southeast Africa "seems to have had a much greater and quicker impact on females than males."[30]

But ironically, the missionary desire to liberate African women from the patriarchal oppression imposed by Zulu religion obscured the importance of women's roles in Zulu society and their limited but traditionally sanctioned opportunities for protection, wealth, and status. Missionary efforts to undermine *lobolo* not only threatened the structure of family and gender relations but also the customary means by which women obtained influence in a patriarchal society. While the Zulu had once been renowned for their universal restraint from casual or unsanctioned sex, by the early twentieth century, sexual promiscuity became a problem that concerned missionaries and African Christians as well as traditionalists. Premarital pregnancies rose sharply with the decline of sex-based initiation groups that instructed young people in the rituals of proper sexual activity, and with the breakdown of patriarchal authority and supervision as mining and other forms of industry drew men away from their homes.

During Pentecost in 1912, missionaries pressed the older women associated with the church in Groutville to exert greater control over their daughters and to end the custom of premarital sexual play. Thus began the *isililo,* or mother's prayer association, which became an important part of twentieth-century African Christianity. In 1919, Sibusisiwe Makhanya, a Zulu woman who had been schooled by Americans, founded the Bantu Purity League for the purpose of controlling the sexuality of young women. The Bantu Purity League encouraged mothers to assume greater control over their daughters and take charge of their sexual education, which had traditionally been managed by female initiation groups and paternal relatives.[31]

In the late nineteenth century, British labor policies drew Africans from Zululand and Natal to mines and cities in increasing numbers, and a proletarian system developed in which Africans were the low-paid workers of an industrialized capitalist society. As African life became increasingly confined within this system, British officials began to look more favorably on the conservative Zulu royal family. Exploiting the respect commanded by the royal family, the British came to view its members as spokespersons for a permanently primitive subculture within white-ruled society. At the same time, the ethnographic term "Bantu" came to be used as the blanket term for most of the indigenous peoples of southeast Africa, and American missionaries participated in efforts to recreate certain elements of traditional African culture.[32]

African women found themselves caught between this reformulated traditional culture, in which British *lobolo* laws and failing kinship structures reduced women's avenues of influence, and an aggressive Christianity that promoted nuclear-family domesticity and conflicted with women's efforts to obtain authority by traditional means. But if African women were subject to a double set of patriarchal religious traditions, neither tradition was devoid of resources for women, and both contributed to the outlook of women who became leaders of less colonized forms of Bantu culture.

The work of Sibusisiwe Makhanya illustrates this point. Born in 1894, she attended the Girls' Seminary at Inanda, which was modeled after Mount Holyoke. She then enrolled in the American Teacher's College at Amanzimtoti and returned to Inanda as a teacher. Makhanya founded the Bantu Purity League in 1919 to protect the safety and reduce the promiscuity of African girls. She received a scholarship from the Phelps-Stokes Fund in New York and attended a Quaker teacher-training school in South Carolina. But she resisted the ideology of accommodation to white supremacy associated with Booker T. Washington and his Euro-American proponents, severed ties with Phelps-Stokes, and enrolled at Columbia Teacher's College along with other Africans who were disaffected with education in the American South. Returning to Natal in 1930, she organized a youth movement, a social center, and a school at Mbumbulu designed to introduce Western innovations in education, communication, and economic production within the context of revitalized traditional customs. In the late 1930s she was a leader of the Zulu Society, founded to restore and modernize traditional Zulu concerns for discipline and male authority.[33]

Makhanya's leadership cannot be understood apart from her dual heritage as an American-educated Protestant and a Zulu woman. Both traditions provided resources for her conception of herself and her vision of African society. And both traditions provided ideal concepts of cultural stability rooted in male authority. It may be ironic that one of her central concerns was the revitalization of this authority, but Makhanya's work represented a common point of agreement between the two traditions. While differences between male authority in missionary and Zulu culture kept missionaries from appreciating any underlying similarity, Makhanya's immersion in both cultures led to her creative role in developing a new culture drawn from both traditional and missionary ideals and deliberately predicated on a commitment to male dominance.

CONCLUSION

Interactions between New England missionaries and non-Western women had significant impact on the lives and cultures of non-Western women, and figured importantly in the early exportation of American culture to the Middle East, India, and Africa. But the impact of Lyon's students and their missionary colleagues in these regions was often contrary to their intentions. Thus in Persia, American missionary efforts to reform Nestorian culture led to the decline of that culture. In Maharashtra, American missionary efforts to promote female literacy contributed to a revitalization of Hinduism. And in Natal, American missionary education helped establish an African Christian elite that chafed against missionary domination. Thanks to the competing power of traditional cultures, and the creative use to which the people of those cultures put the ideas introduced by missionaries, the failure of missionaries to realize their intentions was not without positive outcome. Missionary intervention contributed to the creation of new cultures formed from elements of both traditional and missionary cultures, and in each case, the degree to which missionaries failed to control a new culture was directly tied with that culture's success.

The missionary urge for control was expressed through the aggressively authoritarian quality of orthodox New England theology. This theology drove Americans out of the isolation of their own traditional culture into commitment to the well-being of people in other cultures. It also fueled missionary hostility to non-Protestant religions, and fostered a form of self-righteousness that was all the more pernicious for being hidden from its proponents.

Preoccupation with self-sacrifice skewed missionary thinking, making it possible for missionaries to overlook the arrogance involved in their disdain for other beliefs and to overlook the conflict between this disdain and their commitment to benevolence. The religious and cultural imperialism permitted by this preoccupation with self-sacrifice was deeply tied to commitment to male dominance, which it helped to support. Through this investment in male authority, missionary self-sacrifice also involved investment in the culture in which that authority was enshrined. These commitments prevented missionary women from seeing the underlying commonalities between their own lives and the lives of non-Western women. Despite being prepared for such insight by the advanced education and deliberate cultivation of sisterhood at Mount Holyoke, Lyon's students in Persia, India, and Africa failed to see that they shared with non-Western women a belief in maternal responsibility for maintaining religious tradition and cultural stability, and a loyalty to male authority as an essential aspect of religious tradition and cultural stability.

But at the same time, the concept of benevolence introduced by American missionaries carried salutary impulses to which important elements of today's global consciousness can be traced. In their focus on female literacy and the promotion of women's education, nineteenth-century missionaries were often the first to call attention to the importance of women's roles in the process of social development and reform. In addition, the missionary concept of worldwide sisterhood carried with it the powerful notion that women could be tied to each other across cultures, and obligated to one another through common concerns.

NOTES

1. When Lyon died in 1849, twenty-seven alumnae had become foreign missionaries, and eight had become missionaries to American Indian communities. The next year, the total rose to forty. In 1859, the American Board listed sixty Mount Holyoke alumnae on its rolls, and Baptist and Presbyterian boards listed others. In 1887, fifty years after Mount Holyoke's founding in 1837, one-fifth of all women then serving as American Board missionaries were Holyoke alumnae. See Elizabeth Alden Green, *Mary Lyon and Mount Holyoke: Opening the Gates* (Hanover, N.H.: University Press of New England, 1983; orig. 1979), 264; Edward Hitchcock, ed., *The Power of Christian Benevolence Illustrated in the Life and Labors of Mary Lyon* (Northampton: Hopkins, Bridgman, and Company, 1852), 346.

2. Of course, American missionary women were not alone in triggering these developments; in India especially, British missionary women led the way in inaugurating interchange between Western and non-Western women. But in light of the global power that U.S. culture attained after World War II, the emergent characteristics of American influence in non-Western cultures, and their persisting legacies, take on special interest.

3. David F. Allmendinger, "Mount Holyoke Students Encounter the Need for Life Planning, 1837–1850," *History of Education Quarterly* 19 (spring, 1979), 27–43; Kathryn Kish Sklar, "The Founding of Mount Holyoke College," *Women of America: A History*, ed. Carol Ruth Berkin and Mary Beth Norton (Boston: Houghton Mifflin, 1979), 177–201; and Linda K. Kerber, *Women of the Republic: Intellect & Ideology in Revolutionary America* (Chapel Hill: University of North Carolina Press, 1980).

4. Mary Lyon, *General View of the Principles and Design of the Mount Holyoke Female Seminary*, February 1837.

5. At Mount Holyoke, Lyon and her teachers established a model of giving that involved significant contributions to the seminary's annual mission fund from salaries already set at deliberately penurious levels. Lyon led the way in this strenuous giving, contributing $90 to the annual mission

fund from her salary of $200 a year. In 1843–44, Lyon's twelve teachers received, on average, a yearly salary of $150, of which they donated, on average, almost $30, or 20 percent. See Green, *Mary Lyon*, 254.

6. See Joan Jacobs Brumberg, "The Ethnological Mirror: American Evangelical Women and Their Heathen Sisters, 1870–1910," *Women and the Structure of Society: Selected Research from the 5th Berkshire Conference on the History of Women*, ed. Barbara J. Harris and JoAnn K. McNamara (Durham: Duke University Press, 1984), 108–28; also see Leslie A. Fleming, "A New Humanity: American Missionaries' Ideals for Women in North India, 1870–1930," *Western Women and Imperialism: Complicity and Resistance*, ed. Nupur Chaudhuri and Margaret Strobel (Bloomington: Indiana University Press, 1992), 191–206; and Barbara Fassler, "The Role of Women in the India Mission, 1819–1880," *Piety and Patriotism: Bicentennial Studies of the Reformed Church in America, 1776–1976*, ed. James W. Van Hoeven (Grand Rapids: William B. Eerdmans, 1976), 149–91.

7. Quoted in Justin Perkins, *A Residence of Eight Years in Persia, among the Nestorian Christians; with Notices of the Muhammedans* (Andover: Allen, Morrill & Wardwell, 1843), 26–27. Also see Robert E. Speer and Russell Carter, *Report on India and Persia of the Deputation Sent by the Board of Foreign Missions of the Presbyterian Church in the U.S.A. to Visit These Fields in 1921–1922* (New York: Presbyterian Missions Board, 1922), 315–576; Julius Richter, *A History of Protestant Missions in the Near East* (New York: AMS Press, 1910), 294–317; P.E. Shaw, *American Contacts with the Eastern Churches, 1820–1870* (Chicago: American Society of Church History, 1937), 71–108; and *The Concise Oxford Dictionary of the Christian Church*, ed. E. A. Livingstone (New York: Oxford University Press, 1977), 354–55, 510, 258, 104.

8. Richard Merrill Schwartz, *The Structure of Christian-Muslim Relations in Contemporary Iran*, Occasional Papers in Anthropology No. 13 (Halifax, Nova Scotia: Saint Mary's University, 1985), 41–55; also see Thomas Laurie, *Woman and Her Savior in Persia* (Boston: Gould and Lincoln, 1863), 14; and John Joseph, *The Nestorians and their Muslim Neighbors: A Study of Western Influence on their Relations* (Princeton: Princeton University Press, 1961).

9. Laurie, *Woman and Her Savior*, 18–19; Schwartz, *Structure of Christian-Muslim Relations*, 50, 17–19.

10. Laurie, *Woman and Her Savior*, 20–21. Also see *Nestorian Biography: Being Sketches of Pious Nestorians, Who Have Died at Oroomiah, Persia*, by Missionaries of the ABCFM (Boston: Massachusetts Sabbath School Society, 1857), 25–26.

11. Schwartz, *Structure of Christian-Muslim Relations*, 77–78.

12. See Sima Bahar, "A Historical Background to the Women's Movement in Iran," *Women of Iran: The Conflict with Fundamentalist Islam*, ed. Farah Azari (London: Ithaca Press, 1983), 171.

13. Laurie, *Woman and Her Savior*, 224.

14. Muslim children were welcome in missionary schools, and some elite Muslim families chose Christian schools because of the literary and scientific education they offered, but the religious orientation of mission schools was unattractive to the vast majority of Muslims. See Schwartz, *Structure of Christian-Muslim Relations*, 77–80.

15. See Charles H. Heimsath, *Indian Nationalism and Hindu Social Reform* (Princeton: Princeton University Press, 1964), 9–106; Govind Sakharam Sardesai, "Maharastra Dharma—The Ideal of the Marathas," *The Main Currents of Maratha History* (Patna: Patna University, 1926), 1–29; Datto Vaman Potdar, "Mind of Maharashtra," *Journal of the University of Poona* 9 (1958), 57–64.

16. *Minutes of the General Meeting of the American Missionaries of the Bombay Presidency, Held at Ahmednuggur, December, 1854* (Bombay: American Mission Press, 1855), 56–57; Clifton Jackson Phillips, *Protestant America and the Pagan World: The First Half Century of the American Board of Commissioners for Foreign Missions, 1810–1860* (Cambridge: Harvard University Press, 1969), 32–56; *Memorial Papers of the American Marathi Mission, 1813–1881* (Bombay: Education Society's Press, 1882), ix–xi; R. V. Modak, "History of the Native Churches Connected with the Marathi Mission, and especially those in the Ahmednagar Districts, for the last 50 years," *Memorial Papers of the AMM*, 11.

17. Heimsath, *Indian Nationalism*, 51–53; quotations from 53 and 52.

18. Letter from Mr. Munger, October 15, 1839, *Missionary Herald*, 36 (1840), 275; Hollis Read, "The American Mission," *Memorial Papers of the AMM*, 8. While London missionaries organized the first girls' schools in Calcutta, Americans introduced female education in western India, establishing a girls' school in Bombay in 1824.

19. Letter from Robert Hume, Bombay, June 25, 1850, *Missionary Herald*, 46 (1850), 369–70; Report from Ahmednuggur, *Missionary Herald*, 47 (1851), 269–270; Report from Mr. Hume in Bombay, May 19, 1854, *Missionary Herald*, 50 (1854), 275.

20. Charlotte Staelin, *The Influence of Missions on Women's Education in India: The American Marathi Mission in Ahmadnagar, 1830–1930* (Ph.D. diss., University of Michigan, 1977), 141, 232, 265, 268, 140; quotation from 140.

21. Sushil Madhava Pathak, *American Missionaries and Hinduism: A Study of their Contacts from 1813 to 1910* (Delhi: Munshiram Monoharlal, 1967), 61.

22. Caroline Healey Dall, *The Life of Dr. Anandabai Joshee, A Kinswoman of Pundita Ramabai* (Boston: Roberts Brothers, 1888), 38; Kenneth Ballhatchet, *Social Policy and Social Change in Western India, 1817–1830* (London: Oxford University Press, 1957), 250; Heimsath, *Indian Nationalism*, 16–17.

23. Jyotsna Kapur, "Putting Herself into the Picture: Women's Accounts of the Social Reform Campaign in Maharashtra, mid-Nineteenth to Early Twentieth Centuries," *Manushi* 56 (1990), 28–37; Manmohan Kaur, *The Role of Women in the Freedom Movement, 1857–1947* (Delhi: Sterling Publishers, 1968), 86–89; quotation from 86.

24. Elizabeth A. Eldredge, "Sources of Conflict in Southern Africa, c. 1800–30: The 'Mfecane' Reconsidered," *Journal of African History* 33 (1992), 1–35; James Gump, "Origins of the Zulu Kingdom," *The Historian*, 50:4 (August, 1988), 521–534; Jeff Guy, "Ecological Factors in the Rise of Shaka and the Zulu Kingdom," in *Economy and Society in Pre-Industrial South Africa*, ed. Shula Marks and Anthony Atmore (London: Longman, 1980), 265–89; Lewis Grout, *Zulu-land; or Life among the Zulu-Kafirs of Natal and Zulu-land, South Africa* (Philadelphia: Presbyterian Publication Committee, 1864), 68–78, 201–12.

25. James Dexter Taylor, *The American Board Mission in South Africa; A Sketch of Seventy-Five Years* (Durban: John Singleton & Sons, 1911), 9; Daniel Lindley, Aldin Grout, and Newell Adams to Rufus Anderson, August 22, 1837, Letters and Papers of the ABCFM, Houghton Library, Harvard University; Norman Etherington, *Preachers, Peasants, and Politicians in Southeast Africa, 1835–1880: African Christian Communities in Natal, Pondoland and Zululand* (London: Royal History Society, 1978), 47–48; quotation from Lewis Grout, "A Report of the Umsunluzi Mission Station for the year ending September 1852," Letters and Papers of the ABCFM.

26. Papers of George A. Atkinson, Lydia Bates Grout to Nancy Bates Atkinson, July 31, 1851, Oregon History Center, Portland, Oregon.

27. H. C. Lugg, "The Practice of Lobolo in Natal," *African Studies* 4:1 (March, 1945), 23–27; M. D. W. Jeffreys, "Lobolo is Child-Price," *African Studies* 10:4 (December, 1951), 145–84.

28. Aldin Grout to Rufus Anderson, November 7, 1841, *Missionary Herald* 38 (1842), 339–40.

29. Axel-Ivar Berglund, *Zulu Thought-Patterns and Symbolism* (Bloomington: Indiana University Press, 1989; orig. 1976), quotation from 85; Etherington, *Preachers, Peasants, and Politicians*, 96–99.

30. Jean Comaroff and John Comaroff, *Of Revelation and Revolution: Christianity, Colonialism, and Consciousness in South Africa* (Chicago: University of Chicago Press, 1991), 240; also see Lewis Grout to Rufus Anderson, Umvoti, April 16, 1847, and Lewis Grout to Rufus Anderson, Umsunduzi, November 21, 1848, Letters and Papers of the ABCFM.

31. Deborah Gaitskell, " 'Wailing for Purity': Prayer Unions, African Mothers and Adolescent Daughters 1912–1940," in *Industrialization and Social Change in South Africa: African Class Formation, Culture and Consciousness 1970–1930*, ed. Shula Marks and Richard Rathbone (London: Longman Group Limited, 1982), 338–57.

32. Jeff Guy, "The Destruction and Reconstruction of Zulu Society," and Tim Couzens, " 'Moralizing Leisure Time': The Transatlantic Connection and Black Johannesburg 1918–1936," both in *Industrialization and Social Change*, 167–94; Shula Marks, "Natal, the Zulu Royal Family and the Ideology of Segregation," *Journal of Southern African Studies* 4:2 (April 1978), 172–94.

33. Sheila Marks, ed., *Not Either an Experimental Doll: The Separate Worlds of Three South African Women* (Bloomington: Indiana University Press, 1987), 23, 31–37; quotation from 31.

.11.

Orthodox Christianity, the Nation-State, and Philanthropy: Focus on the Serbian Orthodox Church

MIROSLAV RUŽICA

PRELUDE

This chapter attempts to situate the philanthropic practices of the Serbian Orthodox Church within the history of Serbian society and its background within the Byzantine Empire and Orthodox Christianity. While the latter is necessary for understanding the nature and practice of the Serbian Orthodox Church, without incorporating the distinctive paths of Balkan history any understanding of the concepts and practices of philanthropy within the SOC would be incomplete and misleading.

The first part of this essay focuses on the distinctive nature of the Orthodox Church's understanding of philanthropy as a whole, the presumption being that there exist few substantial differences between the national orthodox churches sharing the Byzantine legacy (Greece, Bulgaria, Romania, Russia, and Serbia).

The second part centers on the Serbian Orthodox Church itself. This story consists mainly of the formulation of numerous survival strategies designed to maintain the essence of the Church unchanged. Unfortunately, the international and local research communities have neglected this domain. The autocephalous churches within Orthodoxy, and the Serbian Orthodox Church in particular, have not encouraged analytical self-studies. There exist, therefore, no critical or reformist lay movements where believers seriously could address key dogmatical or social issues. Additionally, the role played by the Church in constructing Serbian identity and in maintaining its own survival within the context of Balkan history has tended to make all historical narratives partisan by definition. For these reasons this paper must be viewed as a first and mainly conceptual draft for future study.

The attempt to situate the understanding and practice of philanthropy within the historical and societal context of the Serbian Orthodox Church, brought us to a key and paradoxical thesis. Although theological and doctrinal understandings played a major role in shaping the this-worldly role of the Serbian Orthodox Church and its philanthropic practices, historical circumstances, Serbia as a specific type of semimodern society, and the Balkans' distinctive geopolitical realities limited the Serbian Orthodox Church's ability to influence significantly Serbia's national development modernization. These external realities marginalized the Church's philanthropic endeavors and tended to limit its activities to institutional maintenance and traditional charitable activities designed to ameliorate the conditions of the weak and the poor. The Church remained institutionally unable to address and challenge the external order.

THE NATURE OF EASTERN CHRISTIANITY

The best estimates conservatively place the number of Orthodox Christians worldwide at 250 million.[1] Although the titular head of Orthodoxy, the Ecumenical Patriarch of Constantinople (Istanbul) is only *primus inter pares* with the patriarchate functioning primarily as a coordinating center for the various Orthodox churches.

The plural suggests a significant factor within Orthodoxy. The principle that the Gospel should be given to every people (*ethnos*) in its own language and liturgy led to the creation of numerous autocephalous (self-headed) churches within Orthodoxy. To a great extent these are ethnic churches, coextensive with linguistic and historical identities and often national identities.[2]

Although divided by language, culture, and historical animosities, all orthodox churches share adherence to the decisions of the ecumenical synods held between the fourth and ninth centuries. The key dogmas of Orthodoxy—derived from the New Testament, the Holy Fathers, and tradition—as well as the Church's organizational structure and its liturgical forms and procedures were canonized at the Seven Ecumenical

Synods held during that time. The decisions made at these synods remain the basis for Orthodox Christianity today.[3]

Among the Orthodox churches, the Patriarchate of Constantinople retains its central role. Located in the former capital of the Eastern Roman Empire, the Church of Byzantium directly shaped the character of Orthodoxy. Byzantine civilization, which outlived the Western Roman Empire by a thousand years, became the model for the state structure, culture, and religion for many of the countries established within the imperial limits (Bulgaria, Serbia) or under imperial influence (Rumania, Russia). These regions became semi-Greek in administration, architecture, literary forms, and elite life-styles.

Byzantium continued the Roman Empire from the fourth to fifteenth century. A great civilization based on the Empire's organizational tradition with a well-trained central bureaucracy forming its backbone, Byzantium also viewed itself as the premier bearer of the Christian tradition. While the West collapsed into numerous small states, Byzantium continued as a large and relatively unified empire with the emperor retaining significant religio-political functions. Within this political framework, the Church was reduced to its spiritual functions, guarding the purity of doctrine, transmitting religious teaching, and protecting the structure of service to God.[4]

Orthodox theologians interpreted this symbiotic but parallel existence of the Christian Emperor and the Orthodox Patriarch as a symphony, i.e., a partnership in two parallel domains. The Church recognized the Emperor as its protector and as guardian of an integrated faith and directed itself to the spiritual domain, guarding Orthodox truth and maintaining the church. The official laws on the relationships between the state and church, such as the *Epanagoge*, defined the roles of the Emperor and the Patriarch in precisely this way.[5]

This relationship emerged not solely because of the unequal power relationships within the Empire but had roots within Orthodox theology. Orthodoxy views the church not as an organization, but as the visible manifestation of the transcendent spiritual unity of all believers. This unity occurs through the participation of believers in the liturgy. The eucharist becomes a drama during which the advent of the Lord is mystically consummated and the entire history of salvation—the incarnation, death, and resurrection of Christ, the Logos, and the outpouring of the Holy Spirit—is recapitulated.

Even in this short description one can see the three key characteristics of Orthodoxy—traditionalism, ritualism, and mysticism. Although these characteristics often are flung as epithets at the Church, they are not denied by its supporters. The latter value these pillars and cherish them. Nowhere is this clearer than in the conflict over tradition. While many use the term to imply stagnation and even decay, the Church views traditionalism, as the noted Orthodox theologian Georges Florovsky has argued, as continuity, and continuity means truth. The unbroken link of tradition means that the *ethos* of the present church is the same as that of the earliest times. By retaining and transmitting what the earliest witnesses of Jesus' ministry recounted the Church validates its claim to truth.[6] The late Serbian writer Dimitrije Bogdanović expressed this attitude quite directly:

> Orthodoxy is hesitant of drastic change and modernization. This attitude is determined by a consciousness that the message it carries, and the spiritual values it realizes are beyond any time. By the realization that the Church is needed by people of every epoch, and not that people are needed by the Church. Don't be embarrassed by this paradox: it is deeply theological and just. It is not necessary for the Church to be a mass organization; it is not a core problem that it should last and survive; it has not come from some other time. No, it is a church of our time as well, for it is the eternally actual body of salvation. It is not a relic of the past but an assembling around eternal—i.e. contemporary and future truths. Survival is not its goal, but action, to be a witness, to shape life in accordance to Holy Spirit.[7]

While Bogdanović's theological understanding may be valid, traditionalism also carries with it an attitude of reverent preservation of the received inheritance and its defense against innovations. For the Orthodox Church this has been not only an important duty, but is itself practical proof of religious truth.[8] While the Orthodox Church views this positively, its critics have claimed just the opposite. In this context, A. Pollis's conclusions are representative: "Orthodox thinking to date unfortunately has remained frozen in the past; with eternal verities . . . and interpretations culminating in the Orthodox dogma of the eleventh century; the history of subsequent centuries is epiphenomena."[9]

The ritualism of the Orthodox Church produces rich and sumptuous services presenting a complex system of traditional doctrine administrated through standardized formulas and accompanied by symbolic acts.[10] For many believers, however, routinization and the passage of time have divorced these complex rituals from their content and emptied them of meaning. Few communicants have the ability to link the meanings and symbolic forms. This ceremonial ritualism, combined with sacred aphorisms and formulas, has contributed to a process of obscurantism and mystification. When combined with the neglect of preaching, confession, and active lay involvement in the discussion of dogmatical concerns this ritualistic practice became unable to provide the foundation for daily ethical practice.

Orthodox ritual remains intimately linked with mysticism, the third pillar of Orthodoxy. The Church grounds its emphasis on mysticism in its view of itself as the mystical body of Christ and its emphasis on communion with Christ through the eucharistic liturgy. Equally important are contemplation, eremeticism, continuous prayer, and asceticism. These constitute the keys to a pure and virtuous life, being, as they are, central to the Orthodox understanding of salvation as *theosis*, the ongoing process of divinization whereby one becomes "Christ-like." The emphasis on the spiritual being and not the material being made the monk the ideal prototype for the Orthodox believer.

If these three pillars constitute the foundations of Orthodox practice, they imply a particular understanding of the role of the Church in the world. Preeminently it is a view of the Church as not of this world, indifferent toward material reality, and focused on the transcendent. A. Pollis mercilessly concludes that Orthodox Christianity "speaks only to those for whom spiritualism remains the essence of life."[11]

At first glance this statement might strike many, especially Western Protestants, as questionable. The sheer sensuousness of Orthodox services, the emphasis on life-cycle ceremonies, and the grounding of much of Orthodox life in the physical—feasting and celebrating, for example—seem to belie this claim. The point is not that Orthodoxy has denied the ontical status of the material world, only that it has denied the material world any ontological significance.

Orthodoxy's understanding of salvation powerfully illustrates this point. Tellingly, the Orthodox church did not develop the view that temporal (worldly) activities could cause eternal damnation. Orthodoxy regards redemption, rather, as a process in which sinful activities only reduce one's present position, generating a partial loss of substance. Material lapses only slow the process of *theosis*; they do not destroy it. The result, as Demosthenes Savramis has suggested, is an optimistic assumption that human beings can renovate, enlighten, and improve themselves, even to the point of becoming god-like. Such an orientation brings about a reduced consciousness of moral responsibility before God and neighbor. It contains the temptation to spiritual security and moral indolence. The Orthodox Church's focus on the already achieved eschatology explains the lack of direct responsibility for history as such.[12]

This transcendental focus of the Church and its believers has had profound consequences for the worldly role of the Church and its believers. The significance of these facts have been detailed by Demosthenes Savramis and Andreas Buss in their analyses of the Greek and Russian Orthodox Churches respectively. Using the methodology developed in Max Weber's work, especially his *Economy and Society*, they concluded that Orthodox Christianity's other-worldly focus, especially its other-worldly asceticism emphasizing contemplation, isolation, praying in silence, and passivity, prevented it from becoming a viable social actor able to develop coherent and well-articulated social teachings. On the individual side, the Church could provide neither a practical morality nor a psychological stimulus capable of directing believers' economic and social activity. The absence of a *this-worldly* asceticism, i.e., a strict submission to internal responsibility and a religiously sanctioned dedication to secular life, explains why the Orthodox Christianity did not create a rational methodology of everyday life, or religiously conditioned self-control. Worldly success, along with any systematic and practical strategy to achieve it, has been outside the Church's orientation. Although extreme, the conclusions of Pollis are defensible. Given its theological and liturgical emphases, the best the Church could offer to this world has been encouragement on the personal moral level urging believers to avoid sin and to strive for salvation.

THE IDEA OF PHILANTHROPY

There are few studies on philanthropy written by Orthodox scholars or theologians. Historically the Orthodox churches have not addressed social issues in formal documents like the Roman Catholic Church's social encyclicals such as *Rerum Novarum* and *Quadragesima Anno*. Many authors doubt whether the Orthodox churches have a consistent and coherent social doctrine at all. Any reconstruction of the idea and practice of philanthropy, therefore, must retrieve the core cultural traditions of Orthodox Christianity. Preeminently it requires a careful examination of the civilization produced by the Byzantine Empire. The culture, state model, and religious practice of Byzantium so shaped and structured the nature of orthodox churches that the results are felt even today.

In his book *Byzantine Philanthropy and Social Welfare*, D. J. Constantelos has undertaken the only systematic study of Orthodox philanthropy to date. His framework remains relevant for understanding philanthropy and its practice within contemporary Orthodox churches sharing the Byzantine legacy.

Philanthropy in Byzantine culture described man's love for his near ones, his affection and active concern not only for his kin and friends but his fellow man in general. It signified an active feeling of benevolence toward any person, independent of that person's identity or actions. This feeling, however, is grounded theocentrically, on the love of God rather than the love of man.[13] Expressed biblically, it emphasizes such statements of Jesus as "The son of man came not to be served but to serve, and to give his life as ransom for many." This theological grounding of philanthropy meant that its concern was not to please one's fellows but to allow one to please and even imitate God. As Gregory Nazianzenos counseled his people: "Prove yourself a god to the unfortunate, imitating the mercy of God. There is nothing more godly in man than to do good works."[14]

Additionally, the striving to achieve salvation and the eternal King-dom of God implied the possibility of realizing perfection on the earth. "Thus some of them became monks to live of prayer and mortification of material needs, while others distributed their possessions to the poor to free themselves and achieve their theosis as hermits, that is, in con-stant communion with God."[15] John Chrysostom's well-known dictum, "Sell all that you have and distribute it to the poor and you will have treasure in heaven," inspired the donations of many laypersons to mon-asteries, churches, hospitals, and other philanthropic establishments. All this was given for the salvation of the soul and the accumulation of treasures in heaven.

The same principles operated in the formal life of the Church. For Constantelos, the true greatness of Orthodoxy lay in the Church's civiliz-ing and humanitarian work, both among its people and among new tribes and nations. Much of this work devolved upon the bishops who were bound by Church law to undertake such charitable works as visiting prisoners and protecting the weak, widows, and orphans. These obliga-tions, incorporated in canon law, were valid throughout the area of Byzantine cultural influence. An excellent example of these regulations is the Code of St. Sava, a Serbian version of the thirteenth-century Byzan-tine *Nomocanon*. Its chapters on protecting the weak and powerless give us an insight into the concept and practice of the Byzantine common-wealth's philanthropy.[16] The law addresses nearly every aspect of social life and obligates the Church "in close cooperation with the civil author-ities" to organize "charitable 'homes' for the aged, the poor, the sick, the insane, orphans, etc."[17]

Supplied with their own administrative and managerial staff, these homes came under the supervision of the local bishops whom canon law had obligated to support the poor, console the bereaved, and defend those against whom violence had been committed. Particular attention was to be given to those with bodily defects—the blind, deaf, mute, and lame—along with prisoners of war, refugees, and convicts.

As the inheritor of the Greek and Roman traditions, Byzantine philan-thropy also emphasized the role of the emperor. Viewed as the earthly representative of the heavenly ruler, the emperor was obligated to ex-pend effort and monies in easing the plight of his subjects. In fact, only through these activities could the emperor realize his true role. As one medieval writer expressed it, philanthropy was the only activity that made a king an imitator of a God.

In sum, Georges Florovsky's claim that the whole fabric of Orthodox Christianity is social and corporate expresses a key element for under-standing Orthodox philanthropy. The presumption of the ultimate equality of all men, obligated the Church to focus on the needy and unprivileged. In this world the Church served as a hospital for the sick not as a hostel for the well. This function took the form of direct service to the poor and the unfortunate, not elaborate schemes for improving society. Central to this was the Church's emphasis on immediate and intimate human relationship as a significant way of realizing one's religious obligations.[18] When combined with the Church's primary concern with changing human hearts and minds, not the external order, this led to a view of philanthropy that centered on ameliorative charity undertaken on a close personal basis. Negatively, however, it led to indiscriminate charity which ignored the real needs of the poor and created a powerful conviction that Christian love alone could lead to unity and universal solidarity. While rationalizing poverty as poverty of the spirit, it placed the poor and rich in a symbiotic relationship oriented mainly toward salvation. Although almsgiving became a virtue, the Church remained uninterested in the causes of poverty, only its consequences.

Established during the Church's "golden age" of the Byzantine era, these traditional patterns formed the core guidelines for how the Orthodox Church responded to the challenges of modernity and to new historical circumstances. For the Serbian Orthodox Church, however, these theological and historical roots also became entwined with a complex national experience and the struggle to construct and maintain a national identity.

THE SERBIAN ORTHODOX CHURCH

Serbian Orthodox Church would emerge out of this set of cultural realities. These cultural roots, when combined with the particular nature of Serbian history would create a church which remained focused primarily on its role in maintaining Serbian national identity. It, therefore, failed to develop its critical prophetic dimension to any degree whatsoever and, as a result, became increasingly marginalized during the process of modernization.

Christianization of the Serbs began in the ninth century during the reign of the Byzantine Emperor Basil I, and intensified during the mission of Saints Cyril and Methodius at the end of that century. Although culturally, religiously, and politically linked with Byzantium, Serbia emerged as an independent principality during the eleventh century. Although absorbed by Rascia in the next century, it was located farther to the north, in what became the heartland of Serbia. Located within the borders of the Byzantine Empire, the Serbian kingdom often was at odds with its imperial neighbor. Wars were frequent as Serbia attempted to increase its size and power at the expense of declining Byzantium. Historically and mythically, Serbia attained its height of power during the rule of the Serbian King Dušan the Mighty who, intending to replace the old Empire with his dynasty, declared himself Emperor in 1346.

One major result of the emergence of a Serbian kingdom was the formation of the Serbian autocephalous church in 1219. Established by Saint Sava, King Nemanja's son, the Church signaled Serbia's expansion at the expense of its erstwhile imperial ruler. Despite these political conflicts, the new Serbian state and its church remained heirs of Byzantine culture, a fact reflected in the composition of both. Under Archbishop Sava, Byzantine church law, the *Nomos kanones*, was translated into Slavonic. Now known as St. Sava's *Krmcija* it remains the basis for dogmatic, organizational, and liturgical practice within the Serbian Orthodox Church. As in Byzantium, the Serbian Emperor Dušan's *Code of Law* (1349–1354) regulated Church activities and its relations with the state, and forbade proselytism against the state church.[19]

The defeat of the Serbian kingdom at the Battle of Kosovo in 1389 and the final collapse of the Serbian medieval state in 1459 began nearly 450 years of Ottoman rule. The result of this conquest was a decline in state institutions and any independent source of Serbian identity and power, with the exception of the Church. Organized under the Ottoman *millet* system, which allowed different religious communities under their rule to control their internal affairs, the Church remained the sole Serbian organization with some independence.

Although initially under the control of the Patriarch of Constantinople, the Serbian Church was revived in 1557 and retained its independence until 1776 when, in punishment for Serbian support of an Austrian attack on the region, it again was dissolved. Serbian national independence was not the only victim of the Ottoman conquest. The region, a military frontier between empires also fell into an economic decline, eventually becoming a backward, technologically inferior society based on subsistence agriculture. Small, isolated villages with an extended family structure became the basic social unit of a patriarchal, illiterate, and rural society. The Church also suffered from this decline. As a minority religion in an impoverished region its infrastructure decayed—printing shops perished, schools closed, and priestly education became rudimentary. As the number of priests, churches, and monasteries declined, the old pagan Slavic religion resurfaced with its animism and superstition. In the end the Church, impoverished and weakened, served by poorly educated priests, and reeling from Turkish persecution gradually accepted a fusion of Christianity and the ancient faith of its followers.

The reemergence of an independent Serbia began in 1804 with an uprising against the Turks, although nearly seventy-five years of war would pass before Serbia became an independent country in 1878. Conflicts continued until 1912 when Turkey finally relinquished control over the region.

With independence, the Church, previously the center of Serbian na-

tional identity, became increasingly marginalized. As constitutional, economic, and cultural models imported from Western Europe, mainly
Austria, became the basis for Serbian national development, the Church
appeared increasingly irrelevant. Identifying itself with the organic concept of the Serbian nation and refusing to recognize the autonomy of
the secular world, the Church hesitated to accept pluralism, individualism, and Europeanization. Backward-looking, traditionalistic, and
served by poorly educated clergy, the Serbian Orthodox Church, long
indolent due to its years as a monopolistic state church, found itself both
hostile to and unprepared for the challenges of modernization. Unable
to address the new historical realities, the Church cut itself off from any
significant role in the new age.

The modernization of Serbia, therefore, took place with the state in
the role of the sole modernizing agent. In 1844 the government introduced a revised Civil Code based on the Austrian model. Throughout
the nineteenth century Serbia underwent a period of the "canonization
of positivism" to use T. Stoyanovich's phrase. This entailed a rational
approach to economy, politics, and culture, expressed by the contemporary elite through the slogan of progress, order, and modernization, all
meaning, for the Balkans, Western European culture.[20]

Behind this process of modernization lay a large group of ethnic Serbs
who returned from Austria, where many of their families had lived for
over two centuries. They formed the new state's core of educated political professionals, teachers, priests, bankers, and army officers. Bringing
European ideas about government, technology, and education, they
looked to the state as the sole modernizing force. For them, Serbia's
deeply patriarchal, socially undifferentiated, economically backward,
and egalitarian society could be transformed only by a state which stood
against particularism, patriarchalism, medieval customs and practices,
ignorance, and illiteracy. They also supported the central government
against the efforts of local elites to transform themselves into a new oriental patterned nobility.

Given the absence of an independent middle class and a history of
autonomous free cities, there existed no institution other than the central government to fulfill the tasks of modernization. However after the
initial flurry of activity, a strange mixture of native semimerchants, semi-
professionals, semipeasants, semibureaucrats replaced the former emigres. The result was a continuous process of frustration and indecision
about Serbia's core orientation. The permanent dilemma remained
whether to undertake a process of nation building patterned on the
Austrian and French models or to base it on Serbia's mythical and "glorious" past, its patriarchal and collectivist value system, traditional institutions, the extended family, and local autonomy. All Serbian history
for the past 150 years has been a struggle between these two opposite

tendencies. The result has been an entire series of incomplete social, political, and economic accomplishments, only partially modern, and not entirely comparable to their Western European counterparts. An excellent example of the struggle between these two opposite orientations is the story of the parliamentary discussion initiated by the government's proposal to build the first railroad in Serbia in 1884. Briefly, Serbia was obliged by an international contract to build the railroad. Till 1884 Serbia and Montenegro were the only European states without the railroad. The proposal provoked a hot debate and the participants agreed on only one single issue: whatever decision was going to be made it would determine Serbian global orientation—toward the East, where the center was Russia, or toward the West, symbolized by Austria at the time. The opponents were very persistent: the railroad was a terrifying innovation which fundamentally endangered the ideals and historical objectives of the Serbian people; it moved its people away from the ancestors' prophecy, which did not embrace the obtaining of and trading with material goods but was focused on the integration of the dismembered Serbianhood; the railroad would bring foreign ideas and foreigners; it was an instrument to enslave Serbia by the spiritually different, capitalistic West, and that way Serbia would betray not only its own interests but the interests of all of Slavhood as well. Latinka Perović, the commentator of this debate, concludes that this represents the patriarchal and conservative part of Serbia that did not want a modern state. Among the speakers against the agreement were peasants and merchants, big businessmen and intellectuals who had instinctively felt that, by bringing the railroad, the rustic order, quiet work, and the extended family cooperative life would simply perish. A part of the elite had identified itself with the masses. Its own mentality was patriarchal. This part of the elite, however, had built this ideology on the patriarchal basis in order to take control of the government and to create the country in accordance to the people's tradition.[21] The modernizers, the other Serbia, won, of course. Serbia got the railroad. But this belated project, the way this was processed, the sharp polarization of the forces in the conflict even when the technical issues were at stake, had become a pattern of a long, painful, and belated journey to Europe.

The Church played almost no part in the debates over modernization. Tellingly, even local historical studies do not mention any Church role in building modern Serbian society. The Church, in fact, often was viewed as a significant force in hindering modernization and in supporting traditional ways. Therefore, although recognized as the state religion of the Kingdom of Serbia, the Church often came into conflict with the state leading to further marginalization. The kingdom enacted numerous laws limiting the autonomy of the Church, including controls on its public role, ownership of property, and the election of the arch-bishop and bishops.

The twentieth century saw even greater limits placed on the Serbian Orthodox Church. The creation of the Kingdom of Slovenes, Croats, and Serbs in 1918 placed the Serbian Church in a multiconfessional state, stripping it of its establishment status, state protection, and numerous other privileges. Additional laws in the 1920s placed the Church under stricter state control, and in many areas the Church became nothing more than a government agency.[22]

Communist rule (1945–1990) brought the Church under near total state control. Faith became strictly a private matter and the Church limited to its barest sacramental activities and then only inside of religious buildings. The government nationalized most of Church property including 70,000 hectares of land and 1,180 buildings. Many of the Church endowments and foundations also were expropriated. Having lost most of its property, the Church became totally dependent on the government for support, nearly 80 percent of its budget between 1945 and 1965. After 1974 the support decreased dramatically, and by the collapse of the communist state, government monies composed less than 2 percent of the Church's budget.[23]

Although communist Yugoslavia did not undertake an aggressive program of forced atheisation, it did radically limit the social and legal space for the Church. In this hostile environment—with little property and insufficient resources, no strong lay support, denied access to the media, and lacking international support from its sister churches—the Serbian Orthodox Church became a total outsider. This strongly advanced the process of secularization as religiosity became identified with minimal religious activity, such as participation in life-cycle rituals—baptism, marriage, funerals—or the celebration of the feast day of the family's patron saint. Simply insisting on confessional identification became the key to identifying the religious. Few Serbs attend church regularly, participate in the liturgy, fast, or take communion. The typical believer is female, over sixty-four, illiterate, and rural.[24]

The disintegration of Yugoslavia after 1991 and the partial collapse of communism in Serbia created an opportunity for the renewal of the Serbian Orthodox Church, one that proved exceedingly controversial. The long-standing conflict with ethnic Albanians in Kosovo began a process of ethnic identification that intensified as the country began to disintegrate. In this context, the Serbian Communist Party transformed itself into a nationalistic party with the goal of reconstructing the Yugoslav federation under Serbian dominance.

This growth in Serbian populist and national identification provoked strong reactions from the country's other ethnic groups and exacerbated the secessionist tendencies within the other Yugoslav republics.

The collapse of East European communism in 1989 accelerated these tendencies leading to the collapse of Yugoslavia. Religion has not been innocent in these events. Dragoljub Djordjević, a leading expert in religion, claims that the resurgence of ethnic identification promoted a revival of religion in the republics of the former Yugoslavia. He also claims that the religious communities in the former Yugoslavia have been partners in dismantling the country. First, they supported the explosion of the confessional mentality. Second, they legitimized the national leaders. Finally, they abandoned ecumenism among themselves.[25]

The Serbian Orthodox Church actively supported the national cause of the converted communists, thereby creating an opportunity for the Church's renewal. In Serbia, the Church received overwhelmingly favorable media coverage and also undertook a significant expansion of its own book and magazine publishing. Church building became a national priority with construction begun on nearly one hundred destroyed or new churches. The location of new churches became a priority for urban planners, and the principles of church architecture and religious art became topics for serious discussion.

The amicable relations between the Church and the Serbian state lasted from 1990 to 1993. During this time the only significant legal change for the Church was the repeal of the Law on Religious Communities. This provided the opportunity for the Church to rearrange its relations with the government and also produced a series of conflicts with the government. These started with the Church's demand for a return of its nationalized property and increased due to conflicts over public policy relating to education, abortion, divorce, and the status of the Theological College within the Belgrade University.

Disagreements between the Church and the government became particularly heated over the Serbs in Croatia and Bosnia-Hercegovina. The Church supported the secessionist Serbs in these areas and advocated the creation of "Greater Serbia"—the unification of all Serbs in one country. Viewing itself as the only true guardian of the Serbian people, the Church claimed an unassailable moral authority over the issue of Serbian survival.[26]

The Church justified the wars in Croatia and Bosnia-Hercegovina as legitimate defenses of the Serbian people in those countries who found themselves in danger of being destroyed by Catholics and Muslims. The Church argued that Serbian and Orthodox survival required Serbs to enter the wars. While the Church and its Patriarch criticized some of the most virulent excesses, the Church continued to maintain that they were the acts of irresponsible individuals and groups. The Serbian state's eventual acceptance of international calls for the end of the conflict and the withdrawing of support from the secessionists were viewed as traitorous by the leadership of the Serbian Orthodox Church.[27]

This survey of Serbian history ends by emphasizing once more a core ideological matrix that distorted both the Serbian nation-building project and the Church as a social agency. The thesis is simple and straightforward. At no time has the renewal of Serbia focused on modernization as its main goal. The primary goal always has been the establishment of a religio-ethnic state that incorporated within its national borders all area encompassed by the medieval Serbian Kingdom at its height and any geographic regions with large numbers of ethnic Serbs.

This orientation produced what John Plamenatz has called a nationalism of the "Eastern type." Prevailing among culturally insecure peoples, lacking both a well-defined high culture and civil society preceding the formation of the nation-state, nationalism of the Eastern type views the creation of the nation-state as a prerequisite to the elaboration of an authentic culture. With the state as the sole bearer of national identity, the resulting concentration of power in political institutions subsequently obstructs the dispersal of power necessary for the emergence of civil society.[28]

The need to validate the legitimacy of the state results in a mythologization of history. For the Serbs this meant a glorification of the medieval state and the Nemanjić royal dynasty, a romanticization of Serbian people, and the sanctification of those warriors, heroes, and rebels who had struggled for Serbian independence.

Nothing represents this better than the Kosovo myth. The battlefield where the Ottomans defeated the Serbian medieval army in 1389 and ended Serbian independence, Kosovo Polje epitomized the Serbian struggle for identity and independence. The battle's participants became Serbia's national heroes and religious martyrs, celebrated in history, drama, and literature. The date on which it occurred, Saint Vitus's Day, became a national holiday. The Kosovo region itself became a sort of holy land and the desire to "Avenge Kosovo"—to defeat the Turks and liberate southern Serbia—became a key national goal. All other needs and goals took second place to realizing the independence and unification of all of Serbia. The strategy was to build a powerful state apparatus and army, which hindered the processes of industrialization, agricultural modernization, and the development of a comprehensive and progressive educational system.

The Serbian Orthodox Church eagerly adopted Serbian nationalism as its own program and mission. For centuries it had remained the only national institution preserving and shaping Serbian national identity. It participated in the uprisings against the Turks as a leader, a coordinator, a strategist. Nearly all its canonized saints were warrior-heroes. Its music celebrated the Nemanjić dynasty and Kosovo's martyrs. The paintings covering the walls of the beautiful medieval churches are filled with kings, princes, and princesses. The Church completely identified itself with the organic concept of Serbianhood and, since the enemy was an Islamic state, the identification of the nation and the orthodox faith became total.

Additionally, since the Church's corporate and collectivist ethos emphasized the group over the individual, national survival over personal truth, the Church supported nearly every political regime in Serbia, including the communists. Only when the Church viewed the state as retreating from the goal of nationalism, as during the later stages of wars in Croatia and Bosnia-Hercegovina, did relations with the state become cold and distant.

PHILANTHROPIC PRACTICE IN THE SERBIAN ORTHODOX CHURCH: VOLUNTARY GIVING AND SERVICES

Given this complex set of cultural and historical realities any examination of the Serbian Orthodox Church's philanthropic activities and its understandings of its social role requires careful unpacking. This task is made more difficult at this stage because there have been no systematic surveys or analyses of the Church's work, and its archive remains in disarray. The chaos of the past five decades and the recent military conflicts have made any detailed study of this domain nearly impossible since there exist few reliable sources. If we focus on published materials or the broadcast media we see that the core concerns involve Church history, doctrine, personal morality, and Church-state relations. There is little discussion of the Church's social program. Religious philanthropy and the Church's voluntary network are completely absent. A review of the 129 articles on religion/church published in Serbia between 1970 and 1991, turned up only one article on philanthropy.[29] Similarly, an analysis of lectures given at the Orthodox People's University between 1967 and 1977 determined that philanthropy was the subject of only one, and it was delivered by an American Protestant pastor. Therefore, it is unsurprising that a Soros Yugoslavia Fund–sponsored survey of the nongovernmental sector in the Federal Republic of Yugoslavia (Serbia, Montenegro) found only four church-sponsored agencies out of 198. Of these four, the Serbian Orthodox Church co-sponsored only one.[30]

This absence of activity, or at least interest, surprises for several reasons. The first of these is long history of the Serbian Orthodox Church as the location for the preservation and maintenance of Serbian identity and culture along with its history as a source of funding for that maintenance. The significance of this activity is seen clearly in one of the few available resources. This book published in 1933 by a priest of the Serbian Orthodox Church, Mihailo I. Popović, with the revealing title—
Historical Role of the Serbian Church in Guarding National Identity and in

Creation of the State—lists the names of priests and Church officials who made significant donations of cash and land in the period between 1789 and 1933.[31]

The donations break down into two main categories. The first category consists of donations to support the internal life of the Church. These activities included monies to build, reconstruct, repair, and maintain churches and monasteries; to educate seminarians in Serbia and abroad; to support priests, widows, and children; and to encourage religious study and publishing.

The other main category centered on the role of the Church in strengthening religio-ethnic identity. These activities included the creation of scholarships for poor Serbian students, support for national voluntary organizations like the Red Cross, the Mothers' Association, and agencies to aid those with disabilities.

The book also takes pains to describe the Church's centrality in activities vital to Serbian national interest. The chapter entitled "The Role of the Clergy in Guarding the People's Health" exemplifies this work. This chapter's title refers to the role of the Church and local priests in delivering basic health services throughout Serbia. In the first decades of the nineteenth century the Church, as the only national institution, took the leadership role in organizing local health measures such as vaccinations and sanitary education. Later, the Church extended its activities to providing popular medical education and to supporting the first medical associations, agencies, and schools.

The book dwells at length on the clergy's participation in various national, cultural institutions, such as the Red Cross, agricultural cooperatives, the Cultural League, the Saint Sava Society, and numerous educational organizations. The Cultural League's programs, for example, give us clear insights about the directions of the Serbian voluntary sector at the turn of the twentieth century. The lectures and discussions, mostly directed by clergy, had a strongly nationalistic tone. The topics included one's obligations toward the Fatherland, orderly life, the prevention of superstition, patriotism, rational cultivation of land, the duties of youth toward the elderly, citizen-state relations, the German assault on the Slavs, and other nationalistic topics.

The Church's role in strengthening education in Serbia received particular attention. Gifts made by the Church of land, buildings, or materials for schools are listed in detail. It describes how monks and priests often served as teachers or how the local church paid the salaries and provided free housing for teachers in remote rural areas. Particular importance was given to the work of building schools and providing teachers in the so-called "occupied areas," today's Bosnia-Hercegovina, Kosovo, and Macedonia. In those areas the threat to Serbian identity was perceived as being greatest. The Church worked closely with the government in these activities as part of the nation-building project. This generated tensions and conflicts with neighboring countries and many priests were persecuted and even killed, especially in areas still under Ottoman control.

The close links between the Church and the state are demonstrated well by the inclusion of a short chapter praising Serbian and then Yugoslav rulers for their generosity toward the Church. Buttressed by a long list of monetary donations, details of the personal concern of rulers in aiding specific churches and monasteries, and descriptions of the expensive gifts—icons, paintings, and liturgical tools—given for Church use, the chapter draws a close link between the rulers and the Church. That this link was not one-sided is demonstrated by the production of formal and written recognitions of the Church's contribution to the development of Serbian/Yugoslav people.[32]

As this document suggests, the creation of endowments has played a major role in Serbian life since the middle of the eighteenth century. To a great extent, preserving and continuing this medieval tradition rested mainly with Serbian emigres, especially wealthy priests and church officials, in Austria. The Ottomans also deserve some recognition since the long-standing Islamic practice of creating endowments (*waqfs*) for educational, religious, and welfare purposes left its mark on the region. The word for these endowments, *zaduzbina*, retains this historical legacy. The word has a religious meaning describing something one does to aid in the salvation of one's soul, and it also describes an obligation placed on the community to maintain the donor's memory in appreciation for the contribution to the community's well-being. For both of these reasons, many ordinary people adopted this patten of giving for public goods such as bridges, wells, chapels, and schools.

Nearly all these undertakings were linked with the search for national identity and liberation. Most endowments and organizations focused on areas of culture and education as part of the wider national liberation movement. In this struggle, shared by many peoples within the Hapsburg Empire such as the Hungarians, Czechs, Croats, and Slovenes, cultural institutions served as substitutes for political parties and missing national agencies. They also helped to construct national identity by formulating national programs and constructing national symbols. Rulers, wealthy citizens, and artists aided in this by donating book and art collections to a newly established national museum, the university, and the Academy of Science and Arts, the University, the National Library, or some other cultural agency.

By 1913, for example, the Academy of Science and Arts alone administered 13 endowments and 5 funds.[33] The Ministry of Culture's registry listed 75 endowments, 10 foundations, and 286 funds.[34] The vast majority of these were established around the turn of the century or between the two world wars and administered by the Belgrade University and the Academy of Science and Arts. After World War II the communist government nationalized the majority of endowments and funds and by the collapse of their rule in 1989 only six of the thirty-one funds previously administered by the Academy of Science and Arts remained active.

The shift to cultural agencies as managers of these funds illustrates the fact that the Serbian Orthodox Church, despite its role as the primary bearer of Serbian national identity for centuries, found itself increasingly marginalized following Serbian independence. As discussed above, the leaders of the Serbian state saw modernization as a secular process and expected the church to limit its activities to religious affairs. The Church itself did little to resist these pressures, focusing primarily on its religious services and rituals. Its place at the center of Serbian cultural life during times of struggle and crisis was vacated during peace and development.

The Church, however, eventually responded to this increasing marginalization by organizing Christian Charity Action (CCA) in 1932. Designed as the social outreach arm of the Serbian Orthodox Church, the initial implementation failed, requiring its reestablishment in 1966. Although always small, the number of active members increased markedly in the first ten years following reorganization.[35]

The mission of Christian Charity Action is the promotion of deeper religious awareness and commitment through service to others, through charitable activities. According to the available, albeit dated, reports the CCA's main programs are the Orthodox Christian People's University (popular religious education), youth section responsible for missionary activities among youth, an ancillary school for children with learning difficulties, the women's working group which has primary responsibility for maintaining clerical vestments and other liturgical materials, and charity work including visiting the sick and shut-in and collecting used clothes and furniture for the needy. According to the same sources, charity work has been the least successful component.

Following the reintroduction of political pluralism in Serbia by the converted communists in 1990, the Church acted to regain its independence and renew its activities, including the establishment of new funds to support its work.[36] The most significant act by the Church in reasserting its independence, however, came in 1994 when the Patriarchate Board issued its "Declaration on the Renewal of the Serbian Orthodox Church's Endowments and Funds." Aimed at those funds nationalized by the communists in 1959, the resolution authorized the renewal of forty endowments and funds focused mainly on religious education (eighteen), secular education (seven), and charity (seven). Designed in all probability to provide a legal basis for the restoration of Church property, the document elicited no public response from the government and only through behind-the-scenes negotiations did the Church regain any property, namely one palace and several buildings in Belgrade.

The Church apparently based its decision to reestablish endowments and funds on a document listing the Church's endowments and funds dating from March 31, 1938. A copy of this list given to the author in the summer of 1995 by the Patriarchate's staff contains names, purposes, and values of 104 endowments and funds. This list provides the second major document available to scholars interested in reconstructing the history of the Serbian Orthodox Church's philanthropic practices. Examination of the document shows that the majority of endowments and funds emphasized internal concerns. Seventy-nine served the Church's general funding needs—administration, facility maintenance, priestly education—while eight provided retirement and insurance funds for priests, their wives, and their children. The remaining thirteen served some public purpose such as scholarships for poor students, support to hospitals and other social services, and some patriotic purposes—maintaining historical monuments for example. The value of these endowments and funds equaled 80 percent of the Church's annual budget in 1939.

This limited evidence describes part of the historical legacy to which the Serbian Orthodox Church can appeal as it begins its return to public life following the partial collapse of communism in Serbia. The Church, however, still has much to do before it can regain its property, renew its voluntary network, and reformulate its philanthropic activities. One very special factor may contribute much to the development of the Church's voluntary ideas and practice—the refugee issue. Since 1991 more than 400,000 Serbs have entered Serbia from Croatia and Bosnia-Hercegovina as refugees from the war. This issue could re-energize the traditional willingness of the Church and the Serbian people to provide resources and undertake enormous philanthropic activity to ensure the "survival" of the Serbs.

Since the Church saw the end of Yugoslavia and the civil war as threatening "the survival of Serbianhood," it became very active in collecting and distributing humanitarian aid to refugees in Serbia, and later on to Serbs in Bosnia and the Krajina region of Croatia. Although the Church claims that the help is distributed regardless of the ethnic origin of refugees, it appears to be a textbook example of contextual philanthropy, that is, of philanthropy reduced to one's own ethnic fellows.

Initially organized by local priests and dioceses, the Patriarchate made it an institutional priority in 1994, establishing the Humanitarian Fund *Covekoljublje* (Philanthropy), with Patriarch Pavle himself as chairman. The fund's purpose is to collect and distribute donations to impoverished people and refugees. While fund-raising efforts have been directed mainly at emigre Serbs in Western Europe and the United States, there also exists a special action program called "From Brothers to Brothers" to provide assistance to Serbs in Bosnia and Croatia. Although reliable evidence is scant, the organizational network appears quite large, involving significant numbers of lay people and huge amounts of money and goods. It tempts this author to predict that the establishment of such a pattern—especially as human and organizational resources are institutionalized, coordinated, and guided—will survive, reconstructing and redirecting itself toward new ends. This remains only a hypothesis. The Church must transform and shape this network, primarily by overcoming the particularistic and exclusivist legacy it represents. Whether the Church can do this or simply returns to its old patterns remains to be seen.

CONCLUSIONS

Serbia's failure to become the Piedmont of the South Slavs, led to the formation of narrow national strategies and extreme ideological projects which combined with a weak civil society to produce authoritarian or populist governments. This fact, along with Serbia's location between great powers and different civilizations, has deeply shaped the Serbian Church. Sharing its society's extreme ups and downs, the Church has not been challenged by secular and lay movements to explore its this-worldly role or to be a vigorous social actor in the modernizing processes. Instead, it has remained an outsider in addressing social (and even religious) issues of people. This may explain why secularization advanced further in Serbia than in other European countries.[37] The struggle focused on the "Serbian national question" has not produced workable and stable political, cultural, and religious arrangements in the Balkans.

Thus our thesis is that the Church's social environment should be blamed more than orthodox doctrine for its failures to be an active this-worldly agency, including its philanthropic role. While the history of Serbia and the Serbian Orthodox Church outlined above suggested this, we will support our claim by a cursory examination of Orthodoxy in Western Europe and in the United States. These emigre orthodox churches, exposed to Western European and American cultures, and inspired by numerous Protestant churches, have challenged Orthodoxy's traditional other-worldly orientation. They have organized many critical conferences, produced innovative scholarship, addressed numerous social issues, and initiated ecumenical integration. The Institute of Saint Serge in Paris, the Seminary of Saint Vladimir in Boston, Holy

Cross Orthodox Press in Brookline, Massachusetts, and especially the American Orthodox Christian Laity Movement with its Project for the Orthodox Renewal, have demonstrated that the Orthodox church is able to change.[38]

Concerning the potential of the Orthodox Church to transform itself into an inner-worldly agency, a revival and modernization of the parish should be a prerequisite. Unfortunately, the parish has been a center of activity only in times when survival was a crucial strategy, not when the building of community around the Church as centrality of its orientation was expected. It is interesting to see the two completely opposite platforms concerning the role of the parish. For Ch. Yannaras, a known orthodox intellectual from the Institute of Saint Serge in Paris, the parish is crucial if the Church wants to be more inner-worldly focused, to attract new believers, and to revive the faith of old believers, as well as to buffer the secularization processes. The reconstruction of the parish should be the Church's core program. It should include the reduction of its size and even the deprofessionalization of priests. The Serbian writer Ljubivoje Stojanović, on the other hand, thinks that the issue is to keep the liturgical dimension of the parish unchanged. He fears that the parish otherwise may become an association in which the interests and needs of members are key issues. He also thinks that the role of laity within the parish must be subordinated to the priest and be focused on providing logistics for the sacramental service only.[39]

It seems that the Orthodox Church doctrine is neither that rigid nor incompatible with scientific principles. Nothing in Orthodoxy makes it *a priori* incompatible with democracy. In fact its high regard for social relations, equality, social solidarity, and decentralization seem to suggest the opposite. Although Orthodox Christianity denies any autonomy to the profane due to the divine presence in everything, albeit with greater or lesser intensity, this claim is open to numerous interpretations. Orthodoxy's ancient and soft doctrine may be open to new discourses.

The center of its rigidity and traditionalism, however, remains its worshiping practice. But once doctrine becomes a source of renewal, the role of rituals and their meaning also will be transformed. The "openness" of Orthodox churches to the nation-state is new and indirect proof that its doctrine may be open to a variety of this-worldly projects. Maybe a new discourse on philanthropy can replace the nation-state projects? The future is open, but until such renewal occurs, our previous claim remains valid: Orthodoxy's overwhelming emphasis on the transcendental has left the way open for the earthly life of Orthodox believers to be regulated by secular values.

NOTES

1. Elias Oikonomou, "Foundation, Doctrine, and Politics of the Eastern Orthodox Church," *Mediterranean Quarterly* 1993. For more information on

the history and doctrine of Orthodox Christianity see Sergei Bulgakov, *The Orthodox Church* (Crestwood: St. Vladimir's Seminary Press, 1988); James Steve Counelis, *Inheritance and Change in Orthodox Christianity* (Scranton: University of Scranton Press, 1995); Daniel B. Clendenin, *Eastern Christianity: A Western Perspective* (Grand Rapids: Baker, 1994); John Meyendorff, *Witness to the World* (Crestwood: St. Vladimir's Seminary Press, 1987); Alexander Schmemann, *The Historical Road of Eastern Orthodoxy* (Crestwood: St. Vladimir's Seminary Press, 1977); Georges Florovsky, *Christianity and Culture* (Belmont: Nordland, 1974); Kallistos Ware, *The Orthodox Church* (Baltimore: Penguin, 1964).

2. Ernst Benz, *The Eastern Orthodox Church: Its Thought and Life* (Garden City, N.Y., 1963/Sarajevo: Svjetlost, 1989 [Serbocroat]).

3. The Seven Ecumenical Councils are so-called because they were the only major church councils that included both the Western and Eastern churches and dated from First Nicea in 325 to the seventh, again in Nicea in 787. The conflict between the Roman Church and the Church in Constantinople became permanent, and in 1054 the bishop of Rome (the Pope) and the Patriarch of Constantinople mutually placed each other under anathema. This was not removed until 1965 when Pope Paul VI, following the decisions of the Second Vatican Council, renounced the anathema.

4. See Benz, *The Eastern Orthodox Church.*

5. Ibid.

6. Georges Florovsky, "The Social Problem in the Orthodox Church," *The Journal of Religious Thought* 7, 1 (1950–51): 41–51.

7. Dimitrije Bogdanović, "Pravoslavna spiritualnost I iskušenja našeg vremena" [Orthodox Spirituality and Temptations of Our Time], in *Pravoslavlje izmedju neba I zemlje* [Orthodoxy between Heaven and Earth] (Niš: Gradina, 1991).

8. Adolf Harnack, "On Eastern and Western Christianity," in *Theories of Society*, vol. 2, ed. Talcott Parsons et al. (New York: Free Press, 1961).

9. Adamantia Pollis, "Eastern Orthodoxy and Human Rights," *Human Rights Quarterly* 15 (1993): 339–56.

10. Harnack, "On Eastern and Western Christianity."

11. Pollis, "Eastern Orthodoxy."

12. Vladeta Jerotić, *Vera I Nacija* [Faith and Nation] (Beograd: TERSIT, 1995).

13. Demetrios Constantelos, *Byzantine Philanthropy and Social Welfare* (New Brunswick: Rutgers University Press, 1968).

14. Ibid.

15. Constantelos, 1968.

16. Miodrag Petrović, *Krmčija Svetoga Save* [The Code of Saint Sava Concerning the Protection of the Weak and Disenfranchised] (Beograd: Narodna Biblioteka, 1983).

17. Ibid.

18. Florovsky, 1950–51.

19. Paul Pavlovich, *The History of the Serbian Orthodox Church* (Toronto: Serbian Heritage Books, 1989).

20. Traian Stoyanovich, *Balkan Worlds—The First and Last Europe* (Armonk: M. E. Sharp, 1994).

21. Latinka Perović, *A Lesson from the Past—Political Elite and Modernization in Serbia between the Past and the Future* (Beograd: Institute of Social Sciences, 1995).

22. Djoko Slijepčević, *Istorija srpske pravoslavne crkve* [History of the Serbian Orthodox Church] (Muenhen: Iskra, 1966).

23. Patriarchate Board of the Serbian Orthodox Church, *Pismo Predsedniku Miloševiću* [Letter to President Milosević]. A letter sent by the Patriarchate Board in which the return of the nationalized property was requested. The letter is dated January 29, 1990. A copy is in the author's private archive.

24. Mirko Blagojević, *Priblizavanje Pravoslavlju* [Going Back to Orthodoxy] (Niš: Gradina & JUNIR, 1995).

25. Jelena Galić, *Crkva nije kriva za rast nacionalizma* [The Church Should Not Be Blamed for the Growth of Nationalism], in *Politika*, January 23, 1995.

26. Radmila Radić, "Crkva i 'Srpsko pitanje': Srpska pravoslavna crkva u poratnim i posleratnim godinama, 1980–1995" [The Church and the "Serbian Question": Serbian Orthodox Church after World War II, 1980–1995], *Republika* No. 121–123, (August 1–31), 1995.

27. Ibid. Stan Markotich, "Serbian Orthodox Church Regains a Limited Political Role," *Transition* Vol. 2, No. 7 (April 1996), pp. 30–33.

28. Stoyanovich, 1994.

29. Dragoljub Dordjević, *Pravoslavlje izmedju neba I zemlje* [Orthodoxy between Heaven and Earth] (Niš: Gradina, 1991).

30. Branka Petrović and Žarko Paunović, *Nevladine organizacije u FR Jugoslaviji* [Non-Government Organizations in Federal Republic of Yugoslavia] (Subotica: Otvoreni Univerzitet, 1994).

31. It identifies about ninety such churchmen who made over 250 donations—mainly in cash and real estate—during this period.

32. I. Mihailo Popović, *Istorijska uloga Srpske Crkve u čuvanju narodnosti I stvaranju države* [The Historic Role of the Serbian Church in Guarding the People and Creating the State] (Beograd: Nova Stamparija, 1933).

33. Serbia passed its first endowment law in 1897 and saw a tremendous expansion of these types of donations up through the middle of the interwar period.

34. Zoran Avramović, *Zadužbine, fondovi, fondacije I legati u srpskoj kulturi* [Endowments, Funds, Foundations, and Legacies in Serbian Culture] (Beograd: Zavod za proučavanje kulturnog razvitka, 1992).

35. Based on the CCA's Coordination Service membership increased from 7,690 in 1968 to 19,000 in 1976. Ljubica Vuković, "*Osvrt na deset godina rada Versko-dobrotvornog Starateljstva*" [A Review of the Christian Charity Action 10th Anniversary] in *Versko-Dobrotvorno Starateljstvo, 1967–1977* (Beograd: Pravoslavlje, 1978).

36. One such fund was the Church Educational Fund established in 1991 with the goal of improving Church education, libraries, and publications, as well as establishing a scholarship program for students.

37. Djordjević, 1991.

38. Stanley Harakas, *Let Mercy Abound* (Brookline, Mass.: Holy Cross Or-

thodox Church Press, 1983); St. J. Sfekas and G. E. Matsoukas, *Project for Orthodox Renewal—Seven Studies of Key Issues Facing the Orthodox Christians in America* (Chicago: Orthodox Christian Laity, 1993).

39. Yannaras, Ch. 1993, Istorijska i socijalna dimenzija crkvenog etosa (Historic and Social Dimensions of the Church Ethos), in Gradac, 20, 110, pp. 14–32; Ljubivoje Stojanović, *Savremeni trenutak u životu paronije* [Contemporary Moment of the Parish Life], in *Pravoslavije*, 24, 669, pp. 6–7.

PART FIVE
NEW SHOOTS, OLD ROOTS

.12.

Hindu Philanthropy and Civil Society

❧

MARK JUERGENSMEYER AND DARRIN M. McMAHON

In one of his last published essays, Edward Shils contemplated the uncertain relationship between nationalism and civil society. Disagreeing with Jürgen Habermas, Shils insisted that civil society indeed needs the concepts of nation and national society; it cannot exist without them. On the other hand, he somberly warned, "a society in which nationality is driven into the extreme form of nationalism will set many obstacles on the path to being or remaining a civil society."[1]

Nothing sets more obstacles on civil society's path than the extreme forms of nationalism fueled by religious and ethnic passions. In India, the extraordinary rise of religious nationalism in recent years is symbolized by the power of the Sikh separatist movement—now largely quelled—and the electoral victories of the Hindu nationalist party, the Bharitya Janata Party (BJP), still ascendant as a major political force.[2] Surrounding the success of the BJP is the persistent question of what—if any—role religion can play in India in promoting civil society and the national good.

In India, philanthropy—especially religiously motivated philanthropy—is hardly an innocent actor in this grand social drama. Insofar as philanthropic acts help to define a humane society and a just civil order, they carry social weight. For this reason, religiously motivated philanthropy is often seen as encouraging a sectarian political agenda. This essay explores the background of both civil society and generosity in the Indian tradition in order to understand the roots of Hindu philanthropy and its role in shaping India's modern social order.

DHARMA AND HINDU CIVIL SOCIETY

If traditional India does possess the notion of a civil society—a realm of interaction and responsibility separate from the private world of the family and the control of the state—it would be bound up in the concept of *dharma*. This term, often translated as "duty," sometimes as "religion," refers to a moral way of life that undergirds all Hindu notions about society and one's role within it. It is traditionally contrasted with *artha* (the useful) and *kama* (the pleasurable). According to the French Indologist Robert Lingat, "a rule founded on *dharma* [which Lingat's translator calls 'the good'] has an authority superior to that of one founded on *artha*, just as the latter has an authority superior to that of one motivated by *kama*."[3] *Dharma* is also occasionally contrasted with the religious rites and devotion that lead more directly to *moksha* (salvation, liberation of the soul) in that *dharma* prescribes what is worth doing for the here and now, whereas religious rites—including acts of renunciation—are other-worldly and individual in their orientation.[4] Yet the two are connected, for *dharma* is the prerequisite for *moksha*: it is the rule for living a righteous life that makes all other religious acts possible.

Dharma is sometimes compared with the Western notion of natural law, but there are important differences. For one thing, responsibility in the Indian tradition is shouldered by a group rather than individuals; and for another, *dharma* emphasizes obligations that one holds, rather than rights that one possesses or rules that one should follow. A third difference has to do with the particularity of *dharmic* obligations. Unlike rights, which typically are imputed to all persons at all times and places, *dharmic* obligations vary from one stage of life to the next, and from one social group to another. At the heart of *dharma* is the notion that a person's ethical responsibilities depend upon particular circumstances: age, gender, family connections, and social location. Given a social circumstance, *dharma* gives guidance as to what should be done.

We usually think of *dharma* in connection with the social unit known as caste, but there are other social roles that carry *dharmic* weight as well. The *Dharmasastra* literature (writings about *dharma*) goes into great detail about what is expected at each of the traditional four stages of life: the student, householder, forest dweller, and ascetic stages. What is appropriate for one is not suitable for another. Students, for example, are expected to be celibate and retiring—always submissive to their teachers—whereas householders are expected to be sexually active and outgoing, involved in economic and social activities.[5] There are also *dharmic* codes for ordinary day-to-day moral behavior that are incumbent on everyone, outlined in manuals of propriety that are especially well-known in South India, where the sacred *Kural,* a moral guidebook, has become a kind of Hindu bible.[6]

The political implications of *dharma* are associated with the special obligation known as *rajdharma,* the moral responsibilities of those who rule. Religious leaders and military/political leaders were separated by caste; the former were Brahmans, the latter Kshatriyas. By definition, religion and the state were in separate spheres and had separate—but related—*dharmic* obligations. The main role of the state was to provide the "white umbrella" of security and social order necessary for the religious leaders and the caste groups within society to function morally on their own.[7] Although the state and society were separate, it was the role of the state to serve society by maintaining the political and military framework for a *dharmic* social order. The very legitimacy of a ruler was in jeopardy if he or she was perceived as having abandoned his or her *dharmic* obligation to maintain this order.

One of the things that kings could do to demonstrate their *dharmic* good intentions was to give gifts—not only gifts to Brahmans but gifts to the whole of society in the form of good works. Jean Filliozat notes, for example, that the "maintenance of the Good Order" was associated not only with gifts that "permit the rites and assure the existence of the sacerdotal class" but also with "general liberalities as well—good works—enumerated later as consisting of the distribution of food, the digging of wells and ponds, and the building of temples and gardens—those deeds which are, in short . . . the work of kings mindful of their *dharma.*"[8] Such gift-giving to society was expected of non-rulers as well.

Gift-giving was, in fact, one of the links that connected the social and religious worlds of traditional Indian society. The ritual obligation of giving gifts to Brahmans (the notion of *dan*) and the responsibility to serve the gods and *gurus* (the idea of *seva*) became cornerstones of both religious activity and proper social comportment in Hindu civil society.

ROOTS OF HINDU GENEROSITY: *DAN* AND *SEVA*

The act of giving a gift—*dana* (in Sanskrit) or *dan* (in Hindi)—is one of the oldest and most important aspects of Hindu religiosity.[9] It is a central concept in the *Rg Veda,* which dates back at least three millennia; and it is a dominant feature of the *Laws of Manu,* which date from the third century B.C.E.[10] The latter text explains that each of the four great ages in the cycles of cosmic time has its own chief duty. In the first, it is the performance of austerities; in the second, knowledge; in the third, sacrifice; and in the fourth—an age of so enormous a span of time that it includes all of recorded history—"making gifts" is the highest duty that humans can achieve.

What these ancient texts had in mind, of course, were ritual gifts. Jan Gonda defines *dana* in the historical, technical terms of the *Dharmasastra* as "the transfer of property according to sastric [classic textual] rites such as to reach a receiver who is a fit recipient with the idea that the donor will derive from this act some 'metaphysical' or unseen spiritual result."[11] They were to be pure offerings made to the noblest persons: gods, or their surrogates on earth, Brahmans. The texts were exhaustive in their attempts to specify who or what was appropriate for each aspect of the giving process. Classically, there were six elements of *dana*: the donor, the donee, the charitable attitude, the subject of the gift (which must have been acquired by the donor in a proper way), appropriate time, and appropriate place.[12] For each of these there were variations. Not only Brahmans, but ordinary—albeit "worthy"—persons might be recipients of a gift, depending on the time and circumstance. And although the earliest Vedas did not include land—preferring instead cows, horses, chariots, gold, young women, clothes, and food—in later scriptures land became the most meritorious of donations.[13] The following passage from the earliest sacred text, the *Rg Veda*, showers praise on the liberal benefactor, and intimates the metaphysical reward to be earned by those who give generously:

> Those who make gifts of *daksina* [cows or fee] stand high in heaven, those who make gifts of horses stand in the world of the Sun, donors of gold secure immortality [become gods], those who give garments increase the duration of their life. . . . Donors do not die . . . they do not go down to a low goal, they are not harmed, nor do they suffer pain; *daksina* renders unto these donors this whole world and also heaven.[14]

Central to this and other passages of the Vedas is the notion of *ista-purta*, which translates roughly as the "cumulative spiritual result or merit due to one's performance of sacrifices and charitable acts."[15] Spiritual merit, in other words, accrued as a function of giving. And although donations flowed most directly from kings, lords, and other prosperous figures to those who enjoyed the special privilege of *prati-grrah* (acceptance of gifts)—the Brahmans—it is important to note that from quite early on giving in a more general sense took on positive religious connotations. While merit accumulated in greatest quantity when donations were offered to Brahmans, and in direct proportion to the magnanimity of the gift, giving to others was also extolled as an exemplary religious act. The later Vedas explain that "a gift made to one's parents, guru, friend, to a well-conducted man, to one who has laid the donor under obligation, to the poor, to the helpless, or to those endowed with special excellence, leads to reward."[16]

Are these Vedic concepts still prevalent in Indian society? Some scholars claim that they are. Gonda concludes his study of *dan* in the *Dharmasastra* with a brief discussion of Gandhian movements in modern India to show that the "ancient traditions have not been broken off."[17] And Gloria Goodwin Raheja observes in her study of contemporary patterns of ritual prestation in the North Indian village of Pahansu (Saharanpur District) that the discussion of *dan* in the Vedas "is alive and relevant to present-day village life."[18]

The idea of service as a form of giving owes its origins to a development in Hinduism later than *dan*, the Vedas, and the *Dharmasastra*. This development was the practice of giving time and menial duties to the maintenance of temple deities, an activity known as *seva*, "service." In the medieval period, for instance, when devotional love (*bhakti*) became the major genre of religious expression, gifts were often given to God as acts of love, and *seva* became the dominant means of religious dedication.[19] The difference between *seva* and *dan* was not solely a difference between material gifts and gifts of service. In the *bhakti* understanding of *seva*, there was also a difference of motivation: *seva* was a reflexive act of love, whereas *dan* had been an expression of obligation. In *bhakti* Hinduism, God was often experienced through one's teacher, or *guru*, who in many cases became the object of loving service. Still, acts of kindness and generosity to other people counted as *seva* to the *guru*, for they allowed one to share the guru's love and indirectly return it. As with *dan*, the reward for *seva* was *karmic* merit. Whereas the notion of *dan* tends to center on things—gifts—and therefore privileges those economically able to make material donations, *seva* emphasizes gestures and acts. Although it is possible for the poorest villager to offer *dan* in the form of flower petals, a morsel of bread, or sweet well water, *seva* is even more easily accessible to anyone willing to provide time and devotion.

In modern India *seva* is the dominant form of worship in many movements based on the teachings of the medieval *gurus* and their descendants. For example, in the Radhasoami faith, a modern-day North Indian *bhakti* movement, everyone regardless of class or station must perform the most menial tasks of *seva*. Under the watchful eye of the present-day guru (the latest in a lineage stretching back some five hundred years to the great saints, Kabir and Guru Nanak) members undertake on his behalf what the movement calls *mitti seva*, the "service of dirt." Thousands of followers—rich and poor—trek through the dust, moving earth with wicker baskets on their heads as a way of furthering

Radhasoami construction projects and of learning something about submission, humility, and service.[20] There is also, however, "money *seva*," and large social service projects that are *seva* to society undertaken on the master's behalf. Members provide time as well as money, and many become officially recognized as *sevadars* (providers of service) who staff and take part in enterprises such as food distribution, village clinics, eye-care camps, and hospitals run by Radhasoami's *Seva Samiti*, an administrative organization overseeing Radhasoami's philanthropic work.

MODERN HINDU PHILANTHROPY: GANDHI AND THE BIRLAS

It is unlikely that many of India's traditional concepts of giving and service would have been accepted as easily into modern society had it not been for the efforts of that remarkable Indian leader who brought so many aspects of Hindu culture into the modern world: Mohandas Gandhi. The notions of *dan* and *seva* were a significant part of Gandhi's thinking, but he gave them his own interpretation. Gandhi had a habit of taking traditional Hindu religious terms and transforming them in a social and political way, stripping them of sectarian religious affiliation. For instance, the notion of ascetic renunciation, *tapasya*, was transformed by Gandhi into the idea of disciplined political action; and the great battles of the *Bhagavad Gita* were interpreted as metaphors for the moral struggles of daily life.

Likewise, Gandhi construed the gifts and service implied by *dan* and *seva* as social ones. This marked a turning point in the pattern of generosity in India, for Gandhi's social interpretation of ritual offerings made it possible for wealthy Indians to think of such offerings not just as "gifting"—tributes aimed at enhancing the giver's power—but as philanthropy, support for the general welfare of all.[21] Gandhi also made it possible for Hindus to think of this general social welfare as fulfilling Hindu tradition: for in Gandhi's interpretation of Hindu mythology the great epoch of God (*Ram Raja*) was not at the mythical limits of cosmic time but something possible within one's own lifetime. Gandhi's *Ram Raja* was an ideal civil society—a *dharmic* social order that humans created by tapping the spiritual resources within them, especially the divine qualities of love, generosity, giving, and service that lay in the human heart. Gandhi's notions of philanthropy and social service retained some of the essential features of *dan* and *seva*, however: like these concepts, Gandhian ideas of social service included an insistence on the purity of the act, the giver, and the receiver, and the benefit of the transaction for the ultimate transformation of the world.

Specific concepts of Gandhi based on *dan* and *seva* include the idea of *bhoodan* (gift of land), the Gandhian term for land reform, in which people with property are expected to surrender some of their land voluntarily so that it can be reallocated to indigent farmers. A whole village could give itself in the act of *gramdan* (gift of a village), the Gandhian term for cooperative farming, in which villagers voluntarily pooled their land for cooperative use. And one of the most enduring Gandhian concepts based on earlier concepts of ritual giving and service was *sarvodaya* (service to all), the Gandhian term for voluntary labor and an egalitarian, just society. After Gandhi's death, the rural reform movements based on his ideas that have flourished in India and Sri Lanka have been known as *Sarvodaya* movements.

These ideas of Gandhi, and the example set by Gandhi himself, made a great impact on the thinking of many young leaders involved in India's independence movement. Among them were members of the wealthy Birla family, who in this century emerged from a merchant caste in the desert state of Rajasthan to develop into a major industrial dynasty. The patriarch of the family was Ghansyam Das ("GD") Birla, whose personal memoirs, *In the Shadow of the Mahatma* (1953), are a moving testimony to the influence of Gandhi on his moral development and social outlook. As philanthropists, the Birlas are best known for their temples. Usually painted a bright salmon, they follow traditional designs and are done on a grand scale. Over the past fifty years scores of these have been erected at the outskirts of major pilgrimage sites as well as in middle-class suburbs of urban centers. Perhaps more than any other architectural feature on the Indian landscape, they are the very definition of modern popular Hinduism. Beside these temples, albeit architecturally overshadowed by them, one may often find other, more practical gestures of Birla generosity: scores of hospitals, schools, and other projects provided for the common good of all Indians, regardless of religious orientation.

The involvement of merchant-caste people, such as the Birlas, in philanthropic activities was not entirely due to Gandhi, however. As early as the eighteenth century there already were movements throughout India in which newly wealthy groups attempted to increase their status and political influence through strategic acts of giving.[22] In the nineteenth century, middle-class Hindu organizations, such as the *Arya Samaj*, established their own schools and hospitals in order to compete with Christian missionary institutions.[23] Today the Indian tax code recognizes these groups as worthy, tax-exempt objects of generosity.

Still, the example and ideas of Gandhi brought such acts of generosity into the realm of modern philanthropy. Gandhi came from the same caste, class, and upbringing as many of India's most influential businessmen, so it was understandable that he would make an impact on their lives, even if at first reckoning his life-long friendship and collaboration with men such as GD Birla seemed unlikely. Indeed, the image of the ascetic, *dhoti*-clad Bapu, whose later political vision stressed a grass-roots socialism and a vague distrust of the workings of large-scale enterprise, presents a striking contrast with that of the fabulously wealthy Birla. But though the latter never shed his Westernized business attire, and remained until the end of his life an inveterate advocate of economic modernization and capitalist development, he nonetheless shared with Gandhi a number of fundamental conceptions: a committed Indian nationalism, a bitter distaste of the workings of caste and caste discrimination, and above all, a profound belief in the importance of religion as a motivating factor in daily life. The story of their association—to end tragically with Gandhi's assassination on the grounds of Birla House in Delhi in 1948—provides a remarkably acute example of the religious underpinnings of the development of modern Indian philanthropy, and an illustration of the enduring importance of the concepts of *dan* and *seva* in informing this development.[24]

Born in Pilani, Rajasthan, in 1884, GD Birla was the son of a Marwari businessman, Baldeodas Birla, and the third of the four so-called "Birla Brothers," all of whom would earn renown as traders and industrialists in twentieth-century India. Although each of the brothers—and GD most outstandingly—displayed tremendous talents in business from a very young age, they did not begin—à la Horatio Alger—with nothing. Indeed, GD's grandfather, Seth Sheonarayan, had made a considerable fortune speculating in commodities (chiefly opium) in Bombay, and his father continued this practice, branching out to Calcutta, and including wheat, silver, and oilseeds in his portfolio. It was in Calcutta that GD began his career in the family business, but he quickly showed an independent streak, moving out on his own to challenge the British in their monopoly of the brokerage of commodities, a move virtually without precedent. Enduring a considerable degree of resistance in this venture, GD nonetheless prospered, and the snubs he received from the British during this period began to feed an incipient Indian nationalism. At the same time, he maintained a respect for the efficiency of English business practice that allowed him to emulate and innovate with great success. Based on his profits in the trading and brokerage of commodities, he invested in textiles, buying mills and factories, moving from here to banking and mining, eventually establishing a foothold in nearly every facet of Indian heavy industry and financial services. By the 1920s and 1930s he had emerged as one of the wealthiest men in India, and would continue until the end of his long life in 1983 to amass wealth and the social influence it provided him.

GD also inherited from his family a religious obligation to give some of what he earned back to society. His grandfather had established a precedent in this regard, setting up a number of public welfare programs in his native Pilani. GD's father, Baldeodas Birla, also had religious impulses, and following his retirement lived a life of religious austerity and devoted himself to religious contemplation and aesthetics. Baldeodas viewed charity as an integral part of his life: "What one earns in one's youth," he commented, "must be spent in old age for piety or virtuous action. . . . Whatever money I earned in Bombay and Calcutta is being rightly spent in Kashi [the pilgrimage center of Banaras]. What came, now goes."[25] True to his word, the elder Birla rebuilt and resuscitated *ghats* and temples, constructed wells, founded a hospital and a dental clinic, gave millions to Madan Mohan Malaviya's Banaras Hindu University, started a Sanskrit college and a teacher's training college, constructed public lodgings, student hostels, and countless *dharmashalas*, and funded the establishment of the Dr. Bhagwandas Library and numerous other projects.[26] Moreover, he bestowed a legacy destined to pay even greater dividends—the advice to his children and grandchildren to do the same: "Earn and give," he advised them, "since there is no greater sin than earning for one's own self. He who is not of help to others is worthless. There is no use of money if it does not remove the ills of others."[27]

This religious emphasis on the moral imperative to give—to cleanse and purify oneself, acquiring merit through generous philanthropic acts in the tradition of *dan*—proved a dominant influence on GD's life. Moreover, it cultivated in him a receptivity to the teachings of Gandhi—a point that Birla himself would make clearly in his 1953 autobiography, *In the Shadow of the Mahatma*:

> Gandhiji was the dominant influence in my life because of my feeling as a Hindu. I come of a family of merchants which has a tradition of *sanatan dharma*, the eternal religion of duty. My grandfather and those like him may be compared to the Quakers in England and America. Like the Quakers, they prospered miraculously in business affairs but considered it their duty to spend freely on good works. Like the Quakers, they were not "orthodox," that is to say they were not bound rigidly by caste restrictions. . . . My point is that Gandhiji's influence over me was more through his religious character—his sincerity and his search for truth—than his power as a political leader. Often I could not follow his reasoning and sometimes I disagreed with him, but always there was the belief that he must somehow be right in a sense that I could not grasp. Whatever sum he asked from me (and he was, as he put it, an inveterate beggar for the causes he worked for) he knew that he would get it, because there was nothing I could refuse him.[28]

The very terms of this confessional passage—in which Birla at once affirms the importance of his religious upbringing and the tremendous influence of Gandhi—reveal the degree to which GD conceived of his service to the latter as a form of *seva*. As Birla commented in 1931, "One mission of my life has been to serve good causes, and I never hesitated to help Bapu and other friends who ever approached him for my humble service."[29] Describing, in his autobiography, their relationship as "in the nature of a family attachment, of a father towards a son," Birla looked to Gandhi as a gentle master whom he was obliged to serve in whatever capacity.[30] Ceding to the Mahatma the responsibility to designate worthy causes and appropriate enterprises, the otherwise commanding Birla followed humbly, effacing his will in the knowledge that he was secure in the power of a higher authority. A leader in so many capacities, Birla was, with respect to Gandhi, a follower—a *sevadar*—whose business it was to serve with humility, even when Gandhi's policies (the commitment to village-level industry, for example, or his support for labor strikes) worked against his immediate interests.[31]

And serve Birla did. As arguably the greatest single contributor to Gandhi, GD gave vast sums to almost every one of the Mahatma's principal causes from the time of their first meeting at a nationalist rally in Delhi in 1916. The removal of untouchability, the popularizing of basic education, naturopathy, cow protection, *swadeshi*, and Hindu-Muslim unity—all these and a host of other causes were backed by GD. As Birla's biographer, N. M. Jenuja, writes, "there was hardly any social-economic programme of Gandhi which was not generously financed by GD."[32] Birla also contributed extensively to Gandhi's publicity efforts, underwriting newspapers and journals, covering printing costs, and organizing other aspects of the media. Furthermore, GD himself served at Gandhi's appointment in 1932 for twenty-seven years as the founding president of *Harijan Sevak Sangh* (Society for the Service to Untouchables). His own Marwari family having been branded "outcaste" in 1925 when one of his brothers undertook an intercaste marriage, GD felt a particular repugnance for the workings of caste discrimination. He consequently made the cause of the Untouchables a special concern, initiating a great many projects of his own, financing education, the digging of wells, and the building of temples in Untouchable communities. Finally, on a more personal level, Birla fulfilled his duties as *sevadar* as host and keeper, constantly placing his homes and hospitality at the disposal of Gandhi. In light of these facts, it seems somehow fitting, though tragically so, and doubtless with a bitter irony, that Gandhi should spend his final days at Birla House in Delhi. As if to consecrate a lifelong relationship based on service, spiritual guidance, and giving, Birla donated the very home in which the Mahatma died to the Indian people. Birla House now belongs to India's National Trust.

Yet Birla's career as a philanthropist and servant of Gandhi's teachings did not end with the Mahatma's death. He continued his "mission to serve good causes" until his own death in 1983. The thousands of schools established and administered by the Birla Education Trust, the countless orphanages, sanatoriums, libraries, hospitals, and dispensaries, the research clinics founded to improve agricultural productivity and self-sufficiency, the scholarship and exchange programs, the restoration of hundreds of Hindu temples, the Birla Institute of Technology and Science—these all bear witness to GD's continued sense of duty and service. These values, moreover, inscribed in the Indian context of *dan* and *seva*, were shared and furthered by other Birlas as well—GD's brothers, and perhaps most notably his nephew, MP (1918–1990), who in 1986 established the M.P. Birla Foundation, a trust founded to contribute to the "physical, intellectual, moral, and spiritual well-being of mankind." Also deeply influenced by Gandhi, MP conceived of the trust and of his many other philanthropic ventures as a way of dedicating his wealth and properties to God, at once "serving *Dharma* and God's children."[33] The very motto of the foundation, "From God we receive and to God we offer," stresses this conviction, reaffirming the continued resonance of *dan* and *seva* in Indian society.

HINDU NATIONALISM VERSUS CIVIL SOCIETY TODAY

In recent years, however, amidst the climate of resurgent Hindu nationalism, philanthropy of this sort has been interpreted as Hindu sectarianism. Certain secular supporters of the ruling Congress Party have leveled this charge, accusing the Birlas and others, including the prominent Hinduja family of Bombay, of using their wealth to promote a covert religious agenda.[34] To these critics, the Birlas' philanthropy is hardly disinterested. Behind the schools and hospitals, they see the looming, salmon temples. And despite the fact that the Hindujas have sponsored everything from sports programs to art exhibitions and Ravi Shankar concerts, their critics focus on the Hinduja Foundation's promotion of Vedic scholarship, seeing in its support of the study of ancient Hindu texts an attempt to promote Hindu values in the public sphere.

These are charges that confound many members of the Hinduja family and would have genuinely puzzled their philanthropic predecessors, the Birlas. For GD Birla was not only a staunch Gandhian but also, like the Hindujas, a loyal supporter of the Congress Party. Although earlier led by Gandhi, the Congress Party after Independence was shaped by Nehru and his vision of a socialist, secular, modern democracy. Consequently, it does not identify with any single religious tradition or movement, but claims all of India's culture as its heritage, including of course, Hindu culture. For this reason, the Birlas and Hindujas have felt no inconsistency in pledging allegiance to both India's Hindu culture and its secular, political leadership.

Straddling the fence in this manner, however, has become increasingly difficult in the polarized politics of the 1990s. For the rise of the

BJP has rendered religion the central political issue in India today, prompting an extremely heated public debate over whether Indian society can be secular and still be true to traditional Indian values.[35] To the religious activists of the BJP, the answer to this question is a resounding "no": the non-sectarian vision of Indian society promoted by Nehru's descendants in the Congress Party, they charge, is simply a slavish imitation of Western models, at once un-Indian, and irreligious. An authentic Indian nationalism, they argue, must be Hindu. By contrast, Congress secularists respond that these arguments lay the foundations for intolerance and chauvinism. In order to maintain pluralism in a multi-faith society, they challenge, the state and definitions of the nation must remain free from religious affiliation. Understandably chary of Hindu militancy, they are, however, accused of fostering a sort of extremism of their own: a secular extremism that sees all religion as potentially dangerous. In the charged atmosphere of contemporary Indian politics, moreover, it is often the voices that shout the loudest that receive the most attention. Thus, one is faced with the specter of a great political divide: at one extreme are the modernists allied with Nehru's ideas and the Congress Party, accused of selling India's soul to a Western vision of society; at the other, Hindu nationalists associated with Hindu militancy and the BJP, charged with intolerance and chauvinism. Religiously motivated giving, such as that sponsored by the Birlas and the Hindujas, as a result, is caught up in this cross fire of extremes.

There are, however, other moderate Hindu voices seeking to steer a path between the secular and religious fringes—among them some of India's leading intellectuals, who attempt to assert Gandhi's point that a society based on traditional religious values need not be intolerant. Ashis Nandy, a historian and political analyst who is one of the key figures in this group, makes a distinction between the strident Hindu nationalists' political ideology and Hinduism—regarding the latter as a "faith and a way of life" that permeates traditional Indian culture.[36] Nandy implies that the Hindu nationalist party, the BJP, has exploited a legitimate yearning for Indians to create a postcolonial sense of national identity out of their own cultural roots. One of Nandy's colleagues, the distinguished anthropologist T. N. Madan, makes something of the same point in his critique of secularism in India. Although wary of "the real dangers of Hindu communalism," Madan has emphasized that he and his fellow intellectuals in India must "overcome our distrust of India's indigenous religious traditions."[37] His hope is that this substratum of traditional culture can become the basis for a new Indian unity, where the various religious traditions in India may be seen as "members of one family."[38] Along the same lines, the historian Partha Chatterjee has argued that nationalism in India is now poised to launch its "most powerful, creative and historically significant project," namely the creation of "a 'modern' national culture that is nevertheless not Western."[39] While renouncing the extremist forms of Hindu nationalism, the social psychologist Sudhir Kakar claims that the movement has touched on a legitimate need for a society to have what Durkheim termed "a continuity of collective memory" in order for it to move constructively from the past to the future.[40] Thus some of India's leading intellectuals have called for the creation of a sense of civil society in India based on Hindu cultural values, but shorn of the stridency and intolerance associated with the BJP and other Hindu nationalist endeavors.

What this Hindu intellectual circle has argued is that there is indeed an authentic, inclusive Indian cultural tradition. It may be called "Hindu," but it plays no favorites among contemporary religious communities divided by the labels of Hindu, Muslim, Sikh, Jain, Buddhist, and Christian. Although Hindu politicians have attempted to coopt it, this authentic cultural core provides an alternative to the Hindu-secular culture dichotomy, allowing for the cultural integrity of the former and the tolerance of the latter in a modern Hindu civil society that resonates the *dharmic* values of traditional Indian culture. It is a compromise that will probably not please the Nehru secularists or the BJP nationalists. It is, nonetheless, a model of a tolerant society that reconciles both traditional Indian values and the principle of religious pluralism.

This vision of Indian society is one that the Birlas and Hindujas, following Gandhi, wish to foster. The most severe of their secular critics are right in seeing them as supporting a kind of religious agenda, for they certainly rely upon traditional Indian values expressed in Hindu religious language for their understanding of what is virtuous and good in their society, and what is therefore worthy of philanthropic support. When the Birlas go further and actually construct temples, and when the Hindujas go further and support the teaching of classical Hindu texts, it is even more apparent that their vision of the Indian good life is to a large extent a Hindu one. But they see nothing narrowly dogmatic about this vision: their Hinduism is—if one will pardon the term—quite catholic.

Will secular critics of the Hindu philanthropists be persuaded that the Birlas and Hindujas and others are benign, or will they see their public-spirited Hindu generosity as a kind of fundamentalism in disguise? The answer to this question depends in part on current events, and on whether the strident polarization between secular and religious forces increases or diminishes in the public forum. But it also turns on the actions of the philanthropists themselves—on whether they will continue to fund such projects as the construction of temples that appear to be sectarian and divisive, antithetical to the notion of a tolerant Hindu social order, or whether they will increasingly support public enterprises, such as education and health care that serve the whole society, regardless of sectarian affiliation, and thus celebrate the common heritage of India's culture. In the latter case, the Hindu philanthropists must make clear that their vision of *dharma* is not the narrow one of Hindu duty, but a broad notion of social good, and that their observance of *dan* and *seva* is simply an expression of generosity and service that ennobles the social whole. In this way Indian philanthropists can hope to steer between the Scylla of Hindu sectarianism and the Charybdis of Western secularism, and affirm that they are not just imitating the Rockefellers of the West or promoting their own religious cause, but helping to build a modern Indian civil society based on traditional Hindu values.

NOTES

1. Edward Shils, "Nation, Nationality, Nationalism and Civil Society," *Nations and Nationalism* 1, 1 (March 1995), p. 118.

2. For Hindu nationalism see Peter van der Veer, *Religious Nationalism: Hindus and Muslims in India* (Berkeley: University of California Press, 1994). See also Daniel Gold, "Organized Hinduisms: From Vedic Tradition to Hindu Nation," in Martin E. Marty and R. Scott Appelby, eds., *Fundamentalisms Observed* (Chicago: University of Chicago Press, 1991); and the section on Hindu nationalism in Mark Juergensmeyer, *The New Cold War? Religious Nationalism Confronts the Secular State* (Berkeley: University of California Press, 1993).

3. Robert Lingat, *The Classical Law of India*, trans. Duncan M. Derrett (Berkeley: University of California Press, 1973), p. 5.

4. For a discussion of the variety of meanings of the concept of *dharma*, see Wendy O'Flaherty, ed., *The Concept of Duty in South Asia* (Delhi: Vikas Publishers, 1978).

5. Translations from the *Dharmasastra* are found in Ainslie T. Embree, ed., *Sources of Indian Tradition* (New York: Columbia University Press, 1988), pp. 213–33.

6. The classic translation is by G. U. Pope, *The Sacred Kurral* (New Delhi: Asian Educational Services, 1984, originally published in 1886). See also *The Tirukkural: A Unique Guide to Moral, Material and Spiritual Prosperity*, trans. G. Vanmikanathan (Tiruchirapalli: Tiruchirapalli Prachar Sangh, 1969).

7. For translations of ancient writings relating to the political implications of *dharma* see Mackenzie Brown, ed., *The White Umbrella* (Westport, CT: Greenwood Press, 1981).

8. Cited in J. Gonda, "Gifts," in *Change and Continuity in Indian Religion* (London and the Hague: Mouton & Co., 1965), p. 209, ft. 35 (our translation from the French).

9. Useful discussions of the concept of *dan* in ancient Hindu texts may be found in J. Filliozat, *Annuaire du college de France* 55 (Paris, 1955): pp. 229 ff.; J. Gonda, "Gifts," in ibid., pp. 198–228; J. C. Heesterman, "Reflections on the Significance of the Daksina," *Indo-Iranian Journal* 3 (1959), pp.

241–58; and P. V. Kane, "Dana," in *History of Dharmasastra*, Vol. II, Part II (Poona: Bhandarkar Oriental Research Institute, 1941), pp. 837–88.

10. See Wendy Doniger and Brian Smith, trans., *The Laws of Manu* (London: Penguin Books, 1991); and *Manusrmrti: The Ideal Democratic Republic of Manu*, trans. by M. V. Patwardhan (Delhi: Motilal Banarsidass, 1968).

11. Gonda, p. 208.

12. See Kane, pp. 843 ff., for a discussion of each of these constituent elements and the elaborate rules surrounding them in the *Dharmasastra*.

13. In the *Rg Veda* cows, horses, and other animals, as well as chariots, gold, bulls, young women, clothes, and food are cited as gifts. Gonda shows that land is not mentioned in the early Vedas. However, already by the VasDhS.29,l6 land is discussed as the most highly meritorious of all donations. Kane can claim that "the gift of land has been eulogized as the most meritorious of all gifts from ancient times" (p. 858).

14. *Rigveda* x, 107, cited in Kane, pp. 838–39. Kane discusses the principal places where *dan* is discussed in the *Dharmasastra* in *History*, pp. 837–38. See, as well, the so-called eulogies of gifts, the *danastutis* of the *Rg Veda*, compiled in M. Patel, *The Danastutis of the Rg-veda*, trans. B. H. Kapadia (Vallabh Vidyanagar, 1961).

15. This is Kane's translation. As he continues, "The word . . . consists of two parts, *ista* (what is sacrificed) and *purta* (what is filled)," p. 843.

16. Daksa III, 17–18, cited in Gonda, p. 223.

17. Gonda, pp. 227–28.

18. Gloria Goodwin Raheja, *The Poison in the Gift: Ritual Prestation, and the Dominant Caste in a North Indian Village* (Chicago and London: University of Chicago Press: 1988), p. 254.

19. Regarding the genre of devotional love (*bhakti*) and the literature and social movements associated with it, see Edward Dimmock and Denise Levertov, *In Praise of Krishna* (Garden City: Anchor Books, 1967); Friedhelm Hardy, *Viraha-bhakti: The Early History of Krishna Devotion in South India* (Delhi: Oxford University Press, 1984); and J. S. Hawley and Mark Juergensmeyer, *Songs of the Saints of India* (New York: Oxford University Press, 1988).

20. For a further discussion of the importance of *seva* in the Radhasoami movement see Mark Juergensmeyer, *Radhasoami Reality: The Logic of a Modern Faith* (Princeton, NJ: Princeton University Press, 1991), pp. 127–46.

21. This distinction between "gifting" and philanthropy is made by Douglas E. Haynes, "From Tribute to Philanthropy: The Politics of Gift Giving in a Western Indian City," *Journal of Asian Studies* 46, 2 (May 1987), p. 339ft.

22. Haynes, pp. 340–41. See also David West Rudner, "Religious Gifting and Inland Commerce in Seventeenth-Century South India," *Journal of Asian Studies* 46, 2 (May 1987), pp. 361–80.

23. See Kenneth Jones, *Arya Dharm: Hindu Consciousness in 19th-Century Punjab* (Berkeley: University of California Press, 1976).

24. On the life of GD Birla and his relationship to Gandhi, we have relied heavily on Ram Niwas Jaju's *G.D. Birla: A Biography* (New Delhi: Vikas publishing, 1985) and M. M. Jenuja's *The Mahatma and the Millionaire: A Study in Gandhi-Birla Relations* (Haryana: Modern publishers, 1993). In addition to

these works, see also P. Chentsal Rao's *B.M. Birla: His Deeds and His Dreams* (New Delhi: Arnold Heineman, 1983) and V. Gauri Shanker's *To Man, to Country, and to God: A Biography of M.P. Birla* (New Delhi: Har-Anand Publications, 1993) for general family background.

25. Cited in Jaju, p. 34.

26. Ibid., pp. 35 ff.

27. Cited in Ibid., p. 41.

28. G. D. Birla, *In the Shadow of the Mahatma: A Personal Memoir* (Calcutta: Orient Longmans Ltd., 1953), p. 2.

29. Cited in Jenuja, p. 144.

30. Birla, p. xvi.

31. On the other hand, it has been argued that Birla had much to gain by Gandhi's main project—national independence—and the severing of India's economic ties to British industry.

32. Jenuja, p. 65.

33. Smt. Priyamvada Birla, MP's wife, commenting on the reasons for the establishment of the M.P. Birla Foundation. Cited in Shanker, p. 92.

34. Like the Birlas of GD's generation, the Hinduja family today is dominated by four brothers: Gopichand P., Srichand P., Ashok P., and Prakash P. The offspring of Parmand Hinduja, who in 1915 left the province of Sind in what is now Pakistan to come to Bombay as a money-lender and trader, the brothers successfully converted their father's modest legacy into a vast trading and financial empire. Now one of the world's wealthiest families, the Hindujas have, however, been accused of amassing their fortune through illicit arms-trading and other shadowy means. Their principal philanthropic arm, the Hinduja Foundation, nonetheless finances a vast array of altruistic endeavors throughout the world.

35. See Mark Juergensmeyer, "The Debate over Hindu Nationalism," *Contention* 4, 3 (spring 1995), pp. 211–21.

36. Ashis Nandy, "Hinduism versus Hindutva: The Inevitability of a Confrontation," *Times of India*, February 18, 1991.

37. T. N. Madan, "Whither Indian Secularism?" in T. N. Madan, ed., *Religion in India*, 2nd ed. (Delhi: Oxford University Press, 1992), p. 696.

38. Ibid.

39. Partha Chatterjee, *The Nation and Its Fragments: Colonial and Postcolonial Histories* (Princeton: Princeton University Press, 1993), p. 6.

40. Sudhir Kakar, "The New Hindu Identity: A Profile," Electronic Newsstand, an on-line news service, 1994.

.13.

Religious Authority, Reform, and Philanthropy in the Contemporary Muslim World

GREGORY C. KOZLOWSKI

Europeans and Americans have cast the recent history of the Muslim world primarily in terms of religion and its presumed, usually negative, political consequences.[1] They pay little, if any, attention to the ways in which Islam's institutional complexion has changed over the past fifty years. Muslim philanthropic institutions,[2] most notably endowments: *awqaf* (the singular is *waqf*),[3] have altered their aims and style of management in dramatic as well as subtle ways. Those transformations have been much more than simple responses to the stimuli provided by a supposedly innovative and politically aggressive "West." Since the eighteenth century, at least, currents of change within the Muslim world have affected the shape of philanthropic activity probably as much as the examples set by the Ford or Rockefeller foundations.[4] Contemporary philanthropic institutions in the Islamic world have merged, separated and reconfigured both external and indigenous forms. Old and new have blended, sometimes almost imperceptibly, in any given organization. Muslim philanthropy in the context of global history since 1945, therefore, displays a series of unresolved tensions. On the religious level, "scripturalist" approaches to Islam, especially those employing the Oneness of God (*tawhid*) to dismiss "popular" beliefs, such as the efficacy

279

of praying to saints (*awliya*) to intercede with the Almighty, exert considerable international appeal.

Religious reformers of the eighteenth century, among both the Sunni and Shii, in some sense reinvented purificationist approaches that reshaped contemporary readings of the Islamic past.[5] In the late twentieth century, scholars and journalists have usually described that understanding of the faith and its history as "fundamentalist"—though "revivalist" or "reformist" might better suit the character of what are really several different movements.[6] Muslim and non-Muslim observers alike have tended to assume that the fundamentalists have succeeded. If the commentators' opinions can be trusted, fundamentalists have acquired a monopoly on determining Islam's future.

By whatever name, neither revivalists nor fundamentalists have been as successful as the trend spotters have imagined. "Popular" styles of piety within Islam—often apolitical and latitudinarian in their acceptance of the intercession of saints or displaying a certain eagerness to admit that miracles do happen, have survived nearly two centuries of preaching by self-assured reformers. The persistence of those popular inclinations among believers is partly explainable because the beliefs and practices, scorned by the revivalists/reformists, are anchored in tens of thousands of locally controlled endowed/philanthropic institutions.

Because some individual Muslims, as well as groups of Muslims, eschew the most divisive consequences of implicit or explicit confrontations between cosmopolitan and local versions of Islam, Euro-Americans often miss the anxieties which emerge between one set of believers and another. No single trend or movement, whether scripturalist or popular, currently dominates all Muslims in every place in the world.

Muslim philanthropic organizations in the modern world reflect religious tensions and compromises in several ways. An Iranian "foundation" (*bunyad*) might emphasize that Islam is the only religion which genuinely espouses social protest by the poor. A Saudi Arabian "trust" stresses that wealth bestowed on the few meets the highest ethical standards of Islam, so long as a significant portion of the abundance finds its way into the hands of the needy. Both Iranian and Saudi Arabian organizations advance one or another reformist line, which appears contradictory, but countless other institutions hold close to the popular practices of the localities in which most of their activities take place. In the face of bold contrarieties, whether between one or another style of reformism, and both in conflict with populist customs, another set of institutions seeks to avoid all doctrinal as well as doctrinaire wrangling.

The global prominence which Islam has achieved because of such dramatic political events as the Iranian Revolution, the rapid rise in the fortunes of a very few oil-rich states, or the Persian Gulf War, carries with it another knot of uncertainties. While it may be an error to overemphasize the connections of Islam to politics, the interaction between the two should be considered. The melding of religion and politics presents a variety of aspirations. On the one hand, Islam seems to some believers to be returning to the central place in world history it occupied from the sixth until the eighteenth century. Both wealth and revolution engender prominence. At the same time, highly visible Muslim movements must defend themselves against the opprobrium that Euro-Americans almost invariably heap on all things Islamic. Elation over apparent victories stands alongside a persistent fear of imminent defeat. Many philanthropic organizations manifest that fluctuation between bright confidence and a nagging sense of impending catastrophe.

Islamdom's philanthropic institutions operate within international and local environments too rich to be described within the narrow boundaries of a single essay. Muslims live within economies that include very rich nations—Abu Dhabi or Saudi Arabia—and very poor ones—Bangladesh and Sudan. Turkey, Pakistan, India, and Malaysia aspire to industrial prosperity and political power. The middle economic tier, comprising Turkey, India, and Pakistan, already possess sophisticated technological resources in their universities, laboratories, and factories, but still must contend with majority populations directly engaged in agriculture. Nations like Afghanistan still have "internal frontiers" dominated by nomadic or seminomadic groups. Moreover, with a Muslim population exceeding some six million, the United States of America must now be reckoned a significant part of the Muslim world.

Rather than attempting to survey developments in philanthropy throughout the modern Islamic *oikumene*, this essay will focus on Turkey, South Asia—India and Pakistan—and Saudi Arabia, while making occasional references to other regions of the Muslim world. After providing a brief summary of a Quranic view of charity, together with examples from the life of the Holy Prophet Muhammad and the history of endowments (*awqaf*) in the premodern period, the essay then describes a number of philanthropic organizations in nations just mentioned before returning to more general themes in the conclusion.

THE ALMIGHTY, HUMANS, WEALTH, AND HISTORY

The *Holy Qur'an* contains many injunctions to believers to take care of the poor. Giving to the orphan, the widow, the wayfarer, and the needy is a duty which all believers owe to God. Formalized as one of the "five pillars" of Islam, *zakat* is often interpreted as a kind of tax requiring that the prosperous give annually a certain portion of their total wealth—not merely a part of their income, to support the poor. The Holy Book has many warnings about the punishments that await the avaricious: "And let not those who hoard up that which Allah hath bestowed upon them from his bounty think that it is better for them. Nay, it is worse for them. That which they hoard will be their collar on the Day of Resurrection" (III, 180).[7]

Many of Islam's counsels demonstrate a strong egalitarian bent and a fear of the hierarchies that wealth generates.[8] To the present day, Muslim religious thinkers emphasize that the poor have an inherent right to their sustenance and an Islamic state ought to guarantee that right.[9] Thus, "charity" carries no connotation of being a redistribution of wealth to people who do not deserve it. In its strictest sense, *zakat* is not philanthropy—something which arises from a human concern for the disadvantaged segments of humanity. Rather it is a divine command: part of Islam's moral imperative. One must give, because God has ordered it. Making such donations brings the individual closer to God.

Ideal Islamic states would enforce *zakat* as a matter of government policy. However, once the earliest centuries of Muslim history had passed, few governments required all believers to pay alms or punished those who did not. In the present, state enforcement of this regulation is almost unheard of. Even so, the impulse to give to the poor remains strong. Muslims serious about that command have published scores of pamphlets that describe how, in the absence of governmental authority which requires it, any person can calculate for themselves the *zakat* which she or he owes.[10] In their emphasis on alms as a response to divine command and lack of criticism of those who require material assistance, Muslim theological views on charity are very close to those expressed by Christian thinkers in the Late Antique and Medieval periods.[11]

Beginning with the political economists of the seventeenth and eighteenth centuries, however, Euro-American thought on philanthropy gradually divorced itself from a purely theological frame of reference. Philanthropists in Europe and North America have sometimes expressed religious motives for their activities (Andrew Carnegie or John D. Rockefeller, for example), but questions involving the maintenance of public order or the pragmatic benefits provided by assisting the upward movement of the disadvantaged became increasingly prominent in explaining the need for private philanthropic enterprise.[12]

In the history of the United States, philanthropic organizations emerged in the interstices between church, state, and incorporated capitalism. A Ford or Rockefeller foundation developed its own credo that contained aspects of legal-governmental and commercial as well as theological systems of thought. The inherent contradictions in those different *mentalites* could be camouflaged rather than resolved by the actual development of a philanthropic enterprise.[13]

As with the history of Euro-American philanthropy, any attempt to describe the social history of the moral imperative to charity in the Muslim world soon leaves behind the obvious certainties arising from divine commands and the necessity of human obedience to them. Just as in Euro-American philanthropy, complicated webs of intention and activity appear in Muslim benefactions. While the genuinely pious motives of individuals must be considered, placing charitable activity in a social context requires attention to the many economic, cultural, and political exchanges which necessarily accompany any attempt to distribute great wealth to worthwhile causes.

Endowments (*awqaf*) became by the fourteenth or fifteenth centuries (C.E.) the Islamic world's most familiar philanthropic institutions. Within that long period of time and vast geography, the details of any *waqf*'s distribution of wealth had much to do with the values of the individuals who established and managed it. In the eighth century (C.E.) Muslims located the authority to create endowments in the practice (*sunnah*) of the Holy Prophet.[14] Collections of anecdotes (*ahadith*) about the sayings and doings of Muhammad included accounts of his connection to the first endowments. After the conquest of the agricultural oasis at Khaibar, the various orchards and fields of the place were distributed to the warriors by way of booty. Umar us-Sadiq, who eventually became the second caliph, approached the Prophet, asking him what would be the religiously appropriate way of dealing with the property he had acquired. The Prophet told Umar to "tie up" (one of the basic meanings of the Arabic verb *waqafa)* the groves and fields, devoting any income from them to the welfare of all believers.

Apart from those few edifying textual references, the history of endowed institutions in the first Islamic centuries is difficult to trace. The earliest dedicatory inscription for a *waqf* so far uncovered, with the date C.E. 912, comes from Palestine.[15] This endowment mixed a concern for public utility and the kin or dependents of the founder. The income of the *waqf* derived from a rest house for traveling merchants. Those caravanserais usually contained a mosque and were thus pious as well as profitable. Some of the earnings from the hostel went for the upkeep of its buildings, and the rest the founder dedicated to the support of his kith and kin.

The heap of rubble from which archaeologists recovered the inscription just mentioned pointed to one of the major drawbacks for *awqaf:* they tended to fall into neglect and then disappear entirely. Because they were dedicated to God, they were supposed to be permanent— immune from seizure or sale. Yet, very few endowments managed to survive intact over long periods of time.[16] Succeeding generations of the custodians/heirs of *awqaf* lost a living memory of their founders as well as their original intentions. Managers or beneficiaries sometimes feuded among themselves over the disposition of the assets and income of endowments.[17]

New dynasties or changes of faction within a dynasty meant that *awqaf* established by ruling elites faced politically motivated predation.[18] The dissolution of endowments illustrated the many ways in which social, political, cultural, and economic change occurred in Muslim history. Despite the dismal performance of *awqaf* as guarantors of temporal and financial permanence, Muslims who possessed sufficient discretionary wealth continued to turn to *awqaf* when it came time to settle their earthly affairs.

"Religious and charitable trust" is a common textbook definition of a *waqf.* In practice, endowments were much more than that. Personal, familial, and religious concerns mixed easily in all *awqaf.* Some percentage of the endowed income customarily did go to support a mosque, religious school (*madrasah*), and shrine or to a ceremony such as the commemoration of the birthday of the Holy Prophet. Yet, with the appointment of a custodian—often the donor him/herself or some close relative—and the assignment of some of the proceeds to family members or dependents, the endowment bore certain resemblances to Anglo-American testamentary arrangements, such as entailments or trusts.[19] The legal fluidity of *awqaf,* despite their proven inability to grant fiscal or social stability, made them a favored instrument for settling the estates of people belonging to the higher and middling ranks of society.

In the early modern period—the sixteenth to the eighteenth centuries (c.e.)—Muslim rulers built and maintained mosques and religious schools with funds generated by *awqaf.* Because Muslim theology denied any unqualified divine sanction to kings, pious endowments became a way of providing an unacknowledged religious legitimacy. As God alone was (and is) the sole owner (*malik*) of the universe, any human's claim to temporal lordship (also, *malik,* but translated as "king" in the latter context) amounted to blasphemy.[20]

A public proclamation of Islamic devotion through the creation of endowments, therefore, established ambiguous connections between the faith and any rulers of the state claiming to be Muslims. Public benefactions attempted to mollify the suspicions of the "piety-minded" that their rulers must be hypocrites.[21] Religious scholars, even those who accepted employment from sultans, amirs, maliks, and padishahs, found it hard to avoid the moral apprehension that few, if any, temporal lords could be effective sovereigns while remaining at the same time good Muslims. Supplying the patronage which built the schools where those same skeptical specialists in the Islamic religious sciences (*ulama*) studied and taught did not always quiet the scholars' criticisms.[22] Royal philanthropy carried a stigma. Scholars often did their best to avoid imperial patronage entirely. Independent *ulama,* perhaps the majority in any given period, supported themselves through private teaching and preaching. They also seem to have maintained close links of direct kinship and marriage to families of merchants and artisans who provided them with material sustenance.

Building tombs for themselves and their close kin, whose maintenance supposedly permanent *awqaf* guaranteed, was another activity which might enhance a monarch's or a dynasty's reputation.[23] From a puritanical perspective, the construction of ostentatious mausolea smacked of idolatry, but most rulers ignored religious scruple. Dynastic tombs constituted a genealogical argument stressing the historical depth of a royal house and implying that rulers successful enough to build elaborate sepulchers must have enjoyed divine approval.

On a more obvious economic level, endowments might act as a spur for economic development. Mosques and *madrasahs* built in suburbs or near caravanserais in underpopulated regions might become the loci for periodic fairs, which could lead eventually to full-scale urbanization.[24] The encouragement of trade was particularly important because the personal incomes of early modern Muslim kings often came from taxes on the transportation and sale of goods. Thriving commerce helped to fill the privy purse.

In the seventeenth century, Mughal officials in eastern Bengal provided *waqf*-like grants to agricultural entrepreneurs who pioneered the cultivation of the region's delta. Military and religious specialists obtained significant easements on the land revenue so long as they agreed to build mosques and religious schools.[25] Since imperial officials derived their incomes from assignments of land revenue, subordinate officials benefited from any investment which brought new land under the plow.

Women in the various imperial households of the early modern period were significant as the founders and custodians of endowments. Sometimes queens and princesses established the mosques and religious academies. In that way they contributed to the reputation of the ruling house while acquiring their own public personae as benefactors of the faith.[26] By acting as managers of such *awqaf* they not only enjoyed a reputation for piety, but received an income which could assist them in retaining an independent source of wealth should their husband/ father/patron's successors cut off their access to the resources of the state.

Imperial establishments were both big and complex. In the major towns and cities, imperially funded mosques, whose preachers were obligated to begin the Friday prayer with an acknowledgment of the reigning emperor, were a constant reminder of the authority claimed by the state. Most imperial endowments carried provisions for the distribution of alms on important festivals. Only those located near such institutions were able to enjoy the money or foodstuffs offered at imperially sponsored establishments.

Royal endowments have left the most easily accessible and richest documentary evidence. Scholars have been quickest to mine those sources. But all of the activities noted in connection with imperial *awqaf* could be undertaken at subimperial levels by individuals who possessed some kind of power in particular cities, towns, and villages. Locally based strongmen and women established a far greater number of endowments than kings or their wealthiest courtiers ever did.[27]

Paying attention to endowments created by local powerholders permits a somewhat different perspective on Muslim philanthropy in the early modern period. Theological as well as moral doubts about the genuineness of the faith of even the most ostentatiously pious sultans may have inspired some Muslims to employ local endowments to insulate institutions crucial to the daily practice of the faith—mosques, shrines, and schools—from imperial interference. Local endowments helped to defend the faith against the possibly corrupting influences of a state run by hypocritical Muslims.

On a purely political level, locally based *awqaf* anchored the authority of neighborhood, town, and village elites. The founders of local endowments might have attained prominence in one of several ways. Wealthy merchants and artisans were prodigious founders of endowments.[28] The managers and devotees of the tombs of holy men (more rarely women) could parlay control over those endowments into local influence.[29] The rootedness of such places in the political economies of their regions made it possible for the supposedly subordinate individuals who founded or managed those establishments to resist or ignore imperial power simply by surviving on their home turf. Though the early modern states sought to prevent them, provincial officials could create private followings in a given region through the exercise of religious patronage. Court panegyrists may have claimed that their patrons controlled each and every pious foundation within their kingdoms, but such statements did not reflect political realities closer to the ground.

In the early modern Muslim world, therefore, most philanthropy was undertaken in fairly restricted social environments by men and women of "modest substance."[30] The mosques they founded, or the shrines those local authorities contributed to, were often sites for the distribution of charity. Clothing and food were distributed through them. The character of such giving was highly personal. Both donor and recipient knew each other. Offering food or other relief was part of a claim to higher social status. Accepting such gifts implied a certain deference to the benefactor. This exchange did upon occasion give rise to popular resentment. The Persian poet, Hafiz (d. ca. 1390 C.E.) penned the following verses, which hinted at the discontent:

> One day a drunken mullah
> gave his verdict on the Holy Law.

"Drinking wine is bad," he said,
"But having a *waqf* is worse."

Local power holders might be petty tyrants, but they were, at least, a familiar part of the ordinary person's world. Patrons and the patronized shared a common social microcosm. Sultans and padishahs rarely intruded on those smaller universes. The king might be a fellow Muslim, but remained a distant figure to those living in the many thousand towns and villages of the early modern Muslim world. The faith of Islam was practiced for the most part in those local settings. The Meccan pilgrimage (Hajj)—the chief expression of the universal community of faith (*ummah*)—remained an arduous task for the great majority of the faithful. Of all the Ottoman sultans, only one, Yavuz Selim, ever made the pilgrimage.

Beginning in the eighteenth century, much of this world began to change. Though from their inception the early modern states of Islamdom sought the extirpation of local knots of power, they lacked the effective military-bureaucratic means to do so. At the same time, the ideal of a single Islamic community symbolized by the Hajj received practical encouragement from an unlikely source: European imperialists. Relative safety brought by British naval forces deployed in the Arabian Sea and Persian Gulf made the pilgrimage more common. Muslim philanthropy would likewise gain access to the means of globalizing itself.

EUROPEAN EMPIRES AND MODERN MUSLIM STATES

Muslim kings usually took a direct interest only in those endowments founded by themselves or their predecessors. The advent of European rule, however, altered the situation. As the British became the dominant power in India during the nineteenth century, their officials were drawn inexorably into the administration of a number of public *awqaf.* Though some administrators fretted over their involvement in "native" religious institutions, they often found themselves actually managing the day-to-day affairs of such organizations. The "Hughli Imambara" of Calcutta was a case in point. An Imambara is a shrine used by the Twelver (Imami) branch of the Shiis to commemorate the martyrdom of Imam Husain, the grandson of the Prophet. A wealthy resident of Calcutta, Muhammad Mohsin, had dedicated the income of a sizable tract of land to support an Imambara. When not being used for religious services, the building was given over to the teaching of the rudiments of Persian grammar to a few boys in the neighborhood, some of whom were Muslims and some not.

Muhammad Mohsin had never married and was childless. At his death in the 1830s, a friend took over the management of the Imambara. British officials were soon hearing complaints that the custodian was expropriating the income for his gain. At first, the British appointed one of their own Muslim officers, Ali Akbar Khan, to act as an overseer. When he and the guardian could not agree, the British appointed Ali Akbar in the guardian's stead. British officials began sitting on the Board of Trustees of the Hughli Imambara and started to emphasize its educational activities rather than its religious purposes. Eventually the Imambara became "Hughli College," a government-supervised institution which introduced a British-style curriculum taught mostly in English.[31]

By the 1870s, a number of disputes concerning *awqaf* had reached the British courts. Perhaps because these feuds originated among the descendants of the endowments' founders, British judges became ever more concerned that the income of *awqaf* was being devoted primarily to the donors and their kin. British judges considered that practice an evasion of the Muslim's own inheritance laws, which prescribed a specific order of heirs and the shares they should receive. For example, according to a strict interpretation of that system, women inherit a smaller portion of their parents' estates than their brothers. When there are only daughters, their shares do not increase. Most of the portion that would have gone to sons goes to male first cousins. Numbers of Muslims in India, and elsewhere, converted their estates into endowments that named daughters as the trustees and primary beneficiaries. Among other things, this approach preserved control of property within a particular family unit represented in the female line.[32]

Reigning European economic and legal theory in the nineteenth century held that in order to be productive, land or other assets, such as buildings, must be subject to the forces of the market.[33] Inefficient proprietors had to give way to individuals willing, skilled, and eager to respond to the opportunities generated by a "modern" economy. In England itself a lively debate was underway during the same period concerning perpetuities of any sort. Though noted intellectuals such as John Stuart Mill and Henry Sumner Maine argued both for and against taking the pains necessary to perpetuate the original activities supported by trusts, the majority view was against any sort of property arrangement whose terms could not be altered to fit changing circumstances.

British as well as French Colonial courts eventually ruled that *awqaf*, to be legally valid, had to be primarily "religious and charitable trusts."[34] The judgments of European legal organizations may well have created Islamic law and not merely enforced it. Whether the European judges were correct or incorrect in their rulings became irrelevant. Their views became guiding principle for many postimperial nation-states in the Muslim world.

Egypt,[35] Libya,[36] Syria, and Turkey[37] seized the assets of all *awqaf.* Endowments that benefited individual families were generally abolished.

"Public" *awqaf* were preserved when they appeared to be devoted to the preservation of historical buildings, the furtherance of learning, and the distribution of charity. Government bureaus began to take charge of the management of all those institutions deemed charitable and religious trusts. Custodians who had been appointed in the original deeds of endowment either disappeared entirely or acquiesced to bureaucratic overseers. The character of those changes can best be understood by looking at several individual regions of the Muslim world.

TURKEY: THE VEBHI KOÇ *VAKIF*

The Turkish revolution that followed World War I was one of the first and most thoroughgoing attempts to reorganize every aspect of Muslim life. *Law 667* of 13 December, 1925, although aimed at suppressing all Sufi orders and institutions, also abolished all custodial offices and transferred the assets as well of the management of all endowments to a central ministry of *awqaf.* Mosques were part of the Turkish Republic's cultural heritage, and their endowments became the preserve of the government. Those same officials, however, largely succeeded in suppressing the Sufi lodges by forbidding ordinary citizens to act as trustees for the endowments of such places. The simultaneous reorganization of the courts and the complete transformation of civil law, as well as the central role of the army in those activities, made it impossible for the trustees to forestall state annexion by appealing to the traditions of *shariah/fiqh* (Islamic law).

Up to the present day the Turkish state continues to control any endowments created before the revolution. However, a new sort of *vakıf* has appeared over the past thirty years. The founders of those endowments have been Turkey's wealthiest industrialists and financial magnates, such as Vebhi Koç (d. 1996). His *vakıf* provides an example of the process which combined concerns raised by the revolution with the endowment as part of Turkey's "cultural heritage."

Vebhi Koç's investments and enterprises were considerable when he incorporated his foundation on 17 January, 1969. His initial donation amounted to some twelve million Turkish lira (in a period when the TL was stable) or 8 percent of the capital of the Koç Holding Company. Other members of the Koç family made contributions, and in 1988 the Koç Foundation's worth was roughly some twenty million U.S. dollars. The word "Foundation" is frequently employed in its English language reports and the employment of the older term *vakıf* appears in the following statement almost as an act of nostalgia:[38]

> The institution of the *vakıf* (*waqf*) or pious foundation is an ancient tradition in the Islamic world. The earliest such foundations are known

> to have been established in the seventh century (c.e.) and they spread rapidly throughout Anatolia with the advance of the Turks from the eleventh century onward. Thanks to these foundations set up by private individuals and leading members of (sic) state, innumerable schools, libraries, mosques, charitable institutions, hospitals, facilities for travelers, fountains, bridges, roads and commercial buildings were built and operated for the public good. This tradition is still alive in Turkey today. . . . The *Vebhi Koç Foundation* is a direct heir to this rich tradition.

That quotation raises a number of subtle, and possibly controversial, points. In its brief references to the history of *awqaf* a note alluding to Islam's formative era is followed by a reference to the Turkish conquest of Anatolia and the proliferation of charitable institutions associated with the Turks. The Ataturk Revolution was for its first few decades eager to identify "Islam" solely in terms of the cultural heritage of the Turks. The call to prayer, for example, had to be sung in Turkish rather than Arabic (a requirement subsequently abandoned). The Roman script, in place of the modified Arabic script used in the Ottoman period, became the only approved method for writing and printing the Turkish language. Reform of the Turkish language itself meant the purging of thousands of Arabo-Persian words common in the formal language of the Ottoman Court.

Islam itself was nationalized. Perhaps the most telling example of that process can be seen in the cards identifying Muslim sacred objects in the Top Kapı Sarai Museum. After conquering the Mamluks in the early sixteenth century, the Ottomans acquired all the regalia of the caliphs; including some relics attributed to the Prophet himself: his cloak, his staff, his bow and sword. Yet the descriptions of those items in the museum occur only in English or Turkish—not in Arabic. From reading those descriptions, an outsider would never guess that the Holy Prophet had been of Arab stock, that Arabia had been the original heartland of Islam, or that the faith itself was international and not an indigenous Turkish religion. The Vebhi Koç Foundation, therefore, walks a narrow path between affirming the Turkish character of Islam, while admitting somewhat quietly an international dimension to the faith.

Recognizing a possible contradiction between affirmations of nationalism and Islamic universalism, one of the Foundation's reports quotes Vebhi Koç as saying, "It is my sincere belief that the worthiest of acts are those which provide institutions dedicated to the education of Turkish youth, to whom Ataturk has entrusted the future of the Republic." The actual expenditures of the Koç Foundation have been primarily directed to nationalist goals.

Before the incorporation of the Koç *vakıf* in 1969, Vebhi Koç had already made several donations for the following purposes:

1951—For the building of a student dormitory at Ankara University.

1960—A gift to the Ankara Children's Hospital.

1963—A gift to establish an eye bank as part of the eye clinic at Ankara University Medical School.

1967—A gift to establish the Cobalt Pavilion at the Admiral Bristol Hospital in Istanbul.

1967—A gift to build a dormitory at the ME Technical University in Ankara.

1967(?)—A gift to found a library and research facility at Anadolu University in Eskisehir.

After the formal establishment of the Foundation/Vakıf, hospitals and medical/nursing schools continued to receive support. In addition, cultural and educational institutions which the donor's own self-statement emphasized became major foci for the endowment's efforts. The Koç *vakıf* provides scholarships for Turkish students studying in their homeland as well as overseas. A secondary school located in the Findikli quarter of Istanbul has gotten particularly generous treatment. Described as meeting the "challenges of the twenty-first century," the two goals proposed in the school's charter were:

1) To teach a knowledge of and respect for Turkey's traditions, heritage and Ataturk ideals.

2) Provide students with the necessary skills to further intellectual growth and foster success in Turkish and English language universities.

In the furtherance of those goals, the "curriculum combines Turkish and 'Western'[39] materials and systems." The division of linguistic labor dictates that "Turkish language and literature, social studies, religion and morals," be taught in Turkish. English will be employed to develop skills in that language, also to teach mathematics and the sciences.[40] Over the past decade, that secondary school has become Koç University with similar goals and curricula at its core.

Apart from the Findikli educational complex, most of the Koç Foundation's donations resources have gone to the Ataturk Library and the Sadberk Hanım Muzesı. The building of the Ataturk Library began in 1973 and was completed in 1976. "With a commanding view of the Bosporus," the building's design was innovative enough to be nominated for the Agha Khan Prize in Architecture in 1982. The building marked the fiftieth anniversary of the Turkish Revolution and had room for more than a half-million books and videos. Foundation reports describe it as "The most modern public library in Turkey today. . . ." The Koç endowment eventually turned the management of the library over to the Istanbul municipal government.

The Sadberk Hanım Muzesı occupied a nineteenth-century mansion on the Bosporus in the Sariyer district of Istanbul. The Vebhi Koç Vakıf converted it into Turkey's first privately owned museum. The late wife of Vebhi Koç, Sadberk, started the museum's collection of traditional handicrafts: textiles, pottery, manuscripts, jewelry, documents, and artifacts from the Ottoman period. The museum attempts to display the arts and crafts of the Ottoman period as well as depicting, with great sympathy, village life before the revolution.

At once aware of the implications of Ataturk's revolution, Turkish nationalism and the lengthy history of Islam outside of Turkey, the Koç endowment has tended to support institutions and activities that have a national rather than international focus. This has more importance in the present as the political and military elites of the Turkish Republic look with a certain amount of apprehension at the increasingly public display of Islamic piety. Several manifestations of religious militance—a mob attack on a writer's conference attended by Aziz Nesin (a self-professed atheist), which ended up in the burning of the hotel and the deaths of thirty-five people, for example, alarmed the politicians and the generals for whom Islam is primarily a part of Turkey's cultural heritage. The Vebhi Koç *vakıf* presents no revivalist agenda, but adheres rather closely to the Ataturk tradition of putting Islam at the service of nation building.

INDIA AND PAKISTAN: CENTRALIZATION, LOCAL CONTROL, AND BENIGN INTERNATIONALISM

Nearly a century of involvement in the control of *awqaf* by the British raj meant that South Asia experienced a push for the centralized administration of all endowments before most other regions of the Muslim world. As noted above, the courts of the British empire had by 1894 decided that *waqfs* must be for "charitable and religious purposes."[41] Moreover, the British made the first, feeble attempts to register *awqaf*, partly under pressure from rising Muslim political leaders who demanded good management of endowments and the direction of funds to the "betterment of the community."[42]

During the late nineteenth and early twentieth centuries *awqaf* arrived at the center of political debate in British India. In part, the disagreements took place over the court decisions limiting "family" endowments. A seeming legislative success, the *Mussalman Wakf Validating Act* of 1913 turned out to have minimal impact since the bill was not retroactive.[43] The growing intensity of the struggle for independence tended to push the politics of endowments into the background. Likewise, the formation of governments in India and Pakistan after 1947 absorbed the energies of both countries' leaders.

India and Pakistan ended up taking rather different approaches to the regulation of Muslim endowments. As a self-professed secular state, India in many ways attempted to emulate the British by avoiding too much direct involvement in the management of Muslim institutions. A spate of legislation at both the state and all-India levels, however, resulted in a situation with which no one seems to be happy.[44] Semiofficial *waqf* boards have been created at the local, state, and federal levels. Civil servants who are Muslims are sometimes deputed to manage those organizations. Other board members are drawn from Muslim social service organizations, from local mosque councils, and from among prominent figures in individual cities or states. A few states, such as Karnataka, have created ministries of *awqaf*, usually combining them with the state's ministries of economic development.

Complaints about corruption in this system of *waqf* administration remain frequent. Despite laws requiring the registration of endowments, many individuals simply do not comply with government orders.[45] In addition, Muslims are deeply offended when private individuals seize buildings or lands supposedly protected by their status as *waqfs*. The destruction of the Babri Masjid in Faizabad-Ayodhya in December of 1993 was only one dramatic indication of a persistent problem as smaller endowments are absorbed by people looking for housing or new land.

Though the minority status of Muslims in India invariably turns any question about endowments into a debate over political rights and wrongs, many disagreements occur within the community about the proper use of *awqaf*-generated funds. For example, part of the Indian government's control over endowments registered with it is to levy a tax amounting to 6 percent of the income of any *waqf* that is supposed to be dedicated to the support of education. Yet, the relevant laws have never specified the style or content of the instruction to be promoted. At a national meeting held in Delhi in 1979, one of the most contentious issues on the agenda proved to be whether or not contributions from *awqaf* funds could be used for anything except the furtherance of religious knowledge.[46] In the end, proponents of both sides—those favoring a restriction to religious learning and those advocating a broader use for all types of education, especially in science and technology—could agree only to keep disagreeing.

While many, perhaps most, endowments in India suffer from tiny incomes or disagreements about their management, a few new types of philanthropy have emerged. The Hamdard Pharmaceutical Company of India (not to be confused with Hamdard of Pakistan, which will be discussed at length shortly) has directed a considerable portion of its profits to the establishment of an Islamic Research Institute located at

Tughluqabad just south of New Delhi. An impressive multistoried library houses rare manuscripts as well as published books. A museum of Yunani Tibb ("Greek Medicine," which refers to the medical system pioneered by Hippocrates, Galen, and other physicians of the Hellenistic period and further developed by Ibn Sina—Avicenna—and other practioners in the Muslim world up to the present day) attempts to preserve a sense of the scientific progress made by Muslims. Finally, a conference center and publishing house support ongoing research on Islamic subjects.

Apart from such major philanthropic enterprises, a few individuals have taken the first steps to restructure existing endowments to make them more profitable as well as to expand the kind of support they offer to the Muslim community. In the city of Hyderabad, the capital of the modern state of Andhra Pradesh, a retired civil servant, Dr. Hasan uddin Ahmad, set about transforming a small *waqf* into a major enterprise.[47]

The *Bayt ul-Madinah Waqf* was created in 1942 by Dr. Ahmad's uncle. Its economic base consisted of four houses whose rental income was sent to the city of Madinah in Saudi Arabia to support a number of elderly Hyderabadis, most of them women, who had retired to the Holy City where they devoted themselves to prayer and the cleansing of the mosque surrounding the tomb of the Holy Prophet. When the domain of the Nizam of Hyderabad joined the Indian Union in 1948, the founder of the endowment was not allowed to transfer Indian rupees to Saudi Arabia. The founder used the endowment's funds to support a local mosque and for other pious purposes, such as providing scholarships for poor boys or paying for the weddings of poor girls.

Over time, however, the houses that provided the income for those activities became dilapidated. It became difficult to secure tenants willing to pay their rent promptly, and the income dropped off to the point where it barely met the expenses of maintaining the mosque, not to mention the other charitable activities. The founder of the *Bayt ul-Madinah* died childless in 1961; his brother, Dr. Ahmad's father, acted as custodian until his own death three years later. Finally, Dr. Hasan uddin Ahmad became custodian. As part of his duties as a member of the Indian Administrative Service, Dr. Ahmad had acted as secretary to the Central Waqf Board in New Delhi. He embarked on an ambitious scheme to make over completely the *Bayt ul-Madinah*. After securing an interest-free loan (one, therefore, in strict accord with Islamic law's prohibition of usury) from the Central Waqf Council, he had the old houses knocked down and constructed a five-story building of steel-reinforced concrete. When the building was completed in 1982, most of its space was let out to shops, offices, and apartments. In 1989, there were a total of forty-two rent-paying tenants who generated a yearly income of Rs. 309,600.

At present, the greatest portion of the *waqf's* income is taken up in repaying the loan, property taxes, and utility bills. Though Dr. Ahmad confesses that he was probably over-ambitious and a bit naive in formulating his plans, he looks forward to the day—perhaps ten years in the future—when most of the endowment's income will be devoted to a series of educational projects. Dr. Ahmad is a Muslim with strong reformist leanings. A scholar in his own right, he has been invited to conferences devoted to the current situation of Islam in the modern world. He would like the *Bayt ul-Madinah* to support research on Islam by scholars from inside and outside India. Eventually most of the money generated by the *waqf* will be spent supporting public lectures by reform-minded Muslims and on publishing their books.

Dr. Ahmad has, however, retained several benefactions that focus on the neighborhood and the city of Hyderabad. Dr. Ahmad's grandfather (Shams ul-ulama Nawab Aziz Jang), father, and uncle (the founder of the *Bayt ul-Madinah*) had been prominent administrators and scholars at the court of Hyderabad's Asaf Jahi Nizams. The neighborhood in which Dr. Ahmad's house, the mosque and the modern building which provides the *waqf's* income are located was, in effect, founded by his grandfather when he built a house there. Relatives and dependents constructed their homes close to that of Nawab Aziz Jang. The family has numerous personal responsibilities to the less wealthy people connected to it. Therefore, Dr. Ahmad continues to provide scholarships and weddings as well as pay the debts of the poor. The endowment is tied to the locality and thus resembles *awqaf* of an earlier era. At the same time, Dr. Ahmad's own religious interests envision an institution which will be linked to the reformist movement in the Islamic world as a whole. An active septuagenarian, Dr. Ahmad knows that his son will one day become the endowment's custodian, and he looks to him to carry on the work he has started.

Though Pakistan shared with India the same British legal and administrative traditions governing endowments, as a self-declared "Islamic Republic," Pakistan pursued a more aggressive policy toward the management of *awqaf.* In the 1970s, Saudi Arabia became a major source of direct aid to the government of Pakistan as well as an indirect benefactor through the hard currency remitted by Pakistanis employed in the kingdom. Saudi religious scholars and government officials began to pressure Pakistan to enforce a version of Islam more consonant with the reformist Wahhabi movement to which the House of Saud (see below) was deeply committed.

In particular, the Saudis objected to the popular version of Islam preached and practiced in thousands of Sufi shrines that most ordinary

Pakistanis considered basic to Islam. The government's ministry of *awqaf* became the organization primarily responsible for reforming the shrines. Its efforts met with persistent, if covert, opposition from the religious chiefs (*sajjadahnashins*) of the shrines as well as the custodians (*mutawallis*) of the endowments that supported those institutions. Most of them continued to operate their establishments much as they had before the government tried to bring them into line with Wahhabi puritanism.[48]

Official support for a Wahhabi vision of a purified Islam—especially pronounced during the regime of General Zia ul-Haq, drew a positive response from religious scholars affiliated with the Deobandi, Ahl-i Hadith, and Jama'at-i Islami movements. However, another group known as Barelwis held that the veneration of Sufi saints was consonant with the faith. Barelwis have objected strongly to the imposition of Wahhabi standards.[49] A number of Barelwi scholars have argued that any *awqaf* which support mosques and religious academies controlled by them should be exempt from control by the *waqf* ministry of the Pakistan government.[50] Their most extreme argument is that only they (Barelwis) are true Muslims. From their perspective, Deobandis or Ahl-i Hadithis and, by implication, the administrators of Pakistan's bureaucracy, are little better than infidels. In that way, tensions over whose vision of Islam should dominate persist. Controversies of that sort also point to a number of ways in which the involvement of modern states has changed the character of the debate. Supporters of a particular point of view may look to the government to back them up. Opponents, on the other hand, find in the state a large and obvious target for their complaints. In addition, a number of new philanthropic organizations point to other ways in which the character of endowments has shifted over the past few decades.

If local leaders, often known in the Perso-Islamic context as *ra'is*,[51] were the human mainstays of endowments before the advent of modern states, a new type of leader has emerged: an international *ra'is*, whose philanthropic activities take into account the existence of national governments while at the same time evading their strictures. The work of Hakim Muhammad Said, the founder and guiding light of Pakistan's *Hamdard Waqf* provides an example of that new style of philanthropy. In 1947, Hakim Muhammad Said left India. His brother took charge of the Indian Hamdard Company, whose philanthropic enterprise in Delhi was mentioned earlier. In Pakistan, he founded a new Hamdard corporation. Through the manufacture of the herbal medicaments favored by "Greek Medicine" (see above), as well as the popular soft drink, *Ruh Afza*, Hamdard prospered. Hakim Muhammad Said has a reputation in his own right as one of the world's most highly regarded practioners of Yunani Tibb. His frequent journeys to visit patients in the Arab Gulf,

England, and the United States have given him a prominent place on the international scene. These trips also provide him with occasions to lecture about his own vision of Islam and its importance for the modern world.

In the 1960s Hakim Muhammad Said established the entire Hamdard corporation as a *waqf*. Through that endowment, Hamdard supports an impressive array of educational projects. Hamdard frequently sponsors scientific seminars which address physics, biology, and the practice of medicine. The conferences aim at combining modern Euro-American science with a revived awareness of the Islamic world's contributions in those areas of knowledge. The message that Islam can embrace Euro-American science/technology without surrendering its basic ideals forms a crucial part of Hakim Muhammad Said's thought.

Hamdard's biggest project is the building of the Madinat al-Hikmat (literally, "The City of Knowledge/Wisdom").[52] On a big tract of land outside of Karachi, Hakim Muhammad Said has supervised the construction of a complex of buildings which includes a research library, university, school of Tibbiyya, and orphanage.[53] Like Hakim Muhammad Said himself, the Madinat al-Hikmat presents a pacific vision of Islam. The institution is managed along the lines of a Euro-American philanthropic effort: there are many boards of directors/trustees/advisors, each of which includes religious scholars representing every major point of view. Academics, magnates, and government officials also have places on those committees.

In his own writings and speeches, Hakim Muhammad Said emphasizes the irenic and universalistic elements of Islam.[54] He eschews the kind of theological wrangling obvious in the contest between Wahhabi and Barelwi tendencies. He stresses, very gently, moral self-renewal rather than political compulsion. In this way, he garners support from all factions. The Saudis can, with clear conscience, contribute to the completion of the Madinat al-Hikmat, while groups like the Barelwis find nothing in the project to repel them. The *Hamdard Waqf* represents yet another possibility in the future development of Muslim philanthropy as an international force in the modern world.

SAUDI ARABIA: THE KING FAISAL FOUNDATION

Saudi Arabia occupies a unique place in the contemporary Islamic world. For many centuries following the death of the Holy Prophet, the Hijaz was a political backwater. Though the *Haramain*, the Two Holy Shrines of Mecca and Madina, were located there, the centers of the expanding Arab empire shifted to Damascus and Baghdad. Iran, Central Asia, and South Asia eventually became the cultural and intellectual wellsprings of Islamicate life. Pious believers did, of course, make the pilgrimage to the Holy Cities, but their numbers were comparatively few. The Mamluks of Egypt and the Ottomans who conquered the cities claimed the title "Guardian of the Two Holy Places," but few sultans, whether Mamluk or Ottoman, ever bothered to visit them. Those rulers were content to leave the administration of the region to powerful local families. By the end of the nineteenth century, the *de facto* rulers were known as the "Sharifs of Mecca."

Made famous to Euro-Americans by a "Lawrence of Arabia" style of romantic propaganda, the Hashimite rulers of Mecca did not automatically, in the interests of Arab nationalism, rebel against the Ottoman tyrants. Many of the family's sons had gotten their educations in Istanbul. This fact along with other connections meant that the Sharifs of Mecca arrived rather slowly to rebellion against the Ottomans.[55] Nevertheless, a reductionist view of those complicated events has prevailed. The stock view became one of Terrible Turks suppressing Arab nationalist aspirations until British empire builders, like Lawrence, unleashed the Arab will to nationhood.

Given that British imperial history is heavily laden with anachronistic presuppositions, the rise of the House of Saud becomes something of a puzzle. Lawrence favored the Hashimites. A few "Arab hands" in the Foreign Office thought them inadequate to the task of governing a single Arab state—something the British promised the Sharif and his kin. That minority in the Foreign Office and Arab Bureau in Cairo supported the House of Saud. In the end, the forces commanded by the Al Saud defeated the Hashimites and compelled them to leave the Hijaz. In 1926, under the leadership of Abd ul-Aziz ibn Saud, the kingdom of Saudi Arabia was born. The Al Saud family had long been among the most powerful clans in the eastern sections of the Arab peninsula, and in the eighteenth century the family had aligned itself with the purificationist movement led by Muhammad ibn Abd ul-Wahhab. Religious conviction was politically reinforced through intermarriage between the two families.[56]

Even after his political success, Abd ul-Aziz's kingdom remained poor. One American oil explorer remembered that the entire treasury of the kingdom was carried in a small tin box. In the 1920s, 1930s, and 1940s, the Al Sauds' energies were primarily devoted to forging alliances between themselves and the other tribes of the region. Oil production did not reach significant levels until the 1950s, and the rapid inflow of petrodollars only began in the 1970s.

The "moral ambiguity of good fortune,"[57] however, gradually dawned on a few leading members of the Saudi royal family. In particular, King Faisal grasped the urgent need to devote a large portion of the profits from oil production to philanthropy in the larger world of Islam and even in non-Muslim circles. As one of the brochures published by the foundation established in Faisal's honor describes him, "King Faisal was the first modern leader who tried to reactivate Islamic spirit and unity not only for the well being of Muslims, but for their ability to raise their standards and thus contribute to humanity at large."[58]

The significance of these activities can be seen in the fact that open-handedness has become one of the major elements in the political identity of the Saudi Kingdom. An article, published in a magazine directed to an American audience, emphasizes that the spirit of giving to those in need is inherent in the religious and cultural values that form the backbone of the Kingdom of Saudi Arabia. The Islamic concept of extending a helping hand to the needy has long been practiced by Saudi rulers. The sharp increase in the country's oil revenues in the early 1970s provided the Kingdom with the means to do so on a larger scale and become a major contributor of aid to nations around the world. The article notes that the proportion of Saudi Arabia's gross national product devoted to charity is 5.5 percent—a figure which far outstrips that of any other nation. The Islamic Development Bank, various bureaus of the United Nations, the Arab Gulf Programme for Development and many other organizations have received billions of dollars directly from the Saudi government. The King Faisal Foundation (which is always referred to as a *waqf* in its Arabic-language reports), though established by imperial decree (A-134 of 19-5-1396: May 18, 1976) and counting the reigning monarch as its chief executive, was financed primarily by the sons of King Faisal.[59]

To date, the Saudi monarch has been chosen from among the sons of Abd ul-Aziz. Since the youngest of his offspring are men in their early fifties, the likely prospect is that the sons of Abd ul-Aziz will continue to lead the country well into the next century. The sons of the kings who succeeded Abd ul-Aziz have usually taken up subordinate positions in the government or pursued their own business interests outside official politics. That Faisal's sons should embark on a massive philanthropic enterprise in their father's name is both a mark of esteem for their father's example as well as something of a departure from the usual practice within the ruling family of keeping a dead king's sons in the political background.

King Faisal's sons put up one billion Saudi riyals as the initial capital for the Foundation in 1981. Since that time further contributions have been made, and profits from investments have increased the Foundation's assets. Its expenditures during the first year of its operation amounted to SR 144,134,110. Those initial expenditures depleted capital funds too rapidly, and in subsequent years the sums spent were cut back to conserve the initial endowment.

The King Faisal Foundation is self-consciously international in giving grants. Asian countries receive about 50 percent of the total distributed, India being the largest recipient. African countries get about 24 percent, the United States 16 percent, and Europe 10 percent. Many of the Foundation's projects involve the building of mosques and Islamic schools. Cities in India, as noted, are among the most common beneficiaries. Even so, the Bilal Institute of Chicago has obtained the Foundation's support as have projects in the United Kingdom, the Netherlands, New York (where Fordham University received a grant to develop a curriculum in Islamic studies), and New Jersey. The organization has also paid for the building of mosques in the Kingdom of Saudi Arabia.

Educational projects funded by the King Faisal endowment include a range of conferences; for example, a seminar on the life of King Faisal held at the University of Southern California; another on Islam and American society held in Washington, D.C. As with the *Hamdard Waqf,* the King Faisal Foundation displays considerable interest in science and medicine. The University of Texas medical school obtained funds for research on lymphatic cancers, while a center for the study of the history of Arabic and Islamic Sciences was established at Munich.

The list of agricultural reclamation or development projects both within and outside Saudi Arabia is also long. Apart from the obvious Islamic focus of most donations, the activities of the King Faisal Foundation resemble those of Euro-American establishments, such as the Ford or Rockefeller Foundation. The King Faisal Foundation also offers a number of awards to individuals who have made significant contributions to the following fields: serving Islam; Islamic studies; Arabic literature; medicine and science.

Mawlana Abu'l Ala Mawdudi, a much celebrated revivalist thinker and founder of the Jama'at-i Islami movement, was the recipient of the first award for "Service to Islam" in 1979. In the years following, similar awards went to two religious scholars from India, one from Indonesia, two from Egypt, and to Shaikh Abd ul-Aziz Abdullah bin Baz, the most prominent religious scholar in the Saudi Kingdom. Prince Tanku Abd al-Rahman of Malaysia, as well as kings Khalid and Fahd of Saudi Arabia, were also honored.

Between 1979 and 1984, in the years when an award was given (in some years, no prize was awarded) for Islamic studies, a Turkish scholar, two Indians, a Syrian, and an Egyptian received the recognition. The prizes in Arabic literature have been dominated by Egyptians, with four out of six recipients coming from that country, and Palestine and Jordan providing one awardee each. During the same period, awards for science and medicine went to Americans, Britons, a German, and a Swiss.

The priorities implicit in all of those grants reflect the concerns of the Saudis in establishing their role as a leader in the Islamic world, which in modern terms must encompass Europe and North America.

India, Southeast Asia, and Africa, with their vast Muslim populations, are at once a source of strength and a site for aggressive reformism. The numbers of Muslims in any one of those places dwarfs the three or four million Saudis who can claim descent from people living in the region at the time of Abd ul-Aziz. Even so, many Indians still tend to follow popular religious traditions centered on the shrine-tombs of famous saints. The King Faisal Foundation's concentration on educational programs in South Asia demonstrates a commitment to imparting a purer (from the Wahhabi perspective) version of the faith to people in that country. In addition, many of Saudi Arabia's guest workers come from India and Pakistan. Visible support for those poorer countries cannot help but impress and attract Indians and Pakistanis.

Seminars and grants to American or British universities to foster Islamic studies is part of an effort to present the faith in a positive light to a potentially hostile audience. The close ties between the Saudi and U.S. governments so obvious during the Gulf War require an attempt to shift the generally negative impression of Islam held by many Americans. Grants to finance mosques or educational centers in the United States serve the needs of both immigrant and indigenous Muslim communities while they ensure, at least, a hearing for Wahhabi-inspired revivalism.

The King Faisal Foundation also evinces a considerable interest in fostering women's education and health. A number of schools described as being specifically for women have received grants, as have women's medical centers. Without trying to broach the complicated subject of the place of women in the contemporary Muslim world, the shift of women's relationship to endowments does warrant comment. In the early modern period, royal women were prominent as the founders and custodians of *awqaf.* Even in families of comparatively modest means, women took an active and public role in the creation and maintenance of endowments (see above). In the modern period women are no longer prominent as "ladies bountiful," but primarily as the beneficiaries of male largesse. The reports described above, not only of the King Faisal Foundation but of all the organizations, never mention that kind of potentially disruptive issue. It may well be part of the character of philanthropic enterprises to avoid obvious controversy. Nevertheless, theological, political, and practical contests are very much part of Muslim philanthropy.

CONCLUSION

Paper, that compound of partially dissolved fibre which is dried, smoothed, and pressed, has been crucial to Muslim endowments since the eighth century (c.e.), when Muslim peoples learned the craft of making it from the Chinese. Although a strict interpretation of *shariah/ fiqh* ("Islamic law") gives precedence to oral testimony over documentation, the complicated economies of the early modern Muslim world would have been impossible to manage without paper.[60]

Deeds of endowment on paper, where they have survived, have been invaluable sources for the study of the social history of the Muslim world.[61] Old-style scrolls containing deeds and subsequent emendations could be several feet long. Sometimes, thick books containing the same kinds of documents have survived. In either form, they are the "paper trails" which several scholars have followed in interesting ways.

Paper remains crucial to Muslim philanthropy, albeit in a slightly different format. Many philanthropic organizations now produce highly sophisticated, glossy, picture-filled reports and magazines. The newsletter has appeared as an important way of announcing the activities and importance of those establishments. Smiling faces and the obvious benefits of the material succor supplied by philanthropic enterprise reflect a genuine concern to improve the physical as well as spiritual states of individual humans. Reports and pamphlets distributed by philanthropic organizations may be, however, as important for what they do not say or picture as they are for what they do.

In the present, as the Islamic world confronts new possibilities and, in the view of many Muslims, new threats, endowments have retained their place at the center of political, ideological, and societal struggle. While the Saudis present themselves as the guardians of the Two Sacred Places, the revolutionary movement in Iran calls them tyrants and bloodsuckers. Poorer Muslims in South Asia look upon the Saudi bounty with a critical eye. Are Saudi plutocrats genuine Muslims, or do the poor and humble have a superior claim to piety? The faithful ask such questions among themselves.

Muslim reformists often decry the national boundaries that pervade the world envisioned by some of the organizations described above. In August of 1994, the World Khilafat Association meeting in Cairo declared *all* existing Muslim governments illegitimate. The same group issued a demand that the world's Muslims reestablish the caliphate, though the organization can find no one candidate acceptable to all. Thus, the nationalism of Turkey or the assumption that there must always be a Kingdom of the Al Saud rankles some of the faithful as much as it consoles the political elites in those same countries.

Legitimacy may be one of the most overused Weberianisms, but modern Muslim philanthropy does seem to be rooted in a quest to be considered legitimate in religious as well as political terms. Legitimacy is thus more than a passive quality that somehow adheres to certain people or governments; it is an ongoing argument that needs to be repeated constantly. Industrialists, oil shaikhs, preachers, politicians, and gentlemen reformers have all engaged in philanthropy. Indeed, they have replaced the sultans and the *ra'is* who dominated the endowments of the early modern world. Yet each style has its critics. To the reformers, a tomb-shrine borders on idolatry, but the devotees attending celebrations at such sepulchers might well consider the preachers of reform high-handed, over-mighty, and too proud in the face of the humble faith their beloved saint embodied. Every argument seems to have its counter-argument. At present, no one religious, political, or social tendency appears in unchallenged ascendancy in shaping the future of the Muslim endowments and the activities they support. Philanthropy will, no doubt, continue in one form or another, but the political, social, and religious roles that it will play are unclear and are subject to the ongoing dialectics of Islamic history.

ACKNOWLEDGMENTS

The research on and writing of this chapter have been supported by grants from the following: The Committee on the Comparative Study of Muslim Societies of the Social Science Research Council, the Private Sector Research Fund of the Aspen Institute, as well as two of DePaul University's funds: The University Research Council and the College of Liberal Arts and Sciences' Faculty Research and Development Committee.

NOTES

1. Examples from both inside and outside the faith include J. Esposito, *The Islamic Threat* (New York: Oxford University Press, 1992); E. Abrahamian, *Khomeinism* (Berkeley: University of California Press, 1993); and A. Ahmed, *Postmodernism and Islam: Predicament and Promise* (London: Routledge, 1992) and his popular work, *Living Islam* (New York: Facts on File, 1994).

2. Some scholars might argue that "philanthropy" is an inappropriate term to apply to the Islamic world. The author sees no inherent difficulty in using the term. Within the history of the Euro-American world, "philanthropy," though based on Classical Greek vocabulary, is a category invented in the recent past. Scholars have used it to describe organizations that arose primarily in the nineteenth century; see P. Hall, *Inventing the Nonprofit Sector* (Baltimore: The Johns Hopkins University Press, 1992); Muslim institutions have had a similar dynamic history. While their Arabic or Persian reports may employ older terms such as *waqf* (see note 3) or *hibah* to describe themselves, comparable documents in English produced by the same organizations make use of terms such as "trust," whose legal roots are anchored in British and American history.

3. The transliteration, *waqf*, follows the Library of Congress system for transliterating Arabic, Persian, and Urdu with the exception of employing

"w," instead of "v," for the Arabic letter *waw*. Other transliterations are fairly common and reflect either older scholarly forms or attempts to represent the pronunciation of the word in Islamicate languages such as Persian and Turkish. Other transliterations include: *wukf, vakıf,* and *vaqf.* The Arabic plural: *awqaf,* has similar variants; also the Turkish plural: *vakıflar* sometimes appears; see G. Kozlowski, *Muslim Endowments and Society in British India* (Cambridge: Cambridge University Press, 1985), 1–2.

4. For an indication of the importance of eighteenth-century reformist movements, see J. Voll, *Islam: Continuity and Change in the Modern World* (Boulder, CO: Westview Press, 1982), 7–86; M. Cook, "On the Origins of Wahhabism," *Journal of the Royal Asiatic Society* 3, 2, 2 (1992), 191–202; and J. Cole, *The Roots of North Indian Shi'ism in Iran and Iraq* (Berkeley: University of California Press, 1988).

5. The distinction between Great/Scripturalist and Little/Popular traditions follows C. Geertz, *Islam Observed* (Chicago: University of Chicago Press, 1971).

6. "Fundamentalist" is probably next to useless as an analytical category. Nevertheless, the word has become too common to ignore. The capacious volumes published by the University of Chicago Press, e.g., *Fundamentalisms and the State: Remaking Polities, Economies and Militance* (Chicago: University of Chicago Press, 1992), ed. M. Marty and S. Appleby, have enshrined the concept in contemporary scholarly debate. For several innovative, if not entirely successful, attempts to avoid the fundamentalist terminology, see O. Roy, *Islam and Resistance in Afghanistan,* 2nd ed. (Cambridge: Cambridge University Press, 1990), and J. Vatin, "Seduction and Sedition," *Islam and the Political Economy of Meaning,* W. Roff, ed. (Berkeley: University of California Press, 1987), 160–79.

7. Renderings of Quranic verses taken from M. Pickthall, *The Meaning of the Glorious Koran* (New York: New American Library, n.d.).

8. M. Hodgson, *The Venture of Islam,* 3 vols. (Chicago: University of Chicago Press, 1974), I 281, 317–18, 334–44.

9. A. Maududi, *The Islamic Law and Constitution,* K. Ahmad, trans., (Lahore: Islamic Publications, 1960), 55, 151.

10. For example, S. Zainul-Abedin, *Zakat: Quorum (Nisab) and Calculation and Connected Topics of Qurbani, Fitra and Aqiqa.* M. Kamil, trans. (Hyderabad [D]: Minar Book Depot, 1975).

11. See S. Davis, "Philanthropy as a Virtue in Late Antiquity and the Middle Ages," and S. Roberts, "Contexts of Charity in the Middle Ages: Religious, Social and Civic," *The Faces of Charity,* a seminar sponsored by the Indiana University Center on Philanthropy, Baltimore, Maryland, November 19, 1993.

12. R. Schneewind, "Philosophical Ideas of Charity: Some Historical Reflections," in Ibid.

13. P. Hall, *Inventing the Non-Profit Sector,* pp. 3–19.

14. *Sahih Muslim,* A. Siddiqi, trans., 4 vols. (Lahore: Ashraf, 1973), III, 867.

15. M. Sharon, "A *Waqf* Inscription from Ramlah," *Arabica* XXII (1966), 77–84.

16. For one of the rare exceptions, see R. McChesney, *Waqf in Central Asia: Four Hundred Years in the History of a Muslim Shrine, 1480–1889* (Princeton: Princeton University Press, 1991).

17. D. Powers, "*Fatwas* as Sources for Legal and Social History," *al-Qantara* 11/2 (1990), 295–341; also his, "A Court Case from Fourteenth Century North Africa," *Journal of the American Oriental Society*, 110/2 (1990): 229–54.

18. On Safavi seizures of their predecessors' *awqaf*, see A. Lambton, *Landlord and Peasant in Persia* (Oxford: Oxford University Press, 1953), 27–29; examples from every one of Islamdom's regions may be discovered by consulting the other works cited in this article's notes.

19. For an interesting comparison to Muslim endowments and their roles in maintaining dynastic families, see G. Marcus and P. Hall, *Lives in Trust* (Boulder, CO: Westview Press, 1992).

20. W. Madelung, "The Assumption of the Title Shahanshah by the Buyids," *Journal of Near Eastern Studies*, 28/2 + 3 (1968), 84–108, 168–83.

21. C. Petry, "A Paradox of Patronage during the Later Mamluk Period," *Muslim World*, 73/3–4 (1983): 79–88.

22. R. Repp, *The Mufti of Istanbul* (London: Ithaca Press, 1986); the Ottomans are generally credited with being the most orthodox of Sunni monarchs and with having the best-organized "hierarchy" of religious academies as well as scholars. Repp and other Islamicists have probably overstated the vertical power of such systems. However, Repp's account contains several incidents in which prominent religious scholars in the employ of the state indicated that their position was compromised; access to endowed institutions may, however, have helped to make religious scholars of the eighteenth century the only enduring aristocracy within the Ottoman state, M. Zilfi, *The Politics of Piety* (Minneapolis: Bibliotheca Islamica, 1988); for other studies of state patronage and scholars, C. Petry, *The Civilian Elite of Cairo in the Later Middle Ages* (Princeton: Princeton University Press, 1981); J. Berkey, *The Transmission of Knowledge in Medieval Cairo* (Princeton: Princeton University Press, 1992) and *C. Fleischer, Bureaucrat and Intellectual in the Ottoman Empire* (Princeton: Princeton University Press, 1986).

23. C. Asher, "Legacy and Legitimacy," in *Shari'at and Ambiguity*, K. Ewing, ed. (Berkeley: University of California Press, 1988), 79–97.

24. W. McChesney, *Waqf in Central Asia* and his "Waqf and Public Policy," *Asian and African Studies* 15 (1981), 165–190; Pierce, *The Imperial Harem*, 200.

25. R. Eaton, *The Rise of Islam and the Bengal Frontier* (Berkeley: University of California Press, 1993).

26. For Mamluk Egypt, C. Petry, "Class Solidarity versus Gender Gain: Women as Custodians of Property in Later Medieval Egypt," *Women in Middle Eastern History*, N. Keddie and B. Baron, eds. (New Haven: Yale University Press, 1991), 122–42; for the Ottoman empire, L. Peirce, *The Imperial Harem* (Oxford: Oxford University Press, 1993); for India in the Mughal period, C. Asher, *Architecture of Mughal India* (Cambridge: Cambridge University Press, 1992); for transitions between the Mughal and British periods, G. Kozlowski, "Muslim Women and the Control of Property in North India," *Women in Colonial India*, J. Krishnamurty, ed. (Delhi: Oxford University Press, 1989), 114–32.

27. For example, the Ottomans made a highly concerted effort to endow "Friday (*Jami'*) Mosques" throughout their domains. Nevertheless locally founded and controlled mosques were more common; see S. Faroqhi, "A Map of Anatolian Friday Mosques (1520–1535)," *Osmanli Arastirmalari* IV (1984): 161–173a; on the multitudes of locally established *awqaf*, her *Towns and Townsmen of Ottoman Anatolia* (Cambridge: Cambridge University Press, 1984); for a general statement of this argument, Kozlowski, "Muslim Endowments (*awqaf*) and Local Authority in Early Modern Islamic Empires," *Middle East Studies Association*, Phoenix, 18–21 November, 1994.

28. For example, R. Jennings, "Loans and Credit in Early Seventeenth Century Ottoman Judicial Records: The *Sharia* Court of Anatolian Keyseri," *Journal of the Economic and Social History of the Orient* XVI/2 + 3 (1973), 168–216.

29. S. Faroqhi, "*Vakif* Administration in Sixteenth Century Konya," Ibid. XVII/2 (1974), 145–72; also her "Seyyid Gazi Revisited," *Turcica* XIII (1981), 90–102.

30. S. Faroqhi, *Men of Modest Substance* (Cambridge: Cambridge University Press, 1988).

31. G. Kozlowski, *Muslim Endowments and Society in British India* (Cambridge: Cambridge University Press, 1985), 38–39.

32. Kozlowski, "Muslim Women and the Control of Property."

33. A. Smith, *Lectures on Jurisprudence*, R. Meek, et al., eds. (Oxford: Oxford University Press, 1978), 70, and A. Hobhouse, *The Dead Hand* (London: Chatto and Windus, 1880).

34. Kozlowski, *Muslim Endowments*, 131ff.; D. Powers, "Orientalism, Colonialism and Legal History: The Attack on Muslim Family Endowments in Algeria and India," *Comparative Studies in Society and History* 31/1 (1989), 535–71.

35. P. Vatikiotis, *The History of Modern Egypt* (Baltimore: The Johns Hopkins University Press, 1991), 300–311.

36. E. Joffe, "The Role of Islam," *The Green and the Black*, R. Lemerchand, ed. (Bloomington: Indiana University Press, 1988), 38–51.

37. B. Lewis, *The Emergence of Modern Turkey*, 2nd ed., (Oxford: Oxford University Press, 1961), 92–98; 264; 413; 419; 422.

38. The following is based on the official reports in both English and Turkish issued by the Vebhi Koç organization.

39. The quotation marks are provided in the original.

40. For an interesting parallel in a Muslim educational institution founded in India in the 1870s, D. Lelyveld, *Aligarh's First Generation* (Princeton: Princeton University Press, 1978).

41. Kozlowski, *Muslim Endowments*, 137–55.

42. Ibid., 174–77.

43. Ibid., 177–91.

44. For a compendium on the laws governing *awqaf*, M. Qureshi, *Waqfs in India* (New Delhi: Gian Publishing, 1990).

45. S. Rashid, *Wakf Administration in India* (New Delhi: Vikas Publishing, 1979).

46. The author attended the *Kul Hind Awqaf Kanfarans* in Delhi in Febru-

ary of 1979. At that time, he not only observed the proceedings, but obtained copies of the various resolutions and speeches.

47. The author has worked through the papers of the *Bayt ul-Madinah* and had numerous conversations with Dr. Ahmad; a fuller account was provided in a paper, "Problems and Possibilities in the Management of a Muslim Endowment in Modern India (The *Bayt ul-Madinah Waqf* of Hyderabad, India)," presented at the annual meeting of the Association for Research on Nonprofit Organizations and Voluntary Action, Toronto, November, 1993.

48. K. Ewing, "The Politics of Sufism: Redefining the Saints of Pakistan," *Journal of Asian Studies* XII/2 (1982), 251–68; for other important studies of the role of Sufi saints in Pakistan, D. Gilmartin, *Empire and Islam* (Berkeley: University of California Press, 1988), and S. Ansari, *Sufi Saints and State Power* (Cambridge: Cambridge University Press, 1992).

49. For descriptions of those opposing tendencies among the *ulama* of South Asia, B. Metcalf, *Islamic Revival in British India* (Princeton: Princeton University Press, 1982), and U. Sanyal, *In the Path of the Prophet* (Delhi: Oxford University Press, 1996).

50. S. Malik, "Change in Traditional Institutions: Waqf in Pakistan," *Islam, Politics and Society in South Asia*, A. Wink, ed. (Delhi: Manohar, 1991), 81–116.

51. For a discussion of the titles used by local elites, Kozlowski, *Muslim Endowments*, 47–48; on the notion of a "raisocracy" and its relationship to *awqaf*, G. Kozlowski, "The Changing Political and Social Contexts of Muslim Endowments (*awqaf*)," *Le waqf dans l'espace islamique*, R. Deguilhem and A. Raymond, eds. (Damascus: Institut Français d'etudes Arabes da Damas, 1995), 277–91.

52. The use of the terms "Madinat al-Hikmat" and "Bayt al-Hikmat" are conscious references to the center for translation established in Baghdad by the Abbasid caliphs in the ninth century C.E. At the Bayt al-Hikmat Muslim as well as Christian scholars worked together at translating the Hellenistic heritage of learning from Greek and Syriac into Arabic.

53. For a brief description of the project, "Madinat al-Hikmat: Hamdard's Upcoming City of Education, Science and Culture Looks into the Future with Greater Confidence," *Hamdard Islamicus* XVI/1 (1993), 141–47; the photographs following this article are particularly interesting for the messages they send about the institution.

54. For example his *Nuristan* (literally: "the place of divine light"), 2 vols. (Karachi: Bayt al-Hikmat Press, 1988).

55. C. Dawn, *From Ottomanism to Arabism* (Urbana: University of Illinois Press, 1973).

56. For a recitation of the whos, whens, and wheres, see the two books of M. Yapp, *The Making of the Modern Near East* (New York: Longman, 1988), and *The Near East Since the First World War* (New York: 1990).

57. S. Shama, *The Embarrassment of Riches* (Berkeley: University of California Press, 1988), 7.

58. Brochure describing the activities of the King Faisal Foundation.

59. "Aiding the Needy across the World," *Saudi Arabia* 11/4 (1995), 12–17.

60. See *The Function of Documents in Islamic Law,* J. Wakin, trans. and ed. (Albany: State University of New York Press, 1972).

61. McChesney, *Waqf in Central Asia*; Powers, "*Fatawas* as Sources."

.14.

From Repression to Revival: Philanthropy in Twentieth-Century Russia

ADELE LINDENMEYR

> I am sure that a person is born with the ability
> to respond to another's pain. I think that this
> feeling is inborn, given to us along with in-
> stincts and a soul. But if this feeling is not
> used, is not exercised, it weakens and
> atrophies.
>
> —RUSSIAN WRITER DANIIL GRANIN, 1987[1]

Few other countries have experienced the discontinuities and upheavals that have marked the twentieth-century history of the Russian Empire and its successors, the Soviet Union and the loose conglomeration now known as the Commonwealth of Independent States (CIS).[2] Wars, revolutions, Stalinist totalitarianism, experiments in social engineering, and finally, the breakup of the USSR have profoundly affected not only the lives of millions of people, but also the complex of relationships and values that hold a society together. The history of philanthropy reflects these discontinuities: after flourishing under the tsars, private giving experienced a decades-long period of suppression after 1917, then a vigorous but troubled revival since 1985. The little-studied history of twentieth-century Russian philanthropy is a sensitive barometer of how the radical political, economic, and social changes of this century have affected social relationships and ideas about community and social responsibility.

Yet it would be a mistake to see the ups and downs in the history of Russian philanthropy as solely the result of external cataclysmic events. One must also look at the ways Russian society has interpreted philanthropy for features that help to explain the discontinuities in its history.

How have Russians' attitudes toward private giving changed over the course of the twentieth century? What factors contributed to the rejection, suppression, or using Granin's metaphor, atrophy of charity during the Communist period? Were any forms of private philanthropy practiced under Soviet rule? Which ideas and practices of private giving have returned since 1985, and what meaning does charity hold for Russians at the end of the twentieth century? This essay explores these questions to illuminate how cultural beliefs and practices, along with political, economic, and social changes, have shaped twentieth-century Russian philanthropy.

THE CULTURE OF GIVING IN LATE TSARIST RUSSIA

The prerevolutionary philanthropic tradition was composed of three interwoven but distinct strands. The first was a remarkably tenacious culture of private, individual giving, especially of alms. Historians and commentators in the nineteenth and early twentieth centuries often traced the origins of this culture as far back as the Christianization of ancient Rus' in the tenth century, and generally agreed on two factors to explain its persistence into the twentieth. First, Orthodox Christianity historically defined charity as spontaneous, uncritical, individual compassion toward "unfortunates" (*neschastnye*)—the word Russians often used to refer to beggars, criminals, convicts, or the poor generally. Second, Russia was a predominantly peasant country well into the twentieth century. Among the "simple" or "dark" folk, as educated elites called them, ignorance, isolation, and conservatism combined to support premodern conceptions that saw poverty as misfortune and charity as a personal moral obligation.[3]

In fact, almsgiving was more than an atavistic survival from medieval times. Several forces consciously kept it alive and reinforced it in the nineteenth and early twentieth centuries. First, probably, was the underdevelopment and inadequacy of the system of public poor relief. Second, although a few clergy sought to channel popular generosity into more organized and effective forms of assistance, the Orthodox Church continued to laud individual almsgiving. Both Church leaders and the Holy Synod rejected what was regarded as the Catholic Church's emphasis on institutional charity or Protestantism's efforts to discriminate between the deserving and undeserving poor. Outside of the Church, Slavophile social commentators and writers, like the novelist Fedor Dostoevsky, also regarded the widespread practice of almsgiving as uniquely Russian, reflecting a depth of compassion and generosity in the national character that made Russia morally superior to the materialistic West. While the roots of the Russian culture of giving may have lain in medieval religious and social history, and its foundation in the peasant masses, the Church and certain intellectuals also helped to keep it alive in their debates about Russian national identity.[4]

Almsgiving and the begging it helped to perpetuate took many forms in late-nineteenth- and early-twentieth-century Russia. When peasant households ran out of grain in late winter or early spring, they routinely sent children, the elderly, or even entire families with sacks on their backs to beg for "crusts" at huts or manorhouses near and far.[5] The religious pilgrims who crowded roads, churchyards, monasteries, and holy shrines supported themselves by begging from the devout.[6] The merchantry, a social group identified with conservatism, piety, and love of tradition, continued to practice rituals of giving reminiscent of the customs of their seventeenth-century ancestors, such as the distribution of alms every Saturday or in annual commemoration of a death or other family event. The long convoys of convicted criminals who walked hundreds of miles to hard labor in Siberia were in large part sustained along the way by gifts of food and money from other Russians.[7] "No people are so lavish in their charity as the Russians, no people give alms with the same reckless generosity," asserted a knowledgeable English observer in 1905.[8]

A second strand in the philanthropic tradition was giving by members of the ruling family. In some ways this Imperial philanthropy reflected and perpetuated the Russian preference for individual, morally defined charity over legally mandated, publicly funded poor relief. For example, lavish gift-giving to the population invariably accompanied the coronation ceremonies of new tsars in the nineteenth century. The Imperial family also celebrated marriages and births, especially of an heir to the throne, with almsgiving and donations to charities.[9] A more institutionalized form of Imperial philanthropy was the state philanthropic agency, which was headed by an empress or other member of the ruling family, staffed by government bureaucrats, but funded by a combination of state allocations, Imperial gifts, and dues and donations from the populace. These agencies concentrated primarily on managing the numerous charitable, medical, and educational institutions placed under their jurisdiction. Although managed at the top by these state charity bureaucracies, these institutions usually owed their existence to the initiative of private citizens, and survived on a combination of state and private support.

The largest agency was the Department of the Institutions of Empress Maria, founded by Nicholas I in 1828 as a section of his own Chancellery to administer the charities founded by his grandmother, Catherine the Great, and his mother, Empress Maria Feodorovna. The Department expanded steadily until by the turn of the century several hundred orphanages, schools for girls, hospitals, and other institutions came under its jurisdiction, while subagencies created in the 1880s administered institutions for the blind and the deaf. Other special philanthropic agencies continued to be founded to the very end of the dynasty; even the last empress, though painfully shy and alienated from many aspects of court life, did not evade this component of her role. Alexandra served, for example, as patroness and chair of a state agency created in 1895 to provide institutional aid and vocational training to the unemployed (the Guardianship of Houses of Industry and Workhouses), and of another one created in 1913 to sponsor maternity hospitals, creches, and other institutions to combat Russia's extremely high infant mortality (the Guardianship for the Protection of Motherhood and Infancy).[10]

Thus, in Russia, government concern about poverty found its main expression not in poor law reform, as in Victorian Britain, or social insurance legislation, as in Bismarckian Germany, but mainly in the support of state philanthropic agencies and individual charitable institutions under the patronage of the Imperial family. To be sure, members of other ruling families in *fin de siècle* Europe similarly engaged in highly visible, symbolic charitable patronage. In Russia, however, such dynastic philanthropy substituted for a coherent state welfare policy, and continued to be employed in the early twentieth century to address social problems ranging from unemployment and infant mortality to war relief.[11] Even the word used to name most of these agencies—"guardianship" (*popechitel'stvo*)—suggests how far the autocracy was from the concepts of entitlement and redistributive justice that shaped the modern welfare state.

Combining a personalized idea of the ruler's responsibilities with a modern bureaucratic structure, the state philanthropic agencies under Imperial patronage demonstrated the archaic nature of the late imperial autocratic system and the paternalistic ideology that propped it up. Believing in the existence of a sacred bond that united the autocrat with his subjects, Russia's rulers, especially the last tsar, Nicholas II, regarded the Russian people as innocent but impulsive, easily misled children whose protection and welfare was the tsar's personal, God-given duty.[12]

The third strand of prerevolutionary philanthropy—a voluntary sector of privately established, funded, and administered charitable organizations—flourished in the second half of the nineteenth and early twentieth centuries. By the eve of World War I, thousands of private societies and institutions dotted the landscape. Though dampened by the autocracy's suspicious, restrictive policies toward voluntarism, their numbers and diversity testify to the emergence of a viable and growing civil society in Russia. Some philanthropic associations were small, localized, or traditional in their approach to poverty, like the modest monthly pensions granted by Orthodox parish brotherhoods to elderly parishioners. Other organizations were quite large, with thousands of rubles in assets and branches throughout the empire. Many addressed new needs or introduced innovative methods of assistance. Collectively their efforts far exceeded the assistance given to the needy from state or local government sources, and provided most of the aid received by Russia's poor.[13]

Thus private giving in a wide variety of forms was an important element of prerevolutionary social, cultural, and political life. Challenges to all three strands of Russian philanthropy and to the idea of private giving itself multiplied, however, in the late imperial period. First, the basic problem confronting charity virtually everywhere appeared especially acute in Russia: compared to the enormity of need, all the labors and rubles of private philanthropy seemed but a drop in the ocean. Recurrent regional crop failures, beginning with the famine crisis of 1891–92, were interpreted by many Russians as signs of growing impoverishment among the peasantry. Rapid industrialization and the explosive growth of cities were accompanied by pauperization and crime; these dislocations, familiar to other societies that had experienced the effects of the industrial revolution, were new to Russia. Growing urban poverty posed a grave threat to social stability and public safety. The country's future progress and stability were also called into question by recurrent peasant unrest, labor strikes, and student demonstrations, which exploded in revolution in 1905–06 and continued sporadically afterward despite draconian repression. Against such manifestations of popular discontent and despair, many contemporaries criticized philanthropic giving as pitifully inadequate.

The unequal contest between available resources and the scale of need was not the only predicament facing Russian philanthropy. Up to the 1890s, many in educated society retained some belief in the possibility of achieving a measure of social progress by means of what were called "small deeds." But government repression constantly threatened educational and other reform efforts initiated by local governments and private citizens. Writing in her diary in 1887, for example, Moscow feminist and philanthropist Anna I. Volkova praised the progress made by rural local government councils (the *zemstva*) in peasant education and economic development, but expressed fears that the autocracy was about to abolish the *zemstva*.[14] Moderate social activists like Volkova, observing the actions of a suspicious and unpredictable autocracy, struggled against becoming discouraged and disillusioned with gradualist solutions.

Such disillusionment added to growing political radicalism during the last two decades of the monarchy, which further eroded support for "small deeds" and tended to compromise the very idea of private giving, voluntarism, and gradual social improvement. To socialists, of course, the only possible solution to poverty short of social revolution was mass organization and political mobilization, not crumbs from the tables of the rich. Although the pre-1917 membership of parties on the radical left was quite small, their critiques of the autocracy and capitalism, disseminated in countless legal and illegal publications, often found a sympathetic mass audience. Distrust of all but the most radical solutions to social injustice was also embodied in a figure of international renown and enormous moral authority: Leo Tolstoy (1828–1910). Although Tolstoy himself participated in such philanthropic activities as famine relief, his relentless denunciations of organized Christianity, private property, and all forms of government contributed to the loss of faith in such palliatives as private giving.[15]

Another factor in the erosion of confidence in philanthropy was its historically strong association with the Orthodox Church and the monarchy. The prestige of both institutions declined steadily during the last few decades of the old regime, especially after the 1905 Revolution. In the eyes of both radical socialists and moderate liberals, these institutions colluded in trying to prop up a backward, reactionary, incompetent political system founded upon injustice and repression. Two examples illustrate how individuals who personified the state and the Church compromised the idea of charity in the eyes of many Russians. Alexandra's patronage of charities and wartime service to the suffering, for example, do not seem to have diminished her subjects' distrust of their seemingly cold and distant empress. Especially during the war, the "German woman's" interference in government, association with the unsavory Rasputin, and rumored sympathy for the enemy contributed more damage to the Romanov image than any amount of Imperial philanthropy could repair. A more ambiguous figure was Father Ioann of Kronstadt, a charismatic parish priest who was probably the best-known religious figure of the late imperial period. Renowned for his spirituality and preaching, Father Ioann was equally well-known for his own prodigious giving and his sermons on the importance of charity and compassion. At the same time, several factors undermined respect for the priest, especially among the educated elites: an unbecoming element of personal vanity, zealous loyalty to the throne, and his support for the nationalist and anti-Semitic organizations founded in reaction to the 1905 Revolution.[16]

Thus, even before World War I, political divisions and social tensions strained and fractured Russian society's understanding of private giving. The limitations of philanthropy became even more glaring during the years of war and revolution that followed August 1914. World War I placed enormous demands upon the financial and human resources of both the voluntary and government sectors. Several million people were evacuated from the front in western Russia; these refugees needed shelter, food, and clothing. By the end of 1914, 6.5 million men had been mobilized; the total for the entire war exceeded 15 million. Deprived of their breadwinners, soldiers' families needed assistance. In addition to 1.3 million men killed in the war, and another 2.4 million taken prisoner, several million wounded needed medical attention.[17]

The response to such immense need, though eventually unequal to the task, was impressive. Showing the least imagination, the central government adopted the traditional devices of Imperial philanthropy to channel its assistance to the wounded, soldiers' families, and refugees. Empress Alexandra and her four daughters, dressed in nun-like Red Cross nurses' uniforms, visited hospitals to demonstrate their unity with the war effort and its victims. Special committees like the Russian Red Cross or the Committee of Grandduchess Tatiana, composed of members of the Imperial family and high-ranking officials, also channeled Imperial funds into war relief. The true locus of the war relief effort soon shifted, however, to existing or newly created organizations in the voluntary sector. Best known and most active were those established in August 1914 by leaders of the rural and municipal government councils, the Union of Zemstva and the Union of Towns. During the course of the war they assumed an ever larger share of the relief burden, equipping hospitals and hospital trains, organizing the production of uniforms, boots, and medical supplies, and dispensing aid to war orphans, widows, and refugees.[18] From the secondary school students who visited needy soldiers' families to the wealthy who turned their mansions into hospitals, countless volunteers carried out programs initiated by the Unions or non-governmental relief organizations.

By 1917, however, volunteers were exhausted and resources strained to the limit. On the eve of the Bolshevik Revolution, after more than three years of seemingly pointless fighting and suffering, the state of philanthropy presented a tragic paradox: an unprecedented outpouring of voluntary effort, characterized by the dedication of many thousands of people, vigorous new national organizations, and an array of innovative approaches to relief, amid an overwhelming and rising sea of need. One result was undoubtedly to engender support for the abolition of philanthropy and the introduction of state welfare advocated by the Bolshevik Party.

PRIVATE PHILANTHROPY IN THE SOVIET ERA

In certain ways the establishment of the Soviet government in late 1917 and its victory over the White Army in the Civil War by 1920 mark a radical break in the history of Russian philanthropy. Charity was identified with discredited, discarded institutions—the monarchy, the Church, the privileged classes. Socialism's rejection of private assistance in favor of state welfare seemed both logical and just. How much could private voluntary effort accomplish, anyway? Three more years of war, economic devastation, and mass epidemics between 1918 and 1920 had brought additional millions of people to total destitution and had drained remaining resources for charity dry.

The new Soviet government soon dismantled most prerevolutionary philanthropic structures. The state philanthropic agencies were abolished, their funds and institutions nationalized. Private charitable institutions such as orphanages also were nationalized and placed under the new Commissariats of Health, Social Security, or Education. All forms of social activity by the Church, including education and charity, became illegal. Most prerevolutionary, "bourgeois" charities died or were liquidated during the grim Civil War years; hyperinflation and nationalization deprived them of their funds, while death, emigration, and the struggle for survival decimated the ranks of volunteers. Although the Soviet constitutions of 1918 and 1924 proclaimed the right of voluntary association, and Soviet law did not prohibit private social aid organizations, the political, economic, and social climate was extremely hostile to the revival of such trappings of the old capitalist order.[19]

Despite the Soviet state's radical rejection of private assistance, certain kinds of prerevolutionary philanthropy proved resilient or returned in some form after the Civil War. A brief look at the two greatest welfare crises of the 1920s, the famine of 1921–22 and the appearance of millions of abandoned, homeless children, reveals how private assistance fared in the first decade of Soviet rule.

In 1921, drought in the important grain-producing provinces along the Volga River conspired with the legacy of upheaval from the Civil War to produce the worst famine Russia had seen in centuries. According to one modern estimate, one-fifth of the entire population, and one-quarter of the country's rural inhabitants, were affected.[20] Before the famine eased in late 1922 millions of people had died. Although Lenin and other Communist Party leaders loathed the very idea of private charity, the enormity of the crisis and the weakness of the new government made it necessary to call upon both Russian and foreign philanthropic organizations for help.

The leading non-governmental Russian organization in the famine relief campaign was the All-Russian Committee for Aid to the Starving, created in July 1921. Since only thirty years had passed since the last great famine of 1891–92, many of the All-Russian Committee's leaders recalled how members of the intelligentsia then had put aside their political disagreements to unite in the cause of famine relief. This recollection evidently produced a frail hope that this time, too, a united effort by social organizations like the All-Russian Committee with the Soviet government would heal the divisions left by the Revolution and Civil

War.[21] The prominence of erstwhile socialist and liberal opponents to the Bolsheviks among the All-Russian Committee's leadership, however, ensured that the Soviet government would barely tolerate it.

In fact, the Committee hardly had enough time to issue a few appeals to the population for donations in the crisis. Barely six weeks after passing the decree establishing the Committee, the government abolished it and arrested virtually its entire membership. In that short time, however, the All-Russian Committee with its internationally known membership had fulfilled the purpose Lenin had envisioned for it: to elicit sympathy and provide a figleaf of legitimacy abroad, where anti-Soviet sentiment was still strong, while the Soviet government was negotiating with Herbert Hoover over the conditions under which the American Relief Administration (ARA) would operate in Russia.[22]

Unlike the All-Russian Committee, the ARA and a host of other foreign relief organizations, including American Mennonite, Quaker, and other religious organizations, operated with significant success in the famine-stricken region over the next year. Importing millions of pounds of food, clothing, and medicine into Russia, the ARA provided approximately ten million children and adults with daily food rations. Without question the death toll from the famine and related epidemics would have been far greater without the ARA, which provided 83 percent of all the food supplies brought into the famine region. At the time Soviet officials grudgingly admitted the country's great debt to the ARA and other foreign assistance. But subsequent Soviet treatments of the ARA's mission, which interpreted it as an effort either to alleviate a postwar crisis of overproduction in the United States or to camouflage espionage and counterrevolutionary activities, reveal the Soviet government's deep suspicion of foreign philanthropy.[23]

The 1921–22 disaster along the Volga dramatically increased the problem of the *bezprizorniki*—children orphaned or separated from their parents by revolution, civil war, disease, or famine. Estimates at the peak of the problem in 1922 range from 4 to 7.5 million abandoned, homeless children.[24] Once again the Soviet government confronted a problem that far exceeded its capacities, despite the best intentions of the commissariats and social workers involved. As a leading historian has recently written, "As Narkompros [the Soviet Commissariat of Education] put the finishing touches on plans for a network of institutions intended to fashion waifs into a new socialist generation, the famine shifted official priorities to stark survival."[25]

As it had during the famine, the Soviet government again turned to the public with calls for donations. This time, however, it did not make the mistake of creating an independent organization led by prominent public activists from prerevolutionary days. Instead, the appeals for help were issued in Party and government newspapers, and directed especially at such semiofficial organizations as factories, trade unions, and Young Communist (Komsomol) and other Party groups. The campaign contained both new and familiar elements. One striking feature is the effort devoted to informing the public about the problem. Newspaper articles, books, pamphlets, posters, public lectures, and films bombarded Soviet citizens with depictions of the street children's world. At the same time, some of the tried-and-true fund-raising techniques of prerevolutionary charitable associations were revived, such as the sale of artificial flowers or emblems, and the holding of charity lotteries and concerts.[26]

The government also recruited volunteers to help in the difficult tasks of finding, rounding up, supervising, and rehabilitating the abandoned children of the streets. Many of these volunteers belonged to the Friend of Children Society, created in 1923 by the government. The Society operated as a nationwide network of cells, often functioning as units within trade unions, Party organizations, military units, or other organizations, and so enjoying little real autonomy. The official membership reached one million in 1926. Members helped by raising funds, obtaining supplies, supervising shelters and other institutions, and aiding poor families to prevent additional juvenile homelessness.[27]

The Friend of Children Society, the Red Cross (reestablished in 1923 after being abolished in 1918), and other state-sponsored welfare organizations created in the 1920s (such as the Societies of the Blind and the Deaf, founded in 1925 and 1926, respectively) were part of a larger movement to create what Soviet political scientists touted as a new, genuinely democratic form of socialist voluntary association.[28] There is another way to interpret such organizations, however. Invented and supported by the state to serve purposes it defined, yet sustained by the donations and labor of a volunteer or semivolunteer membership, these Soviet-era social organizations bear an uncanny resemblance to the tsarist state's philanthropic agencies. In both periods these organizations supplied rulers with a highly visible way to demonstrate concern about a welfare issue, such as unemployment (as in the case of the Guardianship of Houses of Industry and Workhouses founded in 1895) or juvenile homelessness (as in the 1920s). Government tutelage, a bureaucratic structure, and close links with the ruling elites ensured that the state retained control of the organization's agenda and activities. At the same time, both before and after the Revolution, the shortage of state resources and the low priority given to welfare made the state dependent on whatever private funds and volunteer effort it could solicit to carry out welfare tasks. All that was missing in the Soviet organizations, it would seem, was the symbolic patronage of an empress. (After Lenin's wife Nadezhda Krupskaya, Kremlin wives became noted for their invisibility.)

Another form of philanthropy strongly reminiscent of the prerevolutionary past appeared in the mid-1930s. In tsarist days, service on the boards of local charitable societies, orphanages, schools, or other institutions had been virtually part of the job description for the wives of provincial governors and other civil or military officials. In addition, industrialists' wives often assumed responsibility for organizing and supervising the clinics, schools, bathhouses, or other charitable services that many paternalistic factory owners provided their workers.[29] This tradition was reinvented in 1936 with the inauguration of a women's movement aimed at recruiting the non-working wives of executives, professionals, military officers, and other members of the new Soviet middle class into voluntary public service. The movement, which received the imprimatur of Stalin and other Politburo members, even had its own journal, *The Public-Spirited Woman* (*Obshchestvennitsa*). One group that provided the movement with many members was factory directors' wives, who

> supervised cooks in the factory kitchens so that the food would be edible and hygienically prepared, put up curtains and arranged for the installation of bathtubs in the workers' hostels, advised young girls on morals and personal hygiene, planted trees, and organized day-care centers, drama groups, and study circles.[30]

These reincarnations of bourgeois or Imperial philanthropy in the Soviet Union did not diminish the government's attacks on individual and collective charity as vestiges of the capitalist era that had to be stamped out. Throughout the Soviet period definitions of philanthropy and charity in dictionaries and encyclopedias reflected this hostility; a 1950 dictionary, for example, defined philanthropy as "a means the bourgeoisie uses to deceive workers and disguise its parasitism and its exploiter's face by rendering hypocritical, humiliating aid to the poor in order to distract the latter from the class struggle."[31]

Compassion and charity took on much more serious, sinister connotations during the campaigns against "wreckers" and "class enemies" that began in the late 1920s. The Party portrayed the collectivization of agriculture and rapid industrialization under the first Five-Year Plan as military campaigns in the war to build socialism. As in a real war, pity for the enemy was treason. People who aided or even sympathized with a well-to-do peasant kulak family dispossessed of home, livestock, and personal possessions during collectivization, for example, risked being branded as supporters of a class enemy and opponents of collectivization; they could quickly find themselves dispossessed and arrested, exiled, or shot. In Smolensk a local party secretary was accused of "philanthropy" because he insisted that kulaks be left enough grain for sowing and feeding their children; "[w]hen you are attacking, there is no place for mercy;

don't think of the kulak's hungry children; in the class struggle philanthropy is evil," proclaimed his zealous accuser.[32]

As the denunciations, arrests, and repressions reached a crescendo in 1936–38, and millions were sent to prison, labor camps, or firing squads, a refusal to aid either the victims of the Stalinist terror or their families became, in effect, a matter of self-preservation. In the atmosphere of fear, suspicion, and terror that prevailed in the 1930s, compassion had become a serious crime.

Scattered evidence suggests that almsgiving and other forms of individual charity did not completely disappear in the 1920s and even the 1930s. Most Russians probably became fed up with street children's begging, petty thievery, and hooliganism. Others, however, still responded sympathetically to the urchins' pleas for money, food, and cigarettes, prompting the government and the media to urge citizens repeatedly to donate their money or time to state welfare organizations instead of giving alms.[33] Even during the Stalinist terror, compassion did not die out completely. A woman prisoner among the dozens jammed into railroad car number seven, marked "Special Equipment," later recalled a remarkable incident that took place on her journey to penal servitude in the Soviet Far East in mid-1939. The train stopped at a small station in the Ural Mountains, where peasant women were selling food and drink. One of the emaciated convicts thrust her cup through a small opening in the railroad car door and called out, "water":

> "Saints above, I do believe it's a convict train," said one of the women crouching beside their pails full of cucumbers. "Where, where?" "We must give something to the poor souls. Here, Dasha!" "Bring over some eggs!" "They're asking for something to drink. Manka, bring some milk!" Horny, weather-beaten hands were thrust into our car with pickled gherkins, curds, eggs, and bread. Beneath the kerchiefs which covered the women's foreheads we saw the ancient peasant eyes filled with tears and pity.

The scene made the woman feel "for a moment as if we were not in 1939 but back in 1909."[34]

By the 1950s and 1960s, however, many if not most of the forms of giving that had survived the first decades of Soviet power had probably either "atrophied," to use the metaphor of Leningrad writer Granin quoted at the beginning of this essay, or had been extinguished by force. The outbreak of war in 1941 and the postwar repressions and terror of late Stalinism contributed to the further undermining of the idea of philanthropy. Although veterans like Granin recollect a wartime spirit and practice of mutual aid, extreme privation and suffering during the war must have left the Soviet people with very little to give to their neighbors.[35] The postwar repressions, though more selective than in the

1930s, revived the concept of enemy of the revolution, and a social climate of mutual suspicion returned.

Although the terror ceased after Stalin's death in 1953 and official hostility toward philanthropy moderated somewhat (dictionary definitions lost much of their earlier sharpness, for example), several new factors arose to discourage a revival of private philanthropy. First, the widespread poverty of the Stalinist era, characterized by barely functioning collective farms, miserable wages, substandard housing, high prices, and chronic shortages, abated. In the two decades following Stalin's death, living standards rose steadily. To be sure, poverty still existed in the USSR. According to one expert, a third of the working class was living in poverty in the mid-1960s. But in the words of this same authority, the "Khrushchev years saw poverty . . . cease to be the fate of an overwhelming majority to become that of a sizeable minority."[36]

More important, under Khrushchev and Brezhnev many gaping holes in the state welfare system were gradually mended. All citizens were guaranteed employment, pension benefits (before the mid-1960s, millions of collective farm peasants did not have this right), disability insurance, free medical care and education; and pension and other social security benefits were increased.[37] Under Brezhnev, the Soviet political system became, in the words of one American political scientist, a kind of "welfare state authoritarianism."[38] The diminished poverty and greatly increased social benefits of the post-Stalin years lent some support to the Soviet government's assertions that such bourgeois institutions as philanthropy were not necessary in a socialist state.

At least as important in discouraging Soviet citizens from private giving was the absence of any official recognition of the existence of poverty or need. Gone was the frankness with which the government and media addressed the problem of abandoned children in the 1920s. As a Soviet writer acknowledged in 1989:

> In the 70s and early 80s, when top-level officials tended to hush up the failures of social programmes and to exaggerate achievements beyond reason, it was considered inappropriate and politically disloyal to admit the existence of unhappy people under socialism—people whose wages were barely large enough to acquire the most essential things, handicapped people who led a miserable existence and families dwelling in shared flats or slum houses.[39]

Unemployment, homelessness, pauperism—these were problems judged endemic to capitalism only; under the "developed socialism" of the Brezhnev era, poverty and other social problems were impossible.

Another factor that may have perpetuated public skepticism of philanthropy was the state-sponsored, officially orchestrated "socialist" voluntarism of the Soviet era. Under Brezhnev, the Soviet landscape was filled with thousands of organizations of great diversity, all of which came under the official rubric of "voluntary" or "social" organizations: from trade unions to sporting and chess clubs, from the Red Cross and Red Crescent to the Young Communist League (YCL), from scientific societies to the All-Russia Choral and Philatelic Societies.[40] The inclusion of the Communist Party, the YCL, and the subservient trade unions with more spontaneous (though still tightly controlled) forms of associations, such as clubs, compromised the integrity of the concept of socialist voluntarism. Social welfare organizations such as the Red Cross and the societies for the blind and deaf were simply branches of the state welfare bureaucracy. The state's domination and manipulation of all these organizations turned voluntarism into a travesty that did not escape the notice of many members of the Soviet Union's increasingly urbanized, well-educated, sophisticated population.

Popular cynicism was reinforced by another longstanding, widely practiced form of socialist voluntarism—the *subbotnik* or voluntary, unpaid day of work. The practice began in the enthusiastic days of 1919 as a way for workers to help build socialism by donating one day's wages back to their factory or other enterprise, or to an orphanage, nursing home, or other worthy cause. *Subbotniki* soon became regular occurrences in the Soviet calendar; to commemorate the centenary of Lenin's birth in 1970, the government introduced an annual, nationwide *subbotnik* on the Saturday closest to his birthday in April. Expanding from factories to involve schools, neighborhoods, and other social units, *subbotniki* also were increasingly directed at community service. The Lenin *subbotnik* every April, for example, became a kind of municipal spring cleaning, as students, workers, and others donated their Saturday to picking up litter, cleaning streets, and repairing schools or other buildings. By the 1960s and 1970s, however, the practice was deeply flawed. Voluntary participation had become compulsory. Party and government bureaucrats, not the participants, decided where the money earned at *subbotniki* would be sent.[41] In the public's view the practice, like elections, had become yet another charade of the Soviet system.

THE REINVENTION OF CHARITY IN POSTCOMMUNIST RUSSIA

Given the fate of private philanthropy and voluntarism between 1917 and 1985—reviled, persecuted, and manipulated—their revival in the first years of the *perestroika* era greatly surprised most observers. In the upsurge of voluntarism that swept the country after 1985, thousands of new charitable and mutual aid organizations, foundations, and similar initiatives sprang up.[42] For the first time since 1922, foreign philanthropic organizations were officially allowed to operate on Soviet soil.

Prior to 1985, the history of charity was almost completely unknown and ignored;[43] but as public interest in previously suppressed chapters of Russian history swelled, prerevolutionary philanthropy became the subject of books, discussions, exhibitions, and serious scholarly investigation.

Under President Mikhail Gorbachev's policy of openness or *glasnost'*, newspapers, magazines, and television programs were filled with sympathetic reports of new philanthropic initiatives and discussions of the meaning and importance of private giving. One of the earliest and most influential of these was a moving article by the writer Granin, published in 1987 in the prestigious national periodical, *The Literary Gazette*, in which he lamented Soviet citizens' indifference to the sufferings of others. Within a year after this article Granin himself became the president of a Society of Mercy he helped to found in Leningrad to assist the elderly, disabled, and orphans.[44]

The reasons behind this renaissance of philanthropy are complex and require much further research. A few tentative explanations may be offered here, however. First of all, neither philanthropy nor voluntarism ever entirely disappeared from the Soviet Union. The unrecorded acts of kindness Soviet citizens performed toward their neighbors can never be calculated. One group that played an especially important role in preserving the idea of compassion and the practice of giving during the Brezhnev period was dissident human rights activists. Soviet authorities punished dissidents with lengthy prison terms, arrest, and loss of employment. Their spouses and children also suffered impoverishment and persecution. Faced with these hardships and no other recourse, members of the dissident community provided each other with significant material and moral support, and kept alive a spirit of compassion and a tradition of mutual aid.[45] Future research may reveal close links between the informal or unofficial philanthropic activities carried out by dissidents in the Brezhnev years and the first legally registered private charities that appeared after 1985.

A second factor behind the revival of philanthropy under Gorbachev was the rehabilitation of religion and the great increase in freedom for various faiths. The Orthodox Church, which celebrated with great fanfare one thousand years of Russian Christianity in 1988, was a particular beneficiary of the new policy. Long persecuted and criticized, the Church as an institution, along with figures from its past such as Father Ioann of Kronstadt, now received praise from officials and the press for emphasizing love for one's neighbor and for their charitable works. In press interviews, clergymen pointed to a great upsurge in volunteer social service work by congregations and believers of various faiths, and called for the abolition of laws that prohibited religious groups from engaging in charity.[46]

Third, social problems and needs greatly increased, especially after the Soviet Union broke up in late 1991. Disabled veterans from Afghanistan, refugees from ethnic wars around the former USSR, elderly people subsisting on shrinking pensions, military officers and their families returning from Eastern Europe to homelessness and joblessness in Russia—these are just a few of the new problems that arose.

In addition, poverty became visible again. Once found primarily around the few churches still operating under Soviet rule, beggars now returned to the streets in large numbers, often identifying themselves as war victims or impoverished pensioners. As censorship steadily decreased after 1985, articles about crime, poverty, homelessness, and other social problems, on the one hand, and appalling conditions in state welfare institutions, on the other, began to fill the press. Soviet citizens experienced the shock of suddenly learning some of the true dimensions of domestic problems whose existence had long been denied. As they discovered poverty and need in their own midst, many began to look for ways to help. In addition, disasters of incredible proportions, especially the accident at the Chernobyl nuclear power plant in 1986 and the Armenian earthquake in 1988, received extensive media coverage and added to the misery and shock. Reports of these disasters prompted an unprecedented, spontaneous outpouring of donations from Soviet citizens.

As it had in the early postrevolutionary years, but not under Stalin, Khrushchev, or Brezhnev, the Soviet government under Gorbachev decided not to suppress these charitable impulses. Why? A faltering economy and revelations of huge state budget deficits left the state ill-equipped to deal alone with so many problems of such magnitude. In addition, the state could no longer control or orchestrate all public activities from above; as the processes of *glasnost'* and *perestroika* gained their own momentum, the initiative to organize for philanthropic purposes swelled from below.

The charitable movement of the postcommunist period is a synthesis of old and new. Many organizations and activities that emerged after 1985 consciously modeled themselves after prerevolutionary forms or ideals of giving. In St. Petersburg and Moscow, for example, the Orthodox Church revived the nineteenth-century idea of parish charitable brotherhoods. Once-forgotten philanthropists of prerevolutionary times, such as Empress Alexandra's sister, Elizaveta (founder of a women's charitable religious order), and the nineteenth-century Moscow prison physician F. P. Gaaz, inspired the founding of new organizations.[47] In 1992 a Guardian Society for Penitentiary Institutions was established, in the words of its director, "as a direct, albeit distant, successor to the Guardian Prison Society" that provided assistance to prisoners from 1819 to 1917.[48] As new books and exhibits recalled the extraordinary philanthropy of prerevolutionary Moscow industrialists and merchants, some of the country's new entrepreneurs and private businesses began to contribute to education, the arts, and charity.[49]

Alongside organizations that recall charitable traditions are new kinds of organizations that emphasize self-help, advocacy, or empowerment of the needy. This trend may be found, for example, in the many new societies founded by and for handicapped people in the former USSR, like the All-Russian Society of the Disabled (established in 1989), with more than a thousand businesses employing over 19,000 disabled people.[50] A coalition composed of this society, war veterans, retired army and law enforcement officers, and the Chernobyl Alliance created a political party in 1993, called Dignity and Mercy, and ran fifty-eight candidates in the parliamentary elections of December 1993.[51] Support groups for parents of mentally retarded or hearing-impaired children, refuges for battered women, and counseling for the terminally ill—these are additional examples of new directions taken by postcommunist philanthropy.

One of the most notable factors in the revival of philanthropy is the involvement of foreign organizations on a scale unprecedented in Russian history. At least since the 1988 Armenian earthquake, assistance from foreign governments and non-governmental organizations has poured into the USSR and the Commonwealth of Independent States from Germany, Japan, the United States, and other countries. International organizations such as Care, Project Hope, United Way, and many others now have offices in Moscow and other cities and extensive operations throughout the CIS. Since the breakup of the USSR in late 1991, foreign humanitarian organizations have turned increasingly away from working with government agencies and toward establishing partnerships with non-governmental organizations, in an effort to help indigenous philanthropic organizations eventually become self-sustaining. Since 1985 the flow of funds to the Commonwealth of Independent States from abroad, accompanied by advice and assistance on everything from computer networking to fund-raising techniques, has unquestionably ameliorated the lives of countless individuals in need and strengthened the voluntary sector.

The return of philanthropy has been less smooth than occasional glowing reports in the Russian or foreign press suggest, however. The drafting and implementation of much-needed new laws on non-profit public associations, on charities and foundations, and on charitable gifts have been very slow.[52] Hyperinflation, corruption, and other aspects of the unstable political and economic situations of the postcommunist era greatly complicate the tasks of fund-raising, management, and disbursement. Perhaps most important, Russians must overcome the effects of decades of official condemnation of philanthropy.

American and other foreign aid has become a special focus of Russians' skepticism about philanthropy. As in the 1920s, questions have been raised about the "real" motives behind foreign humanitarian aid. Rumors or press reports about rancid butter or expired oral contraceptives shipped as "aid" from the United States to the CIS feed resentment at having been reduced from a superpower to a "beggar" nation. However good the intentions on both sides, partnerships between American and Russian non-governmental organizations have often been rocky. Cultural differences contribute to miscommunication and frustration on both sides. As Americans and other foreigners rush to do good, they overlook or discount the capabilities of their Russian partners. According to one American participant in these exchanges,

> Perhaps the most often heard complaint from local partners has to do with attitude. The leaders of the emerging third sector in the [CIS] are highly educated, proud people. Many started their work at a time when "private" organizations were still unpopular and even illegal. They are rightfully proud of what they have accomplished on their own under difficult and, even, dangerous circumstances. They are resentful when an American organization comes in with the attitude that nothing of value existed before its arrival and treats the local organization as a "client" rather than a partner.[53]

Irina Kozyreva, a leader in philanthropic assistance to displaced military families and the wife of the former Russian foreign minister, has also criticized the inequity intrinsic to partnerships between wealthy American and struggling Russian humanitarian organizations, while acknowledging that the latter can learn much from their American counterparts.[54]

The humiliation of receiving aid from former enemies of the USSR is not the only or even the major reason for Russians' lingering ambivalence about charity, however. Once, Soviet authorities proclaimed that private giving was no longer necessary under socialism; now, the reappearance of philanthropy, whether homegrown or from abroad, serves as yet another painful reminder of Soviet socialism's failure and the enormity of the social problems confronting the population of the former Soviet Union.

The charitable organizations founded since 1985 also share some responsibility for the Russian public's negative attitude toward philanthropy. A recent survey, based on detailed interviews with Russian businesspeople (currently the only significant source of funds for charity after foreign donations), revealed their "ever growing distrust of specialized charitable organizations engaged in redistributing donations." Bloated staffs, administrative inexperience, and financial malfeasance by some charities have discredited the very concept of private philanthropy in the eyes of potential donors and the public at large.[55]

Finally, there is the mixed legacy of the history of philanthropy in twentieth-century Russia. Many Russians are uncomfortable with words like "charity" and "philanthropy," which carried negative connotations for so long. Granin himself avoids using either the word "charity" or "philanthropy" in his otherwise sympathetic 1987 article on private giving; instead, he uses the terms "mutual aid," "mutual obligation," or the somewhat archaic "mercy" (*miloserdie*). Philanthropy has long been linked to authoritarian paternalism, whether in the form of the tsarist philanthropic agency under Imperial patronage or the Soviet "voluntary" association and *subbotnik*. As private giving has returned, so have phenomena that Soviet propaganda have long associated with it: extreme economic inequality, and a new, post-Soviet bourgeoisie engaged in conspicuous consumption.

But postcommunist Russia also inherited from the prerevolutionary past a rich tradition of compassion and private giving, a tradition that never entirely disappeared during the Soviet era. Since 1985, a thriving—though still chaotic—voluntary philanthropic sector has been constructed on a foundation created from many diverse sources: models from the pre-1917 era, the energy of religious congregations, the expertise and funds of foreign humanitarian organizations and governments, the commitment of members of the legal, medical, social work, and educational professions, and the direct involvement of the needy themselves. Even if the idea of philanthropy has not yet been fully rehabilitated in the former Soviet Union, the practice of it has already contributed significantly to alleviating misery and to building a postcommunist political and social order.

NOTES

1. Daniil Granin, "O miloserdii," *Literaturnaia gazeta*, 18 March 1987, 13.

2. In light of the diversity of these multiethnic entities, this chapter concentrates primarily on the ideas and practices of philanthropy among the ethnic Russian population.

3. See Adele Lindenmeyr, *Poverty Is Not a Vice: Charity, Society and the State in Imperial Russia* (Princeton: Princeton University Press, 1996), chap. 1.

4. See ibid., chaps. 1, 3, and 6.

5. A vivid description of this custom may be found in *Aleksandr Nikolaevich Engelgardt's Letters from the Country, 1872–1887*, ed. and trans. Cathy Frierson (New York: Oxford University Press, 1993), 28–32.

6. A brief description and analysis of this and other religious practices linked to charitable giving may be found in Pierre Pascal, *The Religion of the Russian People*, trans. Rowan Williams (Crestwood, N.Y.: St. Vladimir's Seminary Press, 1976), 39–46. A study of various forms of begging by a nine-

teenth-century ethnographer is S. V. Maksimov, *Sobranie sochinenii*, 2nd ed., vol. 5, *Brodiachaia Rus' Khrista-radi* (St. Petersburg, n.d.).

7. Leo Tolstoy describes this custom in his novel *Resurrection* (1899).

8. Edith Sellers, "Official Poor Relief in Russia; A 'Topsyturvy' System," *The Nineteenth Century* 57 (June 1905): 1029.

9. Alexander II's coronation in 1856, for example, was marked by the lavish distribution of food, wine, and gifts to the population of Moscow, while in 1880, when the Empress died, he designated one million rubles to charity in her memory; N. G. O. Pereira, *Tsar-Liberator: Alexander II of Russia, 1818–1881* (Newtonville, Mass.: Oriental Research Partners, 1983), 47; Direction générale de l'Économie Locale du Ministère de l'Interieur, *L'Assistance publique et privée en Russie* (St. Petersburg, 1906), 81.

10. For a description and analysis of these state agencies by the leading expert on poor relief in the tsarist period, see Evgenii Maksimov, "Nashi blagotvoritel'nye vedomstva," *Trudovaia pomoshch'*, 1903 (January): 1–39; (February): 151–75; (March): 321–50. On Empress Alexandra see Baroness Sophie Buxhoeveden, *The Life and Tragedy of Alexandra Feodorovna, Empress of Russia: A Biography* (London: Longmans, Green and Company, 1928). A brief treatment of the Guardianship for the Protection of Motherhood and Infancy is in Lindenmeyr, "Maternalism and Child Welfare in Late Imperial Russia," *Journal of Women's History* 5, no. 2 (1993): 121–22.

11. See Lindenmeyr, *Poverty Is Not a Vice*, chap. 4, for discussion of the tsarist government's failure to reform Russian poor law in ways that could address the new economic and social needs of a rapidly modernizing society.

12. On the archaic ideology of autocracy embraced by Nicholas see Andrew M. Verner, *The Crisis of Russian Autocracy: Nicholas II and the 1905 Revolution* (Princeton: Princeton University Press, 1990), chap. 3.

13. See Lindenmeyr, *Poverty Is Not a Vice*, chaps. 6 and 9.

14. Anna I. Volkova, *Vospominaniia, dnevnik i stat'i*, ed. Ch. Vetrinskii (V. E. Cheshikhin) (Nizhnii-Novogorod, 1913), 64.

15. For an analysis of Tolstoy's views see Richard Wortman, "Tolstoj and the Perception of Poverty: Tolstoj's *What Then Must We Do*," *Rossia/Russia* no. 4 (1980):119–31.

16. Bishop Alexander (Semenoff-Tian-Chansky), *Father John of Kronstadt: A Life* (Crestwood, N.Y.: St. Vladimir's Seminary Press, 1979); Bishop Alexander defends Father Ioann against such charges on pp. 136–37 and 186.

17. Lieutenant-General Nicholas N. Golovine, *The Russian Army in the World War* (New Haven: Yale University Press, 1931), 48–49, 93–94.

18. See Tikhon J. Polner, *Russian Local Government during the War* (New Haven: Yale University Press, 1930), and Nicholas J. Astrov, "Effects of the War upon Russian Municipal Government and the All-Russian Union of Towns," pt. 2 of *The War and the Russian Government* (New Haven: Yale University Press, 1929).

19. Bernice Q. Madison, *Social Welfare in the Soviet Union* (Stanford: Stanford University Press, 1968), 38; Alan M. Ball, *And Now My Soul Is Hardened: Abandoned Children in Soviet Russia, 1918–1930* (Berkeley: University of California Press, 1994), chap. 4; Dzh. Bredli (Joseph Bradley), "Dobrovol'nye

obshchestva v Sovetskoi Rossii, 1917–1932 gg.," *Vestnik Moskovskogo universiteta*, ser. 8, History, 1994, no. 4 (July-August): 34–44.

20. Mikhail Heller, "O golode, khlebe i Sovetskoi vlasti," introduction to *Pomoshch': Biulleten' Vserossiiskogo komiteta pomoshchi golodaiushchim* (1921, Nos. 1–3; reprint, London: Overseas Publications Interchange Ltd, 1991).

21. The first issue of the Committee's newspaper, *Pomoshch': Biulleten' Vserossiiskogo Komiteta pomoshchi golodaiushchim* (16 August 1921), contains frequent references to 1891–92 (see above note for reprint edition of this newspaper).

22. For a history of the Committee see Heller, "O golode, khlebe i Sovetskoi vlasti," 2–3. A brief discussion of American and British responses to the famine is in Christine A. White, *British and American Commercial Relations with Soviet Russia, 1918–1924* (Chapel Hill: University of North Carolina Press, 1992), 178–81.

23. Heller, "O golode, khlebe i Sovetskoi vlasti," 3, col. 2. Indeed, American motives behind the ARA "were not entirely altruistic," but were impelled in part by commercial interest in the Russian market, according to White, *British and American Commercial Relations*, 179.

24. Ball, *And Now My Soul Is Hardened*, 16.

25. Ibid., 107.

26. Ibid., 139–40.

27. Ibid., 143–44.

28. Ts. Yampolskaya, *Social Organizations in the Soviet Union: Political and Legal Organisational Aspects*, trans. Murad Saifulin and Konstantin Kostrov (Moscow: Progress Publishers, 1975), chap. 1.

29. Lindenmeyr, "Public Life, Private Virtues: Women in Russian Charity, 1762–1914," *Signs: Journal of Women in Culture and Society* 18, no. 3 (1993): 570–71; for examples of philanthropic work for workers by merchant and industrialist wives, see Natal'ia Dumova, *Moskovskie Metsenaty* (Moscow: Molodaia gvardiia, 1992).

30. Sheila Fitzpatrick, "Becoming Cultured: Socialist Realism and the Representation of Privilege and Taste," in *The Cultural Front: Power and Culture in Revolutionary Russia* (Ithaca, N. Y.: Cornell University Press, 1992), 232–34.

31. Vitali Tretyakov, *Philanthropy in Soviet Society* (Moscow: Novosti Publishing House, 1989), 5–11 (quote on p. 7).

32. Quoted in Merle Fainsod, *Smolensk under Soviet Rule* (1958; reprint, Boston: Unwin Hyman, 1989), 241.

33. Ball, *And Now My Soul Is Hardened*, 52.

34. Eugenia Semyonovna Ginzburg, *Journey into the Whirlwind*, trans. Paul Stevenson and Max Hayward (New York: Harcourt Brace Jovanovich, 1967), 304.

35. Granin, "O miloserdii"; John Barber and Mark Harrison, *The Soviet Home Front, 1941–1945: A Social and Economic History of the USSR in World War II* (London: Longman, 1991), chap. 5.

36. Mervyn Matthews, *Poverty in the Soviet Union: The Life-styles of the Underprivileged in Recent Years* (Cambridge: Cambridge University Press, 1986), 11–12.

37. Matthews, *Poverty in the Soviet Union*, 113–25; see also Madison, *Social Welfare*, especially chap. 11.

38. George W. Breslauer, *Five Images of the Soviet Future: A Critical Review and Synthesis*, Policy Papers in International Affairs, no. 4 (Berkeley: Institute of International Studies, University of California, Berkeley, 1978), chap. 2.

39. Tretyakov, *Philanthropy*, 44.

40. See Yampolskaya, *Social Organizations*, 50–74, for discussion of the types of social organizations and laws governing voluntary association in the USSR.

41. Tretyakov, *Philanthropy*, 40–41.

42. Two organizations that have served as clearinghouses for voluntary charitable and other associations in the CIS are the Interlegal International Charitable Foundation for Political and Legal Research, and the Center for Civil Society International. Interlegal was founded in Moscow in 1990 to provide legal consulting services to the emerging non-profit sector and assistance to legislators preparing new laws on voluntary associations; to research charitable, human rights, and other non-profit organizations in the past and present; and to promote development of Russian democracy in general. On the proliferation of charitable associations see, for example, its publication No. 1024, "List of Foundations and Charity Organizations Registered in the Russian Federation," issued in early 1992 (available from Interlegal USA, 165 East 72nd Street, Suite 1B, New York, NY 10021). The Center for Civil Society International, located in Seattle, Washington, has an internet discussion list and website (http://solar.rtd.utk.edu/~ccsi/ccsihome.html) and recently published a guide to non-governmental organizations: M. Holt Ruffin, Joan McCarter, and Richard Upjohn, *The Post-Soviet Handbook: A Guide to Grassroots Organizations and Internet Resources in the Newly Independent States* (Seattle and London: Center for Civil Society International in association with University of Washington Press, 1996).

43. G. N. Ul'ianova, "Noveishaia amerikanskaia istoriografiia rossiiskoi blagotvoritel'nosti (obzor)," *Otechestvennaia istoriia* no. 1 (1995):108.

44. V. Bianki, "Trebuiutsia dobrovol'tsy," *Zhitel'skaia gazeta*, 28 November 1987, 3.

45. See for example, the activities of Tatyana Velikanova, one of the founders of the Movement for Civil, Religious and National Rights in the USSR. Before her arrest in 1980, Velikanova worked tirelessly on behalf of people who had been arrested for their beliefs: writing and receiving letters from people in prison, collecting clothing and money for their children, visiting and comforting victims of persecution or their families; Matthews, *Poverty in the Soviet Union*, 197–98.

46. For example, "Church Spokesman Asks More Opportunity for Charitable Work," interview with Professor Arch-priest Vladimir Sorokin, *Meditsinskaia gazeta*, 30 March 1988, translated and excerpted in *The Current Digest of the Soviet Press* 40, no. 15 (1988): 6–7; A. Mal'gin, "Sotvori dobro blizhnemu," *Nedelia*, 9–15 January 1989, 11.

47. For example, the association founded in Odessa and named in Gaaz's honor; Alexandr Mouchnik, "Dr. F. P. Haaz [sic] Social Assistance Fund,

Odessa, USSR," publication of the Center for the Study of Philanthropy, City University of New York.

48. Andrei Babushkin, "Pages from the History of Guardianship in Russia," *Initiatives in the New Independent States; Newsletter of the PVO/NIS Project* (hereafter cited as *Initiatives*), published by World Learning, Inc., Washington, D.C. (spring 1995): 9.

49. Historian Natal'ia Dumova did much to redeem the reputation of Moscow industrialists with her study of their philanthropy and support of the arts in her 1992 book for a popular audience, *Moskovskie Metsenaty* (see note 29). On giving by Russian businessmen, see Alessandra Stanley, "Russia's New Rich Give in to Philanthropic Urge," *New York Times*, 29 June 1994, 8.

50. Pam Mendelsohn, "The World Institute on Disability in Russia," *Initiatives* (winter 1993–94): 2.

51. Interlegal International Charitable Foundation, Moscow, *Humanitarian Aid and Philanthropy in the ex-USSR*, October-December 1993.

52. In the Russian Federation, new laws on public associations, charitable activity and associations, and non-profit organizations were finally issued in 1995. For summaries and discussion of these laws see: *NGO Law in Brief in the New Independent States: A Publication in the Periodic Series of PVO/NIS Project Bulletins*, published by World Learning, Inc., Washington, D.C., Forum I (winter 1995); "The Russian Law for Nonprofits: A New Era for NGOs," *Initiatives* (spring 1995): 1; Alla Kazakina and Mary S. Holland, "The Law on Charitable Activities and Organizations: A Preliminary Assessment," *CIS Law Notes: Developments from the Commonwealth of Independent States* (published by the law firm of Patterson, Belknap, Webb and Tyler, New York) (February 1996): 24–27; and Vladimir Yakimets, "Toward Third Sector Sustainability in Russia 1991–1996: Critical Factors," *Initiatives* (spring 1997): 27–28.

53. Peter Mahoney, "Letter from Moscow," *Initiatives* (fall 1994).

54. Irina Kozyreva, "American Charity and Russia," *International Affairs*, 1994, no. 10: 26–29.

55. Nina Yu. Belyaeva, "Charity of Strangers? Philanthropy in the Russian Commercial Sector," published by Interlegal USA, 1995.

.15.

State Power and the Philanthropic Impulse in China Today

VIVIENNE SHUE

We hear much about the culture of selfish materialism, the mad desire to get rich, that has gripped the public mind and is transforming the churning social scene on the China mainland these days. Memories of the Maoist past—that not-so-distant revolutionary epoch when the spartan slogan "Serve the People" set the tone—fade rapidly from mind now, displaced by cascades of colorful reports confirming the postsocialist transfigurations of social values that have been taking place in China under Deng and his successors. New affluence, new privilege, and new forms of abuse, conspicuous consumption, crime, corruption, and the intense competition characteristic of Chinese social life today—these are the aspects of economic and social change that have received most emphasis abroad. When there have been signs of greater human concourse—kinder sentiments and gentler acts that also inhabit and animate the contemporary social experience in China—these have tended to be swept to the periphery of our vision.

Yet, as the research reported here reveals, one does not have to look all that far to discover that impressive numbers of Chinese people have in fact been dedicating themselves to "doing good" in recent years, and that all those other widely noted symptoms of social corrosion notwithstanding, the society as a whole has lately witnessed also a rather remarkable resurgence of charitable fund-raising and of philanthropic giving.[1] Money has been donated for lineage halls, ancestral shrines and temples, schools, orphanages and battered women's shelters, old age homes, community recreation centers, the handicapped, sports events, stadiums, zoos, monuments, and other public works, as well as for emergency food aid and disaster relief. Charity drives sponsored now by a widening variety of governmental and non-governmental organizations are reported in China's newspapers almost literally every day. And foundations dedicated to the support of targeted charitable and public service activities have been established by the score.

How should we regard this recent upsurge in charitable activity in China? Are there important ways in which it represents a revival of pre-twentieth-century Chinese cultural practices and ideals? Of Confucian and Buddhist ethical teachings and traditions of humane benevolence? Or should today's charity activism be seen instead as something very new—a quintessentially modern phenomenon in fact—one of the forms assumed by an emerging civil society and part of the process of democratization that should now be expected to follow the demise of state socialism? What has been the role of the authoritarian regime in Beijing in promoting and guiding the current development of philanthropy and charity in China? Is the communist party-state's presence still such a powerful one as to obviate any real return to the ethical values and social philosophies of the prerevolutionary past even as it impedes the formation of genuinely independent organizations of civil association?

ON CIVIL SOCIETY AND CHINA'S OWN LATE-IMPERIAL PUBLIC SPHERE

If the upsurge of charity activism in China is part of an ongoing emergence of a more vibrant civil society than the Chinese people have been allowed to know recently, a civil society that will one day stand in counterpoint to state power and perhaps even challenge that power, then there are certain things we should expect to characterize these charity organizations and their activities. We should expect them not to have been organized primarily at the prompting of the state, for example, nor should they have been formed as a result of an impetus generated within the essentially vertical relationships of authority that characterize state power in China. We should, rather, expect them to be formed voluntarily, to stand relatively independently of state sponsorship, and to be made up of horizontally arrayed associations, groups, and even ordinary individuals, in society.[2] One of the key defining characteristics of a functioning civil society, as that ideal is generally understood, is that civil associations enjoy a fair degree of institutional autonomy from the state, autonomy safeguarded by legally protected rights, by customary freedoms, or by some combination of these. As this essay endeavors to demonstrate, while there is indeed much philanthropic activity taking place in China today, the forms and practices of charity now widely found there do not conform at all well to such standard minimal expectations regarding the relative independence of civil society from the state.

If the civil society model does not fit very well, then is charitable activity in China today more akin, perhaps, to some older forms of public sphere activity that emerged at earlier periods in China's history? Does its development reflect more a revival of specifically Chinese traditions than a latter-day flowering in the East of what, after all, are essentially European notions regarding civil society? According to recent works by a number of leading social historians, at the overlap between state and society in China during the late nineteenth and early twentieth centuries, a lively public sphere with characteristics of its own was in fact evolving. And one of the interesting realms of state-society cooperation and conflict these historians have brought into view through their research on this late-imperial Chinese public sphere is the realm of charitable and philanthropic activity.[3]

Charitable and other civic ventures carried out in China's late-imperial public sphere rested on a moral and social vision shared by members of both the political-official and the non-official social elites which posited the comprehensive and harmonious integration of the upright conduct of social life and of state programs and actions. This comprehensive moral/social vision called ideally for a virtually seamless interpenetration of the activities of local state bureaucrats going about their duties, on the one hand, with the activities of non-office-holding members of local elite families going about their community leadership tasks and responsibilities, on the other hand. Charitable activities carried out in this mode in late-imperial China thus tended to blur the distinction between public (or state) welfare and private philanthropy. Where individual philanthropy activists were concerned, the line dividing official from personal roles was likewise blurred, as was the line between a demonstration of moral duty or social responsibility on their part, and a demonstration of personal kindness or magnanimity. Another line also blurred by this vision was the one which sharply separated pursuit of individual interest from pursuit of the common good. A quest for the one was not necessarily regarded as inconsistent with pursuit of the other.

In a world that rested heavily on assumptions of social hierarchy, such as that of late-imperial China, participation in philanthropic activities often brought with it certain social protections and helped forge socially useful connections for charity activists. Since charities tended to operate in the embrace of this homogenized, universalist, official/non-official moral atmosphere, engaging in philanthropic activities during the late-imperial period was not necessarily regarded as an entirely voluntary affair. Social pressure as well as pressure exerted by government office-holders could and did play a role in shaping what good works were accomplished. The activism of officials in this regard was, indeed, but one way in which the Confucian state might attempt to make good on its claim to safeguard ethical conduct and promote the general moral improvement of human society. For, philanthropic activity historically in Chinese thought, occupied a position as just one component of a broad moral program potentially encompassing people of all social strata. Pre-twentieth-century Chinese treatments of the concept of charity tended to emphasize the moral dimension, in fact, even over the practical delivery of aid, thereby opening to those in society who could by no means be considered rich the possibility of participating in the morally uplifting spirit of philanthropy.[4]

As this essay demonstrates, there is much about the way charity is conceived and organized in China today that is indeed reminiscent of these and other past Chinese cultural practices and ideals. But the essay argues also that we will be disappointed if we expect to find simple or unadulterated recapitulations of antique "traditions" reemerging now in the late, late twentieth century. The many resonances we can find with the Chinese past are fascinating to observe, and they do contribute importantly to the distinctiveness of charitable activity as it is developing in China today. But the collapse of the old imperial system and the last forty years of communist party rule have left a heavy imprint on the way state-society relations are organized and citizens' social obligations are comprehended by everyone in China today. In the final analysis, surviving "traditional" preferences for harmonious state-society collaborations in charity work, as in other realms of public sphere activity in China today, appear heavily beleaguered now by widespread intimations of social tension and mistrust.

DEFINING THE SCOPE OF CONTEMPORARY PHILANTHROPIC ACTIVITY

When asked what is going on in the realm of charity or philanthropy in China today, what seems automatically to come to mind for most people there is just one thing—aid to the deserving poor. We shall turn presently to how precisely the deserving poor are conceived and defined. But first, we may note just how much of what, in the West, we might expect philanthropy to cover is left out of such a definition. Support for organized religious activity is notable for its absence. Organized religions, their activities and their finances, are carefully monitored by the state. Support for the arts of all kinds is generally absent from the common conception of philanthropy as well. Patronage of the arts is still regarded by most people as primarily the sphere of the state. Likewise, with support for public institutions such as museums, galleries, libraries, theaters, and concert halls, as well as most sports and youth recreational activities. Neither are wildlife and environmental protection on the list of philanthropic target activities generally, nor are historical preservation and city beautification projects ordinarily imagined as falling inside the scope of legitimate concerns for charity activists or wealthy individual or corporate philanthropists. These are all areas of public life and public concern for which the state maintains primary responsibility. It is not literally the case that these spheres are entirely ignored by or off-limits to donors, individual and corporate. If we look hard, we *can* find an example here or there of a small project or of a nascent fund or foundation addressing most of the areas of public life just listed. But these kinds of philanthropies are very scarce, most of them precariously under-funded and still, so it seems, in their infancy.

Some Chinese respondents will include support for education as a possible sphere of philanthropic work, if the question is pressed. But they will usually go on quickly to mention that this is an area in which it has been mostly overseas Chinese donors who have tended to take a great interest. The state has accepted some small and some very large gifts from overseas Chinese to establish and run institutions of elementary, secondary, and higher education on the mainland. But by and large, since managing the nation's public education system is very much both the state's responsibility and its jealously guarded prerogative, Chinese citizens with money to give are liable to encounter resistance if they express a desire to give it directly in support of an educational institution. Here for instance is a brief excerpt from an interview with the Shanghai-based manager of a medium-sized Japanese invested joint venture private firm manufacturing and exporting woolen, silk, and cotton clothing. She had donated some of her discretionary company profits in support of children, teachers, and elderly people living in the neighborhood around her company headquarters. She liked, she said, to give locally so she could see exactly how her money was used.

> I've always thought education is important, but since I've been in business, I've come to value education even more. Especially through my exposure to people in Japan. I think that the level of education the people have is related to everything else about a country's development. No matter what sector you care to mention, its development is going to depend on a well educated people. . . . Education is just a basic necessity for running economic enterprises well. I myself wanted to open a private school you know. I've talked with the Bureau of Edu-

cation leaders in my municipal district a number of times about this, but it was never settled. They wouldn't agree. They just will not allow a privately run school here. Actually, there is a[n experimental] school . . . in my district which is very modern and well-run. They have a swimming pool and everything. The Shanghai municipal government has invested directly in this experimental school and runs it. But even though their facilities are good, there isn't enough money in the budget for the school to continue to develop along the lines it would like to. Actually, operating funds are very tight for them. The district Bureau of Education chief asked me therefore if I would consider making a contribution to running this school. It would be half state-run and half privately run. But the Bureau of Education officials up at the municipality level wouldn't even go along with this plan. I think that, if they won't let individuals run private schools, then the schools ought to set up a foundation and accept donations from individuals and enterprises that would like to contribute. That would allow them to accept money from people like me without changing the nature or form of the state-run education system. This suggestion of mine has basically been ignored, though. So, you see, there are some things you'd like to do, but because of the system, it's hard to get them done. In this case, I really wanted to help, but it has just seemed that there was no way to help. It shouldn't be like this, right?[5]

NATIONAL STATE-RUN FOUNDATIONS AND CHARITY DRIVES

Citizens and enterprises may give to Xiwang Gongcheng, "Project Hope," however. Xiwang Gongcheng is a very high-visibility, nationally organized, state-run charitable foundation that collects and disburses funds to build schools and support elementary education in China's poorest communities. It pays school fees for children of families too poor to pay; it buys textbooks and school supplies, builds and weatherizes school buildings, and provides better housing and salary supplements to teachers working in impoverished communities. Xiwang Gongcheng uses public elementary education as its vehicle, but its activities are, it seems fair to say, primarily a form of aid to the deserving poor.

The poor who deserve to receive public and private charity are defined primarily in terms of what are evidently still very vibrant Chinese ideals regarding the family and familism as the bedrock of a stable and healthy society. The honest poor are those for whom the family support system has failed or those for whom the family has come under extraordinary duress. Most conspicuously this group includes orphans, abandoned children, and elderly people whose children have died, left the country, or are unable or unwilling to care for them. In the group also are mentally and physically disabled people, many of whom may be expected never to succeed in finding a mate, and whose impaired earning abilities and afflictions place an unsustainable burden on their families. Two other groups appear to be relatively recent additions to the category. They are the dying—people with cancer or other terminal illnesses who need constant care their families cannot provide—and children of divorced parents whose fathers or mothers neglect their care and support. Disaster victims are also universally regarded as deserving of aid, especially those who have lost not merely material possessions but family members. Other unfortunates may, on an *ad hoc* basis, be included in the catalog of the deserving—for example, victims of fire or accident who have no insurance and sick children needing surgery or other expensive medical treatments their families cannot afford. Members of the "floating population" (i.e., transients) who have bottomed out while in the city are not regarded as among the deserving poor, however. The most they can generally expect is a night or two of shelter courtesy of the local police and a bus or train ticket home to where they originally came from. There, presumably, the remaining members of their families are expected to take them in.

Caring for the deserving poor thus defined was formerly conceived to be the responsibility of the socialist state, often in cooperation with an individual's or a family's work unit (*danwei*). Before the reforms, most of these sick or helpless people fell into the bureaucratic orbit of the Ministry of Civil Affairs and its publicly funded orphanages, old age homes, hospitals for the insane, schools for the deaf, and so on. But with the economic reforms and attendant central and municipal budget crises of recent years, most of these state-run institutions have come under tremendous duress. As allocations from the Ministry and from municipal governments have been cut back, most of these units have been painfully ill-equipped to take the often-recommended route of turning themselves into profit-earning entities producing a product or a service for the market. Many have had to resort instead to further crowding their already packed-in patients and staff members so as to rent out some of their building space in an effort to earn cash income. Others have relied on volunteer assistance, gifts, and charity drives. The Ministry of Civil Affairs, no longer funded well enough to run its homes and schools on budget, has itself become one of the most active forces behind the effort to raise charitable donations. A good face is put on this situation by conceiving it as part of the reformist move to reduce the role of the state in the direct management of social life in favor of mobilizing society's own resources to deal with problems. In large part because the Ministry of Civil Affairs has been out front pressing the concept of individual and corporate charitable donations to a good cause, it is the good causes, the priorities, and specifically the social welfare mission of the Ministry itself that have become most intimately associated with the definition of charity in the public mind today.

This process of definition—the social construction of the neediest—has been abetted also by the activities of the All-China Association of Handicapped People, which was formed under the politically influential auspices of Deng Pufang (Deng Xiaoping's son), and which has set up its own network of funds and foundations at all levels of state administration operating nationwide in collaboration with the Ministry of Civil Affairs. Staff members of the Association, many of whom are disabled persons themselves and who have experienced firsthand the callous treatment that Chinese society generally metes out to handicapped people, can be very militant, even shrill at times, when in pursuit of recognition for their plight and donations to their cause. They have devoted themselves to the effort to train as many handicapped people as possible to perform useful, income-earning work so as to be able to support themselves and their families. They have also devoted themselves to making better wheelchairs, prosthetic devices, hearing aids, etc. available to the disabled. Their organizations have become quite large and bureaucratized—some would say bloated. They also frequently arrange fact-gathering junkets and exchange visitations abroad. Like Xiwang Gongcheng, another nationwide and bureaucratically many-layered institution that collects millions of yuan a year, the Association of Handicapped People has been subject to scandals involving charges of corruption, waste, and misuse of funds. This has undermined the trust of some citizens in these organizations, yet most seem still willing to grant that they do good work and are worthy of support.

Both Xiwang Gongcheng and Ministry of Civil Affairs organs routinely coordinate with other branches of the party-state apparatus to get their message out and to mobilize contributions. They work with the Youth League organizations city by city for example. And, often in the propaganda campaign style, they work with city newspaper reporters and editors, especially those who write on the human interest and social life pages of the weekend or evening editions, to rally support and raise money for specific causes. It is very common for local newspapers to feature a child in need of an operation or an orphan in need of support, appealing directly for contributions from the public with a hotline number to call if readers are willing to contribute. Civil Affairs officials even run what are called "social welfare lotteries" city by city. After about 10 percent in overhead is taken off the top by Ministry officials in Beijing, and after the prize money is paid out, remaining lottery proceeds are put toward the Ministry's most pressing work around the city. Grumbling can readily be heard from businesspeople, factory managers, and ordinary city residents who are under pressure from neighborhood and *danwei* (work unit) officials to purchase lottery tickets. People generally are not shy about expressing a sense of frustration at the number of state-backed appeals for donations to good causes like the social welfare lotteries, or the Asian Games. It is obvious that the patience of many ordinary citizens for this form of privatization—the "charity" approach to raising funds they think ought to be coming out of state revenues—is already getting frayed. But it is also clear that a very large proportion of what is regarded as legitimate charity work in China today is being carried out by institutions organized nationally and staffed throughout the country by the party-state itself.

MUNICIPAL FOUNDATIONS AND CHARITY DRIVES

There are other institutions, equally state-driven, however, that are organized locally rather than nationally and that are assuming responsibility for charity work broadly defined. In early 1994, for example, a Municipal Philanthropic Foundation was set up in Shanghai (*Shanghai Shi Cishan Jijinhui*).[6] The Municipal Foundation is something like a community chest in its fundamental conception. Although it is technically a *minjian* (popular) organization, it was actually set up under the auspices of three state units—the Shanghai Municipal Ministry of Civil Affairs, the *Shanghai Shi Jingshen Wenming Bangongshi* (the Spiritual Civilization Section of the Municipal Committee's Propaganda Office), and *Zhengxie* (Shanghai's Political Consultative Congress). As of April 1995, eight out of the thirteen people on the Foundation's staff were actually Ministry of Civil Affairs officials detailed to work at the Foundation but still receiving their state salaries from the Ministry. Not surprisingly, the charitable mission of the Foundation seemed to parallel very closely the concerns of the Ministry of Civil Affairs, featuring most prominently the elderly, orphaned children, sick children, the disabled, and especially poor households (*tekun hu*). Its first major project was to plan and start building a home for the elderly in one of Shanghai's suburbs for people who are alone and need some care but who can afford to pay the rent for the new flats. The board of the new Municipal Foundation is made up of many prominent people in Shanghai, people in and out of government, including a few famous movie and TV stars, two leaders of the Shanghai Buddhist community, top officials from the Overseas Chinese Affairs Organization (*Qiaolian*), the wife of the Shanghai Municipal Party Secretary, the head of Shanghai's Ministry of Civil Affairs, and various other high city officials. The chairwoman of the Foundation's board is Chen Tiedi, chair also of *Zhengxie*, the Shanghai Political Consultative Congress. If *Zhengxie* had helped draw into service some of the influential backers and personages on the board, and if Civil Affairs had taken the major role in drawing up the Foundation's charitable mission, then the

Spiritual Civilization Section's contribution had been to help with publicity. In under a year, over five hundred reports on the Foundation's work had appeared in Shanghai newspapers, and there had been several special reports on radio and TV as well. A popular hotline program had been set up in cooperation with one of the local radio stations. And Spiritual Civilization had given the Foundation its catchy slogan too: *"Wo ai ren, ren ren ai wo"* ("I love others and everyone loves me"). In under a year they had already collected over ¥40 million, 80 percent of which had come from some four hundred companies and corporations in the greater metropolitan area and from donors in Hong Kong, Taiwan, and Macao, while 20 percent had been collected from individual donors.

As of early 1995, Shanghai was just one of ten provinces and major municipalities in the country which had already established such technically popular (*minjian*) but actually state-organized charitable foundations. And ten more were well into the planning stages. In Hangzhou, where just such a municipal foundation had also been set up, the Civil Affairs official who talked with me about it was less coy about its technically *minjian* status. He said,

> The state is in financial difficulty (*you kunnan*). It can no longer handle providing assistance across the board. So, it is necessary now to develop the energies of society in this sphere. In Hong Kong and in other countries, there is a comparatively complete network of social insurance organizations; the state needn't carry the entire load. Rather, funds are raised from society itself to care for those in misfortune. A good system of social insurance (*shehui baozhang*) ought to include a place for popular organizations (*minjian tuanti*). But in this country, there are certain difficulties (*nandu*) in setting up popular organizations and so our Foundation, though it is theoretically (*dingxing*) a popular organization, actually has a very strong leadership component that belongs to the state. Under Chinese conditions, it is necessary for the State to take the lead.[7]

And in even more provincial Qingdao, where plans were in the works to set up a similar organ, there was even less interest in concealing its essentially statist identity with talk of the elusive *minjian* ideal. There the briefing Civil Affairs official said:

> Yes, we are also just now preparing to set up a Qingdao Municipal philanthropic Commission (*Cishan Hui*). This will be a mass philanthropic organ (*qunzhong xing de cishan jigou*). [Note, he does not use the term *minjian*.] It will seek to raise funds from society to help the poor, the disabled, and so on. We will try to get this set up this year. We meant to get it going in 1994. But the press of work has delayed us. This Commission will help us carry out our social welfare work (*fuli shiye*). It will not be a foundation like the one in Shanghai. . . . It will be

led by municipal government officials. It will be chaired by the Mayor himself. It will be a state (*guanban xing*) organization. The intention is to use the force of the state to mobilize the forces in society. We won't have a philanthropic foundation as they have in Shanghai.[8]

All three cities were doing essentially the same thing, in reality. But in Shanghai they were more scrupulous about the progressive terminology. In Hangzhou, they were more pragmatic in the way they explained the process. In Qingdao, they seemed quite unreconstructed in their actual attitudes, though not unaware that there were terminological differences to be observed. In all three cases a foundation or foundation-like organization was being put in place by the local state to reseize or to preemptively seize any initiative in this realm of charity and social work that might have fallen into the hands of non-state-normalized social forces.

In other talks with officials in Qingdao, it did appear that most of the charity drives there were run like propaganda campaigns. They were interested in raising money, to be sure, but they were at least as much interested in using these charity campaigns to raise the tone of social life, to "raise the quality of the people" (*tigao renmen de suzhi*), a phrase one hears everywhere in China today, to set a good example, and to promote social stability. In an interview with one of the city's vice mayors conducted while he was making a brief, media-covered visit to the municipal orphanage with his wife, for example, I was told the following:

> Last year before New Year, the media, the Civil Affairs Bureau, and the Municipal Government jointly conducted a "Contribute a Little Compassion Campaign" (*"Xian Aixin Huodong"*). The basic value system (*jiazhi guan*) of the Chinese people is undergoing a major change now. Especially among the young people, the concern to make money is becoming the main thing in life. [By running these kinds of campaigns] we hope to make a turn for the better in the social atmosphere (*shehui fengqi*). I personally decided to take on the responsibility of supporting this little orphan boy here last year during the *Xian Aixin Huodong*. . . . The whole campaign made a big impact on everyone. And I have special responsibility in the City Government for social welfare work. It is imperative that someone in my position should set a good example by supporting such a child, by taking him home to spend the New Year holiday with our family, and so on. . . . When we run campaigns like the "Contribute a Little Compassion Campaign" it is a sign that socialist society has developed to a certain level. Especially these days, in the competitive atmosphere of the market economy, we must remember to pay special attention to unfortunate people like orphans. We shouldn't forget them. So, this is what the government intends to be the message of these charitable campaigns.[9]

This concern to use charity as a means of conveying a broadly moral message, as an instrument for raising the tone of social life generally by combating the tendency toward single-minded pursuit of selfish material gain, is characteristic of local officials in the other cities surveyed as well. At this point in his remarks to me, the Vice Mayor in Qingdao made what can also be found to be a very common conceptual link between charity and the maintenance of public security or social order. He said:

> When we find charitable activities (*cishan shiye*) being carried out it signifies that a society has reached a certain level of civilization. . . . Qingdao is one of the leading cities in the country in terms of social peace and stability (*shehui zhi'an*). We have also organized a foundation here that gives rewards to people who [physically] detain and subdue wrongdoers and criminals, for example. . . . And we also recently ran a *"San You Yi Zuo"* campaign ["Three Excellents and One Thing to Do"]—the three Excellents are maintaining an excellent order (*chixu*), maintaining an excellent environment, and maintaining excellent service; the one thing to do is, *zuo wenming shimin*—to be a civilized city dweller.[10]

Where these sorts of local party-state orchestrated charity drives and campaigns to show empathy and compassion are concerned then, the real aims often seem less the accumulated practical benefits that accrue to the needy than the social uplift achieved through the elicitation of morally praiseworthy public behavior from the broadest possible group of ordinary citizens. The amounts individual families can afford to contribute to these campaigns are generally very small, of course. Enterprises and companies, however, can sometimes give substantially more.

MERCHANT-ENTREPRENEUR AND CORPORATION GIVING

Business and corporate giving is another important category of charitable activity. For the sake of broad generalization here, we may include under this heading all kinds of business donors, ranging from fairly humble merchants and self-employed business people (the *getihu*), through the considerably more upscale bracket of successful entrepreneurs, on up to the heads of giant firms, and we may include all forms of business ownership—private, collective, and state-sector industry and commerce. Charitable contributions by these groups of donors generally tend to fall into two broad categories. First, they give to the state-managed funds such as Xiwang Gongcheng and the Association of Handicapped People, they give to state-managed fund-raising drives like those for the Asian Games or for national disaster relief efforts, and they give also to local government-sponsored causes such as the municipal charity drives and the community-chest-type foundations discussed above. Many make contributions to the local public security bureau and to the police who patrol their neighborhoods. Although this certainly seemed in some cases to border on paying a form of protection money, most spoke of it in neutral, euphemizing terms. Just as they spoke of helping the city government take care of the poor and thus alleviate potentially destabilizing inequalities and injustices in society, so they spoke of helping the police carry out their ever more difficult tasks of guaranteeing the security and social peace in the neighborhoods where they do business.

This general type of giving in response to requests and scarcely veiled demands from various units of the state makes up the great bulk of a business's charitable donations in most cases, and it is regarded by many of them as simply part of the cost of doing business. While these contributions are not exactly equivalent to a state tax in the minds of donors— because funds given do go for specified good causes—these donations are not exactly regarded as voluntary or self-initiated either. They are to one degree or another felt to be obligatory. As one manager succinctly expressed the sentiment voiced by many of the businesspeople interviewed: "When the government asks us to help out in these ways we just feel that we have to do it. We always try to give them what they ask for."[11] Most managers express a kind of personal satisfaction with this type of giving nonetheless. They say that they see it as doing their part for a good cause that, one way or another, must get done.

Some managers express disgust at certain businesspeople, however, who try to make these semiobligatory contributions out to be a sign of some special virtue. The implication is either that they are toadying to government officials in hope of gaining some preferments from them, or they are flaunting their charitable giving before their customers hoping that it will bring in more business. Other managers, however, see nothing wrong with using charitable donations as a way of polishing their image with the public. It is part of a virtuous circle, in their minds. As one Shanghai entrepreneur explained his interest in doing good works:

> When we make a contribution to charity, it gives the *laobaixing* [the man in the street] a good impression of our company. They get a feeling of being closer to our enterprise and they have more confidence in our products too. They think that a company that supports charity would certainly not be one to rip them off with fake products or something like that so they trust us. An enterprise that gives money from its own profits for social welfare purposes would not be likely to cheat them, that's what they believe. So this gives our company a good image. And this way, of course, we can make even more money. And with more profits, naturally, we can give more to charity![12]

Some self-styled skeptics in business circles take a harder line, however, claiming that ideally charitable donations should be made anonymously. Otherwise the practice can too easily descend into a competition for fame and glory, something they say they despise and will often describe as ugly, *nankan*.[13] For most, however, it is more a matter of seeking the right balance. Doing good works should and does entitle one to a good reputation in society, they reason. And a good reputation will, and should, help out in business. A company's charitable activity just must not be allowed to become too transparently self-promotional. That, naturally, would repel many people. As one public relations company manager interviewed in Hangzhou put it:

> Companies need to realize this. People will buy the products of one company as opposed to another if they think that the company has a good reputation. Doing good works contributes splendidly to this. It's really the best way there is to develop a good reputation so that consumers will trust your products and patronize your company. . . . But the commercial aspects of your charity work cannot be allowed to become too apparent. If people perceive that you are just promoting your own products, then the whole thing can backfire.[14]

That doing good for others *is* good for oneself seems to be taken for granted by most people. That some kind of benefit to honest donors will come sooner or later, whether they seek it or not, does actually seem to be believed by most businesspeople interviewed. Interestingly, it was sometimes informants who expressed the most violent disapproval of others who they saw as using charity for self-promotion in this world who also said, without any apparent sense of self-contradiction, that their own good works were done in the spirit of accumulating merit (*xingshan jide*) a reference to the Buddhist belief that good deeds done in this life will be credited to us in the next.[15] Most of these people, however, it is important to add, did not profess or admit to any serious belief in Buddhism. They invoked the phrase "*xingshan jide*" as a kind of homily, a cliché, or an expression of folk wisdom.

The second general category of giving by corporations and business managers is to individuals, or sometimes to communities or groups, in some kind of special need. Here the relationships tend to be deeply personalized ones. The individual or family in need may approach a company manager or entrepreneur directly for help. Or the entrepreneur may learn of the need through news reports, or through the grapevine. If the need continues, and if the recipient shows proper gratitude, these donor-recipient relationships can become long-term ones. The gratitude owed, at any rate, is generally expected to be lifelong. One *getihu* restaurateur interviewed in Wuxi, for example, said his major charitable activity was to make a large contribution to Xiwang Gongcheng every year. But he was also sending ¥1,000 a year to a community in Subei (northern Jiangsu Province) where, as a sent-down youth during the Cultural Revolution, he had lived and worked for seventeen years. He knew the poverty and backwardness of the place well, and the money he sent each year was used toward improving local elementary education. "¥1,000 isn't anything to speak of in Wuxi anymore," he said. "But out there [in Subei] you can still do a lot of good with ¥1000."[16] This same petty entrepreneur was paying the education fees and a small living stipend for a child of divorced parents in Shanghai who otherwise would not have been able to afford to go to school. This man clearly liked to give support for education, and when asked why, he explained this way:

> I give money and support to education because people who manage to get an education have greater aspirations in life. They will be able to make a much bigger contribution to society after they have been educated and succeeded at that. So I like to be able to help them get that education. If loafers and idlers who never do anything die of hunger, there's no shame in that, I say. No need to help that sort of people. They'll never make any contribution to society. But people who work hard to get an education are a different matter. And also, that kind of person is going to remember you later on. They will remember that you were the one who helped them at a critical moment. That student I told you about in Shanghai, I've actually never yet even met him. But I do send the money every month and he receives it; and I am sure that in the future he's going to remember that it was me, a *getihu*, who helped him get his education. . . .[17]

If this last remark makes it sound as if this man, as a *getihu* (a self-employed businessman), thinks he has something to prove, the fact is that he does. In China today the *getihu* are mistrusted by the party-state, and they are mistrusted by the public. They are universally assumed to be guilty of sharp trade practices, and their social prestige is, therefore, despite their wealth, still very low. They often use charity as a way of demonstrating personal credibility and claiming a degree of social honor. But their extreme political vulnerability limits the extent to which they can develop their charitable activities as an expression of a personal vision or commitment. This man in Wuxi, for example, who obviously preferred to give his money to education and to those in pursuit of an education, also mentioned that he was prevailed upon by the local leaders (*lingdao*) to make contributions to the elderly and to a family raising some handicapped children.

Managers of larger enterprises in the collective or state sector can, however, sometimes risk flouting local state preferences about the donations they make. One man who runs a very lucrative commercial enterprise and is accustomed to make frequent large donations to state-managed charitable activities can serve as an example.[18] At the time of our interviews he had already been fully enough honored and coopted by local state officials to have agreed to serve on the board of directors of one of their favorite funds for orphans. But he thought their management of the fund was, as he put it, "chaotic." He thought in particular that more should be going into endowment and less paid out on current expenditures. He felt that as a representative of the business community on the board, however, his good financial advice was not being listened to. He explained how he had decided, then, to take matters into his own hands:

> At the end of last year, I made a visit to the orphanage. I took ¥10,000 with me and gave it to the orphanage myself directly and I never told the other members of the board of directors of the fund for the orphans because I didn't approve of what they were doing with their money. I gave the money to the orphanage's director to be used as end of year bonuses for the teachers working at the orphanage. I think these people do a terrific job and make a very big contribution to society, but they are paid very little. The people at the fund for the orphans were pretty upset and angry with me when they found out but I didn't care.

This same man refused to make contributions to Xiwang Gongcheng. He said:

> As for Xiwang Gongcheng, I don't trust them. They've grown into such a bloated bureaucracy. Administrative expenses must add up to half of what they take in. How much of the money contributed is actually used in those schools, I wonder? No systematic auditing is ever done in that organization! So now I do things where I can see and feel the actual outcome of my contribution. If I can't see and feel it, I don't want to get involved. So, I'm not giving any contribution to the orphans' fund this year. They were furious, you know, because I'm still on the board. But I'm not going to the meetings anymore either. If you're going to run a charitable organization you can't run it like gusts of wind, a puff here and a puff there. You need an overall, long-term plan for development and growth. That's the only way to run a charitable foundation successfully. I now have a generally pretty skeptical attitude toward all government-run charity activities. That's why I am getting out of the fund for the orphans. I think it's best to make contributions to the needy as directly as possible without going through so many layers of government organization and bureaucracy. And you should do things that have real, direct, good results.

Fed up with state mismanagement of charitable work, this entrepreneur was turning back to direct, face-to-face patronage, the other form of philanthropic activity characteristic of the re-emerging Chinese business community. Only the very largest and most wealthy firms seem to be in a position to mark out for themselves a distinctive and balanced philanthropic presence. One of these is the Hai'er Group in Qingdao. They manufacture export-quality refrigerators and air-conditioning units and sell also at the top of the line in the home market. The firm has over 6,000 employees, and its 1994 net after-tax profits were approximately ¥200 million.[19] The Hai'er Group's head, Zhang Ruimin, has decided that its charitable contributions will focus on three areas only: children, education, and popularization of science and technology. He and his public relations department resist requests for contributions to other good causes such as support for sports events, the elderly, and the handicapped. The Group does give to Xiwang Gongcheng, and since its contributions are large, it is able to work closely with the Project Hope people to determine exactly how its contributions are used. They have seen to it that Hai'er contributions are used locally, to build a school in a poor Shandong village only one hundred kilometers from Qingdao. Their other major commitment is in supporting the Qingdao Children's Theater, a local drama troupe that puts on plays with moral and inspirational messages for children. Hai'er also helped a youth magazine on science and technology get on its feet. And it has supported the cartoon creators at *Zhongyang Dianshi Tai* (Central Broadcasting in Beijing). Cartoons are expensive to produce and Chinese-made cartoons on TV are increasingly supplanted by Japanese and American imports. In return for the financial support, the cartoonists at Central Broadcasting have been making a series of cartoons featuring the two cute little boys who are on the logo of the Hai'er Group's products. In their cartoon exploits, the boys (the "*Hai'er Hao Xiongdi*") do good deeds and help teach Chinese kids glued to the TV the difference between right and wrong, while presumably also influencing a generation of future consumers who will one day all want to buy Hai'er refrigerators and air conditioners.

Merchant-entrepreneur and corporate philanthropy are still very newly reemerging phenomena on the Chinese social scene. It is perhaps too early to tell what trends will ultimately prevail. So far, however, it appears that giving is generally directed upward, to the state as a kind of semiobligatory form of tribute, or downward through personalized, usually face-to-face, relations of patronage designed to reach selected targets of compassion. Few firms are as independently modernist as Hai'er is in designing and managing its own socially responsible corporate image.

Most businesspeople, on the contrary, in the conduct of their charitable activities, seem to reaffirm not any trend toward a growing corporate independence but, rather, the continued existence of a clearly acknowledged social hierarchy. In this hierarchy, both state officials at the top, through their control over discretionary authority, and needy supplicants at the bottom, through the moral urgency of their plight, exert a kind of leverage over the monied entrepreneur in between. Businesspeople see themselves as obliged, therefore, to give to both. These gifts, as always in Chinese society however, imply reciprocity. Enterprises and businesspeople who extend their gifts both upward and downward in the social hierarchy also stand to gain through these transactions.

THE INDEPENDENTS

One other category of charitable activity should be included to conclude this brief overview. There are a very few truly independent charity workers whose exceptional undertakings do seem to defy all the rules about what is possible in China today. These people embark upon careers of "doing good" neither with the special blessings of state affiliation nor with easy access to money. In none of the cities surveyed was it possible to find more than one or two examples of charity activists in this category, but once found, discussions with them generally proved richly rewarding. Most people encountered in this category provide care for mentally handicapped children, orphans, or the elderly on a nonprofit basis.[20] Most try to set up a small-scale "learning center," or "rehabilitation center." They need to get a license from local state authorities even to do this, and often they encounter bureaucratic suspicion and refusal in trying to do so. They generally accept some payment from the families of the people left in their care, but this typically falls considerably short of real costs and obliges them to seek support from others or draw upon their own family's resources to keep their centers open. To all appearances, these dedicated people generally live hard, and often lonely, lives.

In choosing to follow such a thoroughly unconventional and genuinely strenuous course, these independents naturally court certain types of social and state disapproval. In some cases, there does seem to be a clear awareness on their part that by taking these burdens on themselves they are in effect issuing a kind of indictment of the system as a whole, and of the party-state in particular, for its failure to provide better for the unfortunates whom they then must step in to aid and comfort. In one or two cases encountered, these charity workers seem consciously to regard their social activism as a form of political activism by other means. And even though oblique, there is considerable evidence that their challenges do not go unnoticed by state officials. Still, there may be no grounds upon which officials can move to shut them down.

But indirect social or political criticism would seem to be only one of the possible motivations involved in cases like these. Conversations with the few people found in this category suggest that they tend to be unusually articulate and intelligent people. They may also disproportionately be women and, further, individuals with unconventional personal or family histories. In *all* the cases found in my survey, divorce or spousal separation played a prominent part in the personal stories these people told or in the stories one was told about them by others. Though attitudes about divorce are now in the midst of rapid change in some parts of China, it still remains true for most people that a deep stain of immorality is associated with divorce and this stain adheres to everyone involved, including even the children. And of course because Chinese couples almost always have a child as soon as they are married, when spouses separate there are almost always children involved. Divorce thus entails severing the most sacred of links in the Chinese family system, the link that joins the generations. In their own explanations of why they were motivated to pursue such arduous life choices some of the independent charity activists interviewed made a direct connection with the sense of loneliness, of shame, and the tremendous sense of failure that they endured as a result of their own family catastrophes. In other cases the connection was only implied. But this connection may well be an important one. Charity work, especially as it is defined in China today—as surrogate care when the generally durable but not indestructible Chinese family system fails—may well provide a special sort of arena in which people who have suffered from the stigma of family breakdown can attempt to rehabilitate themselves in their own eyes and in the eyes of society at large. Perhaps the taint of immorality that clings to those who reject traditional family values can be expunged through sufficient devotion to society's surrogate for family values. In any case, the quest these independent activists pursue, while it potentially bears a certain interesting political significance not unconnected to questions about the prospects for civil society in China, does also usually seem to be driven by very deep and very personal pressures.

GENERAL THEMES

What this initial survey of China's coastal urban centers suggests, then, is that there are four major categories of charitable activity now to be found. First there are state-initiated and state-managed nationwide charity causes, projects, and associations like Xiwang Gongcheng. Second, there are local-state-initiated and managed charity drives and community-chest-like provincial and municipal foundations raising donations. Third, there is the category of merchant-entrepreneur and corporate giving which here has been broken down into two subcategories: giving upward (to the state) and downward (to special petitioners and clients). Fourth, there is the tiny but very interesting category of independent charity activists whose operations are tolerated only with suspicion by the state, whose finances are always precarious, and whose permanent existence seems to depend on continuing personal devotion and sacrifice. What has not been found here are any undertakings even remotely resembling the horizontally organized relatively autonomous associations of the civil society model. Western social ideals and wishful expectations of a surge in civil associational activity in urban China are not, in any way, borne out by the findings of this research so far. Have we found then, as suggested above, some contemporary trends and tendencies that more clearly derive from what we might think of as China's own social history? Are there, in particular, any signs that something more closely akin to the style of action in China's own late-imperial public sphere may be reemerging now? Yes and no. We have found a number of quite interesting parallels, but there is no perfect match with the past.

Thinking back to some of the characteristics of late-imperial public sphere charity works briefly outlined at the start of this essay, the parallels with the present should be fairly apparent. An attempt to achieve a comprehensive, harmonious integration of official and non-official actions; the positing of a broad moral-social vision that all members of society might and should be made to share; a preference for blurring the distinction between state (or public) welfare and private philanthropy; a penchant for blending an officeholder's official with his personal roles; a disinclination to separate absolutely pursuit of individual interest from pursuit of the common good; a pervasive consciousness of and attentiveness to social hierarchy as it both informs and is reproduced by charitable action; and a focus that often seems to be less on the practical delivery of aid to those in need than on the general moral uplift associated with the philanthropic impulse. All these parallels should give us confidence that there are salient continuities in Chinese social thought and practice over time that we should be trying to grasp. Reaching back into China's own history for themes and variations by which to set our comparative standards where contemporary state-society relations are concerned may well be more promising than resorting to Western models of development and democratization. But if nowhere in this four-category overview of charity in present-day China do we find Western-style civil associations, neither do we have any very exact analogy to China's own late-imperial-style state-society collaborations either. For the state in China today simply dominates the charitable field *so much more* than was the case at the end of the last century.

Casting our eyes back over China's long and varied social history it is easy to spot what seem like telling continuities—habits of thought and social practice that recur. Thus we can readily discern that statism, social hierarchy, and Chinese family values remain as prominent features today of Chinese philanthropic thought and practice as they were in the past. And yet, pointing out fascinating cultural continuities such as these can never tell us everything we need to know in order to comprehend what possibilities are immanent in contemporary social processes. For, while certain habits of thought and certain practices regarding state power, social hierarchy, or the Chinese family may endure, what the Chinese people have to work with today is a very different state from that of the past, a much altered pattern of social hierarchy, and a profoundly changing Chinese family.

The state's own apparatus is *far* more elaborated now and its informing moral-political philosophy has been greatly secularized and modernized as compared to a hundred years ago. China's basic social structure has been much altered as well. Land reform and other extensive redistributions of wealth during the latter half of this century, years of state ownership and management of all China's major means of production, the spread of public education, mass literacy, and other social transformations have all served to flatten out the *old* patterns of social hierarchy. While at the same time the rise of the communist party elite after 1949, with its unified monopoly over both economic and political power, created a new social status hierarchy even more bureaucratically tied and closely dependent on state authority than before. Meanwhile, the various marriage reform campaigns and efforts to promote women's equality that came with communist revolution, the dramatically changing demographic profile of the nation in the last half century, rapid industrialization and urbanization, and the recent stringent government-mandated controls on fertility have all also been profoundly affecting the lived reality of Chinese family relations and altering the meanings of traditional family values. These changes too, like most of the other changes just listed, have tended on balance to give to the state in China today an even more demanding and intrusive role than it had before.

When we approach our research subject cross-culturally (as is sometimes done here in comparing China with the West), we note that habits of thought and cultural practices, while they are always evolving and are subject to renegotiation and reinterpretation within cultures, do also in important and intriguing ways, endure: distinctive habits of thought and cultural practices survive, and they separate us from each other. But when we approach our subject historically (over time, as it is also suggested here that we do), we note something else. We see that the underlying social raw materials, to which old habits of thought and cultural practices are applied and through which they are renegotiated—these underlying raw materials also evolve and change. And as they evolve, the enduring thoughts that are thought change their meanings, and the surviving practices that are practiced yield different outcomes.

Thus, although as we regard the Chinese scene today we can easily discover ambient attitudes and practices that remind us of the highly collaborative style of the late-imperial public sphere, we do not find any charitable operations that make a true match with that piece of China's past. Perhaps it was the often nearly absolute interpenetration of local official and non-official elite culture that characterized at least some of China's localities during the late-imperial period which made the on-the-surface nearly seamless-seeming collaborations of the old public sphere a sustainable possibility then. But after decades of searing social violence and authoritarian state building, followed by decades more of corroding party dictatorship culminating now in the urgent embrace of crass commercialism operating in transparent service to a nationalistic drive for hegemony in the Asian region—after all this, China's still-communist-party-controlled state apparatus and her opportunistically rising industrial barons and business tycoons of the 1990s cannot any-more regard each other just as imperial petty officeholders and locally embedded landlord and merchant figures once did before.

How should we characterize the salient differences? Clearly the state's claimed prerogatives make it more overpowering of upwardly clamber-ing social elites today than before. But also, there just may be more conflict, cynicism, and suspicion abroad now than can be covered over by striving to keep those dividing lines between official and non-official elites, between state and non-state projects and ventures, or between public and personal morality so conveniently blurred as they might have been in the imperial past. Effective state-society collaborations, in the realm of public charity and private philanthropy, are now more than ever crucially required, needless to say, to deal with China's crushing social problems and demands. But the state-society linkages that are in place in China today seem too fraught with tension and too laden with mutual distrust to produce the harmonious collaborations that are de-sired. Instead, it is greater disharmony and friction that seem more likely to ensue in the organization and development of Chinese charity.

NOTES

1. Between the summer of 1993 and the summer of 1995, I spent eight months in China talking with nearly two hundred people heavily involved in charity and social welfare work in one capacity or another—including private merchant and corporate donors, charity activists, foundation organ-izers, central ministerial and local government officials, along with a num-ber of social workers, and also with a small handful of charity recipients. The research was concentrated in six coastal cities: three of the more cosmo-politan giants, Guangzhou, Shanghai, and Tianjin; and three more provin-cial moderate-sized cities, Hangzhou, Wuxi, and Qingdao. I would like to thank the Ford Foundation, the Indiana University Center on Philanthropy, the National Endowment for the Humanities, and the Committee on Schol-arly Communication with China for their support of this research.

2. On the theory of civil society, see, e.g., John Keane, *Democracy and Civil Society* (London: Verso, 1988).

3. See, e.g., two works by Mary Backus Rankin, "The Origins of a Chinese Public Sphere: Local Elites and Community Affairs in the Late-Imperial Period," *Etudes Chinoises* 9, 2 (Fall): 13–60; and her *Elite Activism and Political Transformation in China: Zhejiang Province, 1864–1911* (Stanford: Stanford University Press, 1986). See also William T. Rowe, "The Public Sphere in Modern China," *Modern China* 16, 3:309–29. And for a study of a slightly later period, David Strand, *Rickshaw Beijing* (Berkeley: University of California Press, 1989). Helpful also are the various contributions to the special issue of *Modern China* devoted to "public sphere"/"civil society" in China?, Vol. 19, No. 2 (April 1992). See also Susan Mann, *Local Merchants and the Chinese Bureaucracy, 1750–1950* (Stanford: Stanford University Press, 1987) and several relevant essays in Joseph W. Esherick and Mary Backus Rankin, eds., *Chinese Local Elites and Patterns of Dominance* (Berkeley: University of California Press, 1990). Interesting and important also are R. Keith Schoppa, *Chinese Elites and Political Change* (Cambridge: Harvard University Press, 1982), and Prasenjit Duara, *Culture, Power, and the State* (Stanford: Stanford University Press, 1988). A useful discussion of some of the most consequential issues involved can be found in Frederic Wakeman, Jr., "Models of Historical Change: The Chinese State and Society, 1839–1989," in K. Lieberthal, J. Kallgren, R. MacFarquhar, and F. Wakeman, eds., *Perspectives on Modern China: Four Anniversaries* (Armonk, N.Y.: M. E. Sharpe, 1991).

4. Note the many interesting parallels here with characteristics of even earlier (late-Ming dynasty) philanthropic thought and practice, as these are analyzed by Joanna Handlin Smith in her chapter in this volume.

5. Interview, Shanghai, 4-13-95.

6. Interview, Shanghai, 4-11-95.

7. Interview, Hangzhou, 4-25-95.

8. Interview, Qingdao, 5-12-95.

9. Interview, Qingdao, 5-13-95.

10. Ibid.

11. Interview, Shanghai, 4-13-95.

12. Ibid.

13. Interview, Guangzhou, 6-17-93.

14. Interview, Hangzhou, 4-26-95.

15. Interviews, Shanghai, 7-1-93; 7-8-93. Interview, Tianjin, 8-3-93. Interview, Hangzhou, 4-26-95.

16. Interview, Wuxi, 4-18-95.

17. Ibid.

18. Author's interview notes, 1995. To be certain to conceal this man's identity, reference to the city where he was interviewed is omitted.

19. Interview, Qingdao, 5-11-95.

20. Interview, Guangzhou, 6-11-93. Interview, Shanghai, 7-1-93. Interview, Qingdao, 5-15-95. Interview, Beijing, 5-25-95.

.16.

Civil Society and Philanthropy in Latin America: From Religious Charity to the Search for Citizenship

ANDRÉS A. THOMPSON AND LEILAH LANDIM

INTRODUCTION

This chapter aims to provide an overview of the different cultural and social factors that have affected the development of non-profit organizations and philanthropy in Latin America. Given that this region contains numerous and varied social, political, and cultural traditions, one must talk about different philanthropic traditions, cultures, and systems. The concept of philanthropy as it has developed over the past century, is not native to Latin America. For that reason, there remains some difficulty in determining the scope of topics to be covered. As we have said in other writings, in Latin America the idea of philanthropy is associated primarily with religious charity and with benevolence. It is viewed, therefore, as an issue for the churches, the oligarchy, and the elites. Though its meaning and practice vary from country to country, the public as a whole generally view philanthropy as a form of social control by the ruling classes. In the case of individual philanthropists, giving has been viewed not as a culturally valuable obligation, but simply as a means of increasing one's prestige and social status.[1]

This popular bias against a particular understanding of philanthropy has been solidified by social science research which, by focusing almost exclusively on the state, has neglected the role played by voluntary action in the making of Latin American societies. Social thinking in Latin America has largely followed the models of the Western European schools and their emphasis on the role of the state in promoting social integration and welfare. Scholars, therefore, have devoted little attention to the development of civil society, and its relationship to the rule of law, to social responsibility, and to the practice of citizenship. The emphasis on economics within social analysis has led to interpretations of Latin American history that focused on the leading role played by the state and the ruling classes in industrialization and economic development. The development of social history within Latin American scholarship is recent, fragmented, and restricted primarily to labor history and the development of the trade union movement. These intellectual factors have hindered the study of non-state actors in the history and development of Latin American nations.

Philanthropic activities as a major component of those non-state actors must receive, therefore, greater attention. There exist significant difficulties, however, in trying to speak about the notion and practice of philanthropy in Latin America given the numerous, different traditions and varying symbolic meanings. How can one include under a common framework the culture and practice of self-help by Jewish emigres to Argentina escaping from the horrors of World War II with the activities of non-governmental organizations struggling to protect the environment in the Brazilian Amazon? Are there points of commonality between the utopia of indigenous people of Michoacan, Mexico, and their tradition of cultural preservation with Colombia's emerging tradition of corporate philanthropy? Are we speaking about the same things? How can we link the Western concept of philanthropy with the various cultural practices emphasizing solidarity and emancipation common to a wide array of social groups throughout Latin America?

Certainly, it would be nearly impossible to present a complete view of the development of civil society and philanthropy in Latin America. This chapter, therefore, intends only to provide an overview of the main trends in the Latin American philanthropic traditions and to suggest how they shaped the voluntary sphere. The aim is to highlight some of the major facts that influenced the cultural constructions of Latin Americans and discuss how they fit (or not) within the present context of philanthropy, civil society, and non-governmental organizations.

The challenge is great, because only recently has philanthropy been understood to include activities such as voluntary and non-profit action for the public good, that emerged from all parts of civil society, even from its lower echelons. The transition has not yet been complete, and for many the term continues to evoke views of elitism and a "hobby" of the wealthy.

Taking the more expansive definition of philanthropy, we can say that voluntary action—the giving of time and money for public benefit—and non-profit activities have been common features throughout Latin America since colonial times. One must admit, however, that charity in Latin America did not begin at home. The practices were brought by the Spanish and Portuguese colonizers of the region who constructed the forms of philanthropy which predominated throughout Latin America, with the possible exception of Uruguay, for more than four centuries.

THE COLONIAL HERITAGE: CHURCH AND STATE
ORGANIZING CIVIL SOCIETY

The conquest and colonization of Latin America was carried out as a partnership between the Catholic Church and the Spanish and Portuguese, in the case of Brazil, colonial states. This fact profoundly marked the developments in the region. Although the first social assistance institutions date from the sixteenth century, the seventeenth and eighteenth centuries saw widespread development of charitable practices and benevolent activities organized under the auspices or the influence of the Catholic church. In Mexico, these undertakings were so important that historians often refer to this period as the "charitable century." In the absence of other sources, religious charity provided nearly all relief to the poor, the needy, and the marginalized. Charitable institutions also served as key instruments for evangelizing native South Americans.

The repressive labor systems of the great plantations established in the region created strong bonds of dependence between laborers and their lords. A system of patronage or clientelism developed out of this bond, with the master of the plantation exercising a paternalistic concern for the needs of his workers. This contrasts dramatically with the typical situation in North America, where the relative independence of workers and laborers led, from its inception, to a situation marked by "pervading voluntarism" where "voluntary collaborative activities were set up to provide basic social services."[2]

While the church and state were partners in power, the church created and built various institutions, such as convents, asylums, schools, and universities. During the pre-Independence period, therefore, all philanthropic activities were deeply marked by the Catholic religion and organized according to its rules. Until the end of the nineteenth century, the counterreformist Catholic church that established itself over practically all the region operated according to a patronage system under which it subordinated itself to the Spanish and Portuguese crowns. To understand colonial society one must understand the church and its various Latin American forms. Despite the variations, the church played a major role in organizing civil society. The role of this church, particularly the work of the religious orders—the Franciscans, Dominicans, Augustinians, and especially the Jesuits through both the Society of Jesus and the Sisterhood of Holy Charity—was central to cultivating the initiatives and values of the philanthropic ventures of the colonial era. Education, health, and social welfare all were the responsibility of the church practically until the middle of the nineteenth century.

In the secular realm, local elites also undertook charitable works and created private organizations for the provision of social services, health, education, and leisure. The traditional, patriarchal, and authoritarian style of these initiatives was framed by the hierarchical system of boon and fealty by which it fell to the "lords" to take the initiative of protecting the "poor" though without an explicit conceptualization of poverty. Lay elites also managed donations from the colonial state for poverty assistance and, even though the recipient was not the church, these donations fell under the realm of Catholic charity.

The cooperation between civilian benevolent activities and religious charity resulted in a peculiar model of non-profit institutions that continues at present—social assistance institutions funded through religious channels but administered by laymen. In a sense, this created a "philanthropic nobility" consisting of exemplary citizens who based their social positions on their religious superiority to the poor. This marked the beginning of "private social services" in Latin America. Though ideological changes within Catholic tradition, particularly in the second half of the twentieth century, challenged this model (as did the "new" non-governmental organizations, or NGOs), it remains the core of the voluntary sector in many countries of the region.

For women, the Sisterhood of Holy Charity formed the core of charitable work. The Sisters of Charity, first funded in 1727 by Don Juan Alonso Gonzalez, were leading activists during the colonial period (until 1820) combining both religious evangelization and social assistance. The Sisters of Charity received financial support from both the church and private charities funded by the upper classes. Colonial elites involved themselves in the work of the Sisters of Charity by providing money and land, as well as moral and political support and personal engagement.[3] The association between the church, the colonial state, and the elites was at the core of all the charitable and philanthropic institutions that developed in Latin America for three centuries. They combined the provision of social assistance to the needy with the control and exploitation of the indigenous people.

The Sisters of Charity developed a rationale for social service based on love, help, and moral precepts. The Sisters assumed active social roles as nurses and social workers, at a time when most women worked in the domestic sphere. Other than economic necessity, religious ideals were the only accepted basis for women to enter the public world. For many women, the life of a nun was much to be preferred over an arranged marriage or remaining at home.

Although institutionally powerful, the diffuse organization of the church provided the room for the emergence of the various lay brotherhoods, sisterhoods, and fraternities that composed a significant component of the voluntary sector. These groups, maintained by their members and recognized by religious and civil law, functioned largely without direct church or state control. Created by the settlers not only for the purpose of worship but also for leisure and socializing, they also provided social services to both members and non-members.

For Brazil, the brotherhoods or fraternities provide the major example of a lay collective association with any significant degree of autonomy. In a vast geographic area such as Brazil, the church apparatus became decentralized and weakened. This fact, along with the tradition of medieval Iberian Catholicism, led Brazil to become home to a wide range of lay-led religious practices and organizations. The most famous and important of these has been the *Irmandade da Misericordia* (Brotherhood of Mercy). The preeminent symbol of philanthropy in Brazil even today, the Brotherhood, founded in Portugal in the late fifteenth century, built countless hospitals, asylums, and teaching establishments around the country supported chiefly by private donations and bequests. In 1739 in Rio de Janeiro they organized the first lay institution for the reclusion of women. Maintained by private donations, its main function was as an orphanage. The Brotherhood also used the building as a retreat center and place for their work in transmitting Christian values and educating couples about the duties of Christian marriage.

Drawing on the labor of large numbers of women religious, the Brotherhood carried out social work on a large scale under the protection of the Portuguese crown. From the nineteenth century on, this work became increasingly undertaken by society women. Their work helped to construct and consolidate a powerful model for women's charitable work in Brazil.

In Mexico, the "charitable century" saw the construction of ninety hospitals and two asylums, along with the establishment of a Royal Lottery for their support. The works of numerous priests and monks, such as Fray Bartolomé de las Casas, remain powerful symbols of the values of humanism and charity as well as of solidarity with the indigenous "underclass."

The "voluntary organizations" established during the first three centuries after European settlement existed under the aegis of the church. The values of Christian charity permeated these institutions. Influenced by the clergy and existing amidst the complex relations between church and state in colonial Latin America, they experienced profound changes during the late 1800s. By the end of the nineteenth century nearly every government in Latin America had separated the Catholic church from the state, although it remained the official religion in many countries. Despite the loss of much state support, the church's strong presence in the social realm continued to permeate the philanthropic and voluntary realm. Even today, in Brazil, Mexico, and Chile the influence remains strong.

THE CREATION OF THE NATION-STATES AND THE RISE OF PRIVATE INITIATIVE

It is not too extreme to say that in Latin America society was created by the state. There, the processes of forming the nation-states preceded the creation and consolidation of civil societies. Civil society throughout the region developed, therefore, in reaction to the state's action and policies.

During the first three decades of the nineteenth century, nearly all the countries of Latin America achieved their independence from Spain or Portugal. The independence struggles significantly altered the relationship between the church and the state. In Argentina, Brazil, Uruguay, and Mexico the new governments removed many public services from the Church with the aim of giving them a more rationalist and secular cast. State assumption of the responsibility for welfare provision was a central component of creating the nation-states, alongside the reorganization of the political regimes and the pacification of the countries divided by fights among *caudillos*.

Mexico provides a representative example. Following independence in 1821 responsibility for beneficent action shifted between various state ministries, including Justice, Foreign Affairs, and Finance. The year 1861 saw the creation of the General Directorate for Beneficent Actions and the development of formal regulations, and by 1899 Porfirio Diaz, inspired by French legislation, decreed Mexico's first Private Beneficence Law.

Despite some advances in social liberalism, as the above-mentioned development of Mexican legislation suggests, Latin America remained heavily controlled by the *caudillo*, clientielistic, vertically loyal state, in which the church continued to play a powerful role. Uruguay, however, provides a significant contrast. As Rodriguez Doldan argues, Uruguay's social order had truly been influenced by liberalism during the mid-

1800s. This led to the development in Uruguay of clear distinctions between charity and philanthropy. "Charity" remained a religious term; it described a particular Christian virtue and became linked with those who supported the church. Philanthropy, understood as a human virtue, was an expression used by those identified as anti-clergy.[4] The government, as the author points out, used beneficence to describe these activities, compromising neither of the two terms. In Argentina, however, where the church continued to predominate in the realm of social services after independence, the terms "charity" and "philanthropy" were indistinguishable. In Brazil, like Argentina, the church remained the preeminent charitable institution, with one major exception. The abolitionist struggle in Brazil saw the establishment of numerous civil associations which provided a significant difference in the tone of its civil life.

The newly independent states, however, were weak and poor with little capacity to deliver the services. This provided the opportunity for different segments of the wealthy classes to organize themselves to undertake charity work. Organizations such as the Uruguayan Ladies Charity Society established in 1853 and the Argentine Society of Beneficence (SB) founded in 1822, exemplified the elite involvement in philanthropic activities.

The Society of Beneficence probably constitutes the most outstanding cases of "patrician" philanthropy. Not only did it receive significant amounts of public funds, it functioned primarily under female leadership. The creation of the SB constituted a milestone in the development of philanthropy and in the history of the Argentine third sector. Until the mid-twentieth century the SB, functioning under private management but with public funds, had the main task of providing aid, beneficence, and social assistance throughout Argentina.

Despite the significant role played by such powerful social actors as the Catholic church and the wealthy, voluntary action and philanthropy played only marginal roles in the process of constructing Latin American nation-states. Authoritarian political systems, land-rich oligarchies, and weak economic systems, along with often violent internal conflicts limited social and political activity. While the Mexican Revolution of 1911 made the greatest movement toward democratization in the region, in several countries the emerging middle classes made similar advances. Little of this movement occurred under the impetus of voluntary organizations. As Leilah Landim argued in the case of Brazil:

> Civil organizations played no leading part in the processes of independence, the abolition of slavery and the proclamation of the Republic. There was no lack of local revolts, regional conflicts and popular campaigns or uprisings as these changes were consolidated and a national

identity constructed in the second half of the nineteenth century. But none of this depended on or produced a consolidated field of strong, durable civil organizations.[5]

What was true for Brazil also was true for all the countries of the region. The newly independent states assumed the responsibility for social welfare, challenging the monopoly of the church and the elites in the social arena.

MIGRATION, URBANIZATION, AND DIVERSITY: THE SEED OF PLURALISM AND SOLIDARITY

Another significant challenge to the traditions of religious and "high-class" charity was provided by the waves of immigrants coming from Western and Eastern Europe and other regions on the eve of the twentieth century. Brazil, Argentina, and Peru received the bulk of these immigrants. Italians, Spaniards, Portuguese, and British, along with Croats, Hungarians, Chinese, and Japanese looking for prosperity, work, and peace overloaded the ships coming to the "new continent." Nearly all of these immigrant groups formed a wide variety of associations designed to help them adjust to life in a new country. These organizations served numerous purposes, from helping the immigrants preserve their cultural traditions and identity, to providing health and funeral services, from securing housing and employment, to building and maintaining houses of worship.

At the close of the nineteenth and the beginning of the twentieth century Latin America experienced a proliferation of mutual benefit, self-help, and self-managed societies. These became common not only among immigrants but throughout the countries. These mutual benefit societies provided their members with medical and pharmaceutical care and financial assistance in case of unemployment, illness, injury, or death. To the extent that the societies attracted workers, they became increasingly politicized and class-oriented, adding to the growth of trade unions. The nascent trade union movement became increasingly radical under the influence of anarchist and socialist ideas brought by the Italian and Spanish immigrants who formed the first ranks of industrial workers. This radicalization was furthered by severe governmental repression of the movement.

Among middle-class and professional groups there also emerged increasing numbers of associations. These included professional associations such as the Brazilian Press Association and employers or manufacturers associations which became channels of communication with the State. The entire period was marked by unprecedented debates over the role of private, non-profit social services, voluntarism, and associativism.

In Argentina, there also developed a large number of non-profit organizations based on the principles of group solidarity, local community control, and self-initiative. These emerged primarily from immigrant collectives, professional associations, political parties, businesses, the Catholic church, and local neighborhoods. These groups organized various types of associations. The first stage of development saw the emergence of numerous self-help societies, with the dual purposes of self-management and group solidarity. Relationships between these groups were not always cordial, and there often were public disputes as to their legitimacy within society and over the definition of "true mutuality." These organizations were followed by the establishment and growth of economic development societies and other neighborhood organizations. These organizations emerged following the end of World War I in response to the increasing numbers of social problems afflicting the city of Buenos Aires. The city's tremendous growth at the end of the previous century forced its inhabitants into neighborhoods farther away from the center of the city. In response inhabitants of these neighborhoods created their own economic development societies. Political parties also played a major role in the development of these societies, representing the strong syndicalism that marked Argentine politics.

While the sources for much of this "politicized" associativism were radical labor views, a counterpoint emerged among Catholics. Preeminent among these organizations in Argentina was Catholic Social Action. Established to prevent the loss of Catholic laborers to the radical trade union movement and to protect Catholic doctrine from liberal and socialist doctrines, Catholic Social Action attempted to address social problems from a Catholic perspective and to show an active concern for the lives of working people. Similarly, the Conferences of Saint Vincent de Paul showed the church's concern for the plight of the poor and laboring classes. Established in Argentina in 1859, the Conferences had both men's and women's groups. Organized around the Workers' Circles the Vincentians were quite successful, even establishing factories that trained women in various industrial jobs.[6]

The Workers' Circles also organized lectures and meetings for women workers with the goal of mitigating social differences and promoting a sense of fellowship between rich and poor. Their goals focused on material and ideological strategies including the diffusion of Catholic ideals focused on love and resignation, resistance to socialist and communist ideologies, strengthening domestic roles, and addressing immediate financial needs.

The Socialist Party of Argentina also promoted the mutual benefit societies, believing that they helped to remove race, political, and national biases in State aid. The Socialists criticized the Workers' Circles, however, because of their ties to the church. The numerous employer-run associations also were condemned by the Socialists, since the dues for these organizations, in which membership often was mandatory, were debited from the workers' salaries. The railroad companies particularly engaged in this. Despite these intramural conflicts, the importance of these groups became apparent with the passage of Argentina's 1913 law officially recognizing these organizations and the organization in 1918 of the National Congress of Mutual Benefit Groups.

Although the extent of these organizations varied from country to country, the establishment of neighborhood organizations and mutual benefit associations owed much of their development to immigration and urbanization. Their emergence from small local groups without state control and oversight really make them the most genuine examples of voluntary, non-profit organizations during this period. Developing locally from people's concerns about their communities and lives, they represent the emergence of a nascent civil society throughout Latin America. Interestingly, while many of these organizations continue as health service providers, few people realize or understand their significance as philanthropic undertakings.

THE RESTRICTIONS ON CITIZENSHIP

Populism and authoritarianism formed the two dominant types of political regimes in Latin America from the 1930s until the present. Both of these regimes, centered on a strong state that restricted civil and political rights, greatly constrained the development of philanthropy and voluntary action in Latin America. While populist regimes organized society in a vertical, corporatist way, the numerous authoritarian regimes restricted the formation of nearly any kind of social organization, thus forcing the emergence of semilegal contra-governmental organizations and guerrilla movements. In both regimes, the state defined itself as the source and arbiter of all social goods, thereby restricting and inhibiting the capabilities of the citizenship to intervene in public causes.

In Brazil, the 1930s ushered in an era of developmentalist, centralist nationalism with authoritarian policies and broad state intervention in the economy and society. Brazil's economic modernization during this period emphasized diversification, industrial accumulation, and social regulation. The government's social policies were marked by corporatism, fragmentation, and selectiveness. Labor legislation and social security occupied a central position in this regulatory regime, much as it did in Peronist Argentina during the 1940s and 1950s. Social scientists speak about a "merit-particularistic" type of system, access to which was conditional upon the individual's position in the labor market. Citizenship and social stratification are thus associated according to criteria defined by the state. A kind of "regulated citizenship" was a typical feature of Populism.[7]

Two main features identified Populism in both Brazil and Argentina: direct state control of social and educational services and the formation of a strong trade union system subordinated to the government. These unions were organized according to a single, standard model and structured vertically by job category. Proceeds from union contributions— deducted from all workers' paychecks—were to be used, via the unions, to promote welfare activities (job training, health services, schools, cooperatives, holiday camps, etc.).

Given the development of centralized and paternalistic governments during this period, it is not surprising that this period also saw the development of the first legislation and agencies designed to regulate relations between non-profit organizations and the government. In 1911, Argentina established within the Ministry of Foreign Relations the Inspector General of Subsidies to oversee recipients of governmental funds. Further institutionalized in 1932 with the decree of the Social Assistance Funds with Congress regulating and designating resources, it became even more formalized in 1937, when the Subsidies Inspection became the National Register of Social Assistance, requiring the registration of all organizations. This gave way to the present system of the National Register of Public Welfare Entities which, after many changes, came under the Secretary of Social Development.

In Brazil, the law providing for the *Declaracaõ de Utilidade Pública* (Declaration of Public Utility) was passed in 1935, followed by the establishment of the *Conselho Nacional de Servico Social* (National Social Service Council, CNSS) in 1938. The CNSS was designed to subsidize the organizations offering care for the vulnerable, health, and education. The *Legião Brasileira de Assistência* (LBA, Brazilian Social Service Legion), through which registered non-profit organizations (caring for children, nursing mothers, pregnant women, and the elderly) received governmental funds, came into being in 1942.

Welfare provision was a combination of social security–granting benefits to workers and a care structure of assistance where the state collaborated (often with clientelistic purposes) with organizations from civil society by granting exemptions, tax incentives, and funding. However, in the case of Argentina, during the Populist period social assistance to those outside the labor market went through only one channel: the Eva Perón Foundation.[8]

During the 1930s Brazil saw the reemergence of a new partnership between Faith and Fatherland, since the Catholic church controlled a great number of the organizations approved by the above legislation or agencies. The church, by agreeing to respect a clear distinction between the temporal and spiritual orders and not question the legitimacy of the state, received numerous privileges. From the 1950s onward, alongside the increasing industrialization promoted by interventionist policy favorable to international capital, there began to consolidate a model of "populism" which began during the Vargas period. This model—similar to Peronism in Argentina—is notable for the presence of a charismatic leader through whom mass support is gained for the government without encouraging any autonomous participation, at the same time that the working classes are controlled and manipulated by paternalistic satisfaction of their aspirations. Populism integrated the "masses" to citizenship through social and labor policies and not through the law and the vote. The irruption of the masses into politics took place in the absence of a democratic institutionality.[9]

During this period, a more autonomous and strongly politicized associativism began to appear in Brazilian society. Several associations with a variety of aims and purposes were organized or revamped. These included small farmers' associations, the National Students' Union, the Rural Assistance Service, and a series of think tanks spanning the political spectrum.[10] All these organizations were suffused by the ideological debates and political forces of the time, and their point of reference was action through or in collaboration with government agencies.

Populism left a deep footprint in the political culture of the region, particularly in those countries where the political regimes achieved success in building welfare states "*a la latinoamericana,*" primarily Argentina, Brazil, and Peru. Negatively, however, populism reinforced the colonization of society by the state. Governments did this not only by limiting and controlling associationalism and non-profit organizations but by arrogating to themselves the right to define both rights and citizenship. The state functioned as the source of collective identities for all social actors and social activities, and anything outside of its control was viewed as suspect or even dangerous. As a result, it had a weak view of individual rights until the occurrence of massive human rights violations during the 1970s and 1980s. That experience led to a major growth in just those organizations focused on civil or minorities' rights that had been particularly absent from the voluntary sector.

The widespread establishment of military regimes throughout the region during the 1960s, 1970s, and 1980s, with the notable exceptions of Mexico, Costa Rica, and Venezuela, was the final touch to the creation of a political culture which excluded the defense of individual rights and respect for the representative mechanisms of democracy. The absence of democratic political regimes and a liberal culture of rights and "the rule of law" reduced to a minimum the space for the development of a philanthropic culture. The values of altruism, solidarity, and giving found political repression, disregard for legal procedures, and limits on association a most inhospitable environment.

However, the closing of the political systems provided the opportunity for the emergence of a new wave of voluntary organizations, which came to be called non-governmental organizations (NGOs). In Brazil and, to a lesser degree, Peru and Chile, society was slowly transformed during the authoritarian period by the emergence and growth of organizations independent of, and often hostile to the state. One fundamental factor in this emergence were positions taken by the Catholic church. As the only institution in civil society that maintained its independence after the military takeover, the church played a leading role in defending human and civil rights. In these undertakings Liberation Theology, especially the statements issued by the bishops' conferences held at Medellín and Puebla in the 1970s, which encouraged a considerable portion of the clergy to "return to the people" and to exercise "a preferential option for the poor," played a major role. Under the church's protective mantle, there emerged secular movements of workers, rural laborers, various professionals, residents of peripheral neighborhoods, along with other groups. In Brazil, the *Comunidades Eclesiais de Base* (Ecclesiastic Base Communities, CEBs) were the most visible example of the activities of this "Popular Church" and produced important leaders for a number of movements and autonomous organizations. In Chile, one cannot think about philanthropy and third-sector activities without taking into consideration the role played by the *Vicaría de la Solidaridad*, which during the military period (1973–1989) served as an umbrella for a wide array of NGOs concerned with human rights, academic freedom, and survival of the poor.

THE PRESENT: PHILANTHROPY AND BEYOND

As we have said, from the 1960s onward there has been an impressive growth of NGOs in every country of Latin America, including to a lesser degree Cuba and Haiti. As has been pointed out in many articles and books, the contributions of international agencies, the role of the Catholic church, and the return to grass-roots social action occasioned by the resurgence of authoritarianism all aided in this development. There remain many questions to be examined. Are there deeper mental and cultural changes lying behind this phenomenon? Has a new sense of helping others emerged in Latin American societies? Has the authoritarian culture left space for a new sense of solidarity and altruism? How extended are these practices in civil society at large?

Certainly, these are difficult questions. As we said in the introduction, the situation varies from country to country and even within countries themselves. Certain issues, however, are common to all of these countries, and we would like to discuss these in closing.

The redemocratization of the region obviously emerges as the first and probably most important common issue. The return to the rule of law, though still precarious, allowed for the free organization of civil society with few political constraints, although some legal restrictions remain. The absence of political constraints means that those who want to do something beyond the individual and family spheres can join with others in their endeavors. While this may appear to be a simple thing, this has had enormous implications for the development of Latin American societies during the past decade, as seen in the emergence of thousands of autonomous organizations of all types. Even though no hard data is available, this implies that resources are being mobilized within civil society (time, money, and talent) to sustain these causes. The investment of millions of dollars in the region by international agencies is an insufficient explanation for this explosion of civil society organizations.

The high level of associativism in the region does not automatically suggest that these countries have strong civil societies. "State-centrism" continues as a strong component of Latin American culture and still shapes people's understandings of the responsibilities between private and public, state and society, the individual and the collective. Democratization, however, brought a new actor into the scene: the market, and with it the centrality of profits. This also has changed the nature of the traditional debates over the roles of state and society in Latin America.

The state throughout Latin America no longer resembles the one that emerged from the period of Populism with an extended apparatus of public agencies and policies. Many of these activities have been or are being privatized, adjusted, and reduced. The state no longer has the capacity to intervene in social life as it did in the past, nor can it respond to the demands of different sectors of the population. The satisfaction of basic social needs now depends very little on the state and increasingly on the capacities for self-help among the deprived populations. While the idea of social citizenship acquired with the expansion of social policies and the labor market over three decades ago declines, a new approach to citizenship within the traditional paradigm of liberalism is emerging. Nevertheless, this trend is full of contradictions. In Brazil for instance, the abandonment of this work by the state has led the Catholic church and other religions to dominate most non-profit organizations in the areas of social welfare, health, and education. Taking advantage of its privileged relationship with the State and social elites throughout most of its history, the Catholic church, along with the Protestants and Spiritists, has managed to reach the marginal and excluded within society. These religious organizations developed a style of operating along with certain values in relation to voluntary action—an emphasis on charity, personal solidarity, self-abnegation, and altruism, along with personal involvement and choice in donations—that have little to do with liberal, individualist views.

The expansion of free-market economies and the privatization of the state provided a new space for business, which now occupies a core place in the Latin American scene. As of yet, there are few signs that social responsibility is being incorporated into the business culture. While Colombia, Venezuela, Chile, Mexico, Brazil, and Argentina show some development in this field, it may simply reflect the size and wealth of their economies along with the greater influence of international businesses. However, the recent Mexican crisis and the "tequila" effect on business behavior may imply a warning signal for the advancement of corporate philanthropy.

It has been said many times that democracy and capitalism are necessary for the development of philanthropy and voluntary action. In Latin America, however, these seem to be insufficient since both "democracy" and "capitalism" need to be qualified. Democracy mostly remains limited to formal, procedural structures adopted by political regimes and has not yet developed into the forms of social organization and participatory decision-making necessary for a democratic culture. Similarly, capitalism in Latin America has not yet managed to improve the quality of life for millions of Latin Americans living in poverty. Perhaps that is why those few who dare to speak about the importance of philanthropy in pluralist societies usually feel compelled to add some qualifications to the term, like "transformational," "social," or "developmental" philanthropy.

We can say that there has never been a "culture of philanthropy" in Latin America as it is understood in the United States. The mixture of cultural and religious heritage, the "state-centered" paradigm permeating politics and social action, the strong belief in charismatic leaders and the "savage" capitalism (as it is called) in all of them combine in different ways in the different countries, and so their outcomes vary. However, a new room for questioning past concepts and practices is emerging. There are signs that the distance the more recent associativism (the NGOs) has placed between itself and the state and the region's traditional social welfare practices, both religious and state-based, is being called into question. According to some analysts, the modern values of citizenship and sociopolitical engagement no longer must be set in opposition to the traditional values of brotherhood, charity, and community. Some indicators suggest that in the struggle to confront the marginalization of the region, what is emerging is a voluntary sphere and a third sector with an awareness of itself as a social and political actor and with language and practices that combine the logic of citizenship and advocacy with solutions to immediate problems.

NOTES

1. For some general background on philanthropy in Latin America, see Rubem Cesar Fernandes, *Privado aunque público: El Tercer Sector en América Latina* (Rio de Janeiro: Civicus, 1994); Andrés A. Thompson, "The voluntary sector in transition: the case of Argentina" (working papers, Center for the Study of Philanthropy, City University of New York, 1990); "Democracy and Development: The Role of Nongovernmental Organizations in Argentina, Chile and Uruguay" in McCarthy et al. *The Nonprofit Sector in the Global Community* (San Francisco: Jossey Bass, 1992); "From Charity to Development: Four Models of Government/Third Sector Relationships in Argentina," paper submitted to the inaugural conference of ISTR, Pecs, Hungary 1994, with Anahí Viladrich; "Democratization and Social Needs: The Role of the Nonprofit Sector and Its Relations with the State in Argentina," final report of a research project submitted to the Aspen Institute, 1995 (mimeo); "*El 'tercer sector' en la historia Argentina*," Doc., CEDES #109, Buenos Aires, 1995; Leilah Landim, "¿Para alem do mercado e do Estado? Filantropia e cidadanía no Brasil" (Rio de Janeiro: ISER, 1993); "Defining the Nonprofit Sector: Brazil," working paper of the Johns Hopkins Comparative Nonprofit Sector Project #9, (Baltimore: The Johns Hopkins Institute for Policy Studies, 1995); "Women and Philanthropy in Brazil: An Overview" (text prepared for the Comparative Project on Women and Philanthropy, Center for the Study of Philanthropy, City University of New York: 1995).

2. Maurice Gurin and Jon Van Til, "Philanthropy in Its Historical Context," in *Critical Issues in American Philanthropy* (San Francisco: Jossey Bass, 1990).

3. For a broader discussion of women's roles and social action see Anahi Viladrich, "Women: Protagonism and Subordination in the Social Action" (CUNY, Center for the Study of Philanthropy, manuscript, 1994).

4. Gonzalo Rodriguez Doldan, "Foundations in Uruguay: Historical Antecedents and the Present Situation" (mimeo), Montevideo, 1994.

5. Leilah Landim, "Citizen's Action Against Poverty and for Life: Philanthropy, NGOs and the Brazilian Crisis" (mimeo), Rio de Janeiro, 1995.

6. Uruguay, in contrast, saw the emergence of a significant important philanthropic movement organized by the Masons. In 1843, the Masonic Order created the Philanthropic Society as a centralizing organization for the charitable work of the different lodges. In 1892 they added the Cristobal Colón Philanthropic Society, traditionally known for providing food for the poor.

7. Wanderley Guilherme dos Santos, *Cidadania e Justica: A politica social na ordem brasileira* (Rio de Janeiro: Campus, 1979).

8. See Eva Peron, *La razón de mi vida* (Buenos Aires: Nueva Nación, 1948).

9. Ines Gonzalez Bombal, "¿Entre el estado y el mercado? ONGS y sociedad civil en Argentina" (Buenos Aires, manuscript, 1994).

10. Similar emergence of think tanks outside the universities' realm took place in Argentina, Chile, and Peru during the decades 1950–1960.

CONTRIBUTORS

LEONA ANDERSON is Professor of Religious Studies at the University of Regina.

SAID AMIR ARJOMAND is Professor of Sociology at SUNY Stony Brook.

G. D. BOND is Professor of Religion at Northwestern University.

STEVEN FEIERMAN is Professor of History and Sociology of Science and of History at the University of Pennsylvania.

JOHN A. GRIM is Professor of Religious Studies at Bucknell University.

ANANDA W. P. GURUGE is Senior Special Advisor to UNESCO's Culture of Peace Program.

WARREN F. ILCHMAN is past Executive Director of the Indiana University Center on Philanthropy and Professor of Political Science and Philanthropic Studies at Indiana University–Purdue University, Indianapolis. He is author or editor of fourteen books, the most recent of which is entitled *Capacity for Change? The Nonprofit World in the Age of Devolution.*

MARK JUERGENSMEYER is Professor of Sociology at the University of California at Santa Barbara.

STANLEY N. KATZ is Senior Fellow in the Woodrow Wilson School of Public and International Affairs at Princeton University and past president of the American Council of Learned Societies.

LESLIE S. KAWAMURA is Professor of Religious Studies at the University of Calgary.

GREGORY C. KOZLOWSKI is Professor of History at DePaul University.

LEILAH LANDIM is a researcher at the Institute for the Study of Religion (ISER).

ADELE LINDENMEYR is Professor of History and Russian Studies at Villanova University.

DARRIN M. McMAHON is Professor of History at Yale University.

DEREK J. PENSLAR is Professor of History, Jewish Studies, Middle East Studies, and Philanthropy at Indiana University.

AMANDA PORTERFIELD is Director of Women's Studies and Professor of Religious Studies at Indiana University–Purdue University, Indianapolis.

EDWARD L. QUEEN II is Director of the Religion and Philanthropy project at the Center on Philanthropy at Indiana University–Purdue University, Indianapolis.

MIROSLAV RUŽICA is Professor of Social Work and Philanthropic Studies at Indiana University–Purdue University, Indianapolis.

VIVIENNE SHUE is Professor of Government at Cornell University.

JOANNA F. HANDLIN SMITH is at the *Harvard Journal of Asiatic Studies.*

ANDRÉS A. THOMPSON is Program Director at the W. K. Kellogg Foundation.

MARY EVELYN TUCKER is Professor of Religious Studies at Bucknell University.

INDEX

'Abbās I, Shah, 126
Ab'l Ala Mawdudi, Mawlana, 300
Abū Sa'īd, Sultan, 122
'Adud al-Dawla, 115
African precolonial philanthropy:
  almsgiving in, 9–10, 18–19; healing
  associations in, 14–18; impact of colonization on, 21; importance of kinship linkages in, 8–9; and labor
  needs, 5–6; leadership-building
  through, 6–8; and marital relationships, 6, 22n6; missionary charity in,
  20–21; and the need for descendants, 4–5, 22n5; parent model of
  giving in, 4, 5; reciprocity in, 4, 6,
  9–11, 14, 15–16, 23n20; shrines as
  sanctuary in, 12–14; in the slave
  trade period, 11, 12; women in, 11,
  15, 16
Agni Puraṇa: *dāna* in, 59; on gifts from
  kings, 68
Ahmad, Hasan ud-din, 294–95
Aitareya Brahmana, 68, 69, 70
Alexander II (Tsar), 328n9
Alexandra (Russian Empress), 312,
  314, 315
Ali Akbar Khan, 288
All-China Association of Handicapped
  People, 339

All-Russian Committee for Aid to the
  Starving, 316–17
All-Russian Society of the Disabled,
  325
Alliance Israélite Universelle, 205,
  212n25
Almsgiving: in African precolonial
  philanthropy, 9–10, 19–20; by Chris-
  tian missionaries, 19–20; in early
  modern Europe, 199; as Islamic tra-
  dition, 18–19, 282; by the Sangha,
  83–87, 95n23; in the Soviet Union,
  320; in Tsarist Russia, 310–11
Alp-Arslan, Sultan, 115, 116
American Board of Commissioners,
  216, 217, 223, 227
American Indian Science and Engi-
  neering Society, 49
American Indian Tribal College Fund,
  37
American Relief Administration
  (ARA), 317, 329n23
Anāthapindika, 88, 89, 92, 99, 102
Analects (Confucius), 173, 174–75
Animals, saving of, xi; in China, 150,
  151; in Theravāda Buddhism, 91,
  92, 96n52
Anishnabeg-Ojibway people, 29–36
Apadāna, 80

373